CINEMA OF CRISIS

CINEMA OF CRISIS

Film and Contemporary Europe

Edited by Thomas Austin and
Angelos Koutsourakis

EDINBURGH
University Press

Edinburgh University Press is one of the leading university presses in the UK.
We publish academic books and journals in our selected subject areas across the
humanities and social sciences, combining cutting-edge scholarship with high editorial
and production values to produce academic works of lasting importance. For more
information visit our website: edinburghuniversitypress.com

© editorial matter and organisation Thomas Austin and Angelos Koutsourakis, 2020, 2022
© the chapters their several authors, 2020, 2022

Edinburgh University Press Ltd
The Tun – Holyrood Road
12(2f) Jackson's Entry
Edinburgh EH8 8PJ

First published in hardback by Edinburgh University Press 2022

Typeset in 10/12.5 pt Sabon
by IDSUK (DataConnection) Ltd,

A CIP record for this book is available from the British Library

ISBN 978 1 4744 4850 5 (hardback)
ISBN 978 1 4744 4851 2 (paperback)
ISBN 978 1 4744 4852 9 (webready PDF)
ISBN 978 1 4744 4853 6 (epub)

The right of Thomas Austin and Angelos Koutsourakis to be identified as the editors
of this work has been asserted in accordance with the Copyright, Designs and Patents
Act 1988, and the Copyright and Related Rights Regulations 2003 (SI No. 2498).

CONTENTS

List of Figures vii
List of Contributors viii
Acknowledgements xi

    Introduction 1
    Thomas Austin and Angelos Koutsourakis

1. Aesthetics of Crisis: Art Cinema and Neoliberalism 25
   Alex Lykidis

2. Beyond Neoliberalism? Gift Economies in the Films of the Dardenne Brothers 43
   Martin O'Shaughnessy

3. The Resurgence of Modernism and its Critique of Liberalism in the Cinema of Crisis 60
   Angelos Koutsourakis

4. Post-Fordism in *Active Life*, *Industrial Revolution* and *The Nothing Factory* 76
   Patricia Sequeira Brás

5. Re-evaluating Crisis Politics in the Work of Aku Louhimies 93
   Kate Moffat

6. Crisis of Cinema/Cinema of Crisis: The Car Crash and
   the Berlin School   105
   Olivia Landry

7. Representing and Escaping the Crises of Neoliberalism:
   Veiko Õunpuu's Films and Methods   119
   Eva Näripea

8. The Future is Past, the Present Cannot be Fixed:
   Ken Loach and the Crisis   136
   Martin Hall

9. It Could Happen to You: Empathy and Empowerment in
   Iberian Austerity Cinema   150
   Iván Villarmea Álvarez

10. The Double Form of Neoliberal Subjugation: Crisis on the
    Eastern European Screen   164
    Anna Batori

11. Housing Problems: Britain's Housing Crisis and Documentary   180
    Anna Viola Sborgi

12. Miserable Journeys, Symbolic Rescues: Refugees and Migrants
    in the Cinema of Fortress Europe   198
    Thomas Austin

13. Frontlines: Migrants in Hungarian Documentaries in the 2010s   215
    Lóránt Stőhr

14. Mongrel Attunement in *White God*   231
    Rosalind Galt

15. Labour and Exploitation by Displacement in
    Recent European Film   244
    Constantin Parvulescu

16. A Hushed Crisis: The Visual Narratives of (Eastern)
    Europe's Antiziganism   260
    Dina Iordanova

Bibliography   277
Index   304

FIGURES

1.1 and 1.2	The competitive ethos of the neoliberal era is portrayed through antisocial framing and blocking in *Chevalier* (Athina Rachel Tsangari, 2015)	37
2.1	Between murder and the gift: *The Son* (Jean-Pierre and Luc Dardenne, 2002)	47
2.2	The toxic gift of the ring: *The Promise* (Jean-Pierre and Luc Dardenne, 1996)	54
3.1	*Prologue* (Béla Tarr, 2004)	64
6.1	The car crash as smokescreen in *Jerichow* (Christian Petzold, 2008)	116
7.1	*The Temptation of St Tony* (Veiko Õunpuu, 2009)	130
10.1	Ryna's tableaux-like positioning in *Ryna* (Ruxana Zenide, 2005)	173
10.2	Jolana's stylised double-framing position in *Touchless* (Matěj Chlupáček and Michal Samir, 2013)	175
11.1	Poster for Paul Sng's *Dispossession* (2017)	192
12.1	Ayiva (left) looking for employment in *Mediterranea* (Jonas Carpignano, 2015)	209

CONTRIBUTORS

Iván Villarmea Álvarez works as a postdoctoral researcher at Universidade de Santiago de Compostela, Spain. He has published *Documenting Cityscapes. Urban Change in Contemporary Non-Fiction Film* (2015) and *New Approaches to Cinematic Space* (2019), the latter co-edited with Filipa Rosário. Since 2011 he has contributed to the online film journal *A Cuarta Parede*, for which he has co-edited the volume *Jugar con la Memoria. El Cine Portugués en el Siglo XXI* (2014) along with Horacio Muñoz Fernández. His current research project is focused on Iberian austerity cinema.

Thomas Austin is Reader in Media and Film at the University of Sussex. He is the author of *Hollywood, Hype and Audiences* (2002) and *Watching the World* (2007), and co-editor of *Contemporary Hollywood Stardom* (2003) and *Rethinking Documentary* (2008). His latest book is the edited collection *The Films of Aki Kaurismäki: Ludic Engagements* (2018).

Anna Batori is an Associate Professor in Film and Television Studies at the Babeş-Bolyai University (Cluj-Napoca, Romania). She has an MA in Film Studies (Eötvös Loránd University) and a PhD in Film Studies (University of Glasgow/Screen). Her book *Space and Place in Romanian and Hungarian Cinema* was published in 2018. She writes and teaches on European and world cinema, modern film theory and digitised narrative techniques.

Patricia Sequeira Brás is a Lecturer in Portuguese Studies at Birkbeck College, University of London. In 2015 she concluded her doctoral research entitled 'The Political Gesture in Pedro Costa's Films'. The relationship between politics and cinema that motivated her doctoral work continues to shape her new research projects. Her current interests include documentary film and feminist practices of storytelling.

Rosalind Galt is Professor of Film Studies at King's College London. She is co-author with Karl Schoonover of *Queer Cinema in the World* (2016) and co-editor of *Global Art Cinema* (2010). She is the author of *Pretty: Film and the Decorative Image* (2010) and *The New European Cinema: Redrawing the Map* (2006), as well as numerous articles on world cinema and the relationships between geopolitics and film aesthetics.

Martin Hall received his PhD at the University of Stirling on British cinema and the radical 1968, in 2019. Prior to his current research, he was Senior Lecturer in Film and Media Studies at the University of Bolton.

Dina Iordanova is Professor of Global Cinema and Creative Cultures at the University of St Andrews in Scotland and the author of a number of books on Balkan and East European cinema. She edited a special issue of *Framework* on the representation of Roma in cinema in 2003, and co-edited, with Paloma Gay-y-Blasco, a special issue on Roma and media representations for *Third Text* (2008). She is currently preparing a monograph discussing aspects of the Romani discourse as seen in transnational film.

Angelos Koutsourakis is a University Academic Fellow in World Cinema at the University of Leeds. He is the author of *Rethinking Brechtian Film Theory and Cinema* (2018) and *Politics as Form in Lars von Trier* (2013), and the co-editor of *The Cinema of Theo Angelopoulos* (2015).

Olivia Landry is Assistant Professor in German at Lehigh University. She is the author of *Movement and Performance in Berlin School Cinema* (2019).

Alex Lykidis is Associate Professor of Film Studies at Montclair State University, New Jersey. His research interests include art cinema, neoliberalism, immigration and political film-making traditions. His work has been published in *The Wiley-Blackwell History of American Film*, *A Companion to Michael Haneke*, *Crossings: Journal of Migration & Culture*, *We Roma: A Critical Reader in Contemporary Art*, *Teaching Transnational Cinema: Politics and Pedagogy* and *Journal of Modern Greek Studies*. His monograph *Art Cinema and Neoliberalism* is forthcoming from Palgrave Macmillan.

Kate Moffat is a Leverhulme Early Career Fellow at the University of Warwick where she is researching the digital networking strategies of the emerging Sámi film and media industries. She earned her PhD from the University of Stirling in 2019 with a thesis based on examining representations of race and ethnicity in contemporary Nordic film culture.

CONTRIBUTORS

Eva Näripea is Director of the Film Archive of the National Archives of Estonia. She serves on the editorial board of *Studies in Eastern European Cinema*, and in 2013–18 was a co-editor of *Baltic Screen Media Review*. She has contributed over thirty book chapters and articles to various internationally published volumes and journals, and co-edited several anthologies on Estonian and Eastern European cinema. Her research interests include spatial representations and peripheral practices in Estonian cinema, histories of Eastern European science fiction film, reflections of neoliberalism in recent Estonian cinema and histories of film preservation in Eastern Europe.

Martin O'Shaughnessy is Professor of Film Studies at Nottingham Trent University. He is the author of *Jean Renoir* (2000), *The New Face of Political Cinema* (2007), *La Grande Illusion* (2009) and *Laurent Cantet* (2015). His research focuses mainly on the politics of cinema. He is currently working on a monograph on French and Francophone Belgian film in (and beyond) the current crisis.

Constantin Parvulescu is Senior Researcher in Film and Media Studies at Babeș-Bolyai University in Cluj and Lecturer in Critical Thinking at University of St Gallen. He specialises in the relationship between audiovisual texts and politics, history and economic issues. He has authored several articles on European film and media, as well as the monograph *Orphans of the East: Postwar Eastern European Cinema and the Revolutionary Subject* (2015). He edited *Recent Quality Film and the Republic of Europe* (a double special issue of *Studies in European Cinema*, 2018), *Global Finance on Screen: From Wall Street to Side Street* (2017) and *A Companion to the Historical Film* (Wiley, 2013/2015).

Anna Viola Sborgi is a Postdoctoral Research Fellow at the University of Genoa and sessional lecturer at King's College London, where she recently completed a PhD in Film Studies. She also holds a PhD in Comparative Literature (University of Genoa). She investigates screen representations of London, housing and gentrification. She co-edited the special issue 'London Is Open: London as a Cosmopolitan City in Contemporary Culture', for *Other Modernities* (2018), and recently wrote on media representations of the Grenfell Tower Fire in *After Grenfell: Violence, Resistance and Response* (2019). She is on the editorial board of *Mediapolis*.

Lóránt Stőhr is an associate professor at the University of Theatre and Film Arts in Budapest. His research fields include film melodrama, documentary and contemporary Hungarian cinema. He has published books on melodrama in the auteur cinema of the late modern period (2013) and contemporary Hungarian documentary (2019). He also writes film criticism for the Hungarian weekly newspaper *Life and Literature*.

ACKNOWLEDGEMENTS

Thanks to Gillian Leslie and Richard Strachan at Edinburgh University Press, and to all the contributors for helping to make this book a reality. Thanks also to Charlotte Adcock.

Chapter 6 by Olivia Landry is a reworking of material from her book *Movement and Performance in Berlin School Cinema* (Indiana University Press, 2019). We would like to acknowledge the support of the Leeds Arts and Humanities Research Institute for providing us with funding to organise a symposium entitled 'Cinema of Crisis: Film and Contemporary Europe' that took place on 9 March 2018.

INTRODUCTION

Thomas Austin and Angelos Koutsourakis

In 2004 *Visions of Europe*, a compilation of twenty-five shorts by selected filmmakers, one from each member country of the European Union, was released. Each director had been given a budget of $41,000 and asked to 'make a film featuring a personal vision of current or future life in the EU'.[1] Hungarian auteur Béla Tarr's entry, *Prologue*, is a wordless black-and-white film comprised of a single shot in medium close-up, tracking across people waiting in line outside a brick building. The camera glides past the more or less impassive faces of scores of men and some women, predominantly middle-aged or older.[2] Entropy is a recurring phenomenon in Tarr's work, an inexorable force gradually gathering pace in films such as *Sátántangó* (1994) and *The Turin Horse* (2011). But in *Prologue* the entropic process is already long developed; we witness it at a relatively late moment. Although the short is deliberately elliptical, it is most readable as a figuration of systemic de-industrialisation. The silent, docile bodies queuing patiently retain the somatic discipline of a workforce, internalised in their corporeal carriage. But this is not the start or end of a shift. Instead they are waiting to collect a small handout of a drink and a snack (whether from a charity or the vestiges of state provision is unclear). These are not workers leaving the factory but ex-workers whose factories, shut down or relocated, have left them.

Since 1989 de-industrialisation has taken on a particular inflection in the formerly state socialist countries of the Eastern bloc (of which more below), but it can also be seen as part of a wider process of economic restructuring, outsourcing and increased financialisation across the global North. As such it is one of a series of interlinked trends and shorter-term shocks that have shaped economies, polities and societies in Europe and elsewhere in the last three decades. We adumbrate them here, alongside an introduction to cinematic responses to these upheavals. The chapters gathered in this book investigate the output of selected European film-makers, encompassing established auteurs and lesser-known directors working in diverse formats (including fiction films, documentaries and videos posted on YouTube), and drawn from not only the dominant, central nations of Europe but also those on its peripheries. Our contributors combine aesthetic, thematic and political analyses in order to explore how films have offered various mediations, understandings and commentaries, both explicit and indirect, on this lengthy period of instability. Together, such filmic interventions constitute what we might call, if a collective noun can stand for such heterogeneity, the cinema of crisis.

Financialisation and De-industrialisation

The accelerating financialisation and de-industrialistion of economies in Europe and beyond began in the 1980s and 1990s, and has continued to the present day.[3] Although dates and details clearly differ from country to country, this radical reorganisation has typically entailed two parallel developments: the growth in significance of deregulated financial sectors in tandem with a decline in the economic and political importance of manufacturing. The former saw a ballooning of 'frictionless' trade in financial products and instruments, including bundling of debt and loan-related derivatives, such as the now notorious credit default swaps which played a part in the financial crash of 2008. By 2007, on the eve of the collapse, $12 worth of derivatives were circulating for every $1 of global income. As Yanis Varoufakis writes: 'the world of finance had evidently grown too large to be contained on planet earth!' (2013: 130, cited in Basu 2018: 37).[4] The latter has been accompanied by the widespread outsourcing of mass production and loss of markets to developing countries that can offer cheap labour and lower environmental standards,[5] and by the dismantling of European workers' rights and protections, wherein 'flexibility' for large employers means insecurity and precarity for their employees.[6] A key driver of these processes has been the prioritisation of returns to shareholders over long-term investment in improving productivity via research and development.[7]

Globalisation has intensified these shifts, and entrenched a rampant neoliberalism across the planet. In 2014 the Marxist economist Ernesto Screpanti noted: 'multinational capital's global domination brings ever greater transfers of surplus value from the [global] South to the capitalists of the North'. However, 'instead of implying improved well-being for workers in [economically] advanced countries, this leads to the increased concentration of income and wealth in the hands of the capitalist class and the impoverishment of the precariat' in both the North and the South (Screpanti 2014: 208).[8] This has in turn led to growing economic insecurity and social anxiety, which has often been amplified and channelled by racist, xenophobic and illiberal politicians pursuing a politics of resentment and scapegoating. In a highly prescient analysis from 2004, Zygmunt Bauman commented:

> Uncertainty and the anguish born of uncertainty are globalization's staple products. State powers can do next to nothing to placate, let alone quash uncertainty. The most they can do is to refocus it on objects within reach [that] they can least make a show of being able to handle and control. Refugees, asylum seekers, immigrants – the waste products of globalization – fit the bill perfectly. (2004: 66)

Ultimately, as Lars Jensen and Kristín Loftsdóttir argued a decade after Baumann, 'the fiscal crisis [. . .] spills into other crises, such as the stalled project of building a pan-European polity' (2016: 1). This is evident in developments such as the Brexit vote of 2016, the new Italian government's increasing reluctance to abide by the fiscal discipline demanded by the EU, and the 2018 failure of Emmanuel Macron's attempt to secure German support for his plans to reform the EU.[9] In the following pages we map the nexus of interlinked upheavals outlined here, pointing to responses from selected European film-makers, which are then analysed further in subsequent chapters.

THE COLLAPSE OF STATE SOCIALISM

While increasingly planetary in their reach and impact, neoliberal policies such as the marketisation of public institutions, reductions in welfare provision and erosion of job security in deregulated labour markets have been particularly rapid and disruptive in the formerly communist states of Eastern Europe. Since the collapse of state socialism in 1989, a lurch towards neoliberalism has resulted in the transformation of social and cultural as well as economic and political spheres, including widespread privatisations and the dismantling of state support, often at breakneck pace. It has also led to the stabilisation of what Immanuel Wallerstein calls processes of 'unequal exchange' (2004: 11) that render peripheral countries dependable on the core ones. The disintegration of the heavy industries in Eastern/Central Europe following the collapse of communism has rendered these states financially vulnerable not only in terms of their trade balance, but also in terms of labour power, since their skilled and unskilled labour force is compelled to seek work opportunities in the core countries.

Wendy Brown notes that 'neoliberalism [is] contoured by globalized capital but given a particular twist in each local context where it dwells' (2006: 692).

Thus, as Constantin Parvulescu argues, one of the problems confronting civil society in a rapidly transforming eastern Europe has been that of subjectivation. He writes:

> Eastern European socialism has not been able to produce strong, ethical, and especially intellectually emancipated subjects, but only second-class citizens of the world, ironically properly prepared to be exploited by capitalism. This is the most disturbing disappointment of socialism, not its economic failure, not even [. . .] the gulag. The post-socialist landscape is populated by subjects perverted by authoritarianism and the corruption of the system. (2015: 158; see also Brown 2006: 693)

Other scholars have drawn on models of postcoloniality to understand post-communist Europe and the discursive positioning of its citizens as 'semi-Europeans' (Kovačević 2018: 3). For instance, Anikó Imre writes of 'parallels between postsocialist and postcolonial states as well as states of mind'. Such states are 'characterized by a sharp opposition between provincial and cosmopolitan cultures; have imbalanced, distorted neoliberal economies; struggle with democratization; fall prey to violent nationalisms; and have troubled relationships with past histories' (2016: 5–6).[10] Moreover, Imre observes:

> While joining the EU has undoubtedly brought more social and economic mobility to a small well-educated or wealthy Eastern European elite, the majority of postsocialist populations have been designated the losers of capitalism, who are themselves to be blamed for their immobility and incapacity to adjust, increasingly by their own governments too. A postcolonial analysis foregrounds the continued sense of inferiority and resentment at the heart of nativist nationalisms. These nationalisms fester beneath the official European rhetoric of a swift generational change that supposedly creates brand-new postsocialist citizens for whom democracy and market rationality are second nature. (2016: 7)[11]

One of the key contradictions in this region of Europe is that oppressive economic, labour and social reforms were imposed unopposed following the transition to free market models. Alexander Kiossev attributes this to feelings of inferiority on the part of Eastern European people and he uses the concept of self-colonisation to describe countries that have 'succumbed to the cultural power of Europe and the west without having been invaded and turned into colonies in actual fact' (2011).

Film-makers in the former Eastern bloc have responded to the crises of postcoloniality and transplanted neoliberalism in diverse ways. For instance, despite their obvious aesthetic differences, Cristian Mungiu's fiction film *Baccalaureat/*

Graduation (2016) and Alexandru Solomon's documentary *Kapitalism: Reteta Noastra Secreta/Capitalism: Our Improved Formula* (2010) offer equally trenchant critiques of cronyism and corruption in Romania's particular version of post-communist capitalism. In her contribution to this collection, Anna Batori explores a recent wave of extreme cinema in Eastern Europe, and asks whether violent and pornographic representations might constitute an indirect response to the capitalist transition. Could images of female humiliation and shock aesthetics be a gesture of self-punishment, part of a process of collective mourning whereby post-socialist nations symbolically punish themselves for their passivity in both the communist past and the capitalist present? For Batori, two key tropes are the father figure and the sexualised and victimised female. She argues: 'The increasing incidence of female rape, domestic violence and physical abuse on Eastern European screens suggests a new repatriarchised social structure that resurrects the socialist father figure as an emasculated, impotent male who, while being colonised by Western powers himself, oppresses his female relatives by their sexual exploitation.'

Eva Näripea's chapter probes the work of Estonian auteur Veiko Õunpuu, an uncompromising critic of the extreme neoliberalism that has, since Mart Laar's premiership in the mid-1990s, dominated both Estonia and other post-socialist states following its lead. Näripea analyses not only Õunpuu's films but also his working practices, in particular two recent collaborations, *60 Seconds of Solitude in Year Zero* (2011) and *Roukli* (2015), which in differing ways resist 'reified cultural production' by attempting new production and exhibition procedures. She concludes that 'Õunpuu's methods acquire a particular urgency at a moment when the emerging generation of young directors appears to submissively conform to the dictates of market-oriented film production that flattens the local cinematic scene by churning out banal variations of the "grand national narrative".'

Post-democracy

As is already becoming evident in this account, neoliberalism has become entwined with growing 'post-democratic' tendencies in the public sphere in the past thirty years or so. In his book *Post-Democracy*, Colin Crouch traces the gradual atrophy of democratic processes across Europe (and the US) from the 1980s onwards. While chronology and details vary from nation to nation, Crouch observes a systemic and relentless trend characterised by the confluence of key economic and political shifts: continuing de-industrialisation and the associated attenuation of the working class as a political force; political parties' increasing reliance on funding and expertise from big business[12] (a process that reached its nadir with the election of Donald Trump to the US presidency in 2016, more than a decade after Crouch published his analysis); the diminution of informed political debate in the media; and the escalating dominance of transnational corporations. For Crouch, 'the global firm' operating beyond the jurisdiction of any single nation-state is 'the key institution of the post-democratic world' (2004: 31). He elaborates:

> while elections certainly exist and can change governments, public electoral debate is a tightly controlled spectacle, managed by rival teams of professionals expert in the techniques of persuasion, and considering a small range of issues selected by those teams. The mass of citizens plays a passive, quiescent, even apathetic part, responding only to the signals given them. Behind this spectacle of the electoral game, politics is really shaped in private by interaction between elected governments and elites that overwhelmingly represent business interests. (2004: 4)

Furthermore, while '[t]he contemporary political orthodoxy that social class no longer exists is itself a symptom of post-democracy [. . .] One of the core political objectives of corporate elites is clearly to combat egalitarianism' (2004: 53, 52; see also Brown 2006: 694). As Screpanti notes:

> There is no doubt that globalization is working to realize the capitalist dream of the minimal state. This does not mean a complete absence of the state. It means that individual states are compelled to give up the role of national collective capitalist and subordinate their domestic policies to the interests of big multinational capital, especially by playing the role of local social gendarme [ensuring law and order, security, etc]. (2014: 205)[13]

We need to note here that post-democratic tendencies vary in Eastern and Central Europe, where the clash for the establishment of hegemonic interests manifests itself differently. On the one hand, pro-Western liberals tend to problematically equate democracy with the free market, limited government and Western institutions, something that perpetuates a top-down governance with limited control by the population (ironically, exactly what Crouch suggests to be the key characteristics of post-democracy). On the other hand, nationalists fight for the establishment of a strong local bourgeoisie (see the current Polish and Hungarian governments), which relies on illiberal forms of governance. Commenting on the present situation in Hungary, Agnes Gagyi suggests that the two conflicting poles are 'democratic antipopulism', which castigates as anti-democratic any protest against neoliberalism, and 'anti-democratic populism', which aims at building a national bourgeoisie (2016: 358). Ironically both of these ideological poles rely on top-down governance. The first fetishises the rational operation of the market, and the second relies on the strong persona of a leader whose policies rely on the building of an imaginary community on the basis of exclusions.

The 2008 Crash and Financial Crisis

The post-democratic tendencies outlined above have been exacerbated in the last decade by the financial emergency that began with the crash of 2008, and by political reactions to these events. As is commonly known, the global financial collapse of 2008 started in the US before spreading to Europe and beyond. The immediate triggers for the crash were financial deregulation, the growth of universal banking, and a speculative bubble that 'swelled from the late 1990s to 2005' in the US, before collapsing under pressure from the subprime mortgage crisis. It is important to remember, however, that deregulation of financial markets in Europe preceded similar policies in the US, and dates back to the late 1980s (Screpanti 2014: 130).[14] But transatlantic influences flowed in both directions, with later US practices taken up in Europe. Screpanti writes:

> an extensive shadow banking system also formed in Europe. Prior to the subprime crisis, it was almost as big as the U.S. system, and afterward it grew even more [. . .] Besides, some countries, like Spain and Ireland, attempted to imitate the American speculation-led growth model, thus helping to trigger real estate bubbles that caused disasters in Europe too. (2014: 131)

One crucial factor in the continuing significance of the crash in Europe more than a decade afterwards is that it effectively licensed national governments as well as the institutions of the European Union, particularly the European Central Bank, to extend and intensify existing neoliberal measures.[15]

Austerity

In his 2011 book, *The Strange Non-Death of Neoliberalism*, Crouch attempts to answer the question: 'how it comes about that neoliberalism is emerging from the financial collapse more politically powerful than ever'. He notes: 'Whereas the financial crisis concerned banks and their behavior, resolution of the crisis has been redefined in many countries as a need to cut back, once and for all, the welfare state and public spending' (2011: xviii–ix). One important answer to Crouch's question comes from Laura Basu's investigation into UK media coverage of the crash and the resulting economic and political fallout from 2007 to 2015. Basu's research shows that the financial collapse was rapidly followed by a period of 'media amnesia', which shaped dominant accounts of the crash, and which still persists across the continent. She identifies three key characteristics: 'a lack of historical explanation; an overly narrow range of perspectives privileging elite views; and a lack of global context' (2018: 2).[16] Basu also observes that 'in response to a crisis of neoliberalism we have seen not a reversal but an *escalation* of neoliberal measures' (2018: 16, 28, italics in original). Similarly, the Eurozone debt crisis, which has been ongoing since late 2009, 'has been accompanied by an extraordinary bout of media amnesia':

> the 2008 crash was almost entirely forgotten as the immediate cause of Eurozone troubles. The majority of coverage gave no explanation for the problems. When explanations were given, they often focused on public profligacy and corruption, regularly using cultural stereotypes and accusing the citizens of the peripheral countries [Greece, Spain, Portugal, Ireland and Italy] of being lazy and corrupt. (Basu 2018: 140)[17]

In this way, a discourse of 'crisis', alongside highly tendentious or fictive accounts of causal factors, was mobilised to justify further extensions of neoliberalism, which entailed more job losses. As James Bloodworth writes: 'A million more people have become self-employed [in the UK] since the financial crisis, many of them working in the so-called "gig" economy with few basic workers' rights' (2019: 2). We can also point to Naomi Klein's work on 'disaster capitalism', whereby disasters and catastrophic events are treated as 'exciting market opportunities' for private companies seeking profits in humanitarian and security initiatives that were once the exclusive domain of state institutions or NGOs (Klein 2008: 6). This model, which Klein applies to events such as the second Gulf War and the rebuilding of New Orleans after Hurricane Katrina, could be revised and extended to national and pan-European responses to the financial crash and the Eurozone crisis. The economic disaster precipitated by financialisation and deregulation was rapidly reframed as an opportunity to deepen neoliberalism under the rubric of austerity as a necessary 'balancing of the books'.

As Iván Villarmea Álvarez notes in his chapter on 'austerity cinema' in Portugal and Spain, the phrase 'We have lived beyond our means [. . .] soon became a mantra for conservative governments, since it allowed them to justify the adoption of austerity measures without having to assume any political responsibility after years of systematic indebtedness'. The expression also offers a simplistic moral reading of what was in fact a complex series of political and economic procedures. By contrast, Olivia Landry's contribution attends to a group of films from Europe's strongest economy both before and after 2008, Germany. Her discussion centres on the car crash as a key trope in three films of the Berlin School: Valeska Grisebach's *Sehnsucht* (*Longing*, 2006) and Christian Petzold's *Yella* (2007) and *Jerichow* (2008). All three are set in de-industrialised villages in former East Germany. Landry writes: 'these are films about wanting more and the price one must pay to achieve such pleasure economies. Their cinematic narratives rigorously echo the logic of neoliberal capitalism and its ominous promise of personal autonomy, sexual freedom and self-development.' Each car crash is a reminder of the costs that accompany these promises, as well as a self-reflexive pointer to cinema's long-standing interest in accidents, and its own much-debated 'crisis' due to the expansion of digital technologies. Landry concludes:

> these crashes are manifest reminders of cinema's open form, its ontology as a mixed medium; they point to the continuing transition from one mode to another. The impermanence of these films' narratives and the fate of their characters does not offer hope or optimism, but it does provide ambiguity in the form of constant change – a continuity of transformation.

To return to Screpanti's Marxist analysis:

> At the root of this crisis lies a social contradiction that the economic policies of the advanced countries are incapable of resolving. Globalization, through the social, fiscal, and environmental dumping enacted by emerging countries, reduces the income and consumption of workers in advanced countries in a way that no fiscal policy can counter without drawing heavily on profits [through taxation]. (2014: 205)

It's vital to note that, while austerity and the other political, economic and social upheavals discussed here have often been designated as exclusively public sphere developments, they have each contributed to a complex and growing crisis that has largely been ignored by dominant discourses, or sequestered as 'merely' a private sphere problem: that of mental health. To make sense of this crisis it must be properly understood as an imbrication of public and private issues, and thus fully politicised, approached as a systemic consequence of neoliberalism rather than a series of isolated individual cases. The late Mark Fisher wrote:

> It does not seem fanciful to see parallels between the rising incidence of mental distress and new patterns of assessing workers' performance [. . .] The current ruling ontology denies any possibility of a social causation of mental illness. The chemico-biologization of mental illness is of course strictly commensurate with its depoliticization [. . .] the task of repoliticizing mental illness is an urgent one. (2009: 37–8)[18]

Relatedly, Peter Coville (2018) asks of the loneliness epidemic evident throughout Europe and beyond, 'Is loneliness the price we pay for an ideology that privileges individual freedom and "choice" above the collective and communal; that sees attachment to others as an obstacle to the pursuit of profit?' Loneliness has political implications because it makes people vulnerable to political groups committed to the re-establishment of a pre-existing pure, national community, which operates on the basis of exclusions. Pascal Bruckner cautioned in 1995 that in an individualistic society, the individual 'may have gained freedom, but he has lost security' (cited in Smith 2019: 8). Security here stands for the feeling of being part of a community, whose loss in neoliberalism has been quickly exploited by right-wing forces across Europe. Furthermore, as Bloodworth notes,

> the disappearance of the institutional affiliations [social clubs and other support networks and traditions] that characterised working-class life for many older people is still keenly felt [. . .] The residual memory of such institutions, passed down to younger generations via word of mouth, heightens the sense of loss for those without access to older collective traditions. (2019: xiii)

The widespread deterioration in mental health that has accompanied increasing inequality and precarity in the past decade is considered in the chapters by Kate Moffat, on self-destructive tendencies in the films of Aku Louhimies, and Alex Lykidis, on the culture of competition and associated feelings of inadequacy in Athina Rachel Tsangari's *Chevalier* (2015).

Austerity has taken differing forms across the continent, with the populations of southern nations such as Greece, Spain and Portugal faring particularly badly. For instance, in Greece, the state's education budget was slashed to one-third of its pre-crash level, and pensions were cut by more than 40 per cent, while healthcare spending collapsed by 20 per cent in just one year (2012), leading to a marked rise in infant mortality (Kershaw 2018: 509, 511). The crisis provides the context for Lykidis's reading of *Chevalier*, set on a luxury yacht in the Aegean Sea, as a coded critique of neoliberalism. 'The characters' anxieties and doubts focus primarily on their physical attributes rather than their social agency and are triggered by gameplay rather than serious introspection. The sublimation of acute crisis into a diffuse and constant state of misplaced anxiety gives the film's narrative an anti-climactic structure.' Thus, Lykidis argues, '*Chevalier* reminds us that neoliberalism survives today by distracting us from the real causes of our misery and by burdening us with a vast array of epiphenomenal concerns.'

Filmic responses to recession, debt and unemployment are also at the centre of the chapter by Álvarez, who considers a range of documentary and fiction films from Spain and Portugal, focusing in particular on dynamics of empathy, victimhood and blame. Álvarez argues that, while some films have produced narratives of self-blame, others have deployed 'a counter-hegemonic strategy against self-blaming discourses that [has] ultimately helped reinforce social bonds'. Thus, although 'the collective imaginary is already full of misrepresentations, the systematic effort of Iberian film-makers to show the plight of the victims has been mainly intended to turn compassion into solidarity and empowerment'. In her chapter, Patricia Sequeira Brás focuses attention on three Portuguese films produced by the cooperative Terratreme, which address the consequences of a process of de-industrialisation that preceded the Eurozone debt crisis, Portugal's financial bailout in 2011, and the further round of closures and layoffs that followed in its wake. Sequeira Brás argues that the documentaries *Active Life* and *Industrial Revolution* and the mostly fictional *The Nothing Factory* are all 'attempt to historicise the event of the economic/debt crisis'. In doing so, the films 'reproach simultaneously the general argument according to which the financial and debt crisis was a delimited moment in time, and the reasoning behind the general acceptance of the imposition of austerity measures'. Drawing on the work of Annie McClanahan, Sequeira Brás finds in the ruins of industrial landscapes in all three films a 'metonymic representation' of the financial crisis: 'the stagnation of the industrial economy [. . .] both prefigured and is the prehistory of the twenty-first-century credit crisis' (McClanahan 2017: 131).

Neoliberalism, austerity and escalating inequalities have also etiolated the previously celebrated welfare states of the Nordic countries (see Loftsdóttir and Jensen 2016). Kate Moffat provides a pertinent reminder that, despite its international reputation, the Finnish welfare state has been subject to a series of assaults, both planned and contingent, since the 1990s. With this context in mind, she explores how Aku Louhimies's social realist fictions *Paha maa/Frozen Land* (2005) and *Vuosaari/Naked Harbour* (2012) 'foreground economic and social inequality'. Moffat also considers how recent accusations that Louhimies bullied and coerced actresses on set have complicated the contexts of reception for his films, problematising his established persona as an auteur who personifies a critical social consciousness.

If, as Pierre Bourdieu, citing Weber, reminds us, every elite has 'a theodicy of [its] own privilege' (1998: 43),[19] under neoliberalism this justification takes the form of the lionisation of private enterprise and the profit motive as engines of achievement that, regardless of negative social impacts (insecure labour, environmental depletion, asset stripping, etc.), should be rewarded morally and politically as well as financially. As long ago as 1991 Bourdieu warned of the impact of neoliberalism on the (French) state, which was increasingly divided between the remnants of social welfare provision and an enthusiastic embrace of the private sector: 'the right hand, obsessed by the question of financial equilibrium, knows nothing of the problems of the left hand, confronted with the often very costly social consequences of "budgetary restrictions"'.[20] Twenty-six years later in London, 72 people died after a council-owned apartment block caught fire. The 2017 Grenfell Tower disaster became a lightning rod for concerns similar to those raised by Bourdieu: inequality, deregulation, outsourcing and gentrification in the housing sector, issues confronting cities across the continent and beyond. As Anna Viola Sborgi notes, London represents a paradigm for 'the deregulation of the real estate market in the neoliberal city'. In her chapter Sborgi considers several documentaries about Britain's housing crisis, and proposes that 'the housing sector [is] a testing ground for a growing social inequality along class, ethnic and gender divides'.[21] Her case studies, from the Channel 4 reality television series *How to Get a Council House*, to the more explicitly political films *Dispossession. The Great Social Housing Swindle* (Paul Sng, 2017) and *Concrete Soldiers UK* (Nikita Wolfe, 2017), 'portray, in different ways and with different purposes, a widening of inequality and social exclusion'.

The hollowing-out and marketisation of the welfare state pursued by neoliberalism and austerity's entwined consolidation across Europe has also been called to account in leftist fiction film. One of the most celebrated exponents of this critique has been Ken Loach, whose *I, Daniel Blake* (2016) was released 52 years after his directorial debut on BBC television. Martin Hall's contribution traces a dualism in Loach's career from 1991's *Riff-Raff* onwards that oscillates between celebrations of past revolutionary struggles in Ireland, Spain and Nicaragua, and stories of more or less isolated workers' sufferings under contemporary capitalism. For Hall, this contrast reveals that 'the films of the director considered to be the most left wing in Britain show no faith in a contemporary transformative Marxist paradigm'. He concludes: 'Loach's films set in the time of the most profound crisis of neoliberalism markedly fail [. . .], instead choosing to set up a dialectic between the individual and the system. The system itself [. . .] is left unexamined politically: what Loach does [instead] is present a moral critique.' A similar move away from collective resistance towards individual, ethical dilemmas can be located in the works of Jean-Pierre and Luc Dardenne. As Martin O'Shaughnessy notes in his chapter, '[w]ith their later fictions, recognising that these [political] traditions had lost their power, they positioned themselves alongside characters who effectively found themselves alone in a struggle of all-against-all'. Drawing on the work of the sociologist Marcel Mauss, O'Shaughnessy proposes that 'there is something akin to a gift economy running through the films that implicitly opens up more politically promising ways forward than their ethical probings'. He concludes: 'The problem with the Dardennes' austere, Levinas-inspired ethics is that it is dependent on that which it opposes: it needs neoliberalism's murderous logic to found its own commitment to the Other and offers no meaningful way to move beyond this opposition.' However, at least some of the gifts that populate the films 'pull bodies into productive collaboration rather than pitting the capacity for violence of some against the vulnerability of others'.

The Rise of Authoritarian Populism

Throughout Europe, the idea of 'crisis' has been put to work to call forth new populist policies, often centred on exclusion, scapegoating and nativism. It is vital to avoid knee-jerk dismissals of populism, however. A significant caution is offered by Kenan Malik:

> contempt for ordinary folk is visible [. . .] in much of the debate about populism [. . .] it's not populist disaffection that is unreasonable, but the policies and institutions that have created that disaffection. Policies that have driven up inequality and driven down living standards. Institutions that have excluded people from the process of decision-making [. . .] Material hardship is [thus] viewed through the prism of political voicelessness. (Malik 2018)[22]

It is also important to understand that the current rise of populist nationalisms is to a degree an intensification of the gradual 'Haiderization of Europe' (Wodak 2015) in the prior decade. In her 2015 analysis of the political success of Jorg Haider's right-wing Freedom Party in Austria during the 1990s and 2000s, and the continent-wide rise of right-wing populism espousing revisionist history, nativist chauvinism, xenophobia and anti-immigration rhetoric, Ruth Wodak cites the 1973 Copenhagen Declaration on European Identity, which enshrines 'social justice [and] respect for human rights'. She comments that 'these values have unfortunately been backgrounded, possibly even forgotten' in the renationalising tendencies of the past twenty-five years (2015: 7). But the ascent of populism, in both right-wing and left-wing variants, has also been an opportunistic strategy, presented as a necessary response to the economic and social dislocations generated by the crash and enforced austerity. As Philip Stephens, chief political commentator of the *Financial Times*, noted in 2018, 'Populism is the true legacy of the global financial crisis'. The historian Ian Kershaw insists that '[c]ivil society, despite the traumas [of the crash and its aftermath, has] proved resilient' across Europe. But he notes that the post-crash decade has also been marked by political volatility throughout the continent (2018: 511).

In his 2016 study *The Populist Explosion*, John B. Judis distinguishes between left-wing populisms, which are largely dyadic (pitting the demands of 'the people' against the entrenched interests of big business and political elites, evident in movements such as Podemos in Spain and SYRIZA in Greece), and right-wing populisms (such as Trump in the US, Golden Dawn in Greece,

UKIP, Marine Le Pen's Front National, Alternative für Deutschland and the Lega Nord in Italy) which, beyond their distinct particularities, are essentially triadic. The third term deployed by these movements is an additional enemy, which they claim is unfairly supported by political and media elites, a part that is usually played by immigrants (and, in the US, African Americans).[23] A key opportunity that right-wing populists exploited enthusiastically, and through which they made significant political gains, from Italy to Germany, from Greece to Hungary, was provided by the so-called 'refugee or migrant crisis' of 2015–16.

The 'Refugee/Migrant Crisis'

The crisis saw well over a million people seek asylum in the EU, and further catalysed nationalist, xenophobic and racist politics.[24] Daniel Trilling offers a useful summary:

> Although the [global] proportion of migrants has not grown significantly, the origin and direction of migration has changed:research by [Hein] De Haas and Mathias Czaika suggests that people are leaving a much wider range of countries than ever before, and they are heading to a much narrower range of destinations than ever before. They are going to the places where power and wealth have become concentrated. Europe, and northwest Europe in particular, is one of those places. (2018, citing Czaika and de Haas 2014)

Trilling adds: 'to see the crisis as an event that began in 2015 and ended the following year is a mistake, because it obscures the fact that the underlying causes have not changed'. This disaster has been shaped by European overreaction and panic, and thus 'has as much to do with immigration policies drawn up in European capitals as it does with events outside the continent' (Trilling 2018). As austerity and neoliberalism accelerate economic and social insecurity throughout Europe, and the sovereignty of nation-states is eroded by globalisation, refugees – readily conflated with economic migrants and 'illegal immigrants' in the language of politicians and commentators[25] – have been repeatedly blamed for these uncertainties.

While notions of 'Europe' as 'a space of imagined possibility' (Osseiran 2017: 192) have informed many of those attempting to travel to the continent,[26] recent outpourings of resentment and hostility against such migrants need to be understood as one facet of an extensive system of violence, past and present, that has been constitutive of the European project. Prem Kumar Rajaram draws on the work of Fanon, Bhabha and Said to emphasise the importance of the cultural and symbolic sphere in this system of dominance:

> The European project is [. . .] colonial not only because colonialism was the condition that allowed for its economic and political emergence, and not only because of its entrenchment in neo-imperialist political economies that generate global insecurities and displacements, but also because of [the discursive] attribution of fullness [to Europe] and the readiness to juxtapose lack elsewhere. (Rajaram 2016: 4)

This Eurocentric perspective is manifest even in some of the well-meaning liberal fiction films interrogated by Thomas Austin in his chapter on the cinema of 'Fortress Europe'. Austin analyses films by Aki Kaurismäki and Emanuele Crialese which primarily focus on the hospitality offered by white European characters towards new arrivals. He contrasts them with two works that attend more closely to the experience of people trying to reach Europe, their dangerous journeys and the problems that await them: Senegalese director Moussa Touré's *La Pirogue* (2012) and American Italian Jonas Carpignano's *Mediterranea* (2015).

In the collision of authoritarian and increasingly illiberal democracies with autonomous flows of refugees and migrants seeking refuge in the EU, the case of Hungary under the leadership of Fidesz party leader and current prime minister Viktór Orbán raises particular concerns.[27] In a consideration of eight years of documentaries made during the Orbán regime, Lóránt Stőhr notes the government's 2011 withdrawal of state funding from film-makers likely to be critical of Fidesz, and a gradual thematic shift from 'empathic documentaries on immigrants integrated into the society and their difficulties in refugee camps' towards more ironic approaches to the installation of physical and psychological boundaries against the Other promulgated under Orbán's rule. Stőhr comments on how long it has taken Hungarian documentaries to recognise the experiences, voices and stories of migrants and refugees, and warns:

> However, it is possible that growing authoritarian tendencies and xenophobic anger at Asian and African migrants will hinder film-makers in making further complex documentaries on asylum seekers. Hungarian documentary has taken a long time to present the individuality of a migrant on screen, but now that the film-makers have found her face, the right to show it might be taken away.

The widespread and ongoing political scapegoating of migrants and refugees across the continent has also deployed the spectre of immigration to divert blame for the damaging impacts of austerity and neoliberal policies on employment and welfare state provision. Like many commentators on the left in the UK, Aditya Chakrabortty noted the intensification of anti-migrant prejudices before and after the Brexit vote of 2016. However, he supplemented this with a more significant observation: 'crucially, migrants were made scapegoats for the misery caused by the government's own drastic spending cuts – for a buckling NHS, a cash-starved school system and falling wages' (2018). Thus, much as with the 2008 crash, right-wing politicians and their allies in the UK media worked to install a fallacious and self-serving narrative which was becoming increasingly difficult to challenge. This second bout of selective media amnesia also conveniently found an alibi for the economically and socially destructive policies enabled by the first.

Both the growing dissatisfaction with the refugee crisis in Europe as a whole and the resurgence of nationalism are indices of what the Hungarian political philosopher Gaspar Miklos Tamas calls 'post-fascism'. For Tamas, post-fascism, like its historical predecessor, operates on the basis of the exclusion of what are considered to be unproductive segments of the population (such as refugees, Roma, people of alternative sexualities and immigrants). The difference is that post-fascism does not rely on strategies of violent *Machtergreifung* (seizure of power), but manages to make its agenda mainstream without going against the established forms of electoral democracy. Post-fascism perpetuates hegemonic capitalist structures but tends to 'ethnicise' class conflicts and geopolitical inequalities. In effect, the politics of exclusion leads to the reversal of 'the Enlightenment tendency to assimilate citizenship to the human condition'. As Tamas writes,

> The scission of citizenship and sub-political humanity is now complete, the work of Enlightenment irretrievably lost. Post-fascism does not need to put non-citizens into freight trains to take them to death; instead, it need only prevent the new non-citizens from boarding any trains that might take them into the happy world of overflowing rubbish bins that could feed them. Post-fascist movements everywhere, but especially in Europe, are anti-immigration movements, grounded in the 'homogeneous' worldview of productive usefulness. They are not simply protecting racial and class privileges within the nation-state (although they are doing that, too) but protecting universal citizenship within the rich nation-state against the virtual-universal citizenship of all human beings, regardless of geography, language, race, denomination, and habits. The current notion of 'human rights' might defend people from the lawlessness of tyrants, but it is no defense against the lawlessness of no rule. (Tamas 2000)

Europe in Crisis

The contributors to this collection do not take 'Europe' to be a self-evident fact or indeed a stable entity in political, social, cultural or economic terms, and the same is true of at least some of the films they discuss. Instead, European exceptionalism and notions of liberty, freedom, the rule of law and common cultural heritage are queried and disrupted. In Anca Parvulescu's pithy phrase: 'if we need to be skeptical of anything, it is Europe' (2012: 727). Similarly, Nataša Kovačević (2018: 3) calls for 'a critical stance towards self-congratulatory multicultural imaginings of community in the EU that occlude neocolonial relations of dependence and exclusion'. However, while selective amnesias and expedient historical mythologies have continued to multiply throughout Europe (see, for instance, Henley 2018), even before Kovačević published her critique, the smug multicultural self-image of the EU had come under increasing pressure, challenged as much by an efflorescence of nativist and racist politics as by postcolonial scholarship. But what this vital critical tradition has served to clarify is precisely the connections between a 'liberal' Eurocentric myth grounded on an (often implicit) hierarchical, civilisational logic that Nico Wilterdink (1993: 120) has called 'Euro-nationalism',[28] and the more explicitly aggressive or 'illiberal' racisms of various chauvinist movements across the continent. Despite their apparent differences, what subtends the work of Wilterdink's 'Euro-ideologists' and the claims of the many nationalisms now (re)igniting within Europe is a violent history of self-definition at the juridical, economic and symbolic expense of others, both inside and outside its borders.[29] As Parvulescu, drawing on Derrida, notes: 'The temptation is to believe that Europeans have left their troubled (colonial) past behind, performed a purifying mea culpa, and emerged as trueborn cosmopolitans. This is perhaps the most insidious form of European nationalism' (2014: 4).[30]

What part have European films played in this dynamic of de- and re-mythologisation? One avenue explored by critical film-makers has been the movements of people seeking work and safety, both internal migrations (often but not exclusively from Eastern to Western Europe) and external flows towards the continent, along with the increasingly technologised, militarised and racialised efforts made to monitor and obstruct these movements. Even in the years of recession and austerity following the crash of 2008, such procedures operated alongside the continued reliance of European economies, both legal and illegal, on cheap migrant labour, notably in agriculture, care work, factories, construction, sex work and other low-status jobs. In his examination of the white benefactor trope in recent fiction films about migration, Thomas Austin turns to Carpignano's *Mediterranea* (2016), a film which dispenses with this model to focus instead on the struggle for subsistence of undocumented African labourers in southern Italy. Austin writes:

> [Capitalism's] persistent, systemic appetite for cheapness has both put to work and immiserated diverse peoples (and natures) in Africa, Asia and South America, and is now often the only way in which a few of their number might be granted a precarious existence inside Fortress Europe.

It is this precarity, and its role in underpinning the (still) relatively prosperous economies of Europe, which is foregrounded in *Mediterranea*. Another film which has attracted critical attention is Maren Ade's *Toni Erdmann* (2016). In both social positioning and direction of travel, the film's (anti-)heroine Ines Conradi (Sandra Hüller), a German corporate strategist working in Bucharest, embodies an inversion of the Eastern European subproletarian (female) care or sex workers of whom Anca Parvulescu writes: 'Although they, too, are theoretically European, certain Eastern Europeans (typically migrant workers coming from countries like Bulgaria, Romania, Albania, Serbia, Moldova, Ukraine) are considered immigrants in [Western] Europe' (2012: 727).[31] *Toni Erdmann* is one of four films explored in Constantin Parvulescu's contribution here, along with *Mediterranea*, *Moon* (Jones, 2009), and *Capital* (*Le Capital*) (Costa-Gavras, 2012). Working across these diverse films, Parvulescu considers the exploitative logics of capitalism, and how it is entwined with migrations of labour, both white-collar and blue-collar. He concludes,

> the so-called demolishing of barriers and disruption of antiquated structures with the aim of making room for free enterprise, coupled with efforts to enhance the circulation of capital, have been accompanied by the establishment of new borders, internal and external, as well as economic and political no-man's lands permissive of unfettered exploitation.

Dina Iordanova's chapter calls attention to a hitherto underexplored phenomenon, the 'hushed crisis' of antiziganism, or hatred of Roma people. While antiziganism is evident in both Western and Eastern Europe, Iordanova concentrates in particular on the latter. 'West European countries can act legally against the Roma without being punished [by the EU], while the East European countries cannot do this and leave it to paramilitaries.' Iordanova investigates three films (from Hungary, Slovakia and Bosnia) that expose and condemn the mistreatment of Roma, before considering an antiziganist trilogy from the Czech Republic, and then a series of Ukrainian anti-Roma pogrom videos uploaded to YouTube. 'Typically, these are short videos showing street confrontations and vigilante groups taking action against groups of Roma who are, allegedly, involved in illegal activities that the authorities do nothing about.' Iordanova concludes: 'It should not be so difficult for us all – academics, educators, social scientists and film-makers – to work together to bring the hushed crisis into the daylight and confront it.'

Aesthetics and Politics

This collection does not simply track thematic linkages between political, economic and social developments of the past three decades and the work of socially engaged film-makers in Europe. Crucially, it also unpacks the diverse aesthetics of these filmic responses, to interrogate the role played by manifold variants of film form in the critiques (or justifications) that they offer. Clearly, even within established designations such as documentary, art cinema, or genre film, a wide spectrum of aesthetic options obtains. So what are the political impacts of the particular choices made by film-makers operating either within or beyond these modalities?

Rosalind Galt opens her contribution by raising the question of 'where we might locate political aesthetics in contemporary European cinema, and in particular the challenge of escaping the various modes of liberal realism that dominate representations of economic crisis and migration'. Her subsequent analysis of Kornél Mundruczó's *White God* (2014), in particular its corporeal and symbolic uses of real dogs, explores a range of possible interpretations of this productively ambiguous film, which refuses the contrasting templates of post-neorealist art cinema and political modernism. Instead, Galt argues, *White God* 'attunes its spectator at once to dogs and to humans, in a process that is increasingly uncertain and dislocating'. Thus, while multiple allegorical readings may be invited by *White God*, wherein 'the dogs are legible as racial, national, ethnic, ecological and animal figures', the film also 'asks us to attune our senses and our empathy towards a collective whose being and desires cannot be so easily exhausted by interpretation'.

Another film-maker whose work confounds the conventions of social realism, but also those of popular genres, is Veiko Õunpuu. In her analysis of Õunpuu's work, Eva Näripea traces his attempts to resist closure and happy or redemptive endings, and to disintegrate narrative structures, 'working with rhythms and atmospheres instead of action-driven stories, in order to provide "a filmic space the meaning of which remains elusive"' (citing Teder 2009). Exploring similar terrain, Angelos Koutsourakis locates a 're-emergence of an aesthetics of modernism' in European film making of the past two decades. He traces a 'reanimation' of modernist devices in films by Béla Tarr, Laurent Cantet and Michael Haneke which, in various ways, offer critiques of neoliberalism's erosion of economic and familial security not just in the 'underdeveloped' countries of the former Eastern bloc, but also among the affluent professional and business classes of Western Europe. For instance, he argues that Haneke's *Happy End* (2017) deploys a modernist structure of aphoristic fragments that recalls the writings of Kafka. Koutsourakis asks whether modernist strategies have 'had a comeback because, far from having overcome past contradictions, late modernity seems to be unable even to offer a positive narrative that justifies its inherent inequalities'.

Haneke also figures in the chapter by Alex Lykidis, which proposes that in Haneke's work in particular, 'multiculturalism is framed as a challenge to class privilege, effectively reversing the displacement of economic issues on to the cultural sphere' whereby cultural panics have blamed immigrants for the economic problems unleashed by austerity. Lykidis also investigates how Tsangari's *Chevalier* 'diverges from the tenets of psychological realism in order to highlight the democratic deficits of the neoliberal era'. In the film, he argues, an aesthetics of crisis is developed, while narrative crisis is withheld. He concludes: 'The bitter truth that *Chevalier* reveals is how an absence of self-awareness facilitates the infiltration of neoliberal values into every facet of our lives.' Finally, Thomas Austin's chapter considers filmic critiques of Fortress Europe's border regime which take contrasting aesthetic forms: from the foregrounded artifice and self-consciously cinephilic and playful address of Aki Kaurismäki's *Le Havre* (2011) to the realist *mise en scène*, hand-held camera and use of available light in Jonas Carpignano's *Mediterranea*. While *Le Havre*'s performative approach may seem more surprising than the verisimilitude and immersive aesthetics of *Mediterranea*, neither style is inevitable or 'best suited' to a socially engaged cinema.

A Planet in Crisis

As this introduction was being written, the UK-based Institute for Public Policy Research published a major report warning of a 'new domain of risk' catalysed by interacting planetary crises across environmental, economic and social spheres. *This is a Crisis: Facing Up to the Age of Environmental Breakdown* warns that

> Human-induced environmental change is occurring at an unprecedented scale and pace and the window of opportunity to avoid catastrophic outcomes in societies around the world is rapidly closing. These outcomes include economic instability, large-scale involuntary migration, conflict, famine and the potential collapse of social and economic systems. The historical disregard of environmental considerations in most areas of policy has been a catastrophic mistake.[32]

In this instance, the catastrophising language appears more than justified. The climate crisis is also important because it draws attention once again to Europe's colonialist past. Simon L. Lewis and Mark A. Maslin have situated the origins of the Anthropocene in European colonialism and the discovery of the 'new world' in North and South America. This historical approach forces us to consider how industrialisation was not something unconnected to colonialism but its direct consequence (Lewis and Maslin 2015: 175; see also Patel and Moore 2018). Naomi Klein issues this warning: 'The age of scientific racism begins alongside the transatlantic slave trade, it is a rationale for that brutality. If we are going to respond to climate change by fortressing our borders, then of course the theories that would justify that, that create these hierarchies of humanity, will come surging back' (Hanman 2019). And Farhana Yamin asserts: 'Ending dominion over nature goes hand in hand with tackling all forms of domination and hierarchy. The struggle for climate justice is also the struggle for racial, gender, sexual and economic equality' (2019: 25). How will European activists, politicians, voters, consumers, film-makers and audiences respond to this planetary emergency? Those urgent questions will call for another book.

Notes

1. Available at <http://www.bfi.org.uk/films-tv-people/4ce2b8abab5b1> (last accessed 12 October 2019).
2. The final eighty seconds of *Prologue*'s five-minute running time is devoted to a list of the names of the 204 people appearing in the film. Presumably these are 'real people', that is, non-professional actors, although Tarr films himself in the queue.
3. De-industrialisation remains an ongoing process in the global North. For instance, at the time of writing, the UK's GMB union reported that between 2007 and 2016, 600,000 more jobs had been lost in the manufacturing sector, taking its share of total national employment down to 9.2 per cent. As a result, 'the manufacturing sector has failed to regain the level of output seen before the financial crash in 2008' (Inman 2018).
4. See also Tooze 2018. On the eve of the crash, the financial sector of Cyprus was 7.5 times the size of its economy, and that of Iceland was 10 times as large (Basu 2018: 37, 46).
5. On differences between Scandinavian, British, German, Austrian, French and Italian experiences of this development, see Crouch 2004: ch. 3. On the role of a rapidly developing China as both outsourcing partner for, and competitive rival to, Europe and the US, see Kynge 2009.
6. Crouch 2004: ch. 2. The increasing polarisation of income as well as wealth was particularly evident in the UK. Ian Kershaw writes: 'Leading business executives had earned forty-seven times the average income of their staff in 1998; by 2014 this had grown to 143 times as much' (2018: 506).
7. There are clearly exceptions to this trend. But John Smith notes that one reason for employers' reluctance to invest in innovation, new equipment or staff training in order to boost productivity has been the low cost of labour. In a deregulated labour market, it is cheaper simply to employ more staff when demand rises, and shed them when it falls, than to spend on sustained efforts to improve productivity. This refusal has been one cause of the historically slow pace of economic recovery after the global slump that followed the 2008 crash. Smith 2016, summarised in Basu 2018: 133.
8. Screpanti concludes: '[An] important political consequence is that the opposition between the immediate interests of the Northern and the Southern proletariat ceases to exist.'

9. On the latter, see Varoufakis 2018. See also Lordon 2018 and anonymous 2018 for analyses of the 'gilets jaunes' protests against Macron's 'extremism of the center' and his neoliberal programme of tax cuts for the rich, increases to fuel duty and other assaults on living standards.
10. Imre is drawing here on Kideckel 2009.
11. Imre is drawing here on Sztompka 2004. For a brilliant account of the 'imitation imperative' in post-Communist Europe, and the feelings of inferiority and resentment towards the initially copied West that it has generated among increasingly anti-liberal politicians and voters, see Krastev and Holmes 2019.
12. The shared reliance of opposing political parties on both corporate funding and a 'consultant class' of experts is most clearly evident in the US.
13. Screpanti adds that in the 'emerging' economies of the global South, global capitalism operates through the 'destruction of traditional cultures and institutions'. It 'not only exports goods and money, but also tends to export firms and ideologies, and indeed to export itself as an exclusive mode of production' (2014: 206).
14. In the US, key measures included Bill Clinton's 1999 repeal of the Banking Act of 1933, which had limited banks' ability to undertake high-risk speculation; the 2002 launch of George W. Bush's housing plan, which encouraged high-risk loans to low-income borrowers; and major reductions in controls on stock exchanges and banks in 2004 (Screpanti 2014: 128–9).
15. By early 2019 commentators were warning of the increasing likelihood of a second global crash. See, for instance, Blakely 2019.
16. Basu's sample consisted of BBC news bulletins, and news stories and comment pieces published by the *Mirror*, the *Sun*, the *Telegraph* and the *Guardian* during two one-week periods each year from 2007 to 2015 (Basu 2018: 29).
17. See also Lapavitsas 2010, cited in Basu 2018: 145: 'Public debt rose in 2009 mostly because states rescued the financial system and tax revenue collapsed as the recession unfolded. Profligacy and public inefficiency had little to do with it.'
18. See also Bourdieu 1998: 40: 'the structural violence exerted by the financial markets, in the form of layoffs, loss of security, etc., is matched sooner or later in the form of suicides, crime and delinquency, drug addiction, alcoholism and a whole host of minor and major acts of everyday violence'. On the contradictory position of the nuclear family under neoliberalism, as both site of the reproduction of labour power and engine of consumption, but also 'a salve for the psychic wounds inflicted by anarchic social-economic conditions', offering temporary and fragile respite from the demands of the workplace, see Fisher 2009: 32–3; Sennett 1998.
19. Bourdieu is particularly critical of neoliberal intellectuals and technocrats who both champion and benefit from 'social neo-Darwinism'. One might compare this 'ideology of competence' with the Blair government's neoliberal version of a 'meritocracy' in the UK.
20. Pierre Bourdieu, interviewed by R. P. Droit and T. Firenczi in December 1991, published as 'The left hand and the right hand of the State', *Le Monde*, 14 January 1992, reprinted in Bourdieu 1998: 5.
21. Kershaw (2018: 506) notes that 'those forced to sleep on the streets more than doubled in number in London between 2010 and 2017 [. . .] The use of food banks to provide meals for the destitute rose by 1,642 per cent over the same period.'

22. He goes on to ask: 'How can we give progressive shape to people's disaffection?' (Malik 2018).
23. Jacques Rancière (2013: 104) offers a vital reminder of linkages between mainstream discourse and 'extreme' populist positions, namely French secularism on the one hand and the Front National's xenophobia and racism on the other: '[Marine Le Pen] really only condenses into a concrete image a discursive sequence (Muslim = Islamist = Nazi) that is present almost everywhere in so-called republican prose. The so-called populist extreme right does not express a specific xenophobic passion emanating from the depths of the body popular; it is a satellite that profits from the strategies of the state and the distinguished intellectual campaigns.'
24. 'In 2015, 1,255,600 first time asylum seekers applied for international protection in the Member States of the European Union (EU), a number more than double that of the previous year. The number of Syrians [. . .] has doubled [. . .] to reach 362,800, while the number of Afghans has almost quadrupled to 178,200 and that of Iraqis has multiplied by 7 to 121,500. They represent the three main citizenships of first time asylum applicants [. . .] accounting for more than half of all first time applicants' (anonymous 2016). As Anatol Lieven notes (2019: 41), the second Gulf War, pursued by George W. Bush, was a key catalyst for the Syrian civil war which then led to the influx of refugees. But the war was also shaped by the climate emergency: 'Between 2006 and 2011, 60 per cent of Syria suffered the worst long-term drought and crop failures in the country's history. Two to three million people became poor and many more were internally displaced. The resulting social instability amplified the political factors that led to war in Syria' (Yamin 2019: 24).
25. The designations 'refugee' and 'migrant' have also often been arranged in a hierarchy which elevates the 'deserving' refugee above the 'undeserving' migrant. This distinction is often a racialised one, which dehumanises and criminalises economic migrants from sub-Saharan Africa in particular.
26. Osseiran also emphasises the significance of movements within the heterogeneous territory of Europe: 'Migrants/refugees' movement *within* the EU space [. . .] is best understood to be, at times, a continuation of their movement *into* the EU space – toward "Europe" [. . .] Syrian migrants/refugees distinguished among various spaces within Europe and set up their own evaluative hierarchies of EU member states' (2017: 191, 196, italics in original).
27. Nicholas De Genova notes that, despite Orbán's aggressive rhetoric, the Hungarian authorities have vacillated 'between vicious violence and begrudging complicity [. . .] in the face of the veritable intractability of migrant and refugee movements' (De Genova 2017: 13).
28. Wilterdink locates three key ideas evident in both state nationalisms and ideas of Europe: 'unity in diversity'; a teleological (and highly selective) model of slow but steady progress across a long history; and a sense that identity is not yet fully achieved but requires further work.
29. Wilterdink suggests that (selected) wars and battles are much more likely to be found in nationalist writings and ideologies than in Euro-nationalist ones (1993: 123). Writing in the early 1990s, he underestimates the possibility of resurgent nationalisms in Europe (1993: 134).

30. Parvulescu is drawing on Derrida 1992b.
31. According to a United Nations report, cited in the *Guardian*: '3.6 million Romanians live abroad, compared with about 20 million left in the country (among EU countries, its diaspora is fourth largest, after the UK, Poland and Germany)' (Ciobanu 2018). The *Guardian* also reports that, following economic collapse and increasing political tensions with Russia, 400,000 Ukrainians now work legally in neighbouring Poland, and the country is now the biggest recipient of wage remittances in Europe, at 11 per cent of GDP (Walker 2019).
32. Available at <https://www.ippr.org/research/publications/age-of-environmental-breakdown> (last accessed 12 October 2019).

1. AESTHETICS OF CRISIS: ART CINEMA AND NEOLIBERALISM

Alex Lykidis

In modern Greek κριση/*krise* means both a moment of difficulty, and judgement or discernment.[1] The etymological origins of the English word 'crisis' are Greek, and its secondary meaning in Greek, that of judgement, was in use in the English language until the early eighteenth century. The first non-specialised definition of crisis in the *Oxford English Dictionary* describes it as a 'vitally important or decisive stage in the progress of anything; a turning-point; also, a state of affairs in which a decisive change for better or worse is imminent; now applied esp. to times of difficulty, insecurity, and suspense in politics or commerce'. This definition shows the crucial link between the two Greek meanings of the word and between the English word's previous and current usages. A crisis is a period of difficulty or insecurity, a moment of decisive change, a turning point. To ensure that this change or turn is a positive one, one must exercise good judgement and sound decision making. As Eugene Hollahan asserts, crisis is used 'as signifier for stressful circumstances, as signifier for dialectical turning points, and as signifier evoking, inducing or even necessitating decisions or judgments' (1992: 4). In other words, crisis challenges our intellectual faculties and compels us to use them.

Throughout its history art cinema has been perceived as an intellectual mode of film making. Avoiding many of the emotional manipulations of popular forms, art films use detachment, analytical style and ambiguity to pose difficult questions to the viewer. Noël Burch defines modernist cinema, of which much of post-war art cinema was a prime example, as a mode of film making that subverts, deconstructs and critically challenges the aesthetic and ideological tenets of classical cinema (1981: 15). Alexandre Astruc saw the development of cinema after 1945, the period in which art cinema became institutionalised and stabilised as a recognisable form, as moving in the direction of philosophy and writing, one in which film language could be used to express abstract thoughts (1968: 18–20; see also Kovács 2007: 37–9). The association of art cinema with an intellectual mode of address presents it as a promising candidate for the facilitation of critical analysis in a time of crisis.

The differentiation of post-war art cinema from Hollywood cinema was based in part on what was perceived to be its heightened fidelity to the complexities of everyday life and human consciousness. Whereas some art cinema directors such as Jean-Luc Godard, Jean-Marie Straub and Danièle Huillet rejected verisimilitude as a mode of address, emphasising instead stylisation and reflexivity, others retained an investment in social and psychological realism. These variants of realist representation have been shaped by two of the most influential theoretical traditions of the modern era, Marxism and Freudianism, both of which formulate crisis as a crucial issue to be understood and addressed. In Marxism, the underlying contradictions of the capitalist mode of production create a series of social, economic and political crises that threaten the survival of the capitalist system by undermining capital accumulation and the social reproduction of the means and relations of production. The social realism of Italian Neorealist films such as *Ladri di biciclette* (*Bicycle Thieves*, 1948) and *La Terra Trema* (1948), as well as certain strains of later art cinema, brought attention to the effects of structural crises and systemic failures on the lives of the working class. In Freudianism, the mental strain created by the competing investments of the id, ego and superego produce psychic crises, managed through defence mechanisms such as denial, rationalisation and repression. The psychological realism of post-war art films such as Federico Fellini's *8½* (1963) and Ingmar Bergman's *Persona* (1966) explored the propensity for crisis of the human psyche, with a special emphasis on the existential alienation of the faithless modern subject (Kovács 2007: 90–9; Bordwell 1985: 208). Art cinema's analytical potential and engagement with crisis are all the more needed in the current conjuncture, one in which neoliberal policies are exacerbating the crisis characteristics of the capitalist system.

Crisis Tendencies of Neoliberalism

The era of late capitalism has been defined by successive crises, the magnitude and frequency of which have far outpaced those of the preceding era (Harvey 2010: 8). After the Second World War, Keynesian state planning, market regulation, fixed exchange rates and welfare benefits were used to stave off systemic crisis. These economic policies were the result of the capital–labour compromise made possible by strong labour parties and unions and by the spectre of the Communist bloc that provided an ideological alternative to capitalism. The social democratic consensus between capital and labour ensured stability but also set limits on capital accumulation, the lifeblood of the capitalist system (Streeck 2014: 24–5). The energy crisis of the early 1970s proved to be the last straw for the capitalist class, which decided to abandon the accommodations of the previous era and usher in a series of neoliberal policies that transformed the relations of power between capital and labour (Duménil and Lévy 2002: 43). Production facilities were moved out of the industrialised West to cheaper and less regulated labour markets, taxation policy became more regressive with steep tax cuts for top income earners, corporations and investors, the power of labour unions and the welfare state was eroded, public enterprises were privatised, financial markets were deregulated and a financial infrastructure was put in place to facilitate the international flow of capital (Harvey 2010: 12–16; Streeck 2014: 28–9, 34–6; Ayers and Saad-Filho 2015: 606).

Neoliberal policies temporarily resolved the crisis of capital accumulation by shifting wealth and power from labour to capital, but in doing so they produced a drop in purchasing power due to wage stagnation (Duménil and Lévy 2002: 54–5). The resulting consumption crisis was managed through the liberalisation of financial markets that enabled the expansion of private and public debt as a way to supplement waning household income (Streeck 2014: 33–9). Public resistance to the increasing social and economic inequality caused by neoliberal policies has been contained by the hollowing-out of democratic institutions and practices. The convergence of centre-left and centre-right party platforms has provided voters with few alternatives to neoliberal orthodoxy and transnational integration has undermined the exercise of popular sovereignty (Mair 2014: 19–55; Ayers and Saad-Filho 2015: 604). In order to justify de-democratisation, mainstream politicians and scholars are increasingly touting technocratic forms of governance and downplaying the importance of elections. Politics has become a dirty word, associated with irrationality and petty self-interest, and political critiques of neoliberal dogma are portrayed as reactionary attempts to inhibit the inexorable forward march and universal reach of market forces (Bourdieu and Wacquant 2001: 4; W. Brown 2015: 42, 123–31; Cammaerts 2015: 528; Davies 2016; Mair 2014: 8–16). While neoliberal ideology presents itself as incontrovertible, political resistance to the precarity and inequality created by neoliberal policies has not been completely eliminated. There have been street demonstrations and occupations against globalisation and neoliberalism for many years, and now popular discontent is beginning to influence election outcomes. One way in which this resistance has been contained is through the scapegoating of immigrants for the immiseration caused by neoliberalism (Feldner, Vighi and Žižek 2014: 3; Balibar and Wallerstein 2011: 29–36, 217–27). The waning legitimacy of the political centre has enabled far-right ideologues to win over disenfranchised working-class voters through a combination of xenophobia, anti-establishment posturing and anti-globalisation rhetoric (della Porta 2017: 36–7; Mair 2014: 19; Mouffe 2005: 66).

The survival of the capitalist system in the neoliberal era has been facilitated by a series of spatial, temporal and ideological fixes of structural crisis. The crisis of capitalist accumulation that began in the 1970s was deferred through a massive transfer of wealth from labour to capital, but this created a consumption crisis that was managed through financialisation and the expansion of debt. The resulting increase in precarity and inequality generated political resistance, which was effectively circumvented by the undemocratic enforcement of neoliberal policies through technocratic governance and transnational integration. Undemocratic governance in turn created a crisis of political legitimacy, which was deflected through the manufacture of cultural crises and moral panics about immigrants and racial and religious minorities. At the heart of this process of crisis management is the mechanism of displacement, which shifts the arena of struggle between economic, political and cultural realms. Displacements may occur organically as unfolding crises reverberate across different sectors of society or they may be deliberately produced in order to disguise the real causes and effects of a crisis (Ayers and Saad-Filho 2015: 605–6; Feldner, Vighi and Žižek 2014: 3; Streeck 2014: 10). In order to explain these transpositions of crisis effects, what is required is an aesthetics of crisis that foregrounds and reverses the direction of the ideological displacements central to the survival of the neoliberal order.

Aesthetics of Crisis

In novels and other narrative forms, historical crisis is usually represented by placing one or more characters in a crisis situation, a narrative turning point that presents both 'danger and opportunity', necessitating critical reflection, good judgement and decisive action (Hollahan 1992: 35). In these instances, the forward momentum of the narrative is interrupted by 'traumatic self-examination', the need to critically reflect on what can be done to resolve the crisis situation (Hollahan 1992: 14). This temporary suspension of narrative development produces a more self-conscious and intellectual prose that often explicitly addresses political or philosophical questions (Hollahan 1992: 6). Narrative crisis may be combined with aesthetic crisis, in which unconventional style takes readers out of their familiar patterns of textual interpretation and comprehension. The transmutation of historical crisis into narrative and aesthetic forms demands a more critical reader, one whose immersion in the narrative is complicated by the intellectual and aesthetic challenges presented by crisis tropes in the text (Hollahan 1992: 10, 24).

The Russian Formalist concept of defamiliarisation and the Brechtian concept of estrangement can provide us with the critical language we need to understand aesthetic crisis. The emergence of a historical crisis suggests that established patterns of thought and action are flawed in some way and that radical shifts in perception and behaviour are required to overcome the current impasse. The aesthetic principle of estrangement seeks to denaturalise and provoke critical reflection on existing practices and beliefs. As Fredric Jameson notes, to 'make something look strange, to make us look at it with new eyes, implies the antecedence of a general familiarity, of a habit which prevents us from really looking at things, a kind of perceptual numbness' (Jameson 1998: 39; see also Brecht 2015: 152, 163–4). Brechtian estrangement portrays human activity 'as something that calls for explanation, that is not to be taken for granted, not just natural' with the aim of making 'the spectators adopt an attitude of inquiry and criticism' (Brecht 2015: 180, 184). For Brecht, social interactions in a work of art 'should be [. . . raised] above the level of the everyday, the obvious, the expected' (2015: 164). Estrangement can be used to historicise and by doing so open up critical perspectives on epistemes such as religion and philosophy that are presented as eternal, self-evident or universal (Brecht 2015: 156, 158, 163; Jameson 1972: 58; Jameson 1998: 40–1). Brecht argues that theatrical actors 'must play the incidents as historical ones. Historical incidents are unique, transitory incidents, associated with particular periods. The conduct of the persons involved in them is not fixed and universally human' (2015: 187–8). Defamiliarisation has a similar aim, seeking to remove 'objects from the automatism of perception' by slowing down and making more difficult our perceptual encounter with descriptions of the world (Shklovsky 1965: 13; see also Shklovsky 1965: 12, 22; Jameson 1972: 51). The objective of both estrangement and defamiliarisation is to induce perceptual renewal by challenging reification and established conventions. What this suggests is that our understanding of historical crisis depends on the cultivation of aesthetic crisis.

Aesthetic displacements or tropological movements produce stylistic turning points that can parallel and help explain historical crises. Defamiliarisation achieves perceptual changes through 'a complex system of [stylistic] mutations and readjustments' which create 'eccentric' reorientations of a reader's perspective (Jameson 1972: 53). Estrangement in Brechtian theatre relies on similar shifts in style, such as the transposition of an actor's role into the third person or into the past (Brecht 2015: 186). Estrangement is often achieved not by changing the fundamental components of style, but rather by reorganising the relations between them. The Brechtian emphasis on contradiction is achieved in part through a reordering of aesthetic elements, which generates conspicuous juxtapositions that reveal the underlying antagonisms of social and aesthetic relationships (Jameson 1998: 83). Defamiliarisation functions in a similar way, providing a new perspective on social phenomena by rearranging them or reorienting our view of them, so as to present them 'out of their normal context' (Shklovsky 1965: 17).

Defamiliarisation and estrangement rely on disorder and disharmony in order to destabilise received ideas and habitual mechanisms of perception. The predictable order and harmony of aesthetic texts must be repeatedly unsettled so that the passive acceptance of conventional thinking does not take hold (Shklovsky 1965: 21, 24). Estrangement and defamiliarisation generate 'abrupt discontinuities' and 'ruptures' within aesthetic traditions, creating what Jameson describes as 'dissonant clarity', a critical understanding of social conditions enabled by the disruption of received wisdom and established pathways of perception (Jameson 1972: 53; 1998: 71). As Brecht put it, 'I was aware of the huge inconsistencies in people's social life, and I did not think it my task formally to iron out all the discordances and interferences of which I was strongly conscious'; instead Brecht aimed to 'show human dealings as contradictory, fiercely fought over, full of violence' (2015: 171).

Throughout its post-war history, art cinema has pursued the disorder and disharmony advocated in theories of estrangement and defamiliarisation (Kolker 1983: 139–95; Perry 2006). Robert Self contrasts art films to the limit texts of the Hollywood studio system that show the strain of their attempts to artificially resolve social problems through narrative coherence and closure. He argues that unlike these limit texts, art films purposely foreground the intractable contradictions of capitalist societies and dominant discourse.

> The art cinema generates its ambiguity as a result of appropriating for itself as subject and form the very problems which constitute the limits of classical narrative. The limit text breaks apart in its effort to recapture in a final unity the disorder that initiates narrative movement; it only partially succeeds in positing a harmonious world of reality characterized by the equivalence of sign and referent, the wholeness of individual identity, the confidence and security of economic exchanges. The distressed aspects of these qualities constitute the art cinema, its ambiguity a function thematically of troubled foregrounding, troubled sexuality, troubled economy, language. What emerges as the excess, the logic of dispersion that exceeds control by the economic narrative in the classical cinema, is given textual primacy by the art film. (Self 1979: 77)

The narrative characteristics of many art films – narrational gaps and delays, lack of resolution, reduced generic motivation and looser cause–effect linkages between narrative actions – align with the representational objectives of defamiliarisation and estrangement by complicating identification and enabling contemplation through a suspension of narrative development

(Bordwell 1985: 205–12; on estrangement's opposition to identification, see Brecht 2015: 151–2). These elements produce the more critical and distanced forms of reading or spectatorship advocated by Shklovsky and Brecht.[2] The deviations from Hollywood style that have come to define art cinema can be understood as transpositions of the kind advocated in theories of estrangement and defamiliarisation. At the most basic level, there is in many art films a reflexive shift in the viewer's attention from story to plot – from what happens in the story to how it is presented to us in the plot – which denaturalises the representation of reality and reminds us of the text's authorship (akin to the anti-illusory style of the epic theatre favoured by Brecht; see Brecht 2015: 77). Our attention is also frequently reoriented from narrative action to characterisation and we are confronted not with the straightforward narrative questions of Hollywood genre films but more difficult social, psychological or philosophical questions that cannot be easily resolved through narrative development or closure (Self 1979: 76–7).

Since estrangement and defamiliarisation depend on the disruption of stylistic conventions, the aesthetic crises produced by contemporary art films should not be measured only against the standards established by mainstream cinema but also against the characteristics of earlier art films. One important development in the content of art cinema has been a change in the causes of narrative crisis, which in contemporary films have more to do with power imbalances and unequal access to information than existential ennui, as in the post-war period. In today's art films narrative crisis is often translated into a corresponding crisis of spectatorship through unusual juxtapositions of or deviations from the conventions of art cinema. It is these stylistic permutations that have enabled contemporary auteurs to challenge the specific strategies of crisis management of the neoliberal era. For instance, in several of Michael Haneke's French-language films, the displacement of neoliberal economic and political crises on to the cultural sphere is reversed by emphasising the class interests that drive French resistance to multiculturalism. By refracting narrative crisis through the distorted lens of bourgeois subjectivity, Haneke's films reveal the way immigrants and people of colour are scapegoated in order to absolve ruling elites of responsibility for the negative consequences of neoliberal policies. Haneke pushes the antagonistic authorship associated with modernist art cinema to its breaking point by creating narrative aporias that can only be resolved if we assign responsibility for the harassment of the film's bourgeois characters to Haneke's authorial agency rather than the immigrant characters suspected of these crimes in the diegesis. The remainder of this chapter will discuss the aesthetics of crisis in Athina Rachel Tsangari's *Chevalier* (2015), which diverges from the tenets of psychological realism in order to highlight the democratic deficits of the neoliberal era.

De-democratisation and the Ethos of Neoliberalism

Supranational institutions such as the World Bank and the IMF have played a crucial role in expanding the reach of neoliberalism, using their influence to propagate neoliberal orthodoxy across the globe. This has exacerbated the economic disparities between the core and periphery of the capitalist world system by opening up vulnerable domestic industries to international competition and heightening the trade imbalances between surplus and deficit countries. The European Union (EU) exemplifies the undemocratic characteristics of supranational governance since its agenda is largely determined by unaccountable agencies such as the European Central Bank (ECB) and the European Council (EC). EU treaties, membership rules and criteria for entry are also used to ensure that neoliberal policies are adopted despite considerable popular resistance to these programmes (Della Sala 2012: 36–7; Heartfield 2009: 722–4; Mair 2014: 99–125; Streeck 2014: 105–16). The ability of supranational institutions to undermine popular sovereignty and delegitimise representative politics is exemplified by the EU's recent imposition of neoliberal policies on the vulnerable populations of the European periphery.

The loans given to the indebted Greek state in a series of bailout agreements since 2010 have been presented as acts of selfless benevolence by the rich countries of the Eurozone, but their real objective has been to protect the German and French banks that purchased much of the Greek sovereign debt. The bailouts have done nothing to stimulate economic growth or to reduce Greece's long-term debt burden. On the contrary, the neoliberal austerity measures mandated by these loan agreements have led to a disastrous reduction in Greek GDP and an accordant rise in poverty and unemployment (Aglietta 2012: 26–8; Blyth 2013: 71–4). The failure of successive Greek governments to resist the neoliberal economic policies dictated by the Troika (EC, ECB, IMF) has led to an unprecedented violation of Greek sovereignty, the latest evidence of a 'post-democratic tendency where democratic procedures remain as formally intact, but are substantially emptied' since 'decisions are now presented as imperative necessities' (Candeias 2011: 59).[3] The formation in November 2011 of an unelected Greek government led by ex-ECB technocrat Lucas Papademos is one example of this post-democratic tendency, as is the acceptance of a third bailout agreement by the Tsipras government in 2015, only days after the Greek people overwhelmingly rejected the agreement in a national referendum (Kouvelakis 2011: 24–6).

The disempowerment that results from de-democratisation is captured in Athina Rachel Tsangari's *Chevalier*, which tells the story of six middle-aged men – Josef (Vangelis Mourikis), Yorgos (Panos Koronis), Dimitris (Makis Papadimitriou), Yannis (Yorgos Pirpassopoulos), Christos (Sakis Rouvas) and the doctor (Yiorgos Kendros) – who gather on a boat in the Aegean Sea off the coast of Athens. Christos works in the same medical practice as the doctor, Josef and Yorgos are business partners in real estate, Yannis is an insurance broker married to the doctor's daughter and Dimitris is Yannis's brother. During the course of the boat trip the men go on diving expeditions, but most of their time is spent playing an elaborate game called chevalier. It involves the staging of contests devised by the participants and the assessment of each player on everything he does; as Yorgos describes it: 'How we speak. Do we speak loudly, softly? What words we use. How we laugh. If our teeth show when we smile. How we look at each other. How we walk. Why we walk and don't sit down. How we think. Everything. And whoever is the best at everything will [win].'[4] Once the chevalier game begins it comes to dominate every aspect of the men's lives, including their daily routines and private interactions. The men's willing immersion in such an all-encompassing competition demonstrates the pervasiveness of the neoliberal ethos that the game embodies and the social impotence of its participants. The game's ubiquitous presence in *Chevalier* undermines the spectator's investment in psychological realism by reducing the differences between characters, the significance of their actions and the expressiveness of their dialogue. Through its defiance of our expectations of realism, Tsangari's film denaturalises the depoliticisation and managerialism at the heart of neoliberal governance.

Gameplay in *Chevalier* exposes all aspects of the men's lives to inspection and assessment, indicative of the way 'neoliberal rationality disseminates the model of the market to all domains and activities' (W. Brown 2015: 31). The mechanics of the game are emblematic of the financial logic that is dominant in the neoliberal era:

> In neoliberal reason and in domains governed by it, we are only and everywhere *homo oeconomicus* . . . *homo oeconomicus* is an intensely constructed and governed bit of human capital tasked with improving and leveraging its competitive positioning and with enhancing its (monetary and nonmonetary) portfolio value across all its endeavors and venues . . . an activity undertaken through practices of self-investment and attracting investors. Whether through social media 'followers', 'likes,' and 'retweets,' through rankings and ratings of every activity, and domain, or through more directly monetized practices. (W. Brown 2015: 10, 33–4)

The chevalier game transforms every casual interaction, quotidian activity, intimate detail and personal characteristic into a potential asset or liability that needs to be evaluated. This parallels the way neoliberal reason transfers the financial logic of portfolio management into the social realm, compelling us to determine the social value of others and to promote ourselves in order to elicit others' attention and approval. The pervasiveness of the chevalier game's evaluative ethos is captured in the early stages of the contest when Yorgos is asked questions by Christos and the doctor about his breakfast preferences. Afterwards, Yorgos writes something down in his notepad, which suggests that his questioners were also being quietly assessed during the exchange. The extension of neoliberal values into every facet of our lives is conveyed in *Chevalier* by the increasingly intrusive contests devised by the players. Early in the game, the participants decide to judge how Yannis sleeps: his posture, choice of sleepwear, etc. Later we see the players call their romantic partners on the phone, with the speaker setting on so that everyone can hear. The point of this is never explained, but it seems that each contestant is evaluated on the basis of whether, and perhaps how, his partner says that she misses him and loves him. The fact that the players deceive their partners by secretly broadcasting their private conversations reveals the fundamentally antisocial nature of the game.

The chevalier game places every player under the constant scrutiny of the others, leading to heightened anxiety and chronic bouts of self-doubt. The men come to expect criticism, often admitting their flaws before anyone else has a chance to point them out. For instance, when the doctor asks Christos how many fillings he has and how often he brushes his teeth, Christos says: 'Maybe I should do it more often. It's not enough.' During a walk by the sea, a mere glance at Josef's hair by the doctor prompts the following exchange (the doctor's words in brackets): 'What are you looking at? My hair? Is it messy? [A little]. Now? [Better.] Was it messy before or only now because of the wind? [Only now. Before you were fine.]' The invasiveness of the chevalier game and its disciplinary effect on the boat's passengers is reminiscent of Foucault's definition of panopticism as a power relation that functions 'in a diffused, multiple, polyvalent way throughout the whole social body', producing 'a society penetrated through and through with disciplinary mechanisms' (Foucault 1977: 208–9). The characters' anticipation and pre-emptive affirmation of external criticism in *Chevalier* highlights the self-regulation undertaken by the panoptical subject who 'inscribes in himself the power relation in which he simultaneously plays both roles; he becomes the principle of his own subjection' (Foucault 1977: 202–3).

The game, despite joining the assembled friends together in a common activity, interpellates them as isolated individuals, which is consistent with the antisocial effects of neoliberalism: 'Integration and individuation, cooperation without collectivization – neoliberal governance is a supreme instance of . . . gathering and separating, amassing and isolating' (W. Brown 2015: 130). The feelings of insecurity and inadequacy that the game engenders are manifested in a series of shots interspersed throughout *Chevalier* that show the film's protagonists preening in front of the mirror, sucking in their stomachs or exercising. The characters are alone in these moments and enclosed by door frames to emphasise their social isolation. The most striking of these shots shows Christos, after discovering that he has high cholesterol, look in the mirror and repeat the phrase 'I'm the best.' *Chevalier* features several instances of shallow focus and unusual blocking that highlight social fragmentation and alienation. This is also conveyed through abrupt shifts in framing that reveal how quickly an apparently cordial encounter can become evaluative. For instance, in one early scene we see Christos and the doctor exercising on adjacent rowing machines. The scene is comprised of three shots: the first features unusual blocking as we see the characters from behind (what David Bordwell [2005] has described as dorsality; see also Colvin 2017); the second uses shallow focus to show the doctor in profile in the foreground while Christos remains out of focus in the middle ground; the third is from the same vantage point as the first but this time only the doctor is exercising while Christos stands next to him and looks at his stopwatch, giving the impression that he is assessing the doctor's performance.

Unusual blocking is again used to highlight the fundamentally antisocial quality of the chevalier game when we observe Christos from behind as he sits on his bed and repeatedly shouts for help. As the others rush to his room to see what's wrong, he calmly informs them that this was a contest designed to test how quickly they respond to an emergency. Christos's dorsality in this scene parallels his diegetic deceptiveness by initially disguising his intentions from the audience. This moment captures the way neoliberal rationality converts the social dynamics of cooperation and solidarity into a competitive framework for assessing individual abilities. Another alienating effect of the game is to drive the characters to be more secretive, since every aspect of their lives is now subject to scrutiny and assessment: the doctor secretly smokes, Yannis threatens to reveal that Dimitris is afraid to sleep alone and Yorgos asks Christos not to tell the others that he recently suffered hypoxia while diving. The inherent individualism of the chevalier game is conveyed in a scene between Josef and Yorgos. Josef is upset because he performed badly in an earlier contest and threatens to end his business relationship with Yorgos, who he feels did not adequately defend him from the other players' criticisms. Yorgos tries to calm Josef down by assuring him that the two of them will win the chevalier game together. The unlikeliness of this outcome is suggested by the framing of this exchange, which isolates the characters in separate shots. This is later confirmed in the film's final image, a high-angle shot of a dock at night that shows the characters get into their separate vehicles and drive away as the camera lingers on the empty parking spaces in a long take that emphasises the social fragmentation of the group.

The penetration of neoliberal values into the private sphere has been accomplished through diffuse 'enforcement with benchmarks and inspection' (W. Brown 2015: 127). In this regard, the Fitbit, a device that constantly monitors and evaluates the wearer's physical activity, might be the paradigmatic gadget of the neoliberal era. In *Chevalier*, the diffuse enforcement of social norms is captured in the contests that comprise the chevalier game, which require the assessment of the contestants against a certain benchmark (for instance, acceptable cholesterol levels) and around-the-clock observation, measurement, comparison and ranking. At the rhetorical level, neoliberal governance has replaced 'moral rules . . . with scientific rules', shifting 'questions of normativity elsewhere, into spheres of expert procedure and methodology, while often ignoring the irredeemably normative constitutions of socio-economic life' (Davies 2016: 14). As Wendy Brown notes, in the neoliberal era 'democracy becomes purely procedural and is detached from the powers that would give it substance and meaning as a form of rule' (2015: 128). This is manifested in *Chevalier* through the proceduralism of character interactions. Even before the chevalier game begins, during the playing of an earlier likeness game, the characters use legalistic language to argue about each other's play. At one point in the discussion, Josef says: 'Retract at once the statement that I am like a pineapple. Take it back right now. It is unfounded. It is unfounded.' There are also intermittent arguments about game rules, such as whether the likeness game should be based on objective standards or subjective assessments. And the characters in *Chevalier* often get hung up on insignificant details. For instance, when Christos tells the others about the rules of the chevalier game, he insists that it cannot be played unless a chevalier ring is given as a prize to the winner.

The procedural discussions in *Chevalier* can be understood as a portrayal of the frustrated political desires of a highly educated Greek middle class that has been shut out of the political process since 2008. The characters in the film apply the skills of negotiation and deliberation associated with politics to a trivial leisure activity. Theodor Adorno described a similar, albeit economic rather than political, function of games in nineteenth-century Vienna:

> The fondness for number games is as peculiar to the Viennese mind as the game of chess in the coffee house. There are social reasons for it. All the while intellectually productive forces in Austria were rising to the technical level characteristic of high capitalism, material forces lagged behind. The resultant unused capacity for figures became the symbolic fulfillment of the Viennese intellectual. If he wanted to take part in the actual process of material production, he had to look for a position in Imperial Germany. If he stayed home, he became a doctor or a lawyer or clung to number games as a mirage of financial power. Such is the way the Viennese intellectual tries to prove something to himself, and – bitte schön! – to everyone else as well. (Adorno, quoted in Jameson 1971: 7)

The procedural discussions in *Chevalier* create a 'mirage of political power' that reflects the paradox of the post-crisis period in Greece, which has seen endless negotiations between the indebted Greek state and its creditors, while

Figures 1.1 and 1.2   The competitive ethos of the neoliberal era is portrayed through antisocial framing and blocking in *Chevalier* (Athina Rachel Tsangari, 2015). In Figure 1.1, Christos's height differential as he monitors the doctor's performance conveys how the chevalier game undermines the camaraderie of everyday interactions. In Figure 1.2, Christos's dorsality captures the deceptiveness of his cries for help, whose sole purpose is to assess how quickly his friends will respond.

at the same time the neoliberal direction of Greek government policies is dictated by the Troika and deemed non-negotiable. The farcical spectacle of politicians participating in never-ending debates about an increasingly narrow and inconsequential subset of economic and political matters is replicated in *Chevalier* by the characters' discussions about the rules and outcomes of the games they play.

From the very first shot of *Chevalier*, we get a sense that the characters, despite their boundless energy, are essentially powerless. We see an extreme long shot of barely visible divers in the sea in front of a massive rock wall. The long duration of this shot emphasises the divers' lack of agency as they make little to no discernible progress in any direction. The wall dominates the shot, the sea a tiny horizontal sliver at the bottom of the frame. This immovable monolith is an apt visualisation of the near-total control of the Troika over the affairs of the Greek state since 2010. The disempowerment of the characters is reinforced in the film's second shot which shows the protagonists exit the water slowly, faltering as the waves turn back from the shore to push them deeper into the sea. Tsangari does not show the men triumphantly catching fish, focusing instead on their ungraceful exit from the water and their exhausted collapse on the shore. These opening shots suggest that the primary purpose of the chevalier game is to distract the characters from their underlying powerlessness.

The limited agency of the characters in *Chevalier* is also hinted at by the intermittent announcements – about the weather, boat performance, schedule, upcoming meals – broadcast over the boat's PA system, which give the impression that the men's interactions are taking place under the auspices of a higher authority. Because we never see a crew member speaking into the PA system, the announcements seem anonymous, distant and uncontestable. Narrative development is frequently interrupted by shots of the waves created by the boat's passage through the water or night-time shots in which only the lights on the shoreline or the lights of the boat are visible. In one such shot, the camera moves slowly around the boat as if to survey it. These glimpses of the boat's operation create a tension between the *mise en scène* and narrative design of *Chevalier*, reminding us that focusing too much on the six passengers and their game will prevent us from understanding the structures that both enable and circumscribe their social interactions. This interplay functions as an apt allegory of the post-crisis political dynamics in Greece, wherein internal activity is largely inconsequential and contained within the parameters established by external authority. More broadly, this is indicative of the curtailment of democratic agency in the neoliberal era, in which, as Wendy Brown notes, 'public life is reduced to problem solving and program implementation, a casting that brackets or eliminates politics' (2015: 127). This notion is affirmed by Tsangari in her description of the game in *Chevalier*: 'No one is really a winner, there's never a clear victory. There's just the game that keeps perpetuating itself' (Veciana 2015).

Aesthetics of Crisis in *Chevalier*

The legalism and proceduralism of the dialogue in *Chevalier* undermine the tenets of psychological realism, a mode of address that was adopted to varying degrees in several strands of post-war art cinema. In traditional or classical art films such as François Truffaut's *Les quatre cents coups* (*The 400 Blows*, 1959) and Tony Richardson's *The Loneliness of the Long Distance Runner*

(1962), alienated protagonists are contrasted to their oppressive environment in a way that emphasises individual psychology. In modernist art films such as Michelangelo Antonioni's *L'eclisse* (*The Eclipse*, 1962) and Ingmar Bergman's *Tystnaden* (*The Silence*, 1963) alienation is much more pervasive, encouraging us to interpret the existential crisis facing the characters through a historical and sociopolitical lens (other strands of modernist art cinema, as mentioned earlier, eschew psychological realism through formalism or reflexivity). In his study of post-war art cinema, András Bálint Kovács argues that classical art films differ from their modernist counterparts by 'develop[ing] psychological motivation for the plot to explain why the character acts the way he does. That is where modern narration differs. Concentration on the characters in modern cinema does not involve psychological characterization' (Kovács 2007: 65). While dialogue is not the only way to produce psychological realism, a common assumption is that many art films allow us to better understand the complexity of human psychology by using dialogue to reveal the interior lives of their characters. In *Chevalier*, our understanding of character psychology is complicated by the impersonal officiousness of the dialogue, which does not communicate personal truths so much as display the characters' over-investment in the competitive dynamics of the chevalier game.

In contrast to the broadly sketched character types found in Hollywood genre cinema, classical art films feature idiosyncratic characters, whose detailed portrayal is achieved not only through extensive dialogue (usually self-description) but also through elements of film style such as framing and *mise en scène* (indirect characterisation). This heightened specificity can, however, lead to social abstraction by preventing the viewer from drawing meaningful connections between individual characters and their historical conditions. The fact that nearly everyone shares the same speaking style and behavioural tendencies in *Chevalier* suggests that characterisation in the film functions as a representation of societal dynamics rather than individual psychology. In an interview about her 2010 film *Attenberg*, Tsangari expressed her aversion to psychologism: 'We had this unspoken pact right from the start: we never discuss character. Our work was pure voice, pure body, pure language. I am not interested in method acting, bringing in back story, talking about psychology' (Nayman 2011).

The similarities in character behaviour in *Chevalier* not only undermine the individualism of psychological realism, they also aptly convey how the logic of neoliberalism has insinuated itself into every aspect of contemporary existence. Tsangari makes it clear that the chevalier game is a symptom rather than a cause of the characters' neoliberal common sense, since their penchant for self-promotion and evaluation precedes and exceeds the confines of the game. For example, before the start of the chevalier game Dimitris asks Yorgos to time him to see how long he can hold his breath. In the next scene, Christos and the doctor exercise together (Christos's words in brackets): 'You have to admit that my endurance is better since I quit smoking. [You have incredible self-discipline. You are doing really well.]' And a short time later Yannis tests Dimitris's knowledge of geometric calculations while they are in the bathroom. Even during activities seemingly unrelated to the chevalier game, such as jet skiing, swimming and windsurfing, the characters are frequently alone and shown isolated in the frame. The competitive ethos embodied by the passengers' gameplay is shared by the boat's crew, who we find out are placing bets on which of the six passengers will win the game.

Chevalier deviates from the individualism of psychological realism in order to critically comment on the democratic failures of the neoliberal era. Our investment in individual psychology is undermined by the similarities between characters in the film, their circumscribed agency and the officiousness of their conversations. The congruence of character actions in *Chevalier* reflects the widespread adoption of neoliberal values, while the inconsequentiality of those actions conveys the disempowerment caused by the undemocratic imposition of neoliberal policies. The legalism of the film's dialogue reveals how the replacement of value-based arguments with purely technical discussions sidesteps and distracts from substantive politics. This displacement lies at the heart of neoliberal crisis management because it prevents any official challenge to market orthodoxies and masks the unpopularity of neoliberal policies. In *Chevalier*, Tsangari foregrounds and denaturalises the transition from representative politics to technocracy by pushing the proceduralism and managerialism of the characters to absurd extremes. The near-unanimity of character behaviour in the film does not allow us to dismiss it as a function of individual idiosyncrasies, forcing us to contemplate its broader implications. And our critical awareness of neoliberal common sense is heightened by its unexpected appearance in the most casual and intimate interactions in the narrative. In these ways, Tsangari cultivates an aesthetics of crisis that draws attention to political questions by defying our typical modes of spectatorship.

While the divergence from psychological realism in *Chevalier* produces an aesthetics of crisis, there is a conspicuous absence of narrative crisis in the film. David Bordwell notes that 'in art-cinema narration . . . the film's causal impetus often derives from the protagonist's recognition that she or he faces a crisis of existential significance' (Bordwell 1985: 208). While the characters of many classical and modernist art films realise at some point that they are facing a crisis, the class satires of Luis Buñuel, such as *El ángel exterminador* (*The Exterminating Angel*, 1962) and *Le Charme discret de la bourgeoisie* (*The Discreet Charm of the Bourgeoisie*, 1972), feature characters whose lack of self-awareness is a crucial component of these texts' social critique (the work of Ulrich Seidl is a more recent example of this satirical tradition).[5] Similarly, in *Chevalier* the boat's passengers appear to be unaware of the limits of their agency and the insignificance of their actions. Their lack of critical awareness means that they do not pause to contemplate or reconsider the direction of their lives. The characters' anxieties and doubts focus primarily on their physical attributes rather than their social agency and are triggered by gameplay rather than serious introspection. The transmutation of acute crisis into a diffuse and constant state of misplaced anxiety gives the film's narrative an anti-climactic structure, something that Tsangari has acknowledged: 'one of the criticisms of [*Chevalier*] is that it doesn't explode, it doesn't reach a point where you actually root for one of them, someone dies, there is a big climax, or a big brawl between all of them. But I . . . felt that in a way, it's much more bitter this way' (Veciana 2015). The bitter truth that *Chevalier* reveals is how an absence of self-awareness facilitates the infiltration of neoliberal values into every facet of our lives. By not combining aesthetic crisis with narrative crisis, Tsangari highlights what William Davies calls the 'politics of anti-crisis' prominent in neoliberal societies, 'through which the very authority of doubt (and hence critical judgment) is challenged, and the time and space of political uncertainty are closed down' (Davies 2016: 150). *Chevalier* reminds us that neoliberalism survives today by distracting us from the real causes of our misery and by burdening us with a vast array of epiphenomenal concerns. Tsangari's film is a testament to how aesthetic crisis can be used to puncture the shibboleths of neoliberal discourse and to redirect our attention to the issues that matter.

Notes

1. This essay is based on material in *Art Cinema and Neoliberalism* (forthcoming from Palgrave Macmillan). After I finished writing the chapter, *Studies in European Cinema* published an article by Richard Rushton on *Chevalier* (Rushton 2019). Rushton's essay engages extensively with the work of Étienne Balibar in order to develop an allegorical interpretation of *Chevalier* in relation to the economic and political consequences of the 2008 financial crisis in Greece.
2. It is worth remembering that it was largely Brecht's influence that led film theorists in the 1970s such as Colin McCabe to criticise the facile acceptance of surface reality and the delusions of epistemic mastery cultivated by mainstream (bourgeois) forms of realism.
3. Colin Crouch argues that contemporary political systems are moving ever closer to a post-democratic model of governance, which he describes as follows: 'while elections certainly exist and can change governments, public electoral debate is a tightly controlled spectacle, managed by rival teams of professionals expert in the techniques of persuasion, and considering a small range of issues selected by those teams. The mass of citizens plays a passive, quiescent, even apathetic part, responding only to the signals given them. Behind this spectacle of the electoral game, politics is really shaped in private by interaction between elected governments and elites that overwhelmingly represent business interests' (Crouch 2004: 4).

4. The dialogue excerpts from *Chevalier* in this chapter are based on the English subtitles and the author's translations of the original Greek dialogue in a digital version of the film made available to the author by Maria Hatzakou at Haos Film.
5. My alignment of *Chevalier* with the modernist anti-psychologism of certain currents in post-war and contemporary art cinema is consistent with the media archaeology approach to art cinema historiography put forth by Angelos Koutsourakis. This approach considers modernist film styles as responses to political circumstances associated with various stages of capitalist modernity. Given that we continue to exist within and against the capitalist world-system, these styles retain their contemporary relevance, which renders problematic any attempt to relegate them to the dustbin of history. Focusing on the modernist genealogy of contemporary slow cinema, Koutsourakis states that 'the re-emergence of slow modernism can be seen as a response to past political problematics against which modernism reacted and which are still applicable in the present' (Koutsourakis 2019: 393).

2. BEYOND NEOLIBERALISM? GIFT ECONOMIES IN THE FILMS OF THE DARDENNE BROTHERS

Martin O'Shaughnessy

Since at least the time of *La Promesse/The Promise* (1996), and without being political film-makers in the conventional sense, Luc and Jean-Pierre Dardenne have resolutely confronted the violences of the neoliberal order and sought to open up ethical routes out of them. In their previous incarnation as documentarians, the brothers worked to keep alive the memory of collective resistances to capitalism or Nazi occupation and the political traditions that accompanied them (Mai 2010: 1–24; O'Shaughnessy 2008). With their later fictions, recognising that these traditions had lost their power, they positioned themselves alongside characters who effectively found themselves alone in a struggle of all-against-all. In a situation of enforced acquisitive individualism and generalised precariousness, and with productive or even protected places rationed, life, their films suggested, had become a struggle to survive, to possess and to belong. One could either make oneself ruthless, as many of their characters do; refuse to fight, but at the cost of accepting one's own elimination; or discover some way to oppose the murderousness of the times. Within this broader context, the young, so often at the centre of the brothers' films, find themselves in a particularly vulnerable position. With their elders either absent, absorbed in their own struggle for survival or actively destructive, they have no one to learn from about how to live productively in the world alongside others. Given the dramatically changed times, the brothers could no longer give their characters access to an elaborated leftist language or the institutional solidarities that would mediate between them and the socio-economic violences that surrounded them or allow them to stand back and map what was occurring. Instead, the characters were effectively immersed in situations, their interactions with others, their decision to kill or not kill, worked out directly in embodied encounters. At the same time, the brothers refused to give themselves or us access to a superior, distanced, spectatorial viewpoint. Instead, they placed their camera in close proximity to their characters, inviting us to follow them, scrutinise their gestures and their interaction with people and things, and track ethical resistances within them as they rise to the bodily surface and disrupt instrumental drives. The same close attention to bodies, gestures and material objects as key loci of meaning (Mai 2010: 57–60) also means that the brothers' films lend themselves particularly well to the kind of study of a cinematic gift economy that will be developed in this chapter.

Given their films' consistent focus on the violences of neoliberalism, we might expect them to respond to the 2008 financial crisis and its sociopolitical consequences. Certainly, *Le Silence de Lorna/Lorna's Silence* (2008) has debt somewhere near its core. It commences as Lorna (Arta Dobroshi), its heroine, celebrates her acquisition of Belgian citizenship, which allows her to take out a bank loan that in turn demands she become a ruthless and predictable repayer (O'Shaughnessy 2014). Rather than probing debt or other themes obviously relatable to the crisis, however, other more recent works – *Le Gamin au vélo/The Kid with a Bike* (2011), *Deux jours, une nuit/Two Days, One Night* (2014) and *La Fille inconnue/The Unknown Girl* (2016) – move in determinedly more positive directions by exploring the potential for greater human connectivity, running against the neoliberal grain even in a time of austerity and aggravated social divisions. In reality, this counter-cyclical reduction of the films' own austerity represents a change of emphasis rather than a radically new departure. On a deeper level, the films have always been traversed by the tension between the destructiveness of the contemporary economic order and the search for an ethical alternative grounded in responsibility for the Other. They therefore defy any simple analysis in terms of pre- and post-crisis films. For their characters and the precarious social worlds in which they move, the crisis has been there from the start, reaching back even before *La Promesse* to at least *Je pense à vous* (1992), their not entirely successful film about the human fallout from the evisceration of the Belgian steel industry. To the extent that neoliberalism, with its assault on the post-1945 social welfare regime and on union power, its financial deregulation and its aggressive globalisation, can be seen as a response to the crisis of capitalist governance and profitability that came to a head in the 1970s (Harvey 2007b: 9–38), the Dardennes' work might indeed be seen as inhabiting the space between two crises.

If the films' interpersonal violences are clearly systemic in origin, the ethical route out of violence is more individual in inspiration, to the degree that any thought is really individual. With Luc Dardenne's academic grounding in philosophy no doubt playing a key part, the brothers are self-avowedly influenced by the ethical thinking of Emanuel Levinas (e.g. Dardenne 2005: 10, 35, 42, 56). Going against much of the European philosophical tradition, Levinas's work asserts the anteriority of the encounter with the Other over any ontology centred on the self. In this context, prioritisation of the latter equates to a form of violence, a denial of the Other in his or her radical otherness. In contrast, the encounter with the Other, or what is revealed of the Other, in his or her vulnerability is a call to the self not to murder, literally or metaphorically, but to become open to a world in which the self, its aims and categories are no longer central. Indeed, because the presence of the Other is always prior, responsibility is no longer figured as autonomy (being responsible for oneself) but as a responsibility before the Other, a being-for-the-Other, an absolute duty of care that precedes any code or order (Levinas 1969, 1978). As some fine scholarship demonstrates (Cooper 2007; Mai 2010), reading the Dardennes in terms of Levinas is apposite and productive not least because the films typically revolve around characters who, when confronted despite themselves with the pressing vulnerability of others, must choose between eliminating them, either in the flesh (murder) or as social beings (instrumentalising or replacing them), and accepting an open-ended responsibility for them. One could indeed say that the brothers' own ethical commitment to their characters is to repeatedly push them to make such a choice, or to force them, when physical or social elimination has taken place, to take responsibility for their acts and commit to addressing their consequences for others.

There are potential problems with such an ethics, no matter how radical it might seem. First, as Alain Badiou has pointed out, it tends to be founded on a sense of human vulnerability rather than, say, a capacity for political resistance or for the creation of the new (Badiou 2003: 22–33). Secondly, it seeks to address at the inter-individual level of self and Other that which can only meaningfully be addressed through collective action and systemic change. It needs neoliberal murderousness against which to set its own ethical commitment but fails to generate a real alternative to it. In this way, it sets up a dichotomous and essentially static opposition between elimination of the Other and commitment to her or him. Some of the more recent films *unwittingly* acknowledge this problem by coming to an apparent impasse. This is the case, for example, in *Lorna's Silence*. Its indebted eponymous heroine conspires with a gang to kill Claudy (Jérémie Rénier), the junkie she has married to obtain Belgian nationality, so that she can remarry and sell on the acquired citizenship rights. Faced with the neediness and vulnerability of Claudy, which is expressed, in typical Dardennes manner, not in an abstract way, but through an importunate, clinging, bodily presence, she repents of this murderousness and the calculating, acquisitive behaviour that accompanies it, but too late. The gang give Claudy a fatal overdose. Lorna convinces herself that she is carrying the dead man's child and becomes an increasingly unreliable accomplice. When the gang seek to make her disappear, she escapes into the woods and takes refuge in a hut where the film leaves her. While the *imagined* pregnancy might seem to embody a commitment to the Other even beyond death, it could also be seen as an implicit admission of both the unreality of any narrowly ethical solution to neoliberal violence and the need for the Other's infant-like vulnerability to ground such an ethics.

Two Days, One Night comes to a similar impasse. Sandra (Marion Cotillard), its heroine, has been off work because of depression. Her employer asks her colleagues to vote on whether to take a bonus or to keep her on the team, these options apparently not both being affordable due to the competitive pressures created by globalisation. Her colleagues have voted to keep their bonus, effectively eliminating her from the company. Their action, a preference for self over Other and for money over the person, is implicitly murderous. Supported by a trade unionist friend, she persuades the boss to rerun the ballot. Over the weekend, another importunate physical presence, she visits each of her colleagues in turn, asking them to put themselves in her shoes, even as she puts herself in theirs. When the ballot is rerun, the vote is tied. The boss offers to retain Sandra and to sack a worker on a fixed-duration contract instead. Refusing to be complicit in another's elimination, she walks away, her head held high. While the film comes close to admitting that only the renewed solidarity of those who support her might effect meaningful change, its virtuoso insistence on the repetition of face-to-face encounters and individual choices suggests a determination to follow a narrowly ethical path even when something more obviously political is required.

Although this political path is never explicitly followed in either *Two Days, One Night* or the other films, I will argue here that there is something akin to a gift economy running through the works that implicitly opens up more politically promising ways forward than their ethical probings. I will further argue that the films require this unacknowledged gift economy to flesh out the relationships they show and give them a future in a way that their ethical narratives cannot. I will initially examine two scenes from *Le Fils/The Son* (2002) to give a more concrete sense of my position. I will then discuss how the gift has been theorised, drawing on Marcel Mauss, the great French anthropologist, and some key critics of his work. I will finally return to the films, looking at how a gift economy has supplemented their deployment of a Levinasian ethics from *The Promise* to the most recent films.

MURDER, CARE AND UNACKNOWLEDGED GIFTS IN *THE SON*

The Son lends itself to a Levinasian reading as much as any Dardenne brothers film. With its austere *mise en scène* and its minimalist cast, it concentrates an ethical drama of a rare intensity. Olivier (Olivier Gourmet) trains juvenile offenders in joinery. He is asked to take charge of the young man, Francis (Morgan Marinne), who murdered his son. Francis had tried to steal Olivier's car radio, was startled by the latter's son who had been left asleep on the back seat and strangled the boy. Only Olivier initially knows who has joined his class. When he tells his ex-wife, she is horrified that he is taking on a task that no one should be asked to assume. In a typical Dardenne brothers oscillation between two opposing pathways – their films never have a conventional linear narrative – Olivier is torn between stalking Francis and taking him under his wing.

The first scene I will look at takes place in the workshop, about 49 minutes into the film. Olivier is helping Francis to construct the type of wooden box that they all use to carry their possessions. The pair are filmed in long takes, with the hand-held camera close to them at all times, panning from one to the other as they interact, tilting from their faces to their hands working wood, measuring and hammering. Olivier insists throughout that Francis work with care and precision. He quizzes him about his family: we learn that the boy is effectively abandoned. As the two males work, we observe the contrast between their bodies, especially when their contrasting arms are brought together by the close framing. Francis is slight. Olivier is heavily built with thick arms (figure 2.1). He wears a wide, weightlifter-style leather belt that points to a weakness (his back) but also underscores his size and power and a capacity for harm that is especially evident when he has tools such as knives in his hands. As is typical of the Dardennes, the dynamics of the scene relate

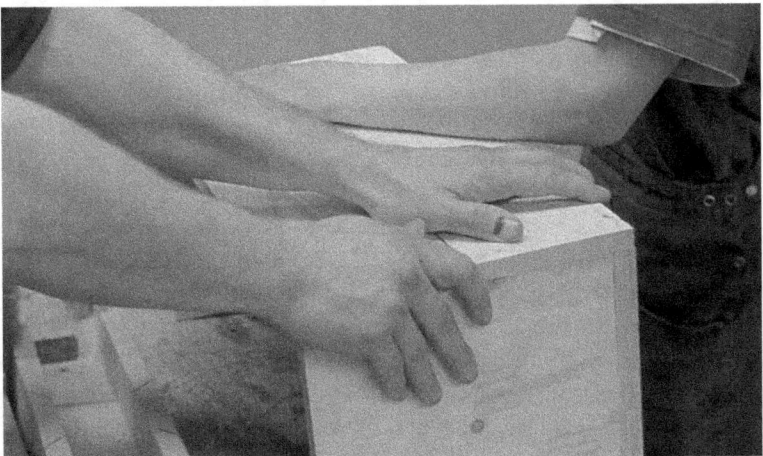

Figure 2.1 Between murder and the gift: *The Son* (Jean-Pierre and Luc Dardenne, 2002).

to what is seen on the surface and what remains hidden but towards which visible elements point. Bodies and gestures are key signifiers of the unsaid. The scene underscores the limits of a rational and instrumental relation to the material world. On the surface, it involves careful attention to the measurable and knowable (the right dimensions, tools and design) but, at a deeper level, it is about the unspoken and unmeasurable moral gap between Olivier and Francis and the ethical decision that the former faces. Will he destroy the vulnerable Francis or take responsibility for him, especially as his abandonment becomes apparent?

However, something in the interaction overflows this ethical dilemma. As the camera's studied attentiveness to objects and gestures underscores, we are witnessing the transmission of a set of embodied skills from one person to another. The younger male is learning to work collaboratively with another on a task neither could do as well alone. The interaction is not without rules, for the young man must commit to learning and obeying while his teacher assumes a duty of care. Yet nor is it narrowly instrumental or centred on the self in any simple way. We might say that what we are seeing is a gift being transmitted, from which the younger man gains without the older man losing, the skills being neither his property nor lost in the interaction or requiring some immediate return. Indeed, the only obvious way for Francis to repay this gift will be by putting the skills to good use at a later date. Drawing on the past, teaching the young man to live productively in the material world and alongside others, the gift fleshes out a future in a way that the ethical encounter alone cannot.

The latent dynamics of the workshop scene come forcefully into the open in the film's conclusion. Olivier drives Francis to his brother's isolated lumber yard and presses the young man on his crime. The latter explains it as a gesture of self-preservation: the child in the car would not release him. Does he regret what he did? Of course he does: it cost him five years of his life. This discussion helps build the tension that simmers in the lumber yard scene beneath the more routine interaction. Olivier tests Francis's capacity to identify different varieties of wood and their qualities. The pair work efficiently to move large planks to the electric saw, cut and stack them, the hand-held camera holding them close, repeatedly panning back and forth from one to the other as if to emphasise the distance between them, but also framing them as they move together as if to underscore how quickly the distance could shrink. Things come to a head when Olivier finally tells the younger man that it was his son whom he killed. Francis takes flight, triggering a cat-and-mouse hunt among the lumber, with the camera closely following the older man, the soundtrack dominated by his heavy breathing and emphasising his threatening physical presence, while rapid pans and tilts and unexpected cuts convey the chaos of the moment. Finally, Francis is caught and pinned down by Olivier. The larger man places his hands round the younger man's throat and squeezes. The camera holds his face in close-up before tilting down to the face of the helpless Francis as he looks imploringly upwards, but also revealing how, as if in response to this supplication, Olivier has released his grip. This decisive scene of the film is wordless, its drama conveyed entirely by bodies, gestures and camera movements. A cut returns us to the woodyard where Olivier is loading the timber into his trailer. Silently, the muddied Francis comes to help him, the two initially only connected by the panning camera but increasingly brought together in the frame, their gestures neatly coordinated, the young man's body actively capable rather than simply vulnerable.

The scene brings the film's ethical oscillation to a head: confronted with the boy's vulnerability, Olivier refrains from murder, while Francis is forced to confront the human consequences of his crime in a way that goes beyond his initial instrumental calculation of lost years. A powerful ethical drama has been worked through. What interests me, though, is what else is happening here. The aborted strangulation indeed lends itself to reading in ethical terms, the strong body responding to the Other's vulnerability. But before and after that there are other dynamics in play. What we again see is a pedagogic, gift-like relationship between two characters, with skills and knowledge being transferred and two bodies working productively alongside each other, the young man taking the lead from his elder. Continuing *after* the decision not to kill, relying on active human abilities beyond the capacity to harm or suffer, it is this relationship that opens a future.

The Gift: Mauss and his Critics

Marcel Mauss is best known for his famous work *Essai sur le don* (*The Gift*), first published in 1925. The book analysed gift-giving practices in traditional societies. Going against accounts that frame pre-modern exchange as a barter-style ancestor of contemporary market economies, Mauss argued that gifts across a range of societies functioned as 'total social facts', at once juridical, religious and moral, these instances not being separable as they are in modern societies (Mauss 2012: 64). Unlike the ideal of modern gifts as entirely without constraint, the gifts described were governed by three rules: the obligation to give, receive and give in return (Mauss 2012: 142–3). A fourth obligation was to give to the gods, not only in recognition of their giving of the world, but also in anticipation of gifts to come (Mauss 2012: 86).

Why, Mauss asked, did people feel obliged to return the gifts they gave? Simply put, each gift was never simply the thing, feast or service given: it bore something of the spirit or identity of the giver and thus exercised a pull on the receiver (Graeber 2001: 33–4, 154–5). A modern sensibility might expect the gift to be aneconomic, a spontaneous and unconditional giving. Involving different forms of rule-governed exchange, the Maussian gift clearly sits badly in such a frame, but also chimes ill with classical models of market exchange. These figure exchange as an instrumental transaction between two individuals whose connection is limited to and ended by the transfer of goods or services of calculable (numerical) value. Despite their diversity, the gift exchanges described by Mauss were typically between groups not individuals, involved extended or open-ended connections, and, breaking down any neat separation of people, services and things, defied simple numerical and instrumental calculation.

Mauss's interest in pre-modern forms of exchange was not simply anthropological. A socialist seeking alternative pathways between the brutality of the capitalist market on the one hand and revolutionary communism on the other, he was drawn to the gift as something that persisted in contemporary society in a range of ways that testified to a deeply embedded resistance to narrow instrumentalism. He wrote of the continuing joy of giving in public, public feasts and hospitality and generous artistic expenditure. He saluted the existence of an emergent social security regime but also celebrated more autonomous institutions such as mutuals and cooperatives which tied groups together in relations of giving and receiving. More prescriptively, he wrote of the need to limit the fruits of speculation and usury and suggested that the rich again needed to be seen as custodians of the common good, able to practise the modern equivalence of 'noble expenditure' in the form of practices such as debt jubilees. With respect to the latter, there is a neglected link to be made between the gift and Mauss's advocacy of a non-punitive system of reparations between France and Germany following the First World War. While many felt that harsh treatment of Germany was needed to pay for war damage and teach the country a lesson, Mauss argued that a more forgiving system of reparations would build long-term trust and collaboration between the ex-foes (Mallard 2011). This chimes with his vision of the gift as a way to build peaceful links between groups that would otherwise be drawn to war.

Mauss was not a sentimentalist. He was aware that gifts always came with strings attached and were often involved in agonistic relationships with the capacity to humiliate those who could give or expend less, as in the famously competitive and destructive expenditure of certain potlatch rites (Mauss 2012: 148–51). His discussion of the potlatch would be taken in a very different direction by Georges Bataille, who repositioned it in his opposition of a restricted (market) economy, built round artificial scarcity, to a heterodox general economics which centred on humanity's repeated need to expend the inevitable production of excess wealth either generously, through giving, art, and festivities, or destructively, as in war (Bataille 1967: 100–15).

One of the most celebrated critiques of Mauss's account of the gift is provided by Jacques Derrida. Derrida noted that Mauss had gathered a series of radically dissimilar practices under the homogenising label of the gift (Derrida

1992a: 26). He suggested that the Maussian gift's inherent conditionality disqualified it as gift, in a way that he himself helpfully summarised during a later discussion with Jean-Luc Marion:

> As soon as a gift is identified as a gift, with the meaning of a gift, then it is cancelled as a gift. It is reintroduced into the circle of an exchange and destroyed as a gift. As soon as the donor knows it is a gift, he already thanks the donator, and cancels the gift. As soon as the donator is conscious of giving, he himself thanks himself and again cancels the gift by re-inscribing it into a circle, an economic circle. (Kearney 1999: 59)

Clearly, Derrida is not simply referring to the giving of things nor to economic returns in a narrow sense. He is describing how all forms of giving and the recognition they generate confirm our sense of individual or collective identity, the power relations existing between donor and receiver and, beyond that, the existing symbolic order (Derrida 1992a: 10–14). To escape this economy of the proper (by which gifts inevitably return to us by confirming existing meanings, hierarchies and roles), gifts must be the subject of a forgetting that forgets forgetting itself, not even leaving an unconscious trace that would bind the receiver (Derrida 1992a: 15–17). The gift, Derrida comments, is therefore not so much impossible, as *the* impossible, something that can have neither donor nor receiver and which cannot be known or calculated, but to which we still aspire (Derrida 1992a: 7).

We are left with what seems an insoluble aporia. Marion offers a solution by suggesting that the gift could be equated not with any interpersonal giving but with the *given*, or that which is given to our consciousness by experience, along the lines of the Heideggerian description of Being in terms of *es gibt* or it (Being) gives (Kearney 1999: 57). Derrida objects that the idea of the *given* suggests something that is a *known* part of experience and therefore not a true gift, which would have to arrive in excess of the known. He equates the gift more with the giving of Time and Being as the preconditions for any specific giving, and compares the gift in this sense to the event, as that which creates an opening for the new within our experience prior to any understanding we may have of it (Kearney 1999: 67).

Pierre Bourdieu, the great French sociologist, takes a very different line. Because the capitalist market economy has become so dominant, he notes, scholars such as Derrida tend to analyse the gift in relation to self-conscious actors making rational, self-interested calculations. Within this context, gifts are seen either as deferred loans or as investments repaid by enhanced symbolic capital, and a 'true' gift must indeed be seen as (the) impossible (Bourdieu 1997: 233–4). But, for Bourdieu, individual actions are always the result of internalised habits and practices that respond to the unspoken rules of specific social fields.

As such, they refuse to be neatly positioned as individual or collective, free or constrained, disinterested or self-interested, and thereby resist the probing of antinomies practised by Derrida (Bourdieu 1997: 236). It is the delay between receiving and returning the gift that enables the subjective experience of the practice as generous and gratuitous (Bourdieu 1997: 231). On a more objective level, however, the gift transmutes economic capital into a capital of recognition through 'the alchemy of symbolic exchanges' (Bourdieu 1997: 235). Recipients of gifts internalise their debt as gratitude and incorporated recognition, love, submission or respect (Bourdieu 1997: 237). Approaching the modern era, however, this more personalised symbolic power gives way to a more impersonal, bureaucratised state authority. Becoming the prime agent of redistribution, the state inherits the recognition and legitimacy that used to result from personal gifts. Looking forward, the task is not to ask whether disinterested giving is possible, but to create societies 'in which, as in gift economies, people have an interest in disinterestedness and generosity' (Bourdieu 1997: 239–40).

What Bourdieu does not explore in any detail, although he clearly acknowledges its existence, is the unequal distribution of the socially acquired disposition to generosity (Bourdieu 1997: 235) and the way some have the means to bestow patronage while others do not. Neither, to any extent, do Mauss and Derrida, the former being more focused on social cohesion, the latter on the (im)possibility of the gift. Yet gift giving has always been marked by inequality, with some able to give due to the unacknowledged labour of others and some turned into effective objects of exchange or of sacrifice. Lévi-Strauss, the great structuralist anthropologist, analysed, for example, how the exchange of women cemented relations between cultural groups, while feminist scholars have explored how the objectification and exchange of women has been used to sustain the homosocial bond (Lévi-Strauss 1977; Irigaray 1997; Rubin 1997).

Where does this leave us? Should we simply jettison the gift as a counterfeit concept that promises something that it can never deliver? Should we recognise the limitations of the gift but build on how it challenges the frame of an instrumental and transactional market economy? Indeed, is it not its conditionality, its ability to join people in collaborative relationships over time, that makes it of political interest? Can we not also learn from how it invites us to understand the object world in ways that exceed or refuse its simple commodification? As argued by Bourdieu, Derrida and others, the gift can lend itself to social conservatism, teaching us to accept that which already exists (an economy of the proper), inviting us to internalise gratitude to the powerful and rendering invisible those whose labour enables the generous giving of benefactors. But, borrowing rather freely from Derrida's equation of the gift with the event, an opening to the unknown, we might consider how the Dardenne brothers' unacknowledged gift economy points to the as yet underdeveloped potential for forms of human interaction based on generous giving and open-ended interdependence. We might also ponder how, taking inspiration from Bataille, such gifts communicate a potential for an economy of plenty rather than a restricted one. I hope my discussion of *Le Fils* has helped pave the way for at least some of these points by underscoring the capacity of the pedagogic gift to open a future based on a shared ability to create and the bountiful transmission of knowledge and gestures that are given without being lost and demand to be passed on again. I also hope that I have shown how, with their close attention to bodies and gestures in their interaction with the material world, the Dardenne brothers' films lend themselves particularly well to such an analysis. I will now return to the films to flesh out my argument.

The Promise

Set against the epic background of now-inactive steel mills, *The Promise* launched the Dardenne brothers' mature style. It tracks its characters in close proximity, observing their bodies and movements, as a polarised ethical dilemma plays out over them. A father, Roger (Olivier Gourmet), and his son, Igor (Jérémie Rénier), make a living by transporting and lodging illegal migrants and putting them to work renovating the house that father and son are buying. Underlying ethical tensions come to a head when Hamidou (Rasmane Ouédraogo), a black African migrant, falls off a ladder at the house while rushing to hide from labour inspectors. Roger lets him bleed to death, effectively involving Igor in the murder of an expendable Other. Igor is given the kind of second chance that the Dardennes give to all their lead characters: before he dies, Hamidou makes him promise to look after his wife, Assita (Assita Ouédraogo), and their child. Igor will attempt to protect Assita while placating his father. Roger's determination to make Assita disappear by trafficking her into prostitution forces the young man to make a choice and to break with his father. His commitment to Assita opens an ethical alternative to the murderousness of interactions in a ruthlessly acquisitive and competitive order. As in *The Son*, however, the ethical drama requires a supplement to flesh out its social world, build a future for the characters and give its bodies capacities beyond murder and vulnerability. It is here that the gift comes in.

The first sequence finds Igor working as an apprentice in a garage. An elderly lady pulls up. He fixes her car but opportunistically steals her purse, which he buries after emptying it of cash. He joins the garage owner to be instructed in how to solder, but the lesson is interrupted when Roger summons his son to help receive a new consignment of migrants. As he leaves work, chided by the owner, Igor takes an exhaust pipe for the go-kart he is building with friends and thanks the owner for it. The sequence clearly establishes an ethical tension that the film will later bring to a head. Igor moves between helping the lady and harming her. The theft of the money and the burial of the purse, with its markers of identity, shows a preference for the depersonalised thing over the person that is inherently violent and anticipates the murder to come and the burial of the body. On the same ethical plane, the garage owner takes responsibility for Igor while the father betrays his duty of care. Yet at the same time, objects and gestures, gifts of one sort or another, are clearly being transferred between people, as the film's close attention to material interactions underscores.

The most obvious gift at this stage is the exhaust pipe. But for Igor to use it and share it with his friends, he has to be able to apply his learned mechanical skills. These are part of a far from unconditional gift from the garage owner. The owner transmits skills that he himself was given, while demanding that Igor commit himself to his work and the hours that go with it. Skills are gifts that circulate and multiply in unpredictable ways. Even though the owner ends the apprenticeship because of Igor's unreliability, Igor will continue to use the skills that he has been taught. When he rescues Assita from Roger's sex-trafficking scheme, he takes her to the garage. There, using a drill, he repairs the sacred statue she carries with her that had been broken when she was attacked by racists. When Roger finds them and is knocked out by Assita, Igor uses the garage's electric hoist to chain up his powerful father, another decidedly unplanned use of acquired skills. Igor will also give the go-kart to his two friends, gifting them the ability to play that was taken from him.

Less positive gifts are also circulating. Roger teaches his son how to instrumentalise others, a toxic pedagogic gift. He gives him money from their illicit dealings and a gold signet ring identical to his own (figure 2.2). After Hamidou's death, he has to scrub blood from Igor's ring. Later, Igor removes it and

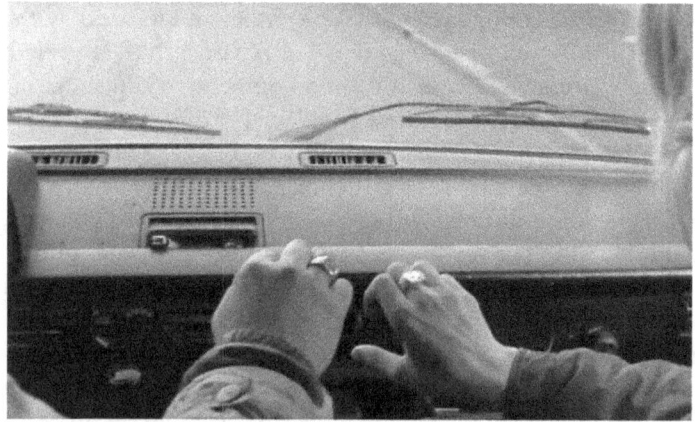

Figure 2.2   The toxic gift of the ring: *The Promise* (Jean-Pierre and Luc Dardenne, 1996).

sells it to raise money to buy a train ticket to send Assita to safety in Italy. The ring's trajectory is instructive. Initially tying Igor into a Derridean economy of the proper, returning to its donor, it made the young man a younger version of his father, underlining a shared attachment to wealth (gold) as it circulates among some but excludes others. The bloodstains underline where such an attachment leads. By selling the ring to be melted down, Igor symbolically breaks out of this murderous economy into something more generous and unpredictable in a way that helps create an opening to the future and to others. Something similar happens with identity cards. To begin with, Roger puts Igor to work faking signatures on the false cards they sell. Later, however, an African woman who has already given Assita money to pay for her child's hospital treatment lends Assita her identity card so that she can travel. Rather than the card returning any material benefit to the woman, it opens a future for the person she helps.

The circulation of gifts within the film invites several overarching comments. To begin with, whether generous or more poisonous, all of the gifts carry something in excess of their existence as commodities. The latter, as Marx famously noted, are fetishised under capitalism in a way that obscures the social relations of production. What our attention is drawn to in *La Promesse* are what we might call the social relations of circulation. These are not always positive, as we have seen, but they do remind us how things work to connect people; memories of their shifting function attach to them, their meanings change and their use value refuses reduction to their exchange value. Secondly, in a way that rather refutes Derrida's homogenising account of conditional gifts tying us to an economy of the proper, we clearly see how, while some gifts do indeed tie people to existing roles and relationships, others establish new connections and open future possibilities. Thirdly, as in *Le Fils*, we observe how pedagogic gifts are particularly fruitful in the way they lend themselves to inventive recycling without the original donor losing what was given. Finally, we again see how, in their capacity for connectivity, circulation and generosity, gifts generate a sense of human potential that far exceeds the interdependent murderousness–vulnerability pair on which the film's more overt ethical economy depends.

Bicycles, Baseball Bats, Bonuses and Panettone: Gifts and their Limits in the Dardennes' Recent Films

The circulation of gifts continues into the brothers' recent films, which are marked, as I noted earlier, by a more pronounced search for social reconnection than their predecessors. Gifts again connect people over time while their more poisonous variants continue to deceive. Yet because they continue to function as a supplement to the brothers' more explicit ethical concerns, their political potential and limits remain underexplored.

The Kid with a Bike has a gift, a bicycle, in its title. Its young hero, Cyril (Thomas Doret), has been abandoned by his father, Guy (Jérémie Renier), and lives in a children's home. In need of money, Guy has sold Cyril's bike. A hairdresser, Samantha (Cécile de France), having been literally grabbed by Cyril in a physical manifestation of the summons of one human to another typical of the Dardennes' film making, buys back the bicycle for him and agrees that he can stay with her. She tries to make him feel cared for, behave responsibly and socialise with local children. When her boyfriend demands that she choose between the child and him, she chooses Cyril. A young local criminal, Wes (Egon di Mateo), tests out the boy's toughness by having a gang member steal his bike and draw him into a fight. Wes pays to have the resultant puncture in Cyril's tyre repaired, invites him into his home, gives him drinks and befriends him. He coaches Cyril in how to mug a local bookseller, using a baseball bat. The mugging goes wrong: the bookseller's son appears and is also assaulted. Cyril tries to give the stolen money away first to Wes and then to his father. Both refuse it, not wishing to be tied to a crime. Samantha makes Cyril hand himself in. In a formal ceremony, Cyril asks the bookseller's forgiveness. The man grants it. Samantha commits to paying the man's medical bills and compensation for loss of earnings. His son is intent on revenge.

The film is a classically simple ethical drama, set in and against a context of social disintegration. A father who can no longer cope prioritises his own survival over that of his son. The child resists his abandonment. A woman, seized by his vulnerability, commits to him at considerable personal cost. Another man-child teaches him to prioritise material wealth over the person, an attitude whose intrinsic ethical violence is given physical form by the mugging. The drama is worked out in typical style, with emotions, attitudes and attachments expressed not as ideas but as movements, gestures and blows produced by bodies caring, collaborating or colliding. But, as in the other films, these interactions need gifts to endow them with durability and to embed them in the material and social worlds.

This is most obviously so with respect to the bike. Always more than a mere thing, the bike initially marks Guy's presumed attachment to his son. When he turns it back into a commodity, it clearly indicates a breaking of ties. Samantha's regifting of it to Cyril removes it once again from a market economy and signals her enduring commitment to him. Later, in probably the film's most joyous scene, the pair cycle together on the river bank and picnic together, their movements in harmony, the gift of the bike bringing forth the gift of the time that she dedicates to him. The bike is a transformative gift. The Cyril who rides it is no longer the vulnerable, abandoned child who clung to Samantha's body but a young man who can move confidently through the world and engage in contact with others. In contrast to Samantha, Wes, the criminal, is a giver of counterfeit gifts that are designed to lure Cyril into becoming an instrument of his ruthless acquisitiveness. The mugging lesson, a poisonous pedagogic gift, reveals its true nature by its failure to circulate. It breaks social connections rather than creating or prolonging them. Tellingly, neither Wes nor Guy accept its fruit, the stolen cash that would tie them to a crime. Their refusal of this last gift confirms their abandonment of Cyril.

The interplay of connective and poisonous gifts continues into *Two Days, One Night*. The initial gift, the bonus given by management to the workers, is the toxic one. Woven into its conditionality, as we noted, is the choice between solidarity with Sandra, the heroine, whose job is to be sacrificed, and material advantage. Some of the workers intend to use the money for home improvements; others need it to pay bills or for their children's education. But whatever the use, the bonus atomises the workers. By making them acquisitive individuals, committed only to privatised, family-centred well-being and beholden to management, it aligns itself with a conservative economy of the proper that places the gift in the service of the status quo and the values, hierarchies and roles it requires. Renunciation of the bonus, which half the workers accept, despite the material sacrifice implied, is, in contrast, a connective gift both to Sandra and to the openly defined collective, with its Belgian and migrant workers, its permanent and temporary staff. Rather than isolating Sandra, it brings her back into relationship with the others while reconstituting them as a group. It is a necessary supplement to the ethics of the face-to-face at the film's heart, but exploration of its potential and limits is curtailed when the film's ethical drama is brought to its ultimately self-defeating close.

The same drive to social reconnection runs through the brothers' most recent film at time of writing, *La Fille inconnue*. Its heroine, Jenny (Adèle Haenel), is a doctor who works with a deprived or elderly clientele but who has been recruited by a much richer practice that will represent a big step forward in her career. She is being shadowed by Julien (Olivier Bonnaud), a trainee medic. The drama is triggered when someone rings the surgery bell an hour after the last appointment. Jenny stops the sensitive Julien from opening the door, saying they have to place limits on their availability. It transpires, however, that the person ringing the bell was an unknown black girl who has been found dead near the surgery. She turns out to have been a prostitute, a commodified and socially disposable individual whose death is not seen to merit much investigation. A classic ethical conflict has been set up within Jenny. Will she seek to atone for not assisting the vulnerable other? Will she pursue her own career, treating medicine instrumentally or, accepting the onerous gift of the practice from the retired doctor who used to run it, will she dedicate herself to her needy patients? Her decision seems to be triggered when Bryan (Louka Minella), a young man she is treating, performs an unexpected song of thanks for her dedication. Jenny will thereafter devote herself to her patients and to finding out who the girl was and how she died, despite the danger this puts her in. A reader of bodies like the directors themselves, she puts her medical skills to work to track the somatic signs of unease that reveal people's guilt or stress. She also works to convince Julien not to give up medicine.

The drama is ostensibly about care given or denied and the way in which embodied emotions have to be repressed so as to erect borders around the self. Somehow, however, the song, which seems insignificant, turns out to be a turning point. A giving back, it implicitly invites Jenny to see her work not so much in careerist terms but as a giving. Alongside it, we find other apparently trivial gifts that are essential to the film's interpersonal economy. An old lady movingly lowers panettone on a string from her window, a gift that she forgot to give the doctor during her visit. A patient with addiction issues makes waffles and gives Jenny some, which we later see her eating. An old man she has helped invites her for a coffee. She repays him by spending time with him. These apparently trivial gifts of time, food and attention confirm the establishment of relations of reciprocity and the capacity of characters to be active agents of connectivity rather than simply vulnerable people. We might also remember how the older doctor gifts his practice to Jenny, who in turn passes on the lessons she has learned to Julien. Things that are never simply objects nor commodities, and that always connect to people, circulate, creating ties and obligations that can only be repaid in the future and in ways that we cannot necessarily predict.

Conclusion

The problem with the Dardennes' austere, Levinas-inspired ethics is that it is dependent on that which it opposes: it needs neoliberalism's murderous logic to found its own commitment to the Other and offers no meaningful way to move beyond this opposition. The dissimilar problem with the brothers' unacknowledged gift economy, one could argue, is that its gifts are either contaminated by the calculating instrumentalism to which they seem opposed or act as a simple sentimental supplement to the status quo. However, not all the gifts in the films are equivalent. Some are indeed calculating and work to support existing relationships and hierarchies. But others offer us repeated glimpses of something with more political potential. They pull bodies into productive collaboration rather than pitting the capacity for violence of some against the vulnerability of others. They invite us to reinscribe objects in a rich network of interpersonal relations, reminding us of their capacity to shift in signification, carry memories and connect people rather than separate them. They remind us too that the embodied skills brought to especial prominence in the Dardennes' films due to their close attention to material interactions belong to no individual and only become bountiful by their giving away (which is not a loss) and through their open-ended, unpredictable circulation. They remind us finally, because of and not despite their conditionality, that generosity calls forth a generosity that is a giving onwards and not just a giving back. And by doing all these things, they offer some essential elements with which to think a future that would not simply be a repetition of our shrunken present but whose social and institutional conditions remain to be found.

What of the films themselves as gifts? The Dardennes clearly owe a debt to Levinas, as well as film-makers such as Robert Bresson, Maurice Pialat, Roberto Rossellini and Ken Loach, who in turn owe debts to a rich array of influences within film-making history. Like other artists, the brothers repay those they have learned from not by a giving back (except to the extent that their films and words pay homage) but through creative labour and a giving on. Their works provide a generous gift to their public while at the same time offering themselves to other film-makers as sources of potential inspiration. Each time the films give, they are enriched rather than used up or diminished by the new readings they generate or the new works they inspire. To this extent, they can be seen as participating in a generous economy of plenty (Hyde 2012: 145–54). Yet as we know, even films by celebrated auteurs are part of the commercial economy of cinema and what one might call the business of authorship, whereby value accrues to a name that in turn becomes a brand that is rendered artificially scarce by copyright and used to sell cinema seats and film-related products (including academic books). Should we therefore suggest that films offer us only counterfeit goods, seeming to give generously all the better to take from us? Or, more realistically, should we acknowledge that, like the gifts that circulate in the films themselves, the works are neither fully outside the market nor totally within it and, as such, refusing dichotomous understandings, invite us to think the social and institutional conditions that would allow artistic creativity and its bountiful fruits to be more generously shared?

3. THE RESURGENCE OF MODERNISM AND ITS CRITIQUE OF LIBERALISM IN THE CINEMA OF CRISIS

Angelos Koutsourakis

The key thesis of this chapter is that there has been a resurgence of modernism in the European cinema of crisis. This revival of a movement that had been declared passé by the majority of contemporary film scholars has to be understood against the backdrop of social crises whose symptoms resemble the crises experienced by modern societies in the first half of the twentieth century. These crises need to be seen in the context of modern societies' separation between the private and public sphere, as well as their inability to generate conditions of economic/social stability and prosperity on account of their vulnerability to economic shocks and pressures. Henri Lefebvre's argument formulated in the 1960s that modernity generates more crises in its 'fruitless attempt to achieve structure and coherence' (1995: 187) is equally applicable to the contemporary experience of late modernity and neoliberal capitalism. As such, to understand the current crisis in Europe, we need to expand its historical parameters and see it not as the exception, but as a systemic reality that has characterised modern societies since the entrenchment of neoliberalism in the post-1989 world.

I am not the first to suggest this. Lauren Berlant famously contended that crisis is part and parcel of a society structured around economic rationalisation and deregulation. For Berlant, the crisis needs to be understood as a systemic reality, a 'crisis ordinariness' (2011: 10), which is part and parcel of the historical experience of late modernity. In a more idiosyncratic way, Teresa Brennan describes the present historical state as exhausting modernity. She contends that neoliberal capitalism exhausts energy resources from nature without replenishing them, while at the same time it imposes exhausting conditions of life on individuals, including those who are materially privileged. Exhaustion is not just a physical symptom of overwork, but the mental status quo of an era unable to envisage and imagine alternatives: 'There is a terrible tiredness around, a sense of having no energy, or of energy departing' (Brennan 2000: 12).

These points can help us understand the crisis as a key constituent of Western societies following the consolidation of neoliberalism. Taking this into account, we can – along with Berlant – consider the European cinema of crisis as something that predates the great financial crisis of 2008 and can be extended to films made in the 1990s and the early 2000s concerned with the devaluation of labour, the endurance of social and historical contradictions following the fall of the Berlin Wall, and the persistence of class as a material process and relation. Under this rubric of the cinema of crisis we can place films by the usual suspects, such as the Dardenne brothers, Carmine Amoroso, Francesca Comencini, Laurent Cantet, Christian Petzold, Angela Schanelec, Béla Tarr, Benedek Fliegauf, Pedro Costa, Teresa Villaverde, Ulrich Seidl, Michael Haneke, Claire Denis and many more. Interestingly, there is a sense of modernist belatedness in the cinema of crisis, given that we experience a reiteration of formal principles and even thematic concerns associated with aesthetic modernism. Here Julian Murphet's definition of modernism as 'family resemblance of formal procedures that crystallized during a systemic media revolution and a series of crises specific to world industrial capitalism' (2017: 1) becomes fully serviceable. Murphet refers to literary modernism, yet his understanding of it as a movement that responds to media transformations and capitalist crises is equally applicable to the cinematic modernism that concerns us here. One should also add that this connection between capitalist crises (post-industrial now) and the modernist aesthetic might enable us to understand why contemporary European cinema gives a nod to aesthetic sensibilities associated with the past. After all, in the cinema of crisis there is little room for postmodern clichés that reality has disappeared in its simulations or that liberal democracy has managed to resolve the past contradictions of modernity. Can we thus hypothesise that modernism has had a comeback because, far from having overcome past contradictions, late modernity seems to be unable even to offer a positive narrative that justifies its inherent inequalities?

In avoiding a statist and linear periodisation according to which modernism has been succeeded by postmodernism, it is imperative to underline that modernism is not to be seen as a series of formal elements but needs to be understood as a gesture of negation that characterises artworks which acknowledge the duality of modernity as a process of liberation and enslavement. As Timothy J. Clark aptly notes, modernism always involved a critique of modernity; it was, as he says, a response to its 'blindness' (1999: 8); this suggests that aesthetic modernism's key contradiction is that it expresses its enthusiasm for the overcoming of the past, which is combined with a persistent anxiety for the present and the future. This modernist angst is noticeable today in the global reanimation of modernism, as evidenced by the novels of Roberto Bolaño, László Krasznahorkai, Jonathan Littell and José Saramago, the plays of Elfriede Jelinek, and the work of all those film-makers misleadingly named as the last modernists, such as Michael Haneke, Ulrich Seidl, Béla Tarr, Jia Zhangke, Lav Diaz, Pedro Costa and many more.

As stated before, many of the contemporary film-makers who recover the modernist aesthetic sensibility combine this with a critique of neoliberal capitalism, and this is why their work can be classified under the umbrella term 'cinema of crisis'. In what follows, I intend to pursue this argument by looking at three contemporary films: Béla Tarr's short *Prologue* (2004), Laurent Cantet's *L'Emploi du temps* (*Time Out*, 2001) and Michael Haneke's *Happy End* (2017). My claim is that this resurgence of modernism in the cinema of crisis is not a nostalgic reiteration of formal principles associated with the past, but a political gesture – a restoration of the modernist critique of modernity and liberal democracy. Michael North's work on modernism's critique of liberalism offers useful insights here. According to North, both left- and right-wing modernism can be seen as reactions to the individualism put forward by liberal democracy. A key aspect of aesthetic modernism was its desire to restore the community impulse and feeling that liberal democracy had abandoned. As he states,

> The promise of modern political movements to win individual freedom and self-fulfillment for all had come to seem a hollow form; the rights and freedoms guaranteed by liberalism seemed mere abstractions, blank checks that could never be filled in or cashed. One source of the power of aesthetic modernism was its implicit claim to effect the liberation that liberal democracy had promised but failed to deliver. Even a reactionary modernism could seem vital in contrast to the ossified remnants of a failed system, and it was reactionaries like Marinetti who promised the most thorough and the most thrilling revolutions. When Ezra Pound called liberalism 'a running sore,' or when T.S. Eliot complained that his society was 'worm-eaten with Liberalism,' they joined the attack on a system that had come to epitomize the failure of modernity. Reactionary critics like Eliot and Pound identified in liberalism the same weakness that Auden had found: the misconception that the individual is 'an absolute entity independent of all others.' In classical political theory, freedom was a social concept, the freedom to participate in the community. Modern, liberal conceptions of freedom are in contrast subjective and personal. (North 2011: 2)

North's comments are focused on literary modernism, but this critique of liberalism is equally applicable to many post-war modernist films concerned with questions of alienation and angst brought about by the changing social conditions in Western societies. This critique of liberal democracy seems to have gained importance in the present, since the contemporary neoliberal model, with its emphasis on economic freedom, negative rights and little government intervention, is a revivification of ideas associated with classical liberalism – against which aesthetic modernism reacted. This is also the case in the Charter of Fundamental Rights of the European Union, where it is stated that the union 'places the individual at the heart of its activities' (European Union 2000: 8), and while the Charter contains a mixture of classical liberalism (focusing on free trade, negative rights) and social liberalism (with an emphasis on positive rights of citizenship, rights to work and trade union membership), a closer look at the economic policies exercised by the EU countries from the 1990s onwards demonstrates clearly that the union has strongly identified with ideas associated with classical rather than social liberalism.

This comeback of classical liberalism may offer a lens through which to make sense of the modernist belatedness that characterises many films that can be understood under the rubric of the 'the cinema of crisis'. Perhaps one way to interpret this belatedness is, therefore, to consider how modernism's key critique of liberal democracy is relevant again. After all, what connects diverse film-makers from Europe, who address questions of social inequality in contemporary neoliberal societies, is precisely their mourning for the lack of a collective spirit that can enable us to envisage alternatives.[1] What interests me in the three films that I use as a lens with which to view this interrelationship between modernist aesthetics and the critique of liberal democracy is the way they foreground mediations between form and the reality of labour in the present. In doing so, they put pressure on the liberal democratic motto that individuals have the capacity to make rational decisions in a labour reality that becomes more alienating either due to the eventual disappearance and devaluation of work, or due to the changing working environment of labour flexibility, which puts pressure even on the economic elite.

Workers without a Factory and Work: Béla Tarr's *Prologue*

Tarr's *Prologue* (2004) is part of an anthology of films released by Zentropa productions entitled *Visions of Europe*. The aim of this anthology was to offer film-makers across Europe the opportunity to create a statement about the present or the future of Europe. Tarr's film is noteworthy because of its pessimism, but also its allusions to other films from the early history of cinema, which intended to represent the collective workforce. The film consists of a tracking shot that registers a group of people waiting in front of a rundown building. As the camera pans to the left, we see more and more faces of motionless individuals looking like workers ready to punch the clock. The camera slowly moves revealing more people waiting in the line, and here the film consciously references the Lumière brothers' *La Sortie de l'Usine Lumière à Lyon* (*Workers Leaving the Lumière Factory*, 1895). The sequence culminates in a static shot of a window, and suddenly a woman appears, smiles and starts to offer each person a small bag of food and a hot beverage in a plastic cup. We realise that these people are actually not workers, but part of what Marx calls the stagnant population, what we now call the precariat, individuals doomed to a life of wagelessness, working insecurity and pauperism.

What we see in this short film by Tarr is the reactivation of the modernist impulse, the view of art as a material intervention that can reveal something about the modern question so as to invite us to resist it. Tarr paints a bleak picture of the present and future of Europe, anticipating a world of increasing inequality, unemployment, wagelessness and deprivation. What is perplexing, however, is that Tarr's melancholic vision of Europe was made in 2004, when Hungary was celebrating its entry into the European Union, after 83.76 per cent of people voted in favour of joining. For Tarr, cinema's potential to reveal rests here on its capacity to show the disappearance of work in an economic environment in which the production of profit is not necessarily synonymous with job creation. The country's entry into late modernity seems to consolidate misfortune rather than producing prosperity.

The film's belatedness is so strong not only because it is shot in black and white and manipulates the modernist trope of the long tracking shot, but most

Figure 3.1 *Prologue* (Béla Tarr, 2004).

importantly because it refutes the narrative categories of individuality, and its main character is the collective. Tarr gestures to modernist predecessors, such as Sergei Eisenstein and his compatriot Miklós Jancsó. Yet the difference is that the collective subject here is not the heroic proletariat, which is ready to signal the coming of a new era. Instead, we see a collective that seems deprived of political agency, not least because it has been bereft of one of its fundamental social and human rights, the right to meaningful, productive labour. Cinema has been historically linked to the reality of work. As the late Harun Farocki (2002) rightly observes, the first film camera (the Lumières') was pointed at a factory, and film-makers from the canon of cinema history such as Chaplin, Lang, Renoir, Eisenstein and Olmi among many others addressed questions of labour and its implications for the subject. Yet as Farocki laments, narrative cinema eventually withdrew its interest from the world of labour and produced stories that took place mostly outside the collective experience of work. Perhaps this was an index of the withering of the optimistic narrative of modernism and its association with political radicalism. But in Tarr's case we experience a recovery of modernist tropes, the collective subject, the tracking shot and the return to the locus of (non) labour. Labour becomes a key theme again, but ironically through its absence.

How can we interpret this vision at a time when the EU symbolised modernisation and democracy, so much desired by the countries of the former Communist bloc? Is it not somewhat perplexing to see a Hungarian film-maker visualising a key country in Central Europe afflicted by collective unemployment and misery? How is that compatible with the general optimism that permeated many countries from the former Communist bloc which joined the EU enthusiastically? After all, in their collective imaginary, Europe stood for prosperity, democracy, modernisation and equal opportunity for all hard-working citizens. Writing in 1996, the Croatian author Slavenka Drakulić idiosyncratically described what Europe signified for all these people coming from countries in Eastern and Central Europe.

> So, what does Europe mean in the Eastern European imagination? It is certainly not a question of geography, for in those terms we are already in it and need make no effort to reach it. It is something distant, something to be attained, to be deserved. It is also something expensive and fine: good clothes, the certain look and smell of its people. Europe is plenitude: food, cars, light, everything – a kind of festival of colours, diversity, opulence, beauty. It offers choice: from shampoo to political parties. It represents freedom of expression. It is a promised land, a new Utopia, a lollipop. And through television, that Europe is right there, in your apartment, often in colours much too bright to be real. (Drakulić 1996: 12)

Yet Tarr, a film-maker who faced political censorship in the Communist years due to his left-wing ideas, and is currently in the black books of the right-wing government of Viktor Orbán, shares here a cheerless vision of a future that is far from being ideal and certainly not colourful (metaphorically but literally also, since the film is in black and white); what has replaced the alienated labour in the formerly Soviet bloc is the devaluation of work and the emergence of a wasted generation with few future prospects. Here the modernist impulse to respond to a new reality of alienation becomes relevant once again, since the historical context forces one to reconsider the canonical politics of time. One is forced to return to some key problematics that have preoccupied the medium since its inception. Whereas in the early days of cinema, the question posed was how long the workers could tolerate structural conditions of inequality and estrangement from their labour, Tarr's film poses the legitimate question of whether these people will ever find work again and have the opportunity to live their lives in dignity.

In typical modernist fashion, the film-maker emphasises the quotidian, the everyday and the mundane so as to invite a critical attitude that can question its self-evidence. The sequence is devoid of any dramatic climax and sentimentality, and if there is any major revelation it is that the collective we see is not a group of workers but of unemployed or precariously employed labourers waiting in line to access basic provisions. As David Trotter explains, the key innovation brought about by literary and cinematic modernism was precisely this emphasis on the ordinary aspects of everyday reality. Modernist film-makers made films that manipulated strategies of mediation and operated within the dialectic of representing and recording reality. The aim of this commitment to the quotidian was to 'put in doubt the very idea of existence as such' (Trotter 2007: 4). Examples from the history of cinema abound, from the 'vernacular modernism' – to invoke Miriam Bratu Hansen – of Chaplin and Keaton, to the European high modernism of Antonioni, Straub-Huillet and Akerman. The 'entry of the real into the fictional'[2] was a key element of film modernism's desire to invite the audience to critically reflect on places and spaces of work, as well as landscapes and individuals affected by the capitalist conditions of labour. Tarr's conformity to the codes of modernism[3] poses pertinent questions regarding both the future of film as medium and the future of work in those structurally underdeveloped countries within the European continent. In a way, the film's stylistic and formal belatedness challenges the prevailing orthodoxy that cinema has lost its radicalism after accepting the postmodern reality of simulations and superficiality. The film subtly suggests that cinema can still be a medium that reveals aspects of reality, which gain limited screen time, but also one that can make us challenge the reigning certainties of our historical present. *Prologue* puts pressure on the hurried, post-1989 optimism that the global reality after Communism would be one of general prosperity and democracy, pointing to structures of underdevelopment that are part and parcel of capitalist growth. In other words, the divisions between East and West, global North and global South, are firmly in place, since poverty is a constitutive part of capitalist development. This is the key contradiction of modernity, the way it reproduces the new and the old, profit and poverty, which remains hitherto unresolved.

This double side of modernisation that simultaneously generates development and underdevelopment might offer a better understanding of the resurgence of aesthetic forms associated with the past. The work of the Warwick Research Collective, which consists of literary scholars such as Sharae Deckard, Nicholas Lawrence, Neil Lazarus, Graeme Macdonald, Upamanyu Pablo Mukherjee, Benita Parry and Stephen Shapiro, can shed some light on this point. These scholars rehearse some key Marxist theses put forward by Marx and Engels, as well as Leon Trotsky, according to which modernity (lived capitalist relationships) coexists with conditions of uneven development, which are not the opposite of the former but its dialectical result (see Warwick Research Collective 2015: 10, 120). The example of colonialism best illustrates this, since it shows how capitalist development in the global North is the direct product of underdevelopment in the global South; this unevenness does not appear *ex nihilo*. Development in the metropoles produces underdevelopment in colonised countries, thanks to the removal of their capacity to self-determine and to utilise their own resources and wealth. Thus, underdevelopment is a core element of the experience of modernity, which produces centres and peripheries. Obviously, conditions of underdevelopment are also immanent in the global North. The ghettoes and the projects in the USA or the different historical experiences of the North and South in England show that the dialectic between development and underdevelopment is a material reality within core capitalist players. If we extend this to Europe, which is still divided into centres and peripheries, we can get a better insight into the current crisis and its dialectical contrast between a strong, prosperous North/West and a weak South/East.

The key lesson that these scholars wish to impart is that by acknowledging this contradiction of modernity we can do away with the established temporal parameters of modernity and modernism, as well as the traditional chronological and geographical approaches to their history. Given that modernism is directly interrelated with modernity and the latter has not overcome the above-mentioned duality, we are encouraged to think of aesthetic forms beyond the canonical aesthetic chronology, and to consider how capitalist developments and crises might render modernism relevant again. One needs to consider films from contemporary Asian cinema, which consciously reanimate tropes from aesthetic modernism, but the same is also applicable in many films from Eastern and Central Europe, which tend to be classified under the imprecise term art cinema. Equally important is to acknowledge that by understanding aesthetic forms in such an archaeological way, we might be able to think beyond the canonical limits of historical temporalisation and consider how previous historical contradictions are applicable in the present and necessitate aesthetic responses associated with the past.

This approach is usefully concrete when trying to understand *Prologue*'s formal/aesthetic belatedness and its pessimistic vision regarding the future of Europe. As Tarr aptly implies, the division of Europe into centres and peripheries will not amount to a better future for the populations of the countries from the former Communist bloc. The film invites us to come to terms with what Svetlana Alexievich calls, with reference to the former Soviet bloc, 'secondhand time', a term that describes people's realisation that the new system in the formerly Eastern bloc did not establish democracy but entrenched social inequality. In a passage worth reproducing, Alexievich quotes one of the people she interviewed as saying:

> In the nineties . . . yes, we were ecstatic; there's no way back to that naïveté. We thought that the choice had been made and that communism had been defeated forever. But it was only the beginning. Twenty years have gone by . . . 'Don't try to scare us with your socialism', children tell their parents. From a conversation with a university professor: 'At the end of the nineties, my students would laugh when I told them stories about the Soviet Union. They were positive that a new future awaited them. Now, it's a different story . . . Today's students have truly seen and felt capitalism: the inequality, the poverty, the shameless wealth. They've witnessed the lives of their parents, who never got anything out of the plundering of our country. And they're oriented toward radicalism.' (Alexievich 2016: 33)

In this passage, one encounters people's realisation that capitalist democracy does not necessarily guarantee a positive narrative of progress, since the key contradiction between combined and uneven development suggests that inequalities will persist in the future.[4] Fourteen years after Tarr's film, the reality pictured is not the exception but the rule, not just in countries of the periphery, but also in the core of Europe including the UK. The film's emphasis on the collective subject points to a structural reality of wagelessness, precarity and dispossession that puts pressure on liberal ideas of individual liberty as the route to prosperity, in an economic environment that renders work superfluous or devalues it by flexibilising and precarising the labour market. The current political climate, with the rise of neo-fascism on a global scale, is a fearful reminder that the critique of liberal individualism can privilege right-wing radicalism in the absence of a concrete left-wing counter-narrative to the status quo.

Tensions Within the Elite: *Time Out* and *Happy End*

The pertinence of modernism as an aesthetic form whose critique of liberalism has validity in the present is evident when considering how films made both in the European centre and the periphery recover the modernist critique of representation. While in the former Communist countries this re-emergence of modernism is to be attributed to experiences of economic unevenness, in the European centre it is the product of an overdevelopment that radically alters the conditions of labour and the historical experience of the welfare state. The expansion of neoliberalism in all spheres of everyday life has entrenched the ideology of individualism, creating a crisis of confidence in community as a social category as well as in social institutions. Modernism has historically flourished in periods of social instability; one needs only to recall German Expressionism's response to the historical conditions before and after the First World War, the Soviet cinema of the 1920s, the left-wing German modernism prior to Hitler's *Machtergreifung*, as well as post-war modernism, which as per Deleuze's famous formulation does away with classical cinema's privileged mode of narration which subordinates time to narrative imperatives (Deleuze 1989: 41–3). Deleuze suggests that post-war modernism thematises 'everydayness' as opposed to narrative, and that this can be seen as part of a crisis of confidence following the Second World War. While this argument has been put under much pressure, there is certainly merit in it, given that much of post-war European cinema emphasises everydayness and mundaneness, which were core features of literary modernism too.

Neoliberalism has brought about a different crisis of confidence that negatively affects even the upper social echelons, who seemed to be impervious to changes in the labour market. Cantet's *Time Out* (2001) is a fine example of a film that reanimates modernist tropes as a response to the material realities of the present. The film focuses on Vincent (Aurélien Recoing), a middle-aged man who loses his job in a consultancy company and pretends to his family that nothing has changed. He keeps on acting as if he is a busy professional, and at one point he even pretends to have obtained a job at the UN in Geneva, so as to justify his long absences from home. He eventually starts making a profit by starting a fake investment scheme and convincing his friends to invest in it with the promise of high returns. Eventually, he joins a professional smuggler, Jean-Michel (Serge Livrozet), only to be found out by his family. Scholars such as Martin O'Shaughnessy have noted how the character's disposition allows him to become the perfect, mobile, free, neoliberal individual. The film's manipulation of the road movie genre becomes a commentary on the mobility of capital, while the character's slow adoption of neoliberal mottos makes him 'more a chameleon than a stable individual' (O'Shaughnessy 2015: 84).

I would add to this that Vincent can be seen as a modernist unreliable agent, since his desire for conformity in a neoliberal environment – which he initially finds it hard to adjust to – leads to the colonisation of his body by capital. His will to adapt to individual performance objectives leads to the total disappearance of individuality, something clearly articulated in many passages in the film where his voice-over does not offer an insight into his persona, but seems like a mouthpiece for capital. At one point, after ending up in a mountain resort, the camera spends significant screen time capturing Vincent reading documents, and the voice-over comments: 'Note on the dynamic evolution between UCDI and NGO. A number of internal agency procedures were revised in order to encourage increased implication of NGO.' Here the character repeats and quotes lines not just to keep on faking business, but also to familiarise and integrate himself into a reality that has been hitherto incomprehensible. At other points in the film he listens persistently to stock market news. Cantet's character follows the post-war European modernist motif of the estranged anti-hero, who responds to a new reality that he or she fails to understand and adjusts her/himself to it. The difference is that the post-war modernist anti-hero, as John Orr observes, is a privileged individual in material terms, who tries to come to terms with her or his spiritual impoverishment (Orr 1993: 15). Yet this existential angst is certainly connected with changes in the material environment. Cantet manipulates the modernist anti-hero motif, but the key innovation is that labour, or rather lack of labour, is explicitly what motivates the character's mobility.

Furthermore, in a modernist fashion, the camera spends significant time capturing everyday details, mostly Vincent trying to acquaint himself with the world of modern capital, and indeed there are very few dramatic highs and lows in the film. This emphasis on everydayness through mobility (travelling) is indicative of a changing environment that privileges impermanence over stability in all domains of social and economic activity. This aspect of the film chimes neatly with Zygmunt Bauman's suggestion that we are currently experiencing the period of liquid modernity, whose key characteristics are job insecurity and ceaseless capital movement. Neoliberal capitalism is 'light capitalism', in the sense that it shows a preference for immediate profit and short-term ventures rather than long-term ones. As he says, 'its lightness and mobility have turned into the paramount source of uncertainty for all the rest' and especially for workers who cannot depend on labour stability (Bauman 2000: 121). But Bauman's thesis becomes a useful conceptual model for understanding how this shift in economy affects community relations. Working flexibility goes hand in hand with emotional flexibility and the inability to commit to steady social relationships. In his words:

> Family, workmates, class, neighbours are all too fluid to imagine their permanence and credit them with the capacity of reliable reference frames. The hope that 'we will meet again tomorrow', the belief which used to

offer all the reasons needed to think ahead, to act long-term and to weave the steps, one by one, into a carefully designed trajectory of the temporary, incurably mortal life, has lost much of its credibility; the probability that what one will meet tomorrow will be one's own body immersed in quite different or radically changed family, class, neighbourhood and the company of other workmates is nowadays much more credible and so a safer bet. (Bauman 2000: 181)

In keeping with Bauman's point, we can uncover the key contradiction put forward by the film, which is how the profit motive can separate one from the community. Vincent, the humiliated worker whose work has been rendered superfluous, eventually learns the new rules of capital, and how mobility, flexibility and short-term relations are the route to individual success and prosperity. Eventually his fake investment scheme allows him to conform to the neoliberal imperatives of egoistic interests and individual profit, at the expense of his small community (family life), but also of his group of friends, whom he tricks out of their money. In a way, the new model of success defined by the free, mobile and emotionally flexible individual clashes even with the basic forms of communal and social interactions such as the private sphere of the family. The more successful Vincent becomes as a businessman, the less time he spends with his wife and children, and his relationship with them deteriorates.[5] This may well be seen in light of what Marx calls the dual nature of money as a means of connecting social groups and individuals but simultaneously as a means of separation. As he says:

> Only through ... the medium of private property does the ontological essence of human passion come into being ... [But] if money is the bond binding me to human life, binding society to me, connecting me with nature and man ... can it not [also] dissolve and bind all ties? Is it not, therefore, also the universal agent of separation? (cited in McClanahan 2016: 48)

For Marx, money can lead to the deformation of individuality by reducing social interactions to exchange ones. This argument gains even more strength in the conditions of liquid modernity, where permanent communal relationships and even family ties act as an impediment to individual ambition and financial success.

The crisis as formalised in Cantet's film is to be attributed to conditions of fast development that render past labour experiences obsolete. Here, unlike Tarr's film, the modernist impulse is reactivated to comment on conditions of overdevelopment, which, however, has a negative effect on labour too. It is noteworthy that the reality visualised in the film is one that impacts negatively even the upper-middle classes; Vincent is a white-collar worker who used to work for a prestigious firm, and yet he finds it difficult to adjust to the liberalised labour market. The film suggests that the compulsive and ceaseless desire for modernisation that characterises late modernity produces conditions of insecurity even for the privileged social strata.

This is also the case in Michael Haneke's *Happy End* (2017), which addresses the persistence of class as a meaningful category and at the same time shows how materially privileged individuals are not exempt from alienation. The film follows the Laurents, an upper-class family in Calais consisting of Anne (Isabelle Huppert), a real estate developer, her brother Thomas (Mathieu Kassovitz), her son Pierre (Franz Rogowski), and George, her father (Jean-Louis Trintignant), who suffers from dementia. The starting point for the narrative is a fatal work accident at a construction site owned by the Laurents, which results in a legal battle with the worker's family, while damaging Anne's relationship with Pierre; another key event is the poisoning of Thomas's former wife (possibly) by her 13-year-old daughter Ève (Fantine Harduin), who moves back in with her father. The film makes use of strategies of multiple protagonists, while in typical Haneke fashion mediation plays a pivotal role.

Haneke's modernism has been acknowledged by scholarship. Catherine Wheatley (2009) locates him in the tradition of counter-cinema, Nikolaj Lübecker (2015: 34) places him in an Artaudian tradition, John David Rhodes and Brian Price (2010: 10) understand his image-critique to be a continuation of the modernist desire to reconcile art with social life, and Roy Grundmann (2010: 387) has discussed his work with reference to Adorno's theses in *Aesthetic Theory*. Tara Forrest places him in a Germanic cinematic and philosophical tradition that understands art as negative utopia. In other words, Haneke reactivates the modernist aesthetic of resistance (Forrest 2015: 142). These are valuable contributions, yet the question that remains unanswered is what this anachronism signifies in the present. Looking at *Happy End*, we can reconsider Haneke's modernism not as a gesture empty of historical significance, but as a reanimation of the modernist critique of individualism as well as a response to the dialectics of development and underdevelopment. Haneke is renowned for his scepticism towards the changing form of social relationships generated by our reliance on new media technologies and modes of communication, and this can be seen in light of this critique.

Consider the film's opening, where action is framed through a smartphone snapchat application. Focalisation is unclear, since the director does not inform us of the identity of the person through whose point of view we experience this scene. Later, we realise that it is the young teenager Ève, who is probably implicated in her mother's drug overdose. The sequence here, along with others in the film focusing on erotic exchanges between her father and his secret mistress (Hille Perl) through social media, refers to social conditions of mediality, which in a neoliberal fashion can reduce sociality to transactional relations. What is of interest in *Happy End* is how mediation becomes a form of separation rather than communication, and indeed this double side of technology as progress and regression has been a key theme of modernist culture since the inception of the railway.[6] Questions of technological mediation figure importantly in the film as a broader commentary on a communication crisis brought about by media expansion that privileges individualism over meaningful interactions. This aspect of the film reanimates modernism's resistance to modernity and its critique of the liberal motto of the private individual which the contemporary new media environment solidifies. Importantly, material privilege does not act as a shield from alienation, and in fact the privileged characters are equally affected by the loss of community, either leading double lives or having affairs that seem to be transactional in scope.

The film's formal organisation relies on fragmented sequences that have a very loose connection with each other. For instance, in a prolonged sequence in the apartment of Laurence (Toby Jones), who is Anne's partner, the camera alternates between BBC footage of Shell workers striking and him talking with Anne on the phone while enjoying his meal. After hanging up, we see the television report through his point of view. There is nothing plot-promoting per se in this sequence, which may well be seen as a commentary on the persistence of class relations. The following scene focuses on Ève preparing to move to her father's house, and has little connection with the preceding one. Similarly, a sequence capturing Thomas's cybersex interactions with his mistress is followed by another showing George in his pyjamas heading to his car to make a failed suicide attempt. This fragmentation recovers the modernistic aesthetic of the aphoristic fragment, which is associated with two literary figures who have been extremely influential on Haneke's oeuvre, Franz Kafka and Heiner Müller.[7] What characterises the modernist aphoristic fragment in Kafka and Müller is a penchant for irony and abstract statements that refuse hermeneutical finality but offer stimuli to which the readers/audiences are asked to respond. The aphorism, as Richard Gray notes, is a typical trope of a modernist aesthetics of resistance. Commenting on Kafka, Gray suggests that his major innovation in terms of narrative technique was the tension between a desire for narrative finality and 'a labyrinthine openness and inconclusiveness which incessantly frustrates this drive for closure' (1987: 2–3). Jean-Michel Rabaté argues something similar, suggesting that Kafka's aphorisms produce 'contrapuntal relationships' (2016: 153). They deconstruct certain doxas but are not committed to reaching definite conclusions.

In *Happy End*, the aphoristic fragment translates to brief, condensed sequences which function as ironic mini-statements. The film points to the contradictions of the conflict between an exclusive world of privilege, which is also susceptible to alienation, and the world of insecure labour, for example the workers employed in Anne's firm and their servants, as well as the war refugees whose unexpected entry into the narrative universe in two sequences has little narrative function. In an emblematic passage towards the end of the film, Pierre appears at his mother's engagement party with a group of refugees, who cause visible discomfort to the guests. In a typical Haneke fashion, the past and the present interact dialectically with each other, since one cannot avoid considering the history of European colonialism, which is largely responsible for the conditions of economic unevenness in the global South.[8] The importance of this sequence is that it invites us to consider the current refugee crisis as something directly interrelated with Europe's problematic colonialist history, which cannot necessarily be restricted to the past. Whereas in the colonies, underdevelopment was the product of the violent plundering of natural resources on the part of European colonisers, currently it is the outcome of problematic economic treaties that force former colonies to sell their resources and the labour of their population cheaply to the former colonisers. This is a form of neo-colonialism, since many of these economic agreements and policies committed to attracting European investment can be realised through non-democratic means, which generate conflicts in the global South. Haneke here asks us to think about the continuing damaging effects of European colonialism. The uncomfortable reactions on the part of Anne's guests are telling indices of Europe's tendency to turn a blind eye to its past and present responsibility for the conditions of underdevelopment in the former colonies.

This connection between the refugee crisis and colonialism and neo-colonialism becomes more nuanced if we consider the connection between media production, material deprivation and conflict in the global South. It is not accidental that following this sequence, Haneke cuts to Ève recording through her mobile phone her grandfather's attempted suicide. The mobile phone, as well as the new modes of communication by means of social media accessed through laptops that are visualised on screen throughout the film, is a reminder of the linkage between development and underdevelopment. The audience is invited to consider the connection between neo-colonial appropriation of mineral resources for the production of technological devices in the global North and the conditions of underdevelopment that force populations from the global South to migrate. One may recall here the role of the tech industry in the civil war in Congo, for the control of the minerals necessary to produce electronic devices, such as mobile phones and computers. The sequence has an aphoristic format in the sense that it activates an encounter with an off-screen historical reality that leaves its mark onscreen without offering a conclusive answer. This passage from the film is a key reminder of one of the major problematics that neither early nor late modernity managed to resolve, that is, that modernisation goes hand in hand with underdevelopment and that the production of profit generates at the same time poverty and conflict. In Haneke's universe, even the leading elite are not protected from the contradictions of late modernity, and as the film suggests, in one way or another, Europe will have to come to terms with its unflattering colonial history.

In conclusion, in her influential study *Dead Pledges: Debt, Crisis, and Twenty-First-Century Culture*, Annie McClanahan suggests that what differentiates the present state of things is the growing disbelief regarding key liberal democratic ideas of social mobility, hard work and what Berlant calls the 'good life'. As McClanahan says, 'we need to know that what unites us today is not the "good-life fantasy" of upward mobility we once clung to but the universal knowledge of that fantasy's historical end' (2017: 196). Yet this historical end has unprecedented effects not just for those at the margins of society, but for the materially privileged too, who come face to face with the antinomies of late capitalism. The end of the fantasy of the good life makes disbelief in the idea of history as progress more widespread, and if we think of modernism as the culture that takes a critical stance towards modernity, we might be able to understand why it is still a valid aesthetic category in contemporary European cinema.

Notes

1. This is the reason why so many contemporary European films tackle the sensitive issue of workers' suicide (see O'Shaughnessy 2018).
2. Jean Renoir suggested that this is the essence of cinema (cited in Rohdie 2015: 141).
3. For more on the persistence of modernism in Tarr's cinema, see Çağlayan 2018: 39–99.
4. According to the City University of New York economist Branco Milanovic, many post-communist countries will have 'at least three to four wasted generations. At current rates of growth, it might take them some 50 or 60 years – longer than they were under communism! – to go back to the income levels they had at the fall of communism' (cited in Ghodsee 2017: 63).
5. As Neil Archer (2008: 142) observes, the film visualises this central contradiction that Vincent fantasises both individual success as well as a happy family life. Yet the question posed by Cantet and not acknowledged by Archer is whether the latter can be reconciled with the former under conditions of labour flexibility.
6. See Laura Marcus's discussion of the anxieties, shocks and traumas associated with railway travel in the late nineteenth and early twentieth centuries (2014: 41–50).
7. Kafka has been extremely influential on Haneke, who has also directed a TV adaptation of *Das Schloß* (*The Castle*). Similarly, he directed a theatre production of Heiner Müller's *Quartet* in 1988 at Theater am Turm in Frankfurt.
8. As Haneke says, 'If you think of the problem that we're all facing today, that of immigration, which is evoked in the background of the film, then you also can't forget that our forefathers and their predecessors were to blame for that situation. I'm referring here to colonialism, which brought about those waves of migration and the social problems that led to it' (cited in Rapold 2017).

4. POST-FORDISM IN *ACTIVE LIFE, INDUSTRIAL REVOLUTION* AND *THE NOTHING FACTORY*

Patricia Sequeira Brás

The US subprime mortgage crisis had its first warning signs with the foreclosure of low-income borrowers' loans in 2006, which culminated in the insolvency of the investment bank Lehman Brothers two years later (Harvey 2010: 2). The American mortgage crisis rapidly contaminated the European financial market, and exposed the weakness of the financial system globally. The catastrophic dimensions of this event consisted of three simultaneous crises: the banking crisis (banks were extending too much credit, selling 'toxic' housing credit investments, and engendering speculative assets to produce fictional capital); the debt crisis (the increase of public borrowing); and the crisis of the 'real' economy (the stagnation of capital and the decrease of productivity) (Streeck 2014: 49). Austerity measures were then imposed as a strategy to reduce public spending and gain 'confidence from the markets' to avoid financial collapse (Streeck 2014: 49). Despite being felt globally, austerity had particularly drastic consequences in Portugal, Ireland, Italy, Greece and Spain from 2010 onwards. Following Greece and Ireland, Portugal asked for a financial bailout in May 2011 (Hewitt 2011). Under the supervision of the IMF, EU and European Central Bank (known as the Troika), the coalition PSD/CDS-PP government imposed a series of austerity measures until 2015.[1]

In a generalised collective hysteria, the themes of debt, crisis and austerity permeated public discourse; and not surprisingly, artists and film-makers produced a wide body of work centring on these topics. In Portugal, many of the films and art projects that emerged during and in the aftermath of the financial bailout have in common the backdrop of the economic crisis and/or austerity.

As Mil e uma Noites (*Arabian Nights*, Miguel Gomes, 2015) is the most prominent project; a triptych that deploys simultaneously documentary and slapstick comedy to ironically dramatise 'real' stories collected from newspaper articles published between August 2013 and July 2014. The trilogy opens with *The Restless One*, specifically with a segment that conflates the layoffs at the shipyards of Viana do Castelo with the unusual story of a man who ingeniously invented a way to exterminate the Asian wasps' nests that were plaguing bee farms in the region. Following this segment, Gomes appears in front of the camera as a film-maker in crisis who is unsure of the viability of his project and his ability to accurately depict the economic crisis and its impact on the Portuguese population. In a rather insincere manner, Gomes claims to be 'too stupid' to piece these two events together (the layoffs and the plague of the Asian wasps), beyond their obvious geographical connection (see Sequeira Brás 2017: 93).

His statement is, however, disingenuous, as I have argued elsewhere, because the Portuguese textile industry was severely affected when textile production was reallocated to the more competitive South East Asian market (Sequeira Brás 2017: 93). Accordingly, Gomes pieces these events together to allude to capital's fluidity and overarching capacity. However, this correlation denotes a superficial critique that fails to address systemic problems and to recognise that capital extrapolates its own cyclical crises by moving to cheaper labour markets. On the other hand, it also conveys a nationalist narrative against austerity that emerged in part because southern European countries felt that their sovereignty was being menaced, since the imposition of austerity measures was administrated by national governments but supervised by the IMF, EU and ECB.

This nationalistic overtone is found again in the third film, *The Enchanted One*, during calls for mass protests, which were already happening, in defence of Portuguese sovereignty against the Troika. In his third film, the director chooses to show demonstrations at which protesters sing the national anthem. Singing demonstrations against the austerity measures were common in 2013, but protesters not only sang the national anthem but also 'Grândola Vila Morena' (1972), a song written by the late Zeca Afonso, a folk singer and political activist. The song was broadcast in the early hours of 25 April 1974 as the signal for the troops to move into Lisbon and begin the military coup that overthrew the dictatorial and colonial regime of the previous forty-eight years. Because of this, 'Grândola Vila Morena' is a symbol of political emancipation, and as such, it can be understood as 'a return of the repressed', capable of including the event of the economic crisis in a historical continuum. The fact that Gomes uses the national anthem instead of 'Grândola Vila Morena' may suggest an exaggerated sarcasm or merely his political affiliation. In any case, it stands out as a nationalistic outburst that refuses to historicise the complexities that resulted in the event of the economic crisis.

The variety of genres and aesthetic choices in films that have taken austerity as subject matter demands an extensive and detailed survey, but in the present chapter I will discuss, in detail, just three films produced by Terratreme, a Portuguese film cooperative. These films are *Vida Activa* (*Active Life*, Susana Nobre, 2013), *Revolução Industrial* (*Industrial Revolution*, Tiago Hespanha and Frederico Lobo, 2014) and *A Fábrica do Nada* (*The Nothing Factory*, Pedro Pinho, 2017). Because these three films address the economic/debt crisis vis-à-vis industrial labour, they appear to belong to a long tradition of *militant cinema*, which, according to Manuel Ramos Martínez, attempts to make 'visible exploitative working conditions and the brutality of industrial transformations' as well as 'make visible and audible the figure of the worker' (2013: 123). Yet the focus of these films is de-industrialisation, so they more appropriately fit into Martínez's category – *post-Fordist cinema* – which refers to films that emerged after 'the crisis of the Fordist model in the 1970s' as well as films that are 'critical of the factory as a site of exploitation and of cinema itself as a medium of audio-visual exploitation' (Ramos Martínez 2013: 124).

In all the films self-reflexivity is deployed, but out of the three, it is *The Nothing Factory* that directly addresses the exploitative capacities of the filmic medium. Nevertheless, the focus on the dismantling of an industry, and consequentially the obsolescence of an industrial landscape and its labour force, is consistent throughout the three films. As such, I will argue that these films offer a critique of work that is aligned with post-Fordist theory and with the Italian autonomist tradition, while producing a narrative in which the obsolescence of industrial work appears as both the cause and result of the Portuguese economic/debt crisis.

The Specificity of the Portuguese Debt Crisis

In comparison with 'other "peripheral" Eurozone members, Portugal did not experience a period of accelerated growth during the years leading up to the global crash' (Finn 2017: 16). Between 2000 and 2007 Portuguese GDP increased 0.6 per cent, 'less than half the figure' of the Eurozone countries; and in 2006 the average 'wage for Portuguese workers was 60 per cent of that earned by their Spanish counterparts' (Finn 2017: 16). On the other hand, even though the Portuguese housing market had substantial growth in the late 1990s, this growth declined after 2000, unlike in Spain and Ireland (Finn 2017: 17–18).

The privatisation of state-owned banks in the 1990s, investment in labour-intensive industries and the subsequent closure of heavy industries, the growth of the tertiary sector and the high percentage of low-skilled workers are some of the factors that preceded the stagnation of the Portuguese economy, but these also contributed to its predicament after the economic global crisis (Finn 2017: 14). The Portuguese population was already impoverished by the time of the financial bailout, yet the cuts in public spending, as part of the austerity programme, worsened their already meagre conditions. This is shown in *Active Life*, one of the first films to address the conditions that paved the way for the financial bailout.

ACTIVE LIFE

Active Life (2013) is a documentary that focuses on the New Opportunities programme, launched in December 2005. This originated from a pre-existing programme implemented in 2001 for the purpose of upgrading the qualifications of the Portuguese 'active' working population by providing formal recognition of informal qualifications acquired through working experience, and certifying competences that differed from the traditional *curricula*. The purpose of the programme was to overcome the fact that the majority of Portuguese workers were, as they are today, less skilled and qualified than their Western European counterparts. Under José Sócrates's government, however, the programme became a tool to address the rising unemployment that preceded the bailout, since the unemployed population was obliged to enrol in it.[2] This measure brought about severe criticism that questioned the legitimacy of the programme before it came to an end in 2011.[3]

The film's opening shot consists of a close-up of files and passport pictures of ex-workers who were enrolled in the programme. The voice-over by director Susana Nobre explains that the film project began in 2006, but gained new impetus in 2007 when she joined the team of the New Opportunities centre as a technician, in Alverca, a peripheral area of Lisbon that was once dominated by the metallurgy industry. The film uses close-up and medium shots, suggesting a degree of proximity that is contrasted with the flat tone of Nobre's voice posing questions outside the shot. That is with the exception of one scene, in which Nobre appears in the middle of a medium shot facing a computer screen, while talking to one of the interviewees. These contrasting registers evidence her double role as film-maker and technician.

The actual process of recognition and equivalence of qualifications was initially the focus of the film, but it gradually became apparent that the film's subject was the interviewees' accounts.[4] The film proceeds, then, from a series of interviews with individuals who had recently become unemployed and were forced to join the programme for fear of losing their benefits. Thus, the film attempts to make visible and audible the story of a pre-existing labour force that is now obsolete.

When the film was shot the financial crisis seemed far from reaching the European arena, but because it was released in 2013, at the peak of the austerity programme, I argue that it enables us to contextualise the event of the economic crisis within a longer historical continuum. The closure of the Portuguese metal industry was the result of the 'liberalisation of trade' in the 1990s, after European integration, which 'drove Portugal to specialize more heavily in labour intensive industries that were less productive than other sectors' (Finn 2017: 15).[5] This means that the workers' layoffs were not the outcome of the financial bailout, since a process of de-industrialisation had been initiated decades before.

Time wasting

Because part of the process of granting qualifications consisted of recognising skills and competences acquired through their working experience, the interviewees had to provide long descriptions of what their jobs had consisted of. In one segment, a woman gives a detailed description of each stage of production in stuffing chorizos, while another man gives an account of all his different jobs for an outsourcing company, confessing only to have enjoyed his work at a record factory, because 'working in an assembly line boxing clothes or tightening nuts means nothing' to him. In Portuguese, 'stuffing chorizos' (*encher chouriços*) is an idiomatic expression that means doing something to fill up time. For that reason, I argue that the combination of these segments is not innocent, since 'stuffing chorizos' coincides with the man's description of meaningless, time-consuming tasks that fill up time, from which surplus value is extracted and transformed into profit.

The workers' accounts testify to how they also wasted their bodies. Interviewees from the metal industry report health and safety issues when explaining how they inhaled the smoke and dust of heavy metals, such as lead and zinc, and how they would open windows in the factory, against their employers' wishes, which often resulted in the destruction of tomato plantations outside, near the factory. One worker even adds that the majority of his older colleagues are now dead due to continued exposure to heavy metals. Yet the similarities between these stories make them appear to repeat, transforming these individual accounts into a collective story. As one interviewee says, while also expressing his resentment:

> each one of us is telling our past life stories, but everyone knows that this is all the same. The story is all the same. Because we earn little . . . because our parents could not afford . . . because of something else . . . because of whatever . . . This is in my opinion 'dirty laundry'.

The workers' commentaries are more or less politically engaged but nevertheless attempt to address the causes of their predicament. For instance, a metal industry worker says: 'I never thought that such a big empire could fall apart [referring to the company for which he worked]. But throughout history [. . .] even the Turkish Empire fell apart. The strength of capitalism . . . ruined it.' Less critically, a woman says that she worked in a clothing factory for almost twenty years, 'but unfortunately the Chinese ruined it'. The interlocutor is unresponsive, so she insists: 'Clients ordered from China.'

China's admission to the World Trade Organization in 2001, and Europe's outsourcing of manufacturing to the competitive East European and South East Asian job markets, severely affected the Portuguese textile industry (Finn 2017: 17). As I have already discussed, such events are the result of the capitalist need to move geographically, to exploit cheaper productive forces. The closure of the metallurgy and textile industries is the consequence of capital's tactics to overcome limitations on growth in order to avoid its own internal crises.

The focus on the obsolescence of a pre-existing labour force may be understood as a nostalgic undertaking, since the film appears to celebrate work by means of lamenting the lack thereof. Yet the director's unresponsiveness to the woman's comment is the result perhaps of an interest in rendering how individual stories (and not simply jobs) became obsolete, rather than offering a theoretical critique of capitalism. The film deliberately attempts to make the worker 'visible and audible', but at no time does it engage with a nostalgic 'narrative of the end of the industrial age' (Ramos Martínez 2013: 127).

Work ethics

Active Life offers a general account of a substantial part of a previously active population which, after wasting their lives and bodies, is now deprived of the means of subsistence, and made more vulnerable due to the decline of the welfare state, as a result of the imposition of austerity measures. The film depicts the gradual effects of a process that anticipates the debt crisis and the subsequent growth of unemployment.

In her discussion of Argentine cinema and the ways in which modes of subjectivity have changed since the 2001 economic crisis, Joanna Page argues that it seems paradoxical that in times of job scarcity, work 'becomes increasingly less central to constructions of identity' (2009: 38). However, I would argue that, on the contrary, it is precisely because of job scarcity and casualisation that work is no longer central in the constitution of our subjectivities. It is instead through consumption that subjectivities are constituted (Graeber 2018). In the late 1990s Pierre Bourdieu proclaimed that casualisation was 'everywhere' (1998: 81), and accordingly, job insecurity deterred workers from organising themselves against the conditions of their exploitation because it prevented 'all rational anticipation and, in particular, the basic belief and hope in the future that one needs in order to rebel, especially collectively' (1998: 82). In this way, Bourdieu argued that the workers' inability to project themselves into the future resulted in their inability to organise in the present. This might explain why, for instance, nostalgia for a past that never was has been successfully exploited in order to create a general consent to austerity measures (Hatherley 2015).

However, some scholars argue that precariousness and casualisation offer an emancipatory potential insofar as they enable the recognition of a common vulnerability and the building of new political alliances (Butler 2006; Lorey 2015; Graeber 2018); on the other hand, Nick Srnicek and Alex Williams (2015) claim that political emancipation can only be achieved by rejecting the glorification of work and, thus, diminishing work ethics. I will further explore the former argument towards the conclusion of this chapter; but, in relation to the latter, I would argue that the diminishing of work ethics is a pointless political demand in itself, because it is already a consequence of increasing precariousness and casualisation.

In *Active Life*, a pre-existing labour force appears 'baffled, emptied out, resentful, impotent, in suspense' (Abrantes 2013). Suspension is also explicit in the fact that these workers' await reinsertion into the job market, even though such a possibility is limited, not only because the great majority are already 50 years old or more, but also because the job market collapsed before the economic crisis. On the other hand, suspension is also emphasised through the repetition implicit within the similarity of these stories. This, in turn, is what allows the transformation of these individual experiences into a collective narrative. Moreover, despite the specificities of the Portuguese context, these stories resonate throughout (more or less) industrialised Western countries.

In the last scenes of the film, Nobre calls the workers to collect their qualifications because the New Opportunities programme is coming to an end. Nobre's voice is superimposed first on to still images of the workers, and then on to long shots that show the uncollected qualifications and related records being destroyed. These last scenes are prescient, since by 2010 the financial crisis had reached the European markets, and by 2011 the imposition of a series of austerity measures would result in cuts in public spending, leading to the dismantling of the programme and, subsequently, the redundancy of a great number of the technicians working under this programme, which aimed to reinsert the unemployed population into the job market.

In general terms, the film registers the degenerative conditions of a working population, composed of both Portuguese and immigrants, as well as the disappearance of an industry as the cause and not the effect of the Portuguese economic crisis. In addition, the film exposes the ways in which capital, by continuously generating its own limits of growth, ultimately causes the destruction of its productive forces, leaving behind a social landscape pervaded by the relics of used labour. Likewise, *Industrial Revolution* shows a similar landscape, offering a critique of capitalism by means of historicising the development of the textile industry.

INDUSTRIAL REVOLUTION

Industrial Revolution (2014) transports us to the valley of the river Ave, in the north-east of Portugal. In the nineteenth century the river's banks were the site of linen manufacturing, paving the way for the development of the cotton industry. Because the river provided water and hydro energy, vital for the different stages of production, the factories were distributed closely, following the river's watercourse. In this way, the film's pace mimics the slow motion of the water; it invites viewers to get on a boat with one of the characters and embark on a journey along the river. In the eerie natural landscape, colonised by industrial ruins, we encounter a misty, oneiric scenario, where a man sings and plays a guitar on the river's bank, or a goat stands on top of a derelict building.

The film offers a historical inquiry into textile development in the region, depicting a landscape that aggregates industrial ruins, while also recollecting the oral histories of the people who inhabit the river's banks and interviewing ex-workers and current managers of operational factory units. Intertwined with the relics of industrial units as well as long shots of secure properties that open their gates only to let out luxurious cars, these stories testify to the exploitative relation between workers and employers. Moreover, their testimonies disclose the economic dependency of the region on textile manufacturing and the impact of living in the periphery of the industrial units, when, for instance, an old couple recounts that an explosion in the nearby factory resulted in the loss of energy supply in their home. On the other hand, the film also addresses how the industry had an environmental impact in the region, showing that the polluted waters do not deter the population from fishing.

From peasants to industrial workers

The film opens with birds chirping and images of nineteenth-century glass photographic plates, depicting the once rural landscape. The voice of one of the co-directors, Frederico Lobo, explains how industrial development transformed the river's force into electricity, and how labour stopped being organised according to dawns and sunsets and began to occupy nights and days; peasants became proletarians. The sound of birds chirping gives way to the sound of a spinning machine that accompanies images of photographic plates showing workers in factories or posing for the camera in their leisure time. This sequence of photographic plates discloses the pre-historical origins that preceded industrial growth; thus, *Industrial Revolution* historicises the present crisis by means of looking back into the past (McClanahan 2017: 123).

The film proceeds with a medium shot of a factory floor peopled by busy female workers, and then by a close-up shot of workers leaving the factory gates. The latter is highly evocative of *La Sortie de l'Usine Lumière à Lyon* (*Workers Leaving the Lumière Factory*, Louis Lumière, 1895), often credited as the first film ever made, and subsequently remembered in Danièle Huillet and Jean-Marie Straub's *Trop tôt/Trop tard* (*Too Early/Too Late*, 1982) and Harun Farocki's *Arbeiter verlassen die Fabrik* (*Workers Leaving the Factory*, 1995), among other films. Thus *Industrial Revolution* alludes, in a self-reflexive way, to the history of cinema as well.

Workers Leaving the Factory provides 'a historical analysis of the invisibility of the factory in cinematic representations' (Ramos Martínez 2013: 127), while *Industrial Revolution* includes long sequences of workers inside the factory, performing repetitive tasks. Yet the latter puts forward a chronological lineage of industrial development that is not unlike Farocki's film. The early sequence of shots that intersects nineteenth-century photographic plates and a contemporary industrial landscape serves to devise a spatial and temporal mapping of the region's industrial history. On the other hand, released in 2014, the film helps to contextualise the economic crisis within a longer historical continuum, as already argued in relation to *Active Life*. Rather than a nostalgic eulogy to a pre-existing labour force, *Industrial Revolution* and *Active Life* facilitate the archaeology of the social and economic conditions that preceded the Portuguese economic/debt crisis.

When discussing the proliferation of photographic projects depicting home foreclosures in the US, Annie McClanahan argues that this photographic genre 'has filled an urgent desire to make visible, legible, and comprehensible an economic crisis whose effects might otherwise remain too complex, invisible, or latent' (2017: 102). On the other hand, McClanahan also points out that Detroit's ruined industrial landscape became a 'metonymic representation' of the financial crisis (2017: 131). This is because 'the stagnation of the industrial economy in the 1970s both prefigured and is the prehistory of the twenty-first-century credit crisis' (2017: 131). Sluggish productivity and the obsolescence of the labour force resulted in widespread borrowing; for that reason, the photographs of Detroit's derelict buildings, and in particularly its industrial empty spaces, 'reveal the relationship between these two historical moments and these two forms of crisis: the crisis of deindustrialization and the crisis of finance' (2017: 132).

In a similar way, the process of de-industrialisation is a 'metonymic representation' of the Portuguese debt crisis. Even though the growth of the housing market had declined after 2000 (Finn 2017: 16), the investment in labour-intensive industries and the closure of heavy industries heralded the financial bailout (Finn 2017: 14). Like the photographs of Detroit, in *Active Life* and *Industrial Revolution* the social and industrial landscapes of dead labour 'stand in for the crisis as a whole' (McClanahan 2017: 104). By means of historicising the economic crisis vis-à-vis industrial development and its obsolescence, these two films rebuke the official interpretation of the financial and debt crisis as a delimited moment in time that requires the taking of an action (Doane 2006: 252), deployed to create a consensus and accept the imposition of austerity measures. However, *Industrial Revolution* not only historicises the economic crisis by devising a temporal mapping of industrial growth, but also outlines its spatial representation when epitomising the role of logistics and circulation for the accumulation of capital.

The container; or, the abstraction of capital

In the film, the water's flow syncopating the slow-paced montage coincides with the display of a natural landscape filled with both foreclosed and operational factories, in order to suggest that the 'social, cultural, ethical or political relations could never be definitely severed from the biological materiality of the water' (Neimanis 2009: 164). The natural and the industrial (read cultural) are never properly distinguished, since weeds, nettles and other invasive plants colonise the derelict factory locations, resisting human entrance. Here, however, lies a significant correlation between water and the fluidity of capital; by this, I mean the sweeping circulation and distribution of people, goods and capital, globally. This interpretation is substantiated by the last sequence of the film, wherein, on the boat, we arrive at the river's mouth to see in the distance a container ship heading out to sea.[6] This last image of the cargo ship appears to stand for global capitalism.

In *Cartographies of the Absolute*, Alberto Toscano and Jeff Kinkle argue that 'a trend [. . .] has emerged throughout the visual arts over the past decade, in which the narrative structure of the art work is parasitic on the global movements of a particular commodity' (2011a: 190). The attempt to trace 'the production and distribution of particular commodities' resulted in what the authors designate as 'the aesthetics and poetics of containerisation', since most commodities are now transported in containers (2011a: 191, 195). Accordingly, the container stands as 'a synecdoche for logistics, circulation and capital in the arts' (2011a: 195). If, on the one hand, the container 'accelerates the volume, speed and scope of trade and production', on the other, it 'signals the devastation of port and ship-labour, the dislocation of transport and production centres in new spatio-temporal fixes [. . .] as well as a kind of radical opacity or invisibility that comes to affect commerce and industry alike' (2011a: 196). In this way, the container emerges in literature, cinema and the visual arts as a sort of device, making reference to recent changes in both production and distribution, while also pointing to 'the constraints on individual and collective action posed by global capital' (2011a: 197).

In the film, the mirage of the cargo ship at the river's mouth not only signals the way in which goods, still produced by the operating textile industry, are distributed, but also gestures towards the obsolescence of part of that same industry, now incapable of competing in the global market. But competitiveness means the diminishing of the workers' salaries, reducing investment in variable capital and, subsequently, the costs of production, to maximise the extraction of surplus value. This is made explicit in a short interview, when we hear an anonymous factory manager saying that an ideal factory has Third World production costs.

Rather than aestheticising and thus fetishising containerisation, in *Industrial Revolution* the cargo ship makes visible the transition from nineteenth-century capitalism to late capitalism. Moreover, the recollection of oral histories and interviews of both ex-workers and managers prevents the tendency found in other symbolic appropriations of the container to dematerialise, homogenise and even hide the social relations inherent in the production and distribution of commodities. The film progresses then from images of an industrial past to end with a shot of a cargo ship transporting containers in order to illustrate the changes that occurred in the social, natural and industrial landscape of the region. In doing so, it also signals the transition from a Fordist to a post-Fordist system of production, discernible in the technological development of new methods of production and distribution as well as in the depiction of the obsolescence of dead labour and of a pre-existing labour force.

Obsolescence

However, obsolescence can acquire an emancipatory character, evidenced in the sequence where the industrial ruins are explored and utilised by a group of young skateboarders. This sequence begins with a shot outside an industrial building, from the perspective of the boat on the river, looking up, and is accompanied by a strong banging coming from inside the industrial plant. It then cuts to a shot in which a group of youngsters attempt to open the building by banging a cylindrical piece of wood against the door; thus, the sound bridges the two shots. Because ruins are 'regarded as forbidden and dangerous spaces, they become spaces of fantasy, places in which unspeakable and illicit acts occur, places of unhindered adventure' (Edensor 2005: 25). For these young skateboarders, the derelict buildings of these factories become spaces for exploration, and the long stretches of concrete floor 'enable the performance of spectacular and dangerous adventures' (Edensor 2005: 25). In these abandoned industrial sites, they also find a great number of objects that are turned into half-pipes, obstacles and surfaces to perform *ollies*, *grinds* and *nose ollies*. In these ruins, beyond the scrutiny of adults, they can carry out 'leisure practices which would be frowned upon in more regulated urban spaces' (Edensor 2005: 30), simultaneously discovering and destroying what is left over on the site.

In this regard, the repurposing of the factory ruins has an anti-authoritarian interpretation. Moreover, obsolescence occurs when the productive function of these buildings is wasted; as such, these young men appear to contest the buildings' previous productive function by means of skateboarding and destroying the site for their leisure. Accordingly, the 'current' occupation of the factory transforms it into an unproductive space. The ways in which the playful occupation of a factory censures the productive function for which it was created will be discussed in the following section.

THE NOTHING FACTORY

The Nothing Factory (2017), which received the FIPRESCI Critics Award in Cannes in 2017, recounts the closure of a lift factory, whose workers mobilise against their employers after discovering that industrial equipment is being taken from the factory. The employers announce the factory's restructuring, and in response, fearing redundancy, the workers organise shifts to prevent more material being taken. During the occupation, they discuss the possibility of self-management and debate the meaning of 'surplus-value' while also singing and dancing. The main character of the film is 'Smith' Vargas, one of the workers and the vocalist of a punk band; the relationship between Smith and his migrant partner and her son serves as a background for the factory's occupation.

The starting point for the film was the play *The Nothing Factory* by Dutch playwright Judith Herzbel, which was adapted by the film and theatre director Jorge Silva Melo. Pedro Pinho and film co-op Terratreme became involved after Silva Melo abandoned the project. Without eradicating the original concept, Pedro Pinho, Luísa Homem, Leonor Noivo and Tiago Hespanha (*Industrial Revolution*'s co-director) wrote the script, while João Matos and Susana Nobre (*Active Life*'s director) produced the film. The film's location was Santa Póvoa de Iria, near Alverca, where Nobre had shot *Active Life*. Finding a location was not an easy process given the subject of the film,[7] until they found Fateleva, a self-managed factory that had been producing lifts since 1975.[8]

The film was a collective effort that would have been impossible to accomplish without the two earlier films (Marmeleira 2017). Despite employing distinct aesthetic choices, all the films provide a portrait of an industrial landscape and a labour force that has become or is at risk of becoming obsolete, and the dismantling of an industry. Even though *The Nothing Factory* is mostly fictional, unlike *Active Life* and *Industrial Revolution*, in all three films crisis is equated with de-industrialisation.

The refusal of work

In the film, the workers occupy the factory to prevent equipment being taken, organising shifts and resisting both the manager's restructuring and the police.

During this time, they discuss the possibility of self-management, aware that it might not be the solution, since it neither challenges the capitalist mode of production nor liberates workers from the realm of exploitation; on the contrary, it means only self-exploitation. This awareness among the industrial workers suggests the film's alliance to the debates put forward by many within *autonomia operaia* in the 1970s, whose theoretical investigations were rooted in the experiences of the workers' struggles in the 1960s in Italy.

After the experience of industrial expansion in the 1950s, and the witnessing of an intensive labour struggle in the 1960s, a strand of Italian Marxism emerged. Emphasising the autonomy of the working class from capitalist exploitation and state power, it departed from the trade unions and the state-centred Italian Communist Party's reformist policies. Accordingly, the workers' movement had to be autonomous from organisations such as parties and unions that did not defend the workers' best interests (Wright 2002: 29), while demands for the improvement of the conditions of the workforce, by for example cultivating working-class consumption and 'greater free time were [considered] meaningless, for it was above all as producers that humans suffered alienation at the hands of capitalism' (Wright 2002: 42). Rather than clinging to self-management, in the 1970s workers and intellectuals alike demanded 'liberation from labour, not the liberation of labour' (Wright 2002: 115). One of the most important arguments that came out from this strand of Marxism was the recognition that relations of production existed beyond the factory floor, since capital colonises all social relations.

The autonomist tradition is present in the film not only because we see the workers discussing the unlikelihood of self-management, but also because the occupation occurs autonomously; even though a trade unionist visits the occupation, the union's involvement is insignificant. Despite their reservations about self-management, the workers do not abandon the factory site; we see them doing nothing inside the factory, or rather, nothing productive. What they do instead is play football, or play games with a lighter and coins, or perform forklift races. These scenes are evocative of the sequence in *Industrial Revolution*, where young skateboarders explore the industrial ruins, challenging the buildings' previous productive function. The ways in which the workers transform their working hours into leisure time challenges the productive purpose of the site. Yet at one moment the film turns into a musical, and rather than working, the workers sing and dance. This functions simultaneously to contest both the factory's productive function and their social position as workers.

When a film-maker, played by the 'real' documentarian Danièle Incalcaterra, becomes interested in the plight of these workers, he decides to make a film about the occupation. With his help, the workers receive an industrial order for 3,000 tilting modules from a self-managed Argentinian factory,[9] and begin to sing and dance. On the one hand, the figure of the director serves self-reflexivity insofar as it problematises the way in which the cinematic medium often exploits the image of the worker. On the other hand, the musical sequence can be understood as a political moment in which the workers themselves withdraw from their social position. This is so because the workers' performance appears to announce a rupture with 'specific' social dispositions (Rancière 2010: 29), and thus to disrupt the 'harmony between the places and functions of a social order and the capacities or incapacities of the bodies located in such or such place' (Rancière 2009: 70).

The film's theoretical engagement is also made apparent in another sequence, in which a group of intellectuals discuss the dilemma of the workers' factory occupation. Anselm Jappe, Isabel do Carmo and Incalcaterra are among them, sitting at a table, eating and drinking as if mythological gods of Olympus commenting on the predicament of mortal proletarians.[10] At the dinner party, Jappe states that self-management is not radical enough insofar as 'a self-managed isolated factory is still a market agent' incapable of going 'beyond the fetishism of the commodity'. The workers' occupation is only 'a short-term solution' as they are doomed to act against themselves; this indicates that his theorisation is aligned with the Italian autonomist tradition.

Throughout the film, a voice-over explicates Jappe's interpretation of Marx's concept of value production under a capitalist system, which informs the film's political discourse. Yet such an interpretation is exclusively focused on the production of value from the perspective of productive labour and commodity fetishism. At the end of the film, Smith, in conversation with the filmmaker, suggests that we are all part of capitalism, and that only a few would want to abdicate from owning a mobile phone, a car, tupperware and other similar commodities. This is inspired by Jappe's own argument when he argues that it is easier to employ a critique against multinationals or demand more work than to expound a critique of value production. 'Because the critique of value is a critique of the world, one cannot accuse multinationals and neoliberal economists without a self-reflexive awareness of one's position' (Jappe 2006: 19). It follows that the critique of value demands a reflexive awareness of our own subject position within the capitalist system, and our participation as value producers and commodity consumers.

Conclusion

The focus of all the films under analysis is the dismantling of an industry, and the critique of the capitalist system from the point of view of production. In the case of *Active Life* and *The Industrial Revolution*, both films explore, in different ways, the image of a social and industrial landscape populated by used labour and the remnants of dead labour. I have argued that these films attempt to historicise the present time, by means of looking back to the pre-history of the great financial crisis. Following McClanahan's argument in relation to the photographs of home foreclosures in the US and Detroit's ruined industrial landscape, I have argued that, likewise, *Active Life* and *Industrial Revolution* advance a critique of capital and of work by means of denying 'the ahistoricism associated with moments of crisis and [by] insistently [returning] our gaze to the prehistory of the present' (McClanahan 2017: 132). De-industrialisation preceded the economic crisis; as such, the films in question signal the shift from productive to non-productive labour, suggesting that rather than being the result of the crisis, de-industrialisation is instead the means by which capitalism reproduces itself.

The attempt to historicise the process of de-industrialisation also appears in *The Nothing Factory*. Shifting from fiction to documentary, the film shows real workers, who are also characters in the film, giving an account of the industrial foreclosures that have swept Santa Póvoa de Iria in recent years. However, unlike *Active Life* and to a lesser extent *Industrial Revolution*, *The Nothing Factory* is explicitly politically engaged and less vulnerable to accusations of nostalgia, because in a rather unambiguous way it puts into question the viability of the factory's occupation through the dialogue of the workers and with reference to Jappe's theoretical arguments.

Unlike films that individualise the crisis by focusing on its effects on families and individuals, *The Nothing Factory* follows the slow disintegration of a family unit in the background of the workers' occupation, until the relationship comes to an end after Smith rapes his partner while she is sleeping. Throughout the film, we also see Smith picking up her son and helping him out with his homework; but again, these interactions are relegated to a subplot. The film's main focus is the workers' occupation, and as such, it offers a critique of capital almost exclusively from the point of view of production. This, in turn, is because of the film's reliance on Jappe's critique of value, which tends to neglect the role of reproductive labour in the production of value.

According to the autonomist tradition, relations of production extend beyond the factory; thus the factory worker can no longer personify the working class, or class struggle for that matter. For this reason, Italian Marxist feminists have argued that any conceptualisation of class struggle has to include the problem of reproductive labour, since 'in performing domestic labour, women not only reduced the costs of necessary labour, but themselves produced surplus value' (Wright 2002: 134). Despite often being unwaged, reproductive labour is not 'outside the wage relation' (Federici 2013). The extraction of surplus value also occurs outside the direct process of production and, as such, a critique of value production within a capitalist system cannot ignore the ways in which surplus value is extracted from non-productive and reproductive labour alike, independently of being waged or unwaged.

On the other hand, the imposition of austerity measures also caused the decline of the welfare state, affecting, in particular, people, mostly women, who perform reproductive labour. For this reason, it seems insufficient to address the economic crisis from the perspective of productive labour. Moreover, some scholars have argued that there is a potential for political struggle from within 'the caring classes', because these have the capacity to reproduce 'the working class as a whole' (Graeber 2018). As David Graeber argues 'most work isn't about producing anything' but is instead 'about maintaining and taking care of things', yet the dominant theory of value is from the perspective of production, which 'is very patriarchal' (Graeber 2018). Following Marxist feminists, Graeber asserts the need to move 'back to a notion of "caring" as the primary form of value creation'. Isabel Lorey posits a similar argument, yet interestingly from the perspective of precariousness and co-vulnerability (following Judith Butler). Accordingly, because 'life is precarious, it is crucially dependent on care and reproduction', which, in turn, emphasises 'the eminent significance of reproductive work' (Lorey 2015: 19).

I have argued that the process of de-industrialisation is a 'metonymic representation' of the Portuguese debt crisis because the investment in labour-intensive industries and the closure of heavy industries heralded the financial bailout (Finn 2017: 16). By focusing on de-industrialisation, *Active Life*, *Industrial Revolution* and *The Nothing Factory* attempt to historicise the economic/debt crisis. In doing so, these films reproach simultaneously the general argument according to which the financial and debt crisis was a delimited moment in time, and the reasoning behind the general acceptance of the imposition of austerity measures. In the case of *The Nothing Factory*, the film is very much informed by a political engagement with a critique of capital according to a reinterpretation of Marx's concept of value production, but the problem with such a critique is that it neglects the role of reproductive labour in value production. As such, I conclude that in different ways, *Active Life*, *Industrial Revolution* and *The Nothing Factory* point towards the origins of the economic debt crisis in signalling the transition from productive to non-productive labour, but fail to notice the potential role that reproductive labour might have for and against capital in future post-work societies.

NOTES

1. In October 2015, after the coalition PSD/CDS (PàF) failed to win a majority in the Portuguese parliament, the second biggest party PS formed a deal with PCP, Left Block and Pan to form a government, known by the deprecatory term *geringonça* ('contraption'). Since then, many austerity measures have been lifted, but the government still abides by neoliberal reforms.
2. Sócrates was the leader of the Socialist Party and the prime minister of Portugal between 2005 and 2011. He resigned in June 2011, after the fourth austerity

package was rejected in Parliament. His resignation resulted in snap elections, won by PSD's Pedro Passos Coelho, whose government imposed severe austerity measures under the supervision of the Troika. In 2017 Sócrates was indicted on corruption charges.
3. *Active Life* press kit, provided by the director.
4. *Active Life* press kit.
5. Labour-intensive industries comprise non-productive labour, such as services, tourism, care work and so on.
6. At the DocLisboa screening of *Industrial Revolution*, Frederico Lobo stated that the image of the cargo ship was sourced from the rushes of another Terratreme film production, *Trading Cities* (Luísa Homem and Pedro Pinho, 2014), a film that reflects the impact of global capitalism in Cape Verde and other north-west African countries. This, in turn, illustrates the collective collaboration sanctioned by this film co-op.
7. Pedro Pinho at the Q&A that followed the screening of *The Nothing Factory* at the ICA, London, on 25 January 2018.
8. The Carnation Revolution on 25 April 1974, which overthrew the dictatorial and colonial regime, gave rise to many experiences of self-management both in factories and farms.
9. After the 2001 economic crisis in Argentina, many factories were occupied and went through a self-managed experience.
10. Anselm Jappe is a philosophy professor, who has published on Antonio Negri (a well-known philosopher from the *autonomia operaia* school) and Michael Hardt, Guy Debord, and on interpretations of the concept of value in Karl Marx. Isabel do Carmo is a well-known Portuguese endocrinologist, who was the founder of the Revolutionary Party of the Proletariat (Partido Revolucionário do Proletariado) and of the armed struggle group Revolutionary Brigades (Brigadas Revolucionárias) against the dictatorial regime, before the Carnation Revolution. Imprisoned several times by PIDE/DGS – the Portuguese political police – she was allegedly involved in a bank robbery in 1978, of which she was acquitted.

5. RE-EVALUATING CRISIS POLITICS IN THE WORK OF AKU LOUHIMIES

Kate Moffat

Over the last two decades Aku Louhimies has established himself as one of Finland's most prominent and critically renowned auteurs. As well as achieving critical acclaim, Louhimies has built a reputation throughout his career for attracting and sustaining large domestic audiences. For example, on its opening weekend his 2017 film, *Tuntematon sotilas* (*The Unknown Soldier*, 2017), the third adaptation of Väinö Linna's celebrated Second World War novel, broke domestic box office records for a Finnish-language film. Louhimies also counts numerous other successful feature films, TV serials and music videos among his portfolio and, in recent years, he has made inroads internationally with the RTÉ-produced miniseries *Rebellion* (2016), based on the Irish War of Independence. His reputation for 'quality drama' has also followed him abroad where his work is consistently well-received on festival circuits across Europe and the United States. Despite the Nordic countries' reputation for welfare-orientated egalitarianism, Louhimies's films frequently foreground economic and social inequality. In the two case studies explored here, Louhimies concentrates on exploring domestic and familial crises in the urban spaces of Helsinki, using these narratives to capture the state of Finnish society in a transitional age of neoliberal economic and political restructuring. In doing so, Louhimies appears to challenge the established perception of Nordic 'continuity', which is understood by historians and sociologists to be a key characteristic of Nordic nation-building rhetoric and one that has served to reinforce a sense of cohesive welfare egalitarianism. Instead, these films appear to disrupt such continuity by casting Finland's status as a pillar of utopian prosperity into doubt.

This chapter unpacks the thematic and ideological representations of crisis in Louhimies's feature films *Paha maa* (*Frozen Land*, 2005) and *Vuosaari* (*Naked Harbour*, 2012). Both explore contemporary life in Helsinki through a patchwork of interconnected and parallel narratives where the characters' lives are marred and intertwined by domestic violence, alcoholism, unemployment and social alienation. However, despite the clear contrasts between dominant historical conceptualisations of social unity and the stark realities represented in these films, I argue that Louhimies appears to reappropriate the theme of continuity. I claim that the central tension in these films revolves around whether they ask us to view crisis as an external affliction of an underlying and established social order, or whether they suggest that crisis is, in fact, a fundamental component of the Finnish social model itself. In other words, I claim that this is a matter of determining whether these films are about crisis *and* continuity or crisis *as* continuity in the Finnish welfare state. We can use this debate to explore the depth and meaning of Louhimies's relationship within the contemporary political landscape.

Other scholars (see Hiltunen 2017) claim that Louhimies's work is not, in fact, explicitly political, but rather reflects a more existential or universal exploration of the human condition in crisis. However, I argue that more recent developments off-screen force us to re-examine such apolitical readings of the films. One pressing reason for reconsidering the relationship between these texts and their production frameworks stems from recent allegations of misconduct directed at Louhimies by several cast and crew members, including those involved in the two films discussed here. These allegations include bullying and subjugation on set, particularly of women, apparently with a view to achieving the desired effect on camera. Consequently, I argue that we must develop a convergent approach to understanding the way Louhimies handles domestic issues by situating them in their broader cultural and political frameworks. I also consider how the theme of crisis spills off-screen and calls into question the values of Louhimies's production practices and contexts. These developments are especially significant because of Louhimies's status in the Finnish film industry, where, historically, auteurs have commanded and reinforced a sense of moral authority, particularly when using their skills and vision to address wider social problems in Finland.

Continuity and Crisis in the Finnish Welfare State

Before looking at Louhimies's work in more depth, we must first explore the origins and context of continuity as the pervasive ideological thread running through the history of Finnish social democracy. According to sociologists

Pauli Kettunen (2001) and Johannes Kananen (2014), the theme of continuity has played a fundamental role in structuring the social, cultural and political institutions of the Finnish welfare state. Specifically, the welfare state was founded on the egalitarian principles of universal equality backed up by high levels of income tax redistribution and investment in public services, education and general infrastructure. In order to create social and economic stability based on such a model, a collective idea of continuity was required. Like its Nordic neighbours, Finland's small population meant that in order to build a sustainable and egalitarian economic model, a significant level of cooperation and consensus was required between the state and its citizens. These pragmatic arrangements developed into a set of 'values' based around sociocultural holism in which prevalent monolithic expectations about social roles and responsibilities emerged. Broadly, this meant that people were expected to behave in accordance with the state's vision of social cohesion (Kananen 2014: 163). As we shall see, themes of continuity and cohesiveness occupy a complex role in Louhimies's films.

The relevance of continuity and its limitations has not gone unnoticed by scholars working in the field of Nordic film studies. Tommi Römpötti (2015: 133–47), for instance, highlights the significance of generational continuity in Finnish road movies, where the resolution to familial crises is found in the restoration of 'togetherness'. Römpötti argues that these trends gesture towards an underlying conservativism in the Finnish road movie, separating it from other national and international permutations where the genre is typically used to express the subversion of social and cultural conventions.

However, economic transitions over the last few decades have also threatened notions of continuity and sociopolitical consensus. Although post-war infrastructure and investment created significant equal opportunities for people, over the last thirty years, the integration of neoliberal policies and a 'revisionist' attitude towards the welfare state has represented a clear departure from the defining mentality of egalitarian collectivism. From the 1980s onwards the basic coordinates of Finnish society, including its economic infrastructure and social policies, experienced significant reform. The same is true for its social and cultural attitudes. As the public's participation in shaping the social order was minimised, the neoliberal free-market mentality, with its emphasis on private ownership over public interests, cast doubt on the sustainability of the welfare state. However, the ideological implications of these cutbacks have rarely occupied public or political debate (Kananen 2014: 141). The emergence of the so-called 'international competition state paradigm' in which competitive economic strategies took precedence over state subsidy in the 1990s continued to confound the previous collectivist logic of the welfare state. The dynamics of the previous role-driven system changed with the new political climate, and the emphasis was now on the 'freedom' of the individual over communal or collective consensus. Although Finland enjoyed a prosperous decade during the 1980s, Finnish welfare politics was severely tested in the 1990s, partly because of the previous decade's financial negligence. Martin Iversen and Lars Thue state that

> scepticism about nationally grounded welfare states was further strengthened by a number of real economic events in the 1990s when the largest Nordic banks were all shaken by a fundamental financial crisis. These crises were particularly deep in Sweden and Finland, and both countries experienced three consecutive years of negative economic growth. The result was substantial national budget deficits, major unemployment and a wave of corporate bankruptcies. (2008: 2)

Further retrenchment policies were justified in the context of this recession. Since the global financial crisis of 2008, austerity measures and associated forms of welfare cutbacks have once again become a central focus across Finland's economic and political agenda. In short, austerity has become a permanent reality. It has also contributed to new ideological divides between those who are perceived as 'entitled' to state benefit, and those who are not. These tensions highlight the contradictions between a universal system of values, which still functions as a key part of Finland's global image, and the individualist-oriented economic reconditioning that the country has experienced over the past three decades. As we shall see, these contradictions find expression in Louhimies's films, in which the fraught lives of the characters mirror the split between togetherness and individualism.

Reel Crises: *Paha maa* (*Frozen Land*) and *Vuosaari* (*Naked Harbour*)

Echoing Louhimies's earlier successes with romantic dramas such as *Kuutamolla* (*Lovers and Leavers*, 2002), *Frozen Land* garnered 172,000 spectators upon its release in 2005 and proved to be the most popular domestic production that year (Solar Films website). The film's aesthetic approach draws on social realism, with a hand-held camera documentary style and an emphasis on domestic space. However, the intense drama of this naturalistic fly-on-the-wall take is mixed with elements of cinematic spectacle, with interludes that include high-octane car chases and a subplot that involves computer hacking. *Frozen Land*'s narrative is based in part on Tolstoy's *The Forged Coupon* (1911) and Robert Bresson's *L'Argent* (*Money*, 1983), which are both cautionary tales about the dangers and entrapments of revenge. In Louhimies's interpretation, contemporary Helsinki serves as the backdrop for a series of overlapping stories triggered by a single event.

When he is suddenly made redundant, charismatic teacher Pertti (Pertti Sveholm) directs his frustrations towards his teenage son Niko (Jasper Pääkkönen). In the first of many instances of retaliation in the film, Niko commits fraud by using a counterfeit banknote. This sets in motion a devastating chain of events, in which the personal crisis of each individual leads to the downfall of the next. The counterfeit note is passed on to the unwitting Isto (Mikko Kouki), who is arrested when the fake money is discovered in his possession. After a humiliating ordeal at the police station, Isto abandons all sense of responsibility and steals a car, the consequences of which set him on course for disaster.

Meanwhile, Niko causes further disruption by conspiring to hack the accounts of a company owned by the wealthy father of his friend Elina (Pamela Tola). Elina and her boyfriend Tuomas (Mikko Leppilampi) are persuaded to join in with the scheme. Like many of the characters, Tuomas is equally dissatisfied with his life and is searching for a purpose beyond empty hedonism. Simultaneously, a recovering alcoholic, Teuvo (Sulevi Peltola), begins his descent into hell after he is cajoled into sharing a drink with an oblivious stranger. Unhappy and isolated in his job as a door-to-door vacuum cleaner salesman, Teuvo crosses paths with a drunken Isto after he manages to evade the police. This encounter, along with other anxieties, leads Teuvo to relapse from his hard-won sobriety. As the two men embark on a heavy drinking session, they pick up an equally drunk woman from the bar and head to a hotel room. As Isto and the woman begin having sex, they deliberately exclude Teuvo and mock his profession. Their evening ends when Teuvo batters them both to death with one of his vacuum cleaners in a fit of resentment, after which he commits suicide.

Dedicated police officer Hannele (Matleena Kuusniemi) also becomes embroiled in the chaos. After discovering the bodies of Isto and his lover, she struggles to contain her emotions at work and begins to take unnecessary risks on duty. One night Hannele leads a dramatic chase, attempting to apprehend Niko and Tuomas, who find themselves on the run after executing their plan to hack the company accounts of Elina's father. During the pursuit, Hannele is struck by a train and killed.[1]

After Hannele's death, Tuomas is arrested and charged with her manslaughter, ultimately taking the rap for Niko. His conviction instigates yet further tragedy when Hannele's husband, Antti (Petteri Summanen), sets out for revenge. Consumed by loss, Antti takes his anger out on his three young children, and they are eventually taken into care. Antti's breakdown culminates in him shooting Tuomas when he is released from prison.

Naked Harbour (2012) also foregrounds the theme of crisis, but this time the narrative is structured around an episodic series of stories about people struggling to find love and acceptance in Vuosaari, a neighbourhood located in the rapidly expanding Eastern district of Helsinki. Like *Frozen Land*, *Naked Harbour*'s ensemble cast of characters find themselves the victims of both circumstantial crisis, such as disease, but also exploitation by others. Pertti's (Mikko Kouki) values and standards centre on an idealised interpretation of the male physique. After failing to achieve this ideal himself, he obsessively pushes the same goals on to his teenage son. For instance, Pertti's neurosis over his son's junk food habits causes him to lash out and punish him. In later scenes when he is alone, Pertti is seen habitually eating excessive amounts of the same prohibited food. Teenager Milla (Amanda Pilke) becomes embroiled in a seedy underground world of internet pornography, where she is cajoled into having sex on camera. Trapped between her misguided desire for fame and recognition and the harsh reality of her situation, she finds herself unable to confide in her oblivious father.

Simultaneously, Marika (Alma Pöysti) struggles to protect her young daughter from the realities of her own terminal cancer, while Robert (Sean Pertwee), a visiting British businessman, preaches the virtues of family life to his Finnish cohort, though in reality, he relies on escorts for company. During brief phone calls to his wife, hidden animosities come to light, as do the contradictions in his personal principles. Running in parallel, a young Russian immigrant boy fights against playground bullies, and another neglected young boy is subjected to his mother's cruelty. The young boy's only companion is his pet dog. As the animal causes an inconvenience, the boy's mother has him destroyed – an act she seemingly carries out herself. Her wilful neglect and lack of maternal instinct represent another violent break with the egalitarian welfare mentality. In each separate story, reality fails to live up to the promise of expectations set by the welfare state. Despite its bleakness, *Naked Harbour* ends on a more affirmative note as the young dying mother Marika is seen playing with her daughter, and the tragedy of her situation is transcended when she embraces acceptance.

Film scholar Pietari Kääpä describes how

> the characters of the films need to be understood as metonymic representatives of wider social problems in Finnish society, as even the titles of the films gesture towards a sense of collective malaise. These films represent Finland as a decidedly fragmented constellation where economic and political structures serve to alienate a large section of the nation's citizens, who, in turn, interpret the social and cultural norms of the society in decidedly negative ways. (2010: 276)

Indeed, few sectors of Finnish society escape crisis, with a sense of despair touching both the middle and working classes. As Hiltunen (2017: 112–14) points out, Louhimies's films are an expression of anxiety surrounding changing social roles in a climate defined by tensions between collective and individual responsibility. In a society conflicted by a commitment to both egalitarian values and competitive neoliberal economic targets, Hiltunen claims that Louhimies exploits a specific brand of 'Finnish melancholia' by drawing on well-established national stereotypes. Emőke Csoma also addresses the perceived marketability of Finnish melancholia and argues that the international success of Louhimies's *Frozen Land* 'is potentially a result of the film using a range of familiar cultural tropes about the Finnish society and the "national character": for example, the use of the drunk Finnish stereotype was often criticized domestically while foreign audiences seem to find such characteristics endlessly fascinating' (Csoma 2012: 161). This self-exoticising 'brand' of misery has a legacy that stretches back in both Finnish and Nordic film cultures.

Many of Louhimies's films are preoccupied with an almost pornographic emphasis on suffering and domestic dysfunction. However, they differ from the work of other renowned auteurs such as Aki Kaurismäki, who have also helped to sustain Finnish melancholia.[2] Kaurismäki's melancholia is typically built on exaggerated stereotypes of the Finnish 'national character', in which dominant (and largely negative) ideas of Finnish masculinity and identity revolve around introspection and self-destructive behaviour. However, simultaneously, Kaurismäki takes social 'realist' themes in an entirely different direction with regard to narrative pace and the aesthetic visualisation of his landscapes. On the surface, the stark brutality of Louhimies's realism arguably offers us a more 'authentic' take on contemporary realities than Kaurismäki's more fantastical or magic realist explorations of the social landscape. Kaurismäki's aesthetic approach is more heavily reliant on the politics of nostalgia, although his relationship with Finnish history is a highly contradictory one, often framed through an ironic detachment. The difficulties in explicitly identifying the relevance of the domestic context in both Kaurismäki's and Louhimies's films may be indicative of the complexities of a Finnish national cinema caught between domestic contexts and the encroaching realities of globalisation.

While Louhimies highlights how the Finnish welfare state fails to live up to people's expectations, the existential nature of each character's dilemma also suggests that his films offer an apolitical take on the theme of crisis. This means that Louhimies might not want us to take the context of the Finnish welfare state too seriously, and instead interpret crisis as a reality of life as opposed to a specific knock-on effect of a badly managed economic or political system. Indeed, with Tolstoy providing a familiar thematic framework in *Frozen Land* and the stories of crisis in *Vuosaari* echoing across generational and class boundaries, we are confronted with a sense that these stories could happen almost anywhere, rendering the Finnish setting almost incidental. Hiltunen claims that there is no 'explicit social criticism or political agenda' (2017: 111) in Louhimies's films. Rather, the universal nature of his themes gestures more towards a moralistic tone that is not necessarily grounded in a historical Finnish context. The characters in *Frozen Land* and *Naked Harbour* are relatable through their flaws and hang-ups, but also through the way in which their experiences differ from the perceived expectations set by the dominant narratives of continuity. There is also a sense that, because crisis is not tied to a specific class, gender or age group, anyone at any time could find themselves at the mercy of a crisis. The only sense of continuity in these films emerges from the characters' mutually self-destructive acts.

However, Louhimies's modification of this theme carries with it an underlying conservatism that is comparable to Römpötti's observations on the Finnish road movie genre. Here, *Frozen Land*'s allusion to Tolstoy's tale of sequential turmoil and the domino effect of one individual's poor choices can also be understood as a conformist take on crisis politics. Louhimies's approach acts as a form of intervention designed to show us that these characters do, in fact, have a set 'destiny' of sorts. This is most evident in *Frozen Land*'s final scenes, where Niko reads Tuomas's eulogy at his funeral. In this closing speech, he makes a poetic reference to a higher order of governance and implies that actions and their consequences can reach beyond a single individual or group. The eulogy appears to reinforce the idea that these crises are in some way predetermined by a higher will or power and are not necessarily the result of a breakdown in the Finnish social system.

Louhimies emphasises a form of continuity in the chaos, and while he may engage with or suggest political issues such as problems with the welfare state, his focus on the dreary commonalities of crises such as domestic disharmony would seem to suggest that there is no specific political agenda here. There is almost a Shakespearean nature to the tragic-comic moments in both films, and the way they expose, and in some cases vindicate, the human flaws and weaknesses in each character. Consequently, we must ask if these films are as historically grounded or as nationally relevant as my discussion of Nordic continuity suggests. By Louhimies's own admission, the characters' circumstances are designed to strike a chord with virtually any audience. *Frozen Land* generates empathy for each character's lack of control over their destiny, and *Naked Harbour*'s emphasis on the search for love and acceptance is not contained by any nation or border. *Vuosaari*, although potentially symbolic of a Finland in transition and confronted with its past histories and futures, could equally be understood as any neighbourhood in a large metropolitan area.

However, if we take *Frozen City* and *Naked Harbour* to represent Louhimies's subtle or coded swipe at the failure of social institutions, I argue that this gesture represents Louhimies asserting and projecting his own sense of moralising universality. In place of narrative consensus, the context of Louhimies's intervention into themes of contemporary crisis signals that we must look more closely at the contradictions in the moral undertones that resonate in these films, and confront the realities of the culture in which they were produced. We must ask if these films become *politicised* when we take their broader production cultures into consideration. Specifically, I claim that in order to understand the role of crisis politics in structuring these films, we must step outside the narrative context and consider precisely whose perspective on crisis is represented here.

Real Crises: Auteur Apologism

Academic discussion of Louhimies's films largely concentrates on how the troubled realities of the characters are woven into a corrupt social fabric.[3] However, the context of these films' production dynamics must also be considered in order to properly understand Louhimies's position as an auteur commentating on such social problems. One cannot account for the narratives without considering them in relation to these contextual developments.

Following the release of *The Unknown Soldier* in 2017, several of Louhimies's prominent collaborators, including Pamela Tola, Matleena Kuusniemi, Pihla Viitala and Jessica Grabowsky, accused him of bullying on set, particularly criticising the way in which Louhimies allegedly placed his artistic goals above their full cooperation and consent (see Rigatelli 2018; Virtanen 2018). These accusations emerged as part of the global #MeToo movement, which has seen a series of high-profile individuals across the global film and television industries facing accusations and charges of assault and misconduct.[4] In Louhimies's case, these involve highly questionable methods for achieving authentic reactions of disgust, such as placing live cockroaches under people's clothing and cajoling (particularly female) actors into compromising and exploitative situations. Some of these alleged incidents occurred during the filming of *Naked Harbour*. Finland's public broadcaster YLE published several articles on the accusations in 2018 and staged a debate between Louhimies and one of his accusers, Matleena Kuusniemi. While Louhimies did not deny or downplay some of the approaches he had used in the past, he has denied other indictments and refuted the way the stories have been framed in sections of the Finnish media.

While Louhimies seems to gesture towards a collective moral order in his films, how do we reconcile these politics of crisis off-screen? The answer to this question is not easy; I propose that we must start by considering how the representational politics work in conjunction with the broader production contexts and frameworks. Although a more extensive examination of these issues is beyond the scope of this chapter, I suggest that the major contradiction lies in how 'exceptionalist' auteur culture fits within the remit of Finland's inclusive, egalitarian agenda and reputation for equality. It is therefore important that we address representational politics in relation to these issues, as the examination of social problems in Finland is embraced by the industry itself as part of its own self-examination and reproach. Here, crisis politics can be manipulated to represent the introspective self-interest of the industry, when in reality, its operations speak of a hierarchical relationship between the director, the cast and crew.

Indeed, these accusations have raised questions about power and crisis politics in the Finnish film industry. Considering these allegations and his response to them, we must re-evaluate Louhimies's legacy and place it in a cultural canon where critical acclaim can potentially overshadow institutionalised production practices that threaten to undermine the moral message of the film narratives.[5] The work of Barbara Klinger (1994) talks extensively about how narratives are informed and influenced by the ideological structures of the wider industry. More recently, and following on from these initial investigations, Stefania Marghitu has explored the term 'auteur apologism' in the post-Weinstein era of film politics. She claims that the term is designed 'to expose the ways that the auteur is not merely a product of individual exceptionalism, but, more importantly, is a product of systematic, cultural, and industrial inequality that keeps women and minorities subject to marginalization' (Marghitu 2018: 493).[6] While an in-depth discussion of these events is clearly beyond the scope of this chapter, by drawing a link between the underlying moral sentiments of these films and the context of the director's status and voice, I hope to highlight how crisis politics can help us consider the relationships between narrative and production practices.

Frozen Land won eight Jussi Awards in 2006, including one for best direction.[7] *Naked Harbour* also met with praise for its sobering exploration of people embracing acceptance. Beyond these accolades, Louhimies is recognised in broader social contexts, having been awarded the prestigious Pro Finlandia Medal in 2017 for his contribution to the arts.[8] Kääpä has suggested that Louhimies's films serve different functions in various national and international contexts, providing a certain commercial allure with his brand of 'Nordic miserabilism' (2012: 129–30) for audiences outside Finland. Equally, Louhimies's success reflects back on the Finnish film industry. Consequently, his auteur stamp of authority requires that his work be taken seriously and considered for its incisive critical commentary and, perhaps above all, its strong sense of moral and social consciousness. The success of Louhimies's work and, specifically, that which has established him as a voice of authority on all things crisis-related in Finland, must also be taken in the context of broader production practices. If, as Hiltunen suggests, we must view Louhimies's films as a reflection of tensions between individual and collective responsibility, we must also apply these themes to the films' production dynamics and consider the contradictions between the power of the individual auteur and their commentary on conformity. This is especially important if those commentaries are complicated by accusations such as those made against Louhimies. This calls for further research on the theme of continuity *as* crisis within the structures and working environments of the Finnish film industry and beyond. The argument against Hiltunen's assertion that there is no political agenda in Louhimies's film must be re-examined in light of these allegations, or perhaps more pointedly, we must look at how our understanding of the wider production culture can transform the way we interpret these texts and their position within a national film canon. One of the reasons why we must reconsider the relationship between text and production is because the identity of these films is shaped by Louhimies as a director with a reputation for provocation and the subversion of 'conventional' narrative expectations.

Conclusion

These two films appear to reappropriate the Nordic theme of continuity by positioning crisis at the centre of the characters' lives and realities. Louhimies seems to suggest that crisis is not something separate from the everyday, but is part of it. In both films, domestic normality is thoroughly shattered. In *Frozen Land*, Tolstoy's tale of cyclical revenge is a fitting analogy for the fraught state of the continuity narrative that lies at the heart of Finnish social democracy. However, in questioning the ways in which this continuity has been tarnished by successive neoliberal governments, I argue that other underlying themes of continuity emerge. In this case, the theme of continuity is built around more existential or philosophical notions of chance and fate. However, I interpret these films, and specifically their crisis themes, as inherently political, especially when placed in the context of their wider production culture. Specifically, the themes of crisis are politicised by the wider cult of the auteur and its contextual significance in Finland.

Although these films deal with existential topics such as freedom of choice and the destructive lure of revenge, Louhimies projects his own moral sense of universality on to his subjects. He is able to emphasise his moral leanings by pitting them against the apparent dysfunction of the social system, allowing his take on these crisis politics to resonate with a certain auteurial authenticity. We must consider the context of this authenticity carefully with regard to recent developments when dominant auteurs such as Louhimies continue to command a strong sense of social consciousness. Arguably, despite the critique of Finnish society in his films, he continues to speak as an establishment voice. When we look at how themes of crisis are articulated onscreen and compare them with the realities of the structural inequalities within the Finnish film industry, a clearer picture of power and the position of auteur culture begins to emerge.

Notes

1. In Hannele's tragic death, Louhimies blurs the boundaries between authority figures and ordinary people caught in the chaos. This is unlike many of the works of fellow Finnish auteur Aki Kaurismäki, who often maintains a clear division between authority figures and those ordinary people battling at the coalface of social dysfunction. In *Frozen Land*, the authorities are shown from two conflicting perspectives, oppressive and unforgiving in their initial treatment of Isto, and yet also over-committed and emotionally involved as with Hannele.
2. Class politics and social criticism are persistent features across Kaurismäki's forty-year career. For some of the most prominent examples, see his 'proletariat trilogy' *Varjoja paratiisissa* (*Shadows in Paradise*, 1986), *Ariel* (1988) and *Tulitikkutehtaan tyttö* (*The Match Factory Girl*, 1990).
3. See Kääpä 2010 for further discussion on the social and political contexts of Louhimies's work.
4. The #MeToo movement in Finland was spearheaded by Finnish director and screenwriter Heidi Lindén.
5. In 2018 the Finnish Film Foundation introduced new guidelines on sexual harassment in the film industry following the #MeToo movement. For the English version, see <https://ses.fi/fileadmin/dokumentit/Guidelines_for_the_prevention_of_sexual_harassment_in_the_film_and_tv_industries.pdf> (last accessed 10 December 2019).
6. The idea that auteurs may reserve the right to treat actors and other members of staff however they wish in the name of art is echoed in criticism directed at distinguished artists such as Hitchcock and Kubrick, whose bullying behaviour became part of their signature style. Reverence for their work allowed them, and many others, a considerable degree of impunity as a result.
7. The Jussi Awards are Finland's equivalent of the Academy Awards.
8. The Pro Finlandia Medal of the Order of the Lion of Finland (Suomen Leijonan ritarikunta) is one of the highest honours in the country and is awarded to artists and writers considered to be of the highest calibre.

6. CRISIS OF CINEMA/CINEMA OF CRISIS: THE CAR CRASH AND THE BERLIN SCHOOL

Olivia Landry

To assert that the Berlin School film movement was ushered in with a car crash requires some qualification. Let us begin with the final shot of Christian Petzold's 2000 film *Die innere Sicherheit* (*The State I Am In*). A close-up image features the profile of the teenage Jeanne (Julia Hummer) after an excessively violent smash-up. Blood wells on her lower lip and her face is smudged with dirt. She bears the signs of the crash, but unlike her parents she has survived. Critics have hailed this image as 'the symbol for a younger German cinema, for the Berlin School and beyond' (Möller 2007: 40). Although this film's crash scene comes at the close of the film, it has been read as marking the beginning of something new, forcibly displaced beyond the film's diegetic borders. Not only does the image offer a striking, albeit ambiguous, conclusion to the film's dramatic final scene and the end of the first instalment of Petzold's so-called Ghost Trilogy, but as the first (relatively) commercially successful film of the Berlin School, *Die innere Sicherheit* and its final frame have also become a sign of the school itself. Some years later, Petzold declared that the car crash is indeed the locus of the birth of cinema: 'Wenn es Unfälle gibt, beginnt das Kino' ('Where there are accidents, cinema begins') (Petzold, qtd. in Suchsland 2007). Despite the particular reference to his own films, Petzold appears to make a sweeping statement about cinema in general.

The car crash is no stranger to cinema. Karen Redrobe goes so far as to call it 'one of film's earliest and most persistent self-reflexive tropes' (2010: 1). It holds an elemental place in early cinema as a response both to the accidental and unstable nature of the medium itself and to the explosion of technology and speed in modernity of the late nineteenth century. Yet its place in the cinema of the Berlin School, a German movement typically dated from the late 1990s to the mid-2010s and frequently characterised as slow and contemplative, is more complex. I have argued elsewhere that the car crash is a component of the performance quality of the Berlin School, motivated by accelerated movement and driven to a cause-and-effect destructive clearing of present forms as a means of opening up to something new at the site of the wreckage.[1] In this essay, I propose an investigation of the car crash in the Berlin School and its engagement with crisis. This is a crisis that permeates both narrative and form. It is at once the crisis unleashed by neoliberal capitalism and all of its ramifications and the crisis of the post-cinematic condition – what some have called the 'end of cinema'. This bumpy kinship between crisis and the car crash poses the urgent question of 'Where do we go from here'? Or better: 'How do we hang on to a dream'? (the titular question of the musical accompaniment to the closing scene glossed above).

Here I revisit some widely known films of the Berlin School: Valeska Grisebach's *Sehnsucht* (*Longing*, 2006) and Christian Petzold's *Yella* (2007) and *Jerichow* (2008). In their diverging narrative treatment of the car crash, these three examples offer a striking cycle of Berlin School films. They were all released within a three-year period leading up to the global economic crisis. Each film portrays the promises, aspirations and failings of neoliberalism via the literal drive for the good-life fantasy, which turns sour. Auto-destruction is an irrevocable feature of each portrayal. Grisebach's film begins with a crash; Petzold's film *Yella* begins and ends with a crash; and his film *Jerichow* ends with a crash. Thus, the crash marks beginning and ending, and the perplexing vortex of borrowed time and space betwixt and between.

Cinema and the Car Crash

If, according to Siegfried Kracauer, 'accidents were the very soul of slapstick' (1997: 62), scholars have more recently expanded on this claim. Indeed, accidents are also the very soul of cinema. In their 2009 special issue of *Discourse*, 'Cinema and Accident', René Thoreau Bruckner, James Leo Cahill and Greg Siegel provided a tremendous forum for critical inquiry into the relationship between cinema and the accident, most prominently the vehicular accident. As they figure it here, the fascination with the car crash in film is often connected to the contingent, the unexpected, the sense of displacement and the anxieties that result in response to the experience of technology. This relation begins with very early cinema, which was prone to technical accidents, and the penchant of 'cinema of attractions' for the accident as staged event. Later came European art cinema's aesthetics of auto-destruction in the 1960s with the films of Jean-Luc Godard, and finally the later, narratively complex films about accidents by film-makers such as David Lynch and Alejandro González Iñárritu. Cinema and the accident have a long and sometimes tortuous history. Bruckner's article 'Lost Time: Blunt Head Trauma and Accident-Driven Cinema' perhaps gets closest to the aims of the present essay inasmuch as it addresses the manifestation of crisis inherent in the cinematic car crash. Bruckner highlights the crash's post-traumatic consequences and their extreme ruptures. The crash violently occasions 'a period of crisis marked by a disituated sense of space and time' (2009: 377). How exactly the car crash not only results in crisis but can also serve as a response to or a comment on crisis is something I will explore further in the course of this essay.

The *Discourse* journal special issue was followed up one year later by Karen Redrobe's monograph *Crash* (2010). With the aim of re-evaluating film studies in all of its transmutations and bastardisations, and at a moment seized by the anxiety of disciplinary erosion, Redrobe documents the extant messiness of the ontology of film through the lens of its history of wreckage. Rethinking the history of cinema via the car crash can provide some perspective for those anxious about the future of cinema. Drawing in particular on the work of Paul Virilio, Redrobe exposes the dialectical tensions of cinema concretised in the car crash: 'stasis and motion, body and image, proximity and distance, self and other, inside and outside' (2010: 1). The framing provided by Redrobe's study is most compelling here. The cinematic crash in cinema delivers a new lens for approaching the apparent crisis of cinema and cinema studies and the fascination with the changing ontology of film in the wake of new media. Cinema purists have perceived the onset of digitisation, streaming and new media as a threat to cinema as both medium and discipline. Redrobe's study suggests, however, that cinema was always a 'mongrel' medium in flux. Both the special issue and Redrobe's book are significant studies of cinema and the crash, which were published simultaneously with the emergence and rise in visibility of the Berlin School as an important German art cinema movement in the late 2000s.

There is some existing scholarship on the car crash and the Berlin School, in particular with regard to the film *Yella*. Consistent with the assessment of much scholarship on the Berlin School as phlegmatic, even stagnant, Lutz Koepnick describes the car crash in Berlin School films as characteristically flat and unavailing. In his words, the crash is incapable of 'derailing the dull automatisms of the day' (Koepnick 2013: 81). For Koepnick, the tendency towards circularity of the crash in its common recurrence in individual films can only reinforce the hegemony of quotidian monotony in the Berlin School and not incite transformation. The recurrence of the crash in some of Petzold's films (consider, for instance, *Wolfsburg* [2003] and *Yella*) is noteworthy, but Koepnick's observation takes us to an interpretative impasse.

Jaimey Fisher, on the other hand, proposes that the car crash in Petzold's films provides a direct commentary on the conditions of existence under neoliberal capitalism. He writes that '[t]he car wreck as narrative culmination underscores Petzold's indictment but also his serious engagement with global capital's constant creative destruction of space and, apparently, individuals' (Fisher 2011: 461). Fisher's account inspires more complex readings of the crash and its narrative and formal possibilities in the Berlin School films. The automobile itself renders visible a profound ambiguity and anxiety vis-à-vis the historical present. The opportunities and convenience that the automobile affords always come at a price. An invocation of Lauren Berlant's much-cited notion of 'cruel optimism' in the neoliberal state, wherein that which 'you desire is actually an obstacle to your flourishing' (Berlant 2011: 1), is germane to this context. The cruelty of this desire and its often destructive force are taken to extremes in crash films both as cautionary tale and opportunity. If, according to Fisher, the car crash engages as much as it indicts the conditions wrought by global capitalism, then Steven Shaviro's Marxist-inspired concept of 'accelerationism' – that is, 'the going through' at full speed – might also be considered here. In Shaviro's words, accelerationism 'exacerbates our current conditions of existence', causing them finally to explode, so that we may 'move beyond them' (2015: 2). The challenge with this potential escape route is that within neoliberal logic, everything is already accelerated in its promise of intensification and maximisation. The car crash is at once consequence and complication of neoliberal capitalism and its persisting states of crisis. This ambiguity is crucial to my reading of the car crash in the Berlin School films in the later sections of this essay.

Crisis of Cinema/Cinema of Crisis

Crisis is a term and concept that needs to be qualified for the present. At the dawn of the last decade, it named conditions of contingency and precarity. Although these conditions had been long familiar to the majority of the world's labouring population, crisis was declared because these conditions had suddenly hit the bourgeois and their sustained good-life fantasy (Berlant, qtd. in Puar 2012: 122). It followed that 'crisis' became a multi-purpose rallying cry for the general politics of our current age. However, it also quickly transformed into a counter-revolutionary mode of stabilising rather than challenging existing conditions and structures (Masco 2017: 65). In political terms, crisis names a struggle and rhetorically manages it. The categorisation of 'crisis' can be therefore a highly misleading performative act. The economic crisis, the euro crisis, the migrant crisis and so forth: these form an affective grammar of both panic and apathy that conditions neoliberal society in the global North. Certainly, this process has been tracked and treated in cinema of the past couple of decades.[2]

Beyond political discourse, 'crisis' as a universal phenomenon simply characterises the stochastic occurrence of events. The modality of crisis is the accidental; it is that which arrives as a syncopated shock and a disturbance to the expected flow of things. In this sense, cinema models crisis. But what of the so-called crisis of cinema? The current discourse surrounding the crisis of cinema in the post-cinematic age has been most poignantly illumined by André Gaudreault and Philippe Marion in their 2015 study *The End of Cinema? A Medium in Crisis in the Digital Age* (published in French in 2013). They raise an updated version of the Bazinian question 'What is cinema?', namely, 'What remains of (what we thought was) cinema?' The proclamatory denouement of 'the end of cinema' is a response to an epistemological upheaval of what we thought we knew was cinema, tinged with a nostalgia that imagines an idealised stability in the past. In reality, the entire history of the medium reveals ontological instability. Echoing Redrobe's claim that cinema has always been a mongrel medium, a riot of accidents and mutations, they argue the following:

> The crisis brought about by the emergence of digital media is not the first upheaval to rock the cinematic realm. It must be said and repeated over and over, tirelessly: *cinema's entire history has been punctuated by moments when its media identity has been radically called into question.* What people have called 'cinema' for over a century has seen a series of technological mutations throughout its history. (Gaudreault and Marion 2015: 2–3)

If we can even speak of the crisis of cinema, then, it must be with knowledge of the past and the present as well as an understanding of the flexible ontology of cinema, which long ago moved away from the mechanics of photography (*pace* Bazin). I propose that the car crash continues to invoke this history of flexibility and anxiety. It reminds us of the ontological instability and precarity of cinema both in its early days of technical experimentation and more recently in an era of new media, with its ebb of traditional film making and viewing. Cahill's suggestion that the car crash in early cinema allegorises 'film's precarious ontological status at the level of content while simultaneously attempting to stabilize it, symbolically controlling the accident as a staged event' (2009: 295) might also be temporally stretched to expound both cinema's early and later history – not so much as calamitous bookends of crisis but as continuity between these two paradigms – a continuous history of crisis. The role of the car crash has in many ways been to symbolically stabilise these ontological crises in its embrace of the medium's accidental nature. Yet the crash also appears to haunt as a spectre, and to call to mind this instability and the danger it can wield. Inasmuch as the car crash allegorises an ontological history of the crisis of cinema, it likewise engages narrative and historical context. Since its inception, cinema has tackled the contingencies of historical and economic tides. To speak of a crisis of cinema also invites its inverse: a cinema of crisis.

In recent European cinema history, the label 'cinema of crisis' has been applied perhaps most consistently to Greek cinema of the 2010s. The first new cinema movement to emerge in the wake of Greece's financial crisis, initiated most famously with Yorgos Lanthimos's celebrated 2009 drama *Dogtooth* and Athina Rachel Tsangari's *Attenberg* (2010), was thought to be a national response to neoliberal capitalism and its destructive ends. As Alex Lykidis (2015) explores, the violence of the overbearing yet impotent authority figure in these films becomes a sign of Greece's diminishing sovereignty in the face of economic downturn. History shows that cinema movements frequently emerge and are shaped by (both in terms of production and reception) prevailing economic, political and social contexts. Similarly in Spain, a group of films released in the early 2010s, which treat social and political precarity in the midst of the economic crisis, have also received the label 'crisis cinema'. An example is Álex de la Iglesia's 2011 drama *La Chispa de la Vida (As Luck Would Have It)*.[3]

However, no such direct equivalent exists in German cinema. While individual films do address social and political precarity, the label 'cinema of crisis' has not been applied to any particular body of films from this period. Relatively unaffected by the throes of economic crisis of the early 2010s that hit its European neighbours (mostly) to the south, if anything Germany has been viewed as the amplifier of the euro crisis with its severe austerity politics. Germany's long-term chancellor, Angela Merkel, has been called the crisis manager *par excellence*. But the tightening knot of global financial crisis and Merkel's tightening fist of neoliberal crisis management have also been felt in Germany, in particular in its former eastern states.

This geographically divisive phenomenon of east and west bears residues of German post-war history and unification that are in no way new to cinematic representation, but its re-emergence as a theme in a number of Berlin School films at a charged moment of global economic crisis locates it once more in the present. Massive de-industrialisation, emigration and dispossession were in part consequences of the unification of the two Germanys in 1990, consequences that continue to attenuate the states of former East Germany. Such topics recur in some of the films of the Berlin School with refreshed urgency. Further, the recurrence of the cinematic car crash as a symptom of and engagement with this crisis moment, in which mobility of all kinds is not only deemed dangerous but even fatal, urges a closer look at the Berlin School in this regard. The following sections offer close analyses of three crash films caught in the tangle of the contingency and precarity of the accidental in chronological order: *Sehnsucht*, *Yella* and *Jerichow*.

After the Crash: *Sehnsucht*

Sehnsucht begins in the aftermath of a car crash. Although Markus (Andreas Müller), the main protagonist of the film, is not directly involved in the accident, he is an eyewitness and the first on the scene. His encounter with this anonymous crash has unexpected effects that play out over the film. Markus is a metalworker and volunteer fireman in the village of Zühlen in Brandenburg, Germany, recently and apparently happily married to his childhood sweetheart, Ella (Ilka Welz). But at fireman's ball held in a neighbouring town, Markus meets and subsequently falls in love with Rose (Anett Dornbusch). Markus's once predictable and harmonious life begins to unravel.

The film opens with Markus's encounter with a wrecked car wrapped around a tree. As we later learn, a man and a woman have attempted to take their lives by deliberately driving head-on into the tree. In the opening shots, however, the *mise en scène* and shot scale do not render the accident legible. The first shot is a close-up of Markus as he desperately attempts to stabilise one of the victims of the crash. The effects of the jittery hand-held camera used in this first shot and the proximity to Markus's head moving in and out of the frame as he frantically performs first aid on the off-screen victim are both claustrophobic and disorienting. It is almost as though Markus symbolically struggles with the film itself in a desperate attempt to try to resuscitate it. 'Hören Sie mich?' ('Do you hear me?'), he seems to say to nobody. To begin there is no image. For the first few seconds, only the soundtrack reveals the approach of an car, which comes to an abrupt halt and from which someone quickly exits. In its opening of the film, the black screen symbolically links cinematic death and the car crash. Only in the second shot (twenty seconds later) does the spectator see the immobile body of the victim lying next to Markus. The second victim (apparently already dead) and the wreck of the car first appear several shots later. There is an underlying impulse in this initial scene that postulates its cinematic reflexivity. Redrobe's formulation elucidates this opening scene:

> Crash films are cinematic quests, undertaken in the spaces whose outer limits are marked by terrestrial speed taking flight on the one hand, and by the mutilated body on the other; by the immobilized corpse, which throws film into crisis, and the speeding imagination taking a camera for a ride. (2010: 7)

Hypostatised here is the crisis of the film and its world. The crash is introduced as the site of formal and narrative crisis. Where does one go from here? Where is the beginning; where is the end?

The crash scene exposes a fragile diegetic world. The film story reflects this fragility insofar as the car crash directly represents the rupture and disturbance of a community and way of life. It is unclear why the couple have attempted suicide, or possibly murder-suicide, but the plot rings with crisis. The long shot of Markus positioned next to the victim cuts to two subsequent landscape shots of scenes of idyllic village life – kids on bicycles and a sunrise over a meadow dotted with family homes. Puncturing these images, however, is the abrasive cry of a siren and dogs barking uncontrollably. This sonic disturbance serves both as a wake-up call to the volunteer rescue workers (common in German villages) and as a sign of a break in momentum, a disturbance in the life of the village as a whole. *Sehnsucht* is not only a film founded on wreckage but also a film about a world founded on wreckage. According to Grisebach, '[she] searched for a story in the wake of a dramatic moment that would be the expression of longing: where something suddenly tears, the framework no longer holds. An event that can no longer be reversed, where something akin to fate occurs' (Grisebach 2006). Grisebach's description of her film resonates with the narrative breaches and horizons opened up by crisis. The car crash performs precisely this dramatic moment and event in the film, in which at once everything begins but also seems to end. The film works on a dimension of borrowed or bracketed time outside the logic of linear rationalisation.

In the case of *Sehnsucht*, the film story emerges as a result of the crash, but its pacing is intersected by the retrograde impulse to return to the moment of the crash and the scene of violence and death, a moment that haunts Markus and the film as a whole. This does not occur by formal means, via flashbacks or even elliptical editing, as one might expect; instead, it returns in the form of an underlying thrust of violence. From the car crash to the way Markus and his wife, Ella, desperately and aggressively make love, and finally to Markus's attempted suicide with a hunting rifle near the close of the film after his wife discovers his relationship with Rose, this so-called love story leans towards brutality. The film's latent violence resonates with Catherine Wheatley's characterisation of *Sehnsucht* as a type of new *Heimatfilm* with its blatantly condemnatory treatment of the rural German landscape. Wheatley posits that *Sehnsucht* employs elements of the *Heimatfilm* genre reflexively as a means of critiquing and reframing it (2011: 145). Unlike the modality of the traditionally parochial *Heimatfilm* and its manifestly apolitical aesthetics (von Moltke 2005), the violence and rupture of the establishing scene of the fateful car crash in this seemingly bucolic village ushers in an alternative and destabilising world in which traditional values and conventions have evidently already begun to disintegrate and new desires and transgressions suddenly manifest themselves.

Are not the crash and attempted suicide at the beginning of the film immediately an unsettling evocation of a crisis mood? The unrest that seems to settle over Markus's life in the wake of the car crash provokes a crisis that could be read as personal but also evokes social dimensions. An unspoken desire for more, for variation, for something new, Markus's affair, as banal as it might narratively seem, signals something beyond itself. Markus is not unhappy in his life with his wife, but it seems that things could be better. This setting, in this almost anachronistic, isolated village, ostensibly cut off from the outside world, is ripped open by the car crash, which leaves its irreparable gash. The desire for more, that good-life fantasy, is and has been a central theme in many films set in the former eastern states of Germany, in which unemployment rates remain high (relative to the rest of the republic) and prospects low. Many East Germans have left for the west as a result. This theme is also patently carried through in Christian Petzold's slightly later film, *Yella*.

The Double Crash: *Yella*

The conceit of Petzold's 2007 film *Yella* is simple enough: a woman from the east desires a better life for herself in the west; a car crash gets in the way. The eponymous protagonist (played by Nina Hoss) reluctantly accepts a fateful ride with her ex-husband, Ben (Hinnerk Schönemann), to the train station that ends in a (attempted) murder-suicide. Yella's attempt to escape Ben's persistent abuse and the dire socio-economic situation of her small town of Wittenberge (in the state of Brandenburg in former East Germany) in order to start a new life in Hanover is interrupted. In an extreme culmination of Ben's brutality and abuse, he tries to hinder Yella's escape by madly racing them both over the side of the Elbe River bridge (the possible thematic connection between the crashes in *Sehnsucht* and *Yella* is evident). In spite of the magnitude of the initial car crash in *Yella* – a plunge into the river from a great height – it pans out as a mere brush with death. Shortly after Ben's Range Rover submerges, Yella pulls herself up on to the shore, sprung from the river as though reborn and still somehow not too late to catch her train. While this miraculous and enigmatic scene of survival initially evokes suspicion in the spectator, it is ultimately played out in a way that appears realistic enough to subdue scepticism. Contrary to its cinematic predecessor, Herk Harvey's cult horror flick *Carnival of Souls* (1962) with its embrace of the supernatural, *Yella* only permits minor slippages and cracks in the verisimilitude of its representation, which at first viewing might easily be overlooked.

That the Range Rover plunges into the murky waters of the Elbe is highly symbolic. An important landmark in German geography and history, the Elbe once divided a stretch of East and West Germany in the area of the North German Plain, not too far from Wittenberge, where the early part of the film is set. The town and its surrounding area are completely infrastructurally depleted. The literal death drive in Ben's car first takes us on a tour through abandoned de-industrialised wastelands, once the home of German firms such as Singer and Veritas – the devastating effects of German unification and neoliberal capitalism. 'Dies ist nicht der Weg zum Bahnhof, Ben' ('This is not the way to the train station, Ben'), Yella remarks. No, it's a *de*-tour of bust and a mortuary foreshadowing of more destruction to come, what Ben refers to as 'ein kleiner sentimental Umweg' ('a short sentimental detour'). *Yella*'s crash site is thus already framed as a historical, geographical and political boundary that drives the basic structure of this filmic narrative.

With added visceral impact (here we see and experience the crash), the first car crash in *Yella* echoes that in *Sehnsucht* as a violent opening that throws the film world asunder. In Anke Biendarra's words, 'The spectacular move effectively breaks the narrative trajectory of the film after barely ten minutes and throws the viewer into speculative turmoil about the continuation of the story line' (2011: 467). But positioned at the beginning of the film, the crashes of *Sehnsucht* and *Yella* are to be perceived 'not simply as nihilistic spectacles of disaster, but . . . rather as sites for exploring the condition of living on after "the end"' (Redrobe 2010: 205). In myriad ways, the Berlin School examples here exist in extended time and space; they are the bastard offspring of the physical and allegorical scrapheap of the car crash and the temporality of sudden crisis. The bracketed time of *Yella* advances in the crisis mode of contingency and the accidental.

After her narrow escape from death, Yella arrives in Hanover to take up her new position as an accountant only to discover that her company has been seized by the authorities because of illegal activity, and with it her immediate hope for a new start. As chance would have it, Yella encounters Philipp (Devid Striesow), an independent venture capitalist eager to take her on as an unofficial partner. They also become lovers. But through a stunningly ruthless modus operandi, Yella takes things too far in her pursuit of financial gain and even provokes the suicide of a client. From the start, Yella does not quite fit into this world; she does not know its rules and does not recognise its boundaries, unstable as they may seem. Yet it is not clear if Yella stands outside this world or is a figuration thereof. Petzold's images of neoliberal capitalism and its abstract operations in the film's scenes of ominous business transactions involving hedge funds, those high-risk capital modes of investment, explicitly invite the crisis mood and consequently reflect Yella's own precarious condition between life and death. The film's narrative is also punctuated by incidental symptoms, which repeatedly return Yella to the moment of the crash and threaten to destabilise her present reality. These are forms of micro-crises, including hallucinations of visits from Ben and occasional loss of hearing. Eventually, Yella's energetic denial of the power of death catches up with her.

There is a return to the crash in the final sequence of the film and with it all illusion of continuity is exploded. Bruckner might refer to this second crash as the 'desituation' of the film: 'it is the end of the line, so to speak, but also a point along the narrative loop that cannot be located' (2009: 394). The transgression of spatial and narrative boundaries unleashed in *Sehnsucht* and reprised in *Yella* returns with a jolt in the double car crash of the latter. In the wake of the second crash, which deviates in formal detail only in minor ways from the first, the police arrive on the scene and a large crane lifts the submerged Range Rover out of the river. The corpses of Yella and Ben are retrieved from the water and laid out on the shore. The two are dead, but death does not feel like a permanent state, especially if we consider that according to the film's ending Yella has been dead for much of the film. As much as the circular crash might appear to point to the systematicity of an open-and-shut narrative, the repetition of the crash refuses to tie up loose ends. Crisis, that durational loop of chance and change, never ceases. Narratively speaking, mobility of all sorts becomes fraught with the cruelty of neoliberal reality. Indeed, when pushed on the point of politics in his films, Petzold affirms his engagement with mobility as both a critique of capitalism and a demonstration of the machinery of film making (Abel 2005). Automobility is political. Further, the 'dream machine', as Paul Ginsborg dubs the automobile, can at any moment transform into the 'death machine' (Ginsborg 2003: 83). Nowhere does this ring so true as in *Yella*.

The phenomenon of the dream machine qua death machine begins in slow drive in the final film examined in this essay. *Jerichow* comes to a crashing end. Yet closure is also not the promise of this violent final act.

The Terminating Crash: *Jerichow*

The terminal car crash in Petzold's 2008 film *Jerichow* bears out the logic of the excessive final act *mutatis mutandis*: it goes out with a bang. The film's triangular narrative draws on James M. Cain's novel *The Postman Always Rings Twice* (1934) and its classic film noir adaptation by Tay Garnett (1946). Laura (Nina Hoss) is married to the slightly older, boorish, alcoholic and abusive Ali (Hilmi Sözer). It is a marriage of convenience. She has debts, he has money. She is willing to submit to his pleasure economy to achieve her own goals of economic stability, even prosperity. In the village of Jerichow in Saxony-Anhalt, directly on the border with Brandenburg in north-eastern Germany, there is widespread unemployment and economic hardship. One day Thomas (Benno Fürmann) comes along. He has recently been dishonourably discharged from the army and is in search of a job but unable to get a foothold. A minor accident provokes an encounter between Thomas and Ali. The two find common ground and even develop a quasi-friendship. But then Thomas falls for Laura. A clandestine affair ensues and the two devise a plan to get Ali out of the way. They plot a car crash.

As with its narrative precursors, in the final scene of *Jerichow* the murderous plot by Laura and Thomas backfires. In Petzold's version, however, Ali ends up committing suicide out of rage and wrath when he discovers their plan. He drives himself off a cliff that borders the Baltic Sea. The crash as the Range Rover hits the embankment below and the attendant explosion are heard but not seen, as the spectator is positioned with Laura and Thomas as they first retreat from the scene. But the violent sonic disruption forces them to turn around and Laura rushes to the edge of the cliff. The spectator watches from Thomas's distanced perspective as the beautiful seascape is quickly and menacingly consumed by an enormous plume of black smoke. While there is a dark and apocalyptic aesthetic to this final tableau of Laura's silhouette dwarfed against the rush of smoke on the edge of the cliff, this final shot is aesthetically evocative of a smokescreen (see figure 6.1). Could this accident be a ruse for something else, something hidden? Is this ending no ending at all? In cinema, the smokescreen traditionally proffers either a diegetic means of transition or a means of resetting the scene and of decelerating it, by means of which chronological time is intercepted (Bruckner 2009: 396). The appearance of the smokescreen at the close of the film confounds. It suggests a possible transition but no true conclusion.

Too many questions are left unanswered and problems unsolved at the close of the film. Crises persist. The cruel realities of neoliberal capitalism, domestic and sexual abuse, and racism form a cycle of violence in the film that is present yet never directly addressed.[4] In many ways, the film implicitly exemplifies a national crisis (though not tragedy) in the global economy. But in *Jerichow*'s grim neoliberal noir tale, all three protagonists are presented as at once exploited and guilty. None receives our sympathies in their death drive towards the good-life fantasy. Unlike in Cain's novel and Garnett's filmic adaptation, which even more problematically and less self-reflexively explore similar themes, Petzold's version ends abruptly with the car crash and Ali's death, and not with the typical noir turn to narrative justice, that is, to Laura's and Thomas's punishment

Figure 6.1   The car crash as smokescreen in *Jerichow* (Christian Petzold, 2008). Hans Fromm, © Schramm Film.

for adultery and (at least attempted) murder of Ali. It would be erroneous to presume that Ali's death alone delivers justice or redemption. Such a reading eschews the critical ambiguity of the car crash. According to Mark Osteen, cars in noir films function broadly as 'amoral spaces' and as 'overdetermined symbols of characters' aspirations and disappointments' (2008: 184). Redrobe adds that the 'car becomes a figure through which to engage the complex question of individual and collective responsibility in the face of uncontrollable and sometimes antisocial drives, addiction, and sexual desire' (2009: 318). Transgression and punishment are the pared-down narrative points of the noir genre. The destruction of the automobile thus follows this logic with what Robert Rushing would characterise as the 'didactic impulse' of the crash (2017: 22). But if the car transgresses the boundaries of a given world, the crash is not the car's retribution; instead, it just accelerates transgression; it tears right through the boundaries.

Petzold ends *Jerichow* with a perplexing car crash that does not discipline or smooth over the bumps and fault lines, but rather yields a (literal) descent into violence and destruction. From *Yella* to *Jerichow*, the plummet of the Range Rover is repeated a third time. This third explosive descent eludes our cognitive reflection and instead occasions the imperative force of the violence enacted both on and by Ali. Whether we choose to read the close of the film narratively as Ali's act of sacrifice to or resistance against Laura and Thomas, what is resonant in this act is the residue of violence and pain that lingers and sticks like the black smoke to the atmosphere. It is in these traces that an interstice appears. This aperture is not a narrative cliff-hanger (pardon the pun); it is a place of rift and detour from the through line. In all three of these crash films, the route of neoliberal promise – portrayed by the 'dream machine' – is not simply a rut, to borrow Berlant's phrase (2007: 275); it has reached the level of repeated disaster. Once opened, the gash refuses to close.

Accidental Means and Ends . . . (A Conclusion)

Risk, desire and violence (over-)drive this cycle of films. On the face of it, *Sehnsucht*, *Yella* and *Jerichow* are clearly distinct. In particular, Grisebach's film, with its more restrained mode and only implicit political orientation, might at first appear aesthetically and narratively out of place. Yet the themes of all three of these films bear important affinities. All set in various de-industrialised villages in former East Germany between 2006 and 2008, these are films about wanting more and the price one must pay to achieve such pleasure economies. Their cinematic narratives rigorously echo the logic of neoliberal capitalism and its ominous promise of personal autonomy, sexual freedom and self-development. For as Steven Shaviro reminds us, 'these often take on the sinister form of precarity, insecurity, and the continual pressure to perform' (2015: 33).

Neoliberalism thus always works in the crisis mode of the accidental and the unpredictable. In a similar manner, so do these films. The introduction of the car crash to films already beset by crises serves as a compelling amplification, or better, acceleration, of the present.

At the same time, the car crash has long been a symbol of cinema and its accidental nature. It represents and nurtures cinema's penchant for contingency, dramatic acceleration and hyperstimulation. Cinema's privileging of the crash has a self-reflexive bent insofar as it draws a through line from form to content and from history to narrative. A sentient return to the car crash in German cinema leading up to a moment of heightened financial crisis and in an era of post-cinematic digitisation and new media trends offers a double commentary on this age-old kinship of cinema and crisis. Incurring violence and even death, the crash in these Berlin School films introduces a new level of impact and precarity that is so far gone that it has often already hit bottom. Finally, these crashes are manifest reminders of cinema's open form, its ontology as a mixed medium; they point to the continuing transition from one mode to another. The impermanence of these films' narratives and the fate of their characters does not offer hope or optimism, but it does provide ambiguity in the form of constant change – a continuity of transformation. Within these changing paradigms the new emerges, as frightening or exciting as it may be.

Notes

1. This study draws partly on my investigation of the car crash in the Berlin School films in my 2019 book *Movement and Performance in Berlin School Cinema*.
2. Consider most famously the films of Belgian directors Jean-Pierre and Luc Dardenne and British director Ken Loach.
3. Allbritton (2014) provides an informative overview of Spain's 'crisis cinema'.
4. It may be noted that Ali is Turkish German. His racialised representation is an added dimension in Petzold's version of this story that bears address. Miller (2012) explores the elements of racialisation present in the film in a comparative reading with *Yella*.

7. REPRESENTING AND ESCAPING THE CRISES OF NEOLIBERALISM: VEIKO ÕUNPUU'S FILMS AND METHODS

Eva Näripea

We will have to get used to living with the crisis.
Because the crisis is here to stay.

Carlo Bordoni (Bauman and Bordoni 2014: 7)

On 28 December 2018 a press release from the Estonian Film Institute, the country's principal film fund allocating public subsidies, announced triumphantly that 2018 had been a landmark year for Estonian cinema – domestic productions, including 14 new narrative features, had attracted over 650,000[1] admissions (compared to about 347,000 admissions in 2016 and 282,000 in 2017), with the market share of domestic films reaching over 16 per cent (compared to 10.5 per cent in 2016 and 8 per cent in 2017). This self-commendation, based primarily on statistical values, exemplifies well how Estonians have internalised the neoliberal 'Newspeak', which determines quality in terms of quantitative dimensions (cf. Mitric and Sarikakis 2019: 428) and follows the logic of the marketplace, reducing 'all facets of human life ... to their economic aspect, quantified in monetary terms and assigned a barcode' (Bauman and Donskis 2016: 15).

A closer look at these popular films indicates a tendency towards accessible productions targeted at the 'average' audience, frequently combining nodal points of the 'national narrative' (Tamm 2018), which presents the past as a teleological struggle towards the independent nation-state, with the toolbox of the so-called 'orthodox chronotope' of 'Hollywood Aristotelianism', characterised by 'dramatic realist aesthetic', 'seamless diegetic continuity' and emotionally satisfying finales (Stam, Porton and Goldsmith 2015: 225, 226–7). In the Estonian context, this constellation becomes politically loaded because the particularities of the Estonian version of neoliberal capitalism stem from a combination of an uncompromising laissez-faire philosophy, a fierce rejection of the Soviet legacy and an ardent quest to build the nation-state. Inspired by Milton Friedman, the political elite of the early 1990s equated economic freedom with national independence (see, for example, Bohle and Greskovits 2012: 125). As a result, Estonia has become one of the most liberal market economies in the European Union, frequently applauded as a success story of rapid neoliberal reforms, while paying for it with steep inequalities in distribution of income, precarious conditions of employment, erosion of the social welfare system and severe ethnic dispossession of the sizeable Russian minority (a legacy of Soviet colonisation) (see, for instance, Kideckel 2002; Notermans 2015). Most recently, these imbalances have led to an extreme nationalist backlash (see Tuch 2019).

In the field of the arts, neoliberalisation has had the effect of commodifying culture and glorifying the 'creative industries', which, according to the dominant political position, should, ideally, be self-sufficient and independent of any state subsidy, either surviving in the 'free market' or perishing if there is no demand. The project-based film-funding model, adopted in the late 1990s as very much a symptom of the neoliberal economy, has turned creative talent, as well as technical staff, into a modern-day precariat, without a stable income, basic social guarantees and overall sense of security. According to David Harvey, this commodification of cultural forms is an expression of 'accumulation by dispossession', the key feature of neoliberal order (Harvey 2005: 148), which testifies to 'a radicalized return to nineteenth-century principles of the free market' (Kapur and Wagner 2011: 2) and which affects most severely the weakest cohorts of society.

While 'disseminating human kindness' (Sepp 2019), the majority of recent Estonian productions rely on audiovisual and narrative strategies that, by evoking ostentatious visuals and providing gratifying endings, subdue critical thought and normalise 'invisible hegemonic ideological apparatuses' (Mitric and Sarikakis 2019: 429), that is, the modus operandi of neoliberal capitalism and its loyal servant – the neoliberal nation-state. In a way, neoliberal capitalism imposes its own peculiar form of censorship, not only on cinema but also across the entire cultural terrain, as eloquently outlined by Kiwa, a local 'multi-channel meta-artist':

> The new culture is flattened at its roots due to commercialism and political correctness. . . . Experimentalism in any form or shape is filtered out and the entire context is degenerated. This results in events and formats that

faithfully follow textbook formulas and guidelines of funding schemes. Such cultural impoverishment is propelled by the fear that the state, fund or sponsor might refuse to back the 'extremes'. Sustainable culture relies on plurality and heterogeneity, but these are drowned into the mainstream. . . . Innovation and experimentation is replaced by reproductions of conformist worldview or stimulations of low passions. . . . Censorship is redundant when the marketplace prevails. (Kiwa 2016)

It is precisely this predominance of the capitalist marketplace, which affects human creativity and quality of life alike, against which Veiko Õunpuu rebels. A commitment to undermining the foundations of neoliberal capitalist hegemony[2] and reified cultural production informs all aspects of his work, as signalled by seeking alternative modes of production and exhibition, experimenting with audiovisual and narrative techniques, and portraying the nauseating consequences – both local and global – of rampant neoliberalisation. Indeed, Õunpuu's films can be productively interpreted as critiques of neoliberal 'accumulation by dispossession', the central element of which is management and manipulation of crises (Harvey 2005: 162–3). As summarised by Ewa Mazierska, 'crisis is a structural feature of capitalism', but in the neoliberal variety the crisis is perpetual rather than intermittent (Mazierska 2018: 105; see also Bauman and Bordoni 2014: 59).

Propelled by this notion of a perpetual state of crisis that affects all aspects of human existence, as well as drawing on a Marxist frame of reference in general, and some of the ideas developed by left-wing scholars such as Zygmunt Bauman and David Harvey in particular, the following discussion concentrates on Õunpuu's cinematic output in terms of practices, techniques and representations. After looking at the ways in which Õunpuu has responded to the effects of neoliberal capitalism on cinematic production and expression, I will investigate his filmic depictions of various forms of crisis, ranging from private to social and from local to global.

Addressing the Crisis of Creativity

Õunpuu's first feature films were produced firmly within the framework of institutionalised funding schemes typical of European cinema, which subsidise film making in the name of proclaimed 'diversity'. However, instead of facilitating cinematic experimentation and innovation, these policy measures have been criticised for leading to increased standardisation of narrative and audiovisual form catering to the widest audience possible, thus jeopardising rather than fostering cultural heterogeneity. Alongside the global expansion of neoliberalism, the idea that cinema is first and foremost an art form – a long-standing view held in relation to film making in Europe – is steadily losing ground to a market-prioritising approach, which treats cinema as merchandise that is to be valued in correlation with its commercial success (Mitric and Sarikakis 2019). In response to this populist-entrepreneurial drive and the growing crisis of creative freedom, succinctly summarised by Kiwa as quoted above, Õunpuu has set out to test alternative modes of image-making practice that would challenge the constraints of this system and the flat results that it tends to produce.

His first attempt to do so was *60 Seconds of Solitude in Year Zero*, a project developed in collaboration with Taavi Eelmaa, which materialised as one of the concluding events of the European Capital of Culture year in Tallinn on 22 December 2011.[3] 'Flying in the face of the cynicism of marketing, production, business operators and the moral majority', the curators invited 56 directors from all over the world to make an anthology film 'dedicated to preserving freedom of thought in cinema' (Eelmaa and Õunpuu 2011), in commemoration of the waning era of analogue technology.[4] To escape the commercial circulation of reified culture, the resulting piece was only shown once, free of charge, in near-freezing temperatures on an open-air screen in the cruise ship dock of the Port of Tallinn, and the 35mm reels of what was reported to be the only copy were burned on-site after the screening.

The curators provided a one-minute-long slot to each of the participants, asking them to reflect, without the use of dialogue, on the theme of the death of cinema, and to focus their contribution on one of the five elements – earth, wind, fire, water or spirit. Apart from these rather flexible guidelines, the only predetermined part of the project was the score, composed by Ülo Krigul, which shaped the final order of the sequences. Divided into minute-long segments, the music was made available to the directors as an online interactive schedule, so that each author could book the one that felt most appropriate. In this way, the authors were liberated from the restrictions typically imposed by a definite point of departure for any film – a screenplay that posits a story-plot nexus. Downplaying the role of a story (the petrified framework of conventional narrative form), as well as the written word in general, and instead favouring music (one of the most elusive yet potent components of cinematic texture) as the foundation of the overall design is particularly noteworthy in the light of Õunpuu's deep-seated antipathy towards the mechanisms of commercialised film production, which normally requires a predefined (verbalised) structure, leaving little room for contingency and spontaneity – something that was later central to the production process of *Roukli* (2015).

Just as conceptual art of the 1960s primarily questioned the assumption that the principal purpose of art is to create a certain kind of material object (Kosuth 2002), the main goal of the authors of *60 Seconds* was to give a priority to a concept and to avoid leaving behind an artefact, a commodity that would inevitably enter the 'streams of exchange values', as the manifesto of the project declared. The significance of *60 Seconds* lies in ephemeral aspects – in the way it was conceived, in its non-conventional process of production and exhibition, and most of all in the performance of destruction as a protest against 'commercial pragmatism' and 'practical mind' that, according to Õunpuu, 'will effectively (by taking our game, our love away, by turning it into utilitarian exchange of commodities or power machinations) murder us and our dreams'. Declining 'the invitation to the abattoir' of neoliberal cultural production, he preferred to 'see our work burned' (Gray 2012).

By subscribing to the intellectual premises of conceptual art, Õunpuu and Eelmaa stand out as proponents of the idea of autonomous art applauded by the modernist critique of the culture industry. Although the conclusions of Max Horkheimer and Theodor W. Adorno on the insurmountable division of 'high art' and 'popular culture' (Horkheimer and Adorno 2002: 94–136) in particular have frequently been accused of elitism, the idea that resistance to commodification can have political, emancipatory power has gained renewed urgency in the context of rampant neoliberalism that strives to maintain the status quo instead of inspiring purposeful action, thereby 'homogenis[ing] culture [and] rendering it deadly for the soul' (Mazierska and Kristensen 2014: 4; see also Bauman and Bordoni 2014: 43).

Yet the question remains to what extent the voices of such counter-hegemonic expressions and ideas reach society at large and what impact they could have. It certainly looks as though the resonance in the local arena was somewhat limited, as *60 Seconds* did not really spark any substantial discussion among Estonian critics. The project's (now defunct) website did list over thirty media items in English, German, French, Finnish and Italian, testifying to widespread international attention, but most of the texts were quite brief and appeared shortly after the event. In spite of these doubts, *60 Seconds* remains a fascinating experiment in search of alternative methods of cinematic production and expression, as well as a rather rare example of inherently political film making in post-Soviet Estonia, dealing directly with the increasingly precarious conditions of creativity and creators.

In 2014 Õunpuu embarked on another project designed to break away from the clutches of reified cultural production dominated by corporate and commercial interests. While the contributors to *60 Seconds* had been allocated no financial resources whatsoever, *Roukli* was made on a shoestring budget of approximately €45,000, raised to a significant extent by a crowdfunding campaign through Hooandja, an Estonian equivalent of Kickstarter. In fact, *Roukli* was the first Estonian film to rely on such an alternative funding scheme. To accommodate the creative process, a not-for-profit Roukli Filmiühistu (Roukli Film Association) was set up, which provided a legal umbrella for the crew members and actors who formed the film's collective of producers and authors. Significantly, the talent and crew worked without remuneration, and would be compensated in equal parts only if *Roukli* yielded profits at the box office

(Tuumalu 2014). This emphasis on joint authorship, as well as shared responsibility and symmetrical distribution of any possible revenues, is especially important, since it disrupts the typically exploitative patterns and hierarchies of the capitalist production mode, which serves the purpose of capital accumulation by appropriating the surplus value of wage-based labour. The arrangement of work for which Õunpuu and his collaborators opted decidedly reshuffles the clear-cut roles (producer, director, screenwriter, actor), as well as the income brackets commonly allocated to each participant in the film industry. Blurring the borders between these accustomed positions signals the desire to eschew the chains of capitalist professionalism – a manifestation of alienated work as defined by Marx (1844). Not respecting the conventional division of labour is also a boldly 'amateurish' move and, as such, indicates an ambition to pursue a non-specialised and hence non-alienated form of work (see Marx and Engels 1947: 22).

Circumventing the established, institutional sources of funding was important for Õunpuu and his partners, because these tend to come with various strings attached. First, the makers of *Roukli* consciously sought the opportunity to choose their own rhythm and pace of working, following their own will rather than the 'ticking clock' of a shooting schedule (Delfi 2014) and, in turn, capital. Of course, this objective should be understood in relative rather than absolute terms, because it would be practically impossible to shed all limits of time. Indeed, the period of principal photography, only 16 days, was quite short, especially for a feature-length film.

The second, and perhaps the most important, advantage of this escape is related to Õunpuu's well-documented scepticism towards the process and benefits of 'script development', especially in the way practised by the institutional backers of cinema. For example, in a speech he wrote on the occasion of receiving the annual award from the Union of Estonian Film Journalists for *Sügisball* (*Autumn Ball*, 2007) in 2008, Õunpuu stated that

> The good people of the Estonian Film Foundation should forget about the screenplays analysed to death by brainy experts, the meticulous storyboards and the call for dull dramatic structures – this kind of risk management is nothing but repressive. We need more playfulness and ecstasy; we need creativity, freedom and the courage to risk. (Õunpuu 2008: 127)

Indeed, Õunpuu's films have become more and more 'unscripted'. Starting with two adaptations – *Tühirand* (*Empty*, 2006) and *Autumn Ball*, both (loosely) based on Mati Unt's much-celebrated texts, Õunpuu has moved further away from the constraints of a preconceived screenplay with each successive film (although, admittedly, never discarding it completely).

Untrammelled by the need to commence the production process of *Roukli* with a meticulously polished scenario, a space of spontaneity opened up to the team that granted the performers more room to improvise and allowed the director-scriptwriter to modify the scenes and the flow of situations as they unrolled (Delfi 2014). In Õunpuu's own words, they regarded the shooting period 'not as a process of the visual codification of the script, but as a creative test tube for mixing the impulses of talented actors, divine accidents and an unrelenting desire to speak only about what is on our minds at the moment' (Delfi 2014). Hence, the central working method of the team of *Roukli* was improvisation. Apart from demonstrating Õunpuu's programmatic hostility towards the value of the written word, this strategy has a clearly political dimension, as noted by Gilles Mouëllic in *Improvising Cinema*: 'Today more than ever, opting for the freedom of improvisation on a film set implies resisting a system in which filmmaking is reduced to a faithful adaptation of a script rewritten as the result of compromise with the backers' (Mouëllic 2013: 35).

While recognising the symbolic significance of the multiple ways in which the authors of *Roukli* strove to counteract the hegemonic structures and politics of the commercially driven cinematic establishment, it is disputable whether they succeeded in providing a viable alternative to it. On the one hand, they were indeed liberated 'from the obligation to please market researchers and massive audiences' (Dixon and Foster 2002: 1), as well as from the guilt of spending 'the taxpayers' hard-earned cash' on realising their own 'individual fantasies' (Tuumalu 2014). On the other hand, the meagre financial resources, which is an inevitable side-effect of such independent mode of production, imposed a considerable strain on the key figures of the group, so much so that Õunpuu has sworn never to do it again (Kilumets and Valme 2015). Even if a lack of resources might fuel filmic creativity to a certain extent (Dixon and Foster 2002: 1), there is a limit beyond which it becomes a burden.

Contesting the Mass-produced Form

Since Horkheimer and Adorno introduced the concept of the *Kulturindustrie* in 1944, it has been repeated *ad infinitum* that the conventions of psychological realism, stemming from nineteenth-century literature and theatre, and constituting the very foundations of 'classical' narrative structures, serve the 'quick-profit-oriented mentality' (Tuumalu 2009) of the entertainment industry and reproduce the hegemony of capitalism. Given Õunpuu's left-leaning allegiances, it is not surprising to note his ingrained distaste for the 'orthodox chronotope' of 'Hollywood Aristotelianism' (Stam, Porton and Goldsmith 2015: 225). In Õunpuu's own words, the classical narrative formulas belong 'to the sole domain of the Ego', result in escapist stories and ultimately belittle the spectator's 'intelligence and ability to understand the world and reflect on it' (Teder 2009). Instead, he makes conscious efforts to disintegrate rigid narrative structures, working with rhythms and atmospheres instead of action-driven stories, in order to provide 'a filmic space the meaning of which remains elusive' (Teder 2009). Õunpuu subscribes to a familiar ideological critique of commercial cinema and its desire for closure and happy or redemptive endings. He prefers to 'open doors, rather than close them' (Teder 2009). Instead of 'unity of meaning' imposed by montage, his artistic credo proposes 'ambiguity of expression' (Bazin 1967: 36), claiming to challenge audiences and demanding Brechtian, active spectatorship, as opposed to the presumed passivity of consumers.

Õunpuu's cinematic expression has a clearly discernible inclination towards loosened, fractured and open-ended narrative structures, cinematography of extended takes and widened shots, and austere or desolate *mise en scènes*. His films typically unroll in a contemplative manner, lingering on situations and characters that are, at best, loosely interconnected, rather than galloping through the formulaic, strictly causal and forward-looking movements of a traditional three-act plot. These choices make him a counterpart of the ambitions and aesthetic strategies of 'slow cinema'. First coined in the early 2000s in reference to the cinematic style of film-makers such as Béla Tarr, Tsai Mingliang and Abbas Kiarostami (Ciment 2006), this term has come to label a style founded on 'the employment of (often extremely) long takes, de-centred and understated modes of storytelling, and a pronounced emphasis on quietude and the everyday' (Flanagan 2008). The discourse of slow cinema is generally perceived as a 'reaction to an increasingly fast world and cinema' (de Luca and Barradas Jorge 2016: 10), providing 'resistance to the destructive pace of capitalism' (Nagib 2016: 26), challenging 'dominant notions of progress and goal-oriented activity' and 'introducing the prospect of taking the time to think differently, and of thinking time differently' (Davis 2016: 102).

Indeed, time plays a crucial role in Õunpuu's project of counteracting the hegemonic forces of the capitalist culture industry. In addition to the slowness/speed nexus, in which deceleration takes on political significance as indicated above, his films are increasingly characterised by jumbled temporalities. While 'dominant cine-aesthetics relays time as a linear succession of events' (Stam, Porton and Goldsmith 2015: 228), Õunpuu's films regularly interrupt and scramble the continuous flow of (narrative) time, combining different chronological moments. This proclivity for dissonant temporalities that disregard the coherence of diegetic space-time and disrupt causality underpins all of Õunpuu's films. However, it reaches an extreme in *Roukli*, the main strategy of which is decidedly palimpsestic. Deriving from Ancient Greek, this word denotes, according to the *Oxford English Dictionary*, 'a parchment or other writing surface on which the original text has been effaced or partially erased, and then overwritten by another; a manuscript in which later writing has been superimposed on earlier (effaced) writing'. In film studies, Robert Stam has used the term 'palimpsestic' to describe the chronotopic multiplicity that is characteristic of the alternative cine-aesthetics of postcolonial cultures. Stam argues that the world's avant-gardes employ a paradoxical and oxymoronic temporality as 'a means for breaking away from linear, cause-and-effect conventions of Aristotelian narrative poetics, a way of flying beyond the gravitational pull of verism, of defying the "gravity" of chronological time and literal space' (Stam 1999: 64). Something similar happens in *Roukli*, which merges conceptual, visual and auditory references from a wide range of time periods (the Viking Age, the Second World War, the 'cowboy capitalist' 1990s), belief systems (paganism, Ancient Greek religions, Christianity, Buddhism) and geographical points of origin. Restructuring – or, rather, de-structuring – the regimes of (cinematic) time and history, *Roukli* conjures a spatiotemporal constellation that challenges the orderly, easily comprehensible and predictable clockwork universe of the Newtonian paradigm. In addition to disturbing the force fields that shape the cinematic products of the capitalist culture industry in general, *Roukli* mobilises its specific temporal frame of reference in order to critique the Estonian 'grand national narrative' in particular – an idea to which I will return in due course.

Representing the Crises of 'Negative Globalisation'

From the very beginning of his film-making career, Õunpuu has been drawn to characters in distress. *Empty*, his debut short, focuses on the failing marriage of Mati and Helina, with Marina and Eduard serving as accelerators of desire and jealousy, doubts and turnarounds. *Autumn Ball* presents an extensive ensemble of miserable individuals and dysfunctional relationships, ranging from bored couples to desolate divorcées and perverted loners. Both Tony, the titular character of *Püha Tõnu kiusamine* (*The Temptation of St Tony*, 2009), and Fred, the protagonist of *Free Range* (2013), undergo a severe existential crisis, although in Fred's case the prospects are presented as significantly brighter. Finally, *Roukli* observes four urban 'bohemians' (Dalton 2015) in a remote farmhouse, driven out of their natural habitat by an unnamed war – the ultimate manifestation of crisis.

The individual predicaments that lie at the core of Õunpuu's oeuvre typically function as symptoms of the contemporary socio-economic order, conveying his critique of the personally devastating, morally corrupting and socially erosive effects of neoliberal capitalism. Even *Empty*, which is based on a short story written in 1972, hence in a radically different ideological context, can be argued to have broader significance in terms of evoking an overwhelming sense of isolation that transcends both the intimate sphere and the diegetic spatiotemporal situation of the story, thus talking less about late socialism and more about the neoliberal 2000s. In addition to the general atmosphere of solitude that ties the characters of *Empty* to the post-Soviet zeitgeist, the impression of contemporary significance is intensified by moments of temporal dissonance, minute palimpsestic 'ruptures' of the film's diegetic space in the form of small markers of the new material culture, that is, objects that cannot belong to the early 1970s. While the Soviet period was certainly not without its own alienating qualities, especially for a small nation violently forced into the 'friendly family of Socialist Republics', the private crises of *Empty* can be read as standing for today's 'crisis of *agencies* and *instruments of effective action* – and its derivative: the vexing, demeaning and infuriating feeling of having been sentenced to *loneliness*', which, according to Zygmunt Bauman lies 'at the bottom of all the crises in which our times abound' (Bauman and Bordoni 2014: 95; emphases in the original).

It is equally important to note the professions of the characters in *Empty* – Mati is an artist, Eduard a violinist and Marina a student of painting. The creative class plays a paramount role in Õunpuu's films, the protagonists of which are frequently engaged in artistic lines of work, with only a few exceptions, most notably Tony, who is a mid-level manager of a factory. In *Empty*, the intellectuals seem to lead a rather carefree life in terms of material security, made possible by strong unions during the Soviet period that ensured a regular income and a place to live, even if for a certain price. By contrast, the cultural workers in *Autumn Ball* have largely been left to their own devices in making a livelihood, forced either to take on menial jobs (like Anton, a sculptor who has had to resort to a job at a security company) or to adapt to the tastes of the masses at the expense of their creative freedom and dignity (like the Stage Director specialising in relationship comedies and sinking his despair into excessive amounts of alcohol). In addition to the artists, the universe of *Autumn Ball* includes a number of representatives of the working class, such as Laura, a single mother working in a sewing factory; Theo, a sex-addicted doorkeeper at a restaurant; and August Kask, a perverted barber. Brought together to the same dreary terrain, a seedy-looking Soviet housing estate filled with countless decaying prefab high-rise blocks, plus an odd newly developed residence, the film suggests that all of them are affected by the collapse of the former socio-economic hierarchies and the twilight of the socialist welfare state, as well as by the newly emerged forces of neoliberal 'accumulation by dispossession' (Harvey 2005: 160–2), which, as explained above, hit Estonia with particular vigour (Kideckel 2002: 115; Bohle and Greskovits 2012: 96–137). In a different context, which nevertheless also perfectly applies to the Estonian situation, Andrew Ross has aptly pointed out that

> workers in low-end services . . . and members of the 'creative class', who are temping in high-end knowledge sectors, appear to share certain

experiential conditions. These include the radical uncertainty of their futures, the temporary or intermittent nature of their work contracts, and their isolation from any protective framework of social insurance. (Ross 2009: 6)

Returning to Zygmunt Bauman's idea quoted above, I would add that Õunpuu's underlying concern is related to the realisation that, despite these shared conditions, the individuals lack agency. Caged into the new, atomising neoliberal reality, they are incapable of changing their situation for the better, failing to form meaningful (personal) relationships, let alone taking any collective action. Therefore, while predominantly scrutinising the difficulties of two quite distinct 'classes', Õunpuu's critique cuts across the entire social spectrum, pertaining to Estonian society as a whole and perhaps even to what Bordoni dubs the 'global citizen', characterised by 'a state of isolation and solitude'. Bauman and Bordoni suggest that this state is a consequence of 'demassification', a process that results from a 'divorce between power and politics' and has led to 'the absence of agency' – to the inability to choose a way out of the current, all-embracing and permanent state of crisis (Bauman and Bordoni 2014: 12, 59). Furthermore, Bauman argues that

> The new individualism, the fading of human bonds and the wilting of solidarity are engraved on one side of a coin whose other side shows the misty contours of 'negative globalization'. In its present, purely negative form, globalization is a parasitic and predatory process, feeding on the potency sucked out of the bodies of nation-states and their subjects. (Bauman 2007: 24)

According to Bauman, the present crisis is characterised by globally produced, 'extraterritorial' problems, the solving of which is quite impossible with the 'instruments of political action' available to the essentially 'territorial' nation-states:

> Each formally sovereign territorial unit might serve nowadays as a dumping ground for problems originating far beyond the reach of its instruments of political control – and there is pretty little it can do to stop this, let alone pre-empt it, considering the amount of power left at its disposal. (Bauman and Bordoni 2014: 22)

The notions of devastating individualism, negative globalisation and impotence of the nation-state stand at the core of *The Temptation of St Tony* and, in particular, *Roukli*. In the former, Tony, 'a self-made, middle-aged mid-level manager', is struck by a full-blown existential crisis upon realising that his prosperity has been built 'on the foundation of corpses' (Tõnson 2010). In the film, this macabre phrase is not just an abstract trope, but quite the contrary. Driving back from his father's funeral in the muddy, impoverished countryside, Tony accidentally runs over a dog and, hauling its carcass to the road-side forest, discovers a ghastly pile of disjointed human hands. In the final part of the film, Tony himself faces the threat of being sawn into pieces in a 'meat factory' that is the likely source of the severed body parts. Captured by a mysterious and powerful gang calling themselves 'the last people', Tony finds himself undressed and strapped on to an operating table in what appears to be a human slaughterhouse. He is fortuitously saved from death after his executioner trips and kills himself with the chainsaw that was meant to penetrate Tony's flesh. Making a hasty exit from the butchery, Tony notices an Estonian tricolour – the ultimate symbol of the nation-state – hanging next to the door and wraps it around his naked body, in a futile attempt to shield it from the freezing temperatures.

This scene visualises quite strikingly the concept that, in today's negatively globalised world, the nation-state has virtually no power to protect its citizens. Instead, individuals and societies are left at the mercy of the 'supranational economic power' (Bauman and Bordoni 2014: 31), essentially opaque global forces operating largely beyond (local) political control (Bauman and Bordoni 2014: 11), dominated by secretive and undemocratic institutions, such as the International Monetary Fund, the World Bank and the World Trade Organization. Indeed, such enigmatic and predatory global forces find a vivid embodiment in the mysterious Herr Meister and his entourage, the monstrously

Figure 7.1 *The Temptation of St Tony* (Veiko Õunpuu, 2009).

clownish ringmaster Count Dionysos Korzbyski and the servile sidekick Kleine Willy – 'the last people' who snatch Tony because he wants to rescue Nadezhda from their eerie brothel. In the words of Count Korzbyski, Herr Meister is 'the connoisseur of all great secrets, terrestrial and subterranean, the master of mysteries' – far more powerful than any state institution. If anything, the grotesquely inadequate police appear to serve Herr Meister's interests, rather than enforcing the law, as testified by a scene where Tony's complaint about the human remains he found in the woods is disregarded in favour of dealing with Nadezhda, who has once again escaped from the brothel. This outlandish institution, preposterously called Das Goldene Zeitalter (The Golden Age), caters to the kinky tastes of the elite, pimping enslaved young women to the highest bidders. Herr Meister and the privileged class literally feed on the misery of the less fortunate, as the final scene of the film tellingly suggests – in the middle of a foggy ice rink stands a table with Nadezhda's lifeless body, her stomach ripped open; Tony, struggling with gag reflex, sits at the table and gobbles up the bloody pieces of her flesh, still steaming as the bodily warmth meets the chilly air. Alongside the aforementioned human butchery, which seems to be another 'branch' of Herr Meister's exploitative empire, processing the human leftovers once their resources have been exhausted, this finale provides a dramatic image of the cannibalistic and predatory practices internalised by capitalism in general and financial capital in particular (Harvey 2005: 148). The crux of the ferocious neoliberal world order is eloquently summarised in Herr Meister's words: 'Come now, the times of the corpse, the times of the blade and of murder, the times of shameless lust; the fish die in the ocean, man on the street.'[5]

A sense of the fundamental vulnerability of both individuals and nation-states in the face of the all-encompassing, obfuscated forces of negatively globalised capital(ism) is perhaps even stronger in *Roukli*, which seems to pick up where *The Temptation of St Tony* left off. While in the latter the national flag still signals the existence of a nation-state, even if it is essentially incapable of saving its citizens from harm, in *Roukli* the tokens of sovereignty are lacking altogether and the audience meets the protagonists in the midst of a war – the ultimate manifestation of crisis and destruction. Spaces of ruin are a prominent feature of Õunpuu's entire oeuvre, principally signalling the detrimental effects of neoliberal capitalism on individuals, environments (both natural and man-made) and communities. Yet *Roukli* focuses on the destruction itself, imagining a world in anticipation of an apocalypse.

Set in and around a remote farmhouse during what appear to be the last days of the capitalist world, *Roukli* presents four central characters – Jan, a scathingly sarcastic writer; Eeva, his diligent sister; Villu, a failed composer and Eeva's husband, frustrated with their childless and passionless marriage; and Marina, a painter and Jan's ex-girlfriend, a sensitive and soulful beauty. These representatives of the urban creative class have been forced into internal exile by an unnamed war that razes the city and approaches their rural shelter, signalled by the ominous sounds of jet fighters and exploding bombs. Deprived of their social roles and professional identities, the foursome find themselves confronted with their deteriorating relationships and inner demons. The already perilous situation of the group escalates when Lowry and Indrik, a pair of pitiful vagabonds, arrive at the farm in search of a hiding place from the men of Peedu, a local 'warlord'. Finally, Peedu's gang invade the farmstead and take Jan with them, while Lowry and Indrik flee to the woods with Marina.

Earlier commentators have read the film as a representation of a personal end of the world (Karjatse 2017: 150). Indeed, Õunpuu has suggested that his intention was to scrutinise the total loss of an individual identity, personal as well as professional, and the disintegration of all social roles as a means of a certain kind of liberation (Kilumets and Valme 2015). While I agree that the individual crises of the four protagonists play a significant part in Õunpuu's critique, as the frequent close-ups of the characters confirm, I suggest that the notion of destruction that is so central to *Roukli* can also be interpreted in collective terms. In particular, the film can be seen as a breaking down of the Andersonian imagined community (Anderson 2006)[6] and the established 'national narrative' (Tamm 2018) on the one hand, and the evaporation of the nation-state into the neoliberal global space (Bauman 2007: 25) on the other.

Õunpuu has never concealed his profound contempt for nationalism and the concomitant Estonian 'grand narrative of nation'. According to him, 'our paralysing sense of the nation is cartoonish. Likely because it is actually very weak, almost non-existent; it lacks a positive content; it is defined merely through certain historical confrontations' (Teinemaa 2011: 7). Indeed, as Marek Tamm has demonstrated, the Estonian national historical narrative is constructed as a grand struggle for independence, involving a series of clashes and rebellions (Tamm 2018: 18) and teleologically leading towards the predetermined triumph of sovereignty. In a model proposed by Homi K. Bhabha in his famous article 'DissemiNation: Time, Narrative, and the Margins of the Modern Nation', this type of narrative falls into the 'continuist, accumulative temporality of the pedagogical' (Bhabha 1990: 297), celebrating particular nodal points of the historical timeline and arranging them into a coherent, linear and causal sequence.

The war that wreaks havoc in *Roukli* might be construed as another battle, simply a setback in this overarching scheme. Yet the narrative form of the film decisively renounces this possibility by rejecting any teleological linearity and instead offering multiple superimposing images of various historical crises and armed conflicts, ranging from the incursions of Estonian pirates into Sweden and the retaliating conquests of Nordic Vikings in Estonia, to the waves of deportations and emigration during the Second World War and the clashes of the local underworld in the early capitalist 1990s. The sense of numerous historical moments collapsing into a palimpsestic 'montage' is introduced at the very beginning of the film, with a motto borrowed from Uku Masing, a prominent figure of Estonian religious philosopy:

> This I feel that all the dead are alive in me
> From ancient times and still
> But am I a mirror or a lens in an amalgam, from which they break through.

Importantly, the constitutive elements of this palimpsest are not limited to episodes of local and national history. The scope of the multi-temporal and poly-spatial galaxy of *Roukli* is distinctly transnational, incorporating numerous references to impending global catastrophes, such as nuclear threat and refugee crises, as well as a broad spectrum of symbols extending from paganism and Greek mythology to Buddhism and Christianity. All in all, the dilapidating universe of *Roukli* articulates the destructive momentum of capitalism that 'dismantles all existing social and cultural structures, norms, and models of the sacred' (Magagnoli 2013: 729; see also Harvey 2005: 3), drowning 'the most heavenly ecstasies of religious fervour . . . in the icy water of egotistical calculation' (Marx and Engels 2008: 37). In fact, the image of the godless world of capitalism also made an appearance in *The Temptation of St Tony*, embodied in a preacher who had lost his faith. In *Roukli*, the spiritually detrimental effects of capitalism manifest as tainted or mocked biblical symbols – a rotten apple; the self-inflicted stigmata on Indrik's hands and feet; Jan's reaction – 'total fucking nonsense' – to Villu reading aloud the Scriptures.

The national narrative is further undermined by the way *Roukli* portrays the countryside. Instead of the bucolic images so typical in Estonian culture, both literary and visual (see, for example, Peil and Sooväli 2005; Näripea 2012: 250–6; Magnus 2014), the film depicts the rural environment as impoverished and uncultivated. In a striking contrast to the established understanding that the countryside is both the cradle and the fortress of the Estonian nation, the backbone of national identity, in *Roukli* it fails to provide a refuge, either physical or mental, for the urban intellectuals. Instead of offering a safe haven, the rural environment comes across as hostile and dangerous, infested with vagabonds and (neo-)Vikings. The traditional homestead has been obliterated, leaving the characters with an acute sense of dislocation, of not belonging – not unlike the refugees mass-produced in many corners of the negatively globalised world.

By refusing to subscribe to the grand national narrative, Õunpuu provides a penetrating critique that is perhaps particularly timely at a moment when the world is faced with the dire consequences of negative globalisation, which advances hand in hand with 'nationalism, religious fanatism, fascism and, of course, terrorism' (Bauman 2007: 8). The understanding that nationalism and negative globalisation (that is, neoliberal capitalism) are two sides of the same coin is particularly relevant in the Estonian context where radical neoliberal reforms were from the very beginning 'intrinsically tied to the agenda of nation-state building', serving 'the purpose of forging national identities' and paying little attention to mitigating 'the accompanying social hardship' (Bohle and Greskovits 2012: 96). Hence, Õunpuu's desire to undo national identity overlaps with his aspiration to denounce the appalling ramifications of unbridled neoliberalisation.

Conclusion

As argued above, the notion of crisis plays a paramount role in Veiko Õunpuu's work, which strives to expose the worldwide consequences and crises of 'negative globalisation' in terms of representations, as well as to counteract the detrimental effects of a neoliberalised film industry in terms of production practices and narrative techniques. While his various attempts to escape the institutional frameworks of cinematic production have perhaps not been entirely successful in offering sustainable alternatives – as demonstrated, for example, by his recent return to the more 'traditional' mode of film making with *Viimased* (*The Last Ones*, which was scheduled to be released in 2019), their value as intentional acts of resistance should not be underestimated. Rather, Õunpuu's methods acquire a particular urgency at a moment when the emerging generation of young directors appears to be submissively conforming to the dictates of market-oriented film production, which flattens the local cinematic scene by churning out banal variations of the 'grand national narrative'. In this context of populist 'accessibility', Õunpuu's complex, ambivalent and irrational universes, which often frustrate audiences and critics alike, serve as precious enclaves of the inquisitive mind that continues to ask uncomfortable questions and refuses to provide easy answers.

Acknowledgements

Research for this essay was funded by Eesti Teadusagentuur, grant no. IUT31-1. I would also like to thank the Estonian government for continually keeping up our hopes about raising research funding to 1 per cent of GDP.

Notes

1. Four narrative features and two documentaries resulting from a programme dedicated to the centenary of Estonian independence in 2018 accounted for more than half (352,000) of the admissions. However, the most popular film, with over

146,000 admissions, was *Klassikokkutulek 2: pulmad ja matused* (*Class Reunion 2: A Wedding and A Funeral*), directed by René Vilbre, a remake of the Danish film *Klassefesten 2: Begravelsen* (*The Reunion 2: The Funeral* (2014), directed by Mikkel Serup.
2. The majority of the Estonian population cannot imagine a leftist alternative to neoliberal capitalism, even if the post-Soviet 'liberal shock-therapy' (Notermans 2015) resulted in soaring social inequality, because the experience of extended Soviet occupation (1944–91) has led to widespread suspicion of any left-leaning initiatives.
3. Eelmaa has also frequently appeared in Õunpuu's films, most significantly as the protagonist in *The Temptation of St Tony* (2009).
4. Including celebrated figures such as Iranian Amir Naderi, Japanese Naomi Kawase, Singaporean Eric Khoo, Americans Ken Jacobs and Mark Boswell, Korean Park Chan-wook, Thai Pen-ek Ratanaruang and German Tom Tykwer, as well as a number of promising young talents.
5. While Tony is certainly complicit in the atrocities of the capitalist system, the film clearly concentrates on his increasing awareness and discomfort with his own condition and that of the surrounding world. This makes him an ultimately sympathetic character whose growing sense of unease determines the essentially agonising spectatorial experience and patterns of identification.
6. Anderson defines a nation as 'an imagined political community' that is 1) imagined because its members 'will never know most of their fellow-members . . . yet in the mind of each lives the image of their communion'; 2) limited because it 'has finite, if elastic boundaries beyond which lie other nations'; 3) sovereign 'because the concept was born in an age in which Enlightenment and Revolution were destroying the legitimacy of the divinely-ordained, hierarchical dynastic realm', envisioning freedom in the form of the sovereign state; and 4) a community 'because, regardless of the actual inequality and exploitation that may prevail in each, the nation is always conceived as a deep, horizontal comradeship' (Anderson 2006: 6–7).

8. THE FUTURE IS PAST, THE PRESENT CANNOT BE FIXED: KEN LOACH AND THE CRISIS

Martin Hall

As the contemporary version of the crisis brought on by the financial crash of 2008 reaches its second decade, the cinema of Ken Loach presents something of a conundrum for the politically radical spectator. Since his return to frequent feature film production as the Cold War began to end in 1990, his work has predominantly been focused in two areas: the everyday struggle for existence in the contemporary world: for example, *Riff-Raff* (1991), *Ladybird, Ladybird* (1994), *Sweet Sixteen* (2001), *It's a Free World* (2007) and *I, Daniel Blake* (2016); and the historical, revolutionary struggles of working people against capitalism and imperialism, such as *Land and Freedom* (1995), *Carla's Song* (1996) and *The Wind that Shakes the Barley* (2006). There have also been documentaries made for television, notably *The Flickering Flame* (1996) and *Spirit of '45* (2013).

In this chapter, the defeatism of the British left since the 1980s and the positions taken by its reformist wing following that period, one in which Francis Fukuyama (1992) pronounced 'the end of history', will be posited as a seam running through Loach's contemporary cinema. A binary is set up by Loach's films during this period: a Gramscian War of Manoeuvre is represented in the revolutionary time of the historical films, but in the contemporary period texts, there is no complementary War of Position, which is the form that the struggle takes in order to fight the hegemony of bourgeois culture; instead, we have a working class that is atomised and ground down, with any victories presented being on an individual level.[1] Moreover, as the neoliberal model has lurched further into crisis since 2008, and as social movements attempting to combat neoliberalism have risen since the Seattle World Trade Organization protests of 1999, no change in Loach's cinema can be discerned. In order to ascertain why this might be, Alain Badiou's work on the constitution of the subject will be used to suggest that what is missing from Loach's worldview is faith in what Badiou calls 'the Idea of Communism', which he situates as one 'related to the destiny of generic humanity' (2009a: 79). We may more commonly refer to this as a grand narrative. Through this analysis, a case will be made that the films of the director considered to be the most left-wing in Britain show no faith in a contemporary transformative paradigm.

Moreover, Mark Fisher's concept of 'capitalist realism' will be of use in specifying exactly what relationship Loach's contemporary subjects have to the present, a cinematic time that is haunted by the ghosts of the past and of lost futures. Fisher suggests that late capitalism is infused with 'the widespread sense that not only is capitalism the only viable political and economic system, but also that it is now impossible to even *imagine* a coherent alternative to it' (2009: 2). Furthermore, borrowing Derrida's neologism of hauntology, Fisher writes at length in a later volume (2014) of the various ways in which contemporary popular culture is haunted by what *might* have been. This untimely position is represented by a number of Loach's subjects in his films set in the present. For Badiou, the time of the subject is the future anterior, which he considers to be 'what supports belief' (2006: 418) in the subject; what *will* have been. The gap between these two conceptions of the future corresponds to the differing positions taken by Loach in his historical and contemporary films: his historical subjects are fixed by choices, and anterior reflection cannot bring those struggles into the present. Much has been made in popular discourse and in the social democratic imagination of the ways in which the various twentieth-century revolutions and attempts at anti-capitalist societies failed. There is an anterior inflection to this, seen from our contemporary situation: the revolution will not have taken place; instead, we get 1989 and the supposed 'end of history'.

It must be stated at this stage that capitalist realism does have antecedents and can perhaps be seen as a recurring thread throughout the crisis, and, indeed, before it. At a moment when the first creaks in the social democratic post-war consensus and the Keynesian model were yet to be felt, Theodor Adorno, in a 1964 conversation with Ernst Bloch on utopian longing, stated that 'what people have lost subjectively in regard to consciousness is very simply the capability to imagine the totality as something that could be completely different' (cited in Bloch 1988: 3–4). Adorno's proto-postmodernism hints at a problem with the future conception of 'the end of history'; namely, that perhaps we have been here before, suggesting that the teleological stasis of late capitalism is less determined than Fukuyama, postmodernism and even Fisher would have us believe. Economically, the consensus would grind to a halt and force a reaction after Richard Nixon's unpegging of the US dollar from gold in 1971 and the subsequent breaking up of the Bretton Woods system that had been set up in 1944. Following that, the Yom Kippur War and the oil crisis brought about by the oil embargo of October 1973 saw a dramatic rise in the price of oil and attempts to freeze wages by the British government. The reaction was the beginning of the neoliberal era, though few were calling it that then. What is the case is that the attempt to recalibrate the relationship between labour and capital in favour of the latter was set in motion at that point, after the relative gains of the working class in the West in the previous sixty years or so.

Loach, of course, was working during the beginning of the collapse of the post-war consensus. In the early to mid-1970s he made one feature film, *Family Life* (1971), and one major television series for the BBC, *Days of Hope* (1975). The binary this chapter is setting up can be seen coming into view during this period, which suggests that the tendency outlined in the previous paragraph was in genesis here. *Family Life* is a fairly typical social realist film about a young woman being forced into an abortion, while *Days of Hope* concentrates on the period from the middle of the First World War to the General Strike of 1926, seen through the lens of one family. Jacob Leigh (2002: 91–113) is of the view that the radicalism of the series[2] – and of much of Loach's work during the late 1960s and early 1970s – can be attributed to the influence of screenwriter Jim Allen, whose revolutionary politics permeate Loach's television at this point. Allen would also work with Loach on a series of feature films in the 1990s and will be returned to below, specifically in the discussion of *Land and Freedom*. For now, it is enough to suggest that a split between the revolutionary and the despairing subject can be seen in germ form at this stage in Loach's career.

In terms of Loach's response to the most recent manifestation of the crisis from 2008 onwards, which was set in train by the collapse of the US subprime mortgage market and the consequent crisis of international banking, what is of note is the extent to which it can be argued that he presents a contemporary-set cinema that would like to fix capitalism, but cannot reform it, never mind overturn it. We can suggest that this parallels to some degree the response from nominally social democrat governments in much of the West, which was to pump money into the economy via quantitative easing and to prop up the banking system via nationalisation; in other words the socialisation of debt in a world governed by the privatisation of profit. Along with this in Britain has come nearly a decade of austerity, which has seen a further transfer of wealth from the poor to the rich, and from the public to the private. While Loach, as a socialist, clearly does not support such measures and has aligned himself strongly with the leadership of the Labour Party in Britain since Jeremy Corbyn was elected in 2015, it is still noteworthy that his cinema post-2008 has not presented a subject who has the means to organise collectively and effect change. Loach is not alone in this: a quick survey of film-makers considered to be on the left throughout Europe would produce similar results. However, where Loach differs is in his continuing adherence to the Trotskyist tradition, unlike, for example, Béla Tarr or Michael Haneke, which would lead the spectator to expect the continuing representation of the revolutionary subject. Prior to analysing a number of Loach's films in detail, let us briefly consider what has happened politically since 2008, in order to provide greater context for what I will suggest is key to understanding Loach's recent cinema.

Badiou names 'the short century' (2007: 31) as the one that begins with the Russian Revolution in the middle of the First World War and ends with the termination of the Cold War.[3] This century is in opposition to the one in which neoliberalism has risen, which he describes as one which 'calls for renunciation, resignation, the lesser evil, together with moderation, the end of humanity as a spiritual force, and the critique of "grand narratives"' (2007: 31). This world, which Badiou calls an 'intervallic period' (2012: 38), and which has held sway since the 1980s in the West, appears to be drawing to an end. Since the crisis of 2008 and the seismic shocks that it set in train, there has been, to varying degrees, a return to oppositional politics and a subsequent rise of the left and the right. With the exception of Emmanuel Macron's in France and to a degree Angela Merkel's in Germany, governments of the centre that propose a third-way, supposedly non-ideological politics of managerialism are thin on the ground. Instead, we have seen the rise and failure in Greece of Syriza's challenge to the European Union and austerity; the election of Trump; Bolsonaro, who can legitimately be called a fascist, taking power in Brazil; the rise of Corbyn in Britain; the contested space that is Brexit; the rise of Sanders in the US; the election of fascists to parliament in Germany for the first time since the Second World War; an alliance between populists and the far right in Italy; the continuing drive rightwards of some of the countries on the eastern periphery of the European Union; and an independence insurgency in Catalonia, of varying political colours.

In terms of the rise of the left specifically, there has been a notable uptake in political engagement in a variety of Marxist and non-Marxist movements since the aforementioned protests in Seattle, taking in Occupy, Stop the War and Black Lives Matter along the way. This phenomenon has begun to be analysed in a variety of ways in recent publications by, among others, Jodi Dean (2016), Chris Nineham (2017) and Liz Fekete (2018). We are returning to a world of division, one in which the grand narratives of yesteryear are proving themselves alive and well. Furthermore, for the first time since the 1980s, it can be suggested that 'the long night of the left is drawing to a close' (Douzinas and Žižek 2010: vii). This is the disavowed context in which Loach presents his contemporary subjects.

Let us look at Loach's historical cinema first, in order to situate the War of Manoeuvre in his films that present the subject of Badiou's short century. Since the end of the Cold War Loach has made four historical feature films that present class struggle to varying degrees: in *Land and Freedom* we have the Republican side of the Spanish Civil War in 1936, seen through the eyes of a volunteer from the Communist Party of Great Britain (CPGB). He is assigned to the POUM (Partido Obrero de Unificación Marxista), or the Workers' Party of Marxist Unification, an anti-Stalinist party formed as an alliance of left communist Trotskyists and the right opposition in 1935, though it quickly broke with Trotsky, who did not support it. In *Carla's Song*, which is set in 1987, a much more recent struggle is represented, namely that of the Sandinistas in Nicaragua against the US-backed Contras. *The Wind that Shakes the Barley* takes place during the Irish War of Independence (1919–21) and the civil war that followed after the island was partitioned. *Jimmy's Hall* (2014) is set in the Ireland of the early 1930s and concerns the deportation of revolutionary Jimmy Gralton (Barry Ward) after his revivification of the eponymous hall, which he uses as a centre of political education and culture, in so doing incurring the wrath of both Church and state. Each of the films also has a romance plot, with *Carla's Song* making it the central driver of the narrative. I will concentrate on *Land and Freedom* and *The Wind that Shakes the Barley*, as they are the texts that are concerned with grand historical struggle and indeed grand narratives, specifically communism.

Eleftheria Rania Kosmidou, in a discussion of *Land and Freedom*, makes a persuasive case that 'Loach's melancholy and reflective nostalgia . . . makes him an allegorist commentating on the present' (2012: 56). This notion of commenting on the present can be extended to all four of the historical films, though I do not agree with the notion that Loach is predominantly using allegory as a form; rather, I am suggesting principally that his historical texts comment on the present via their presenting of the struggle as past, and as contingent upon historically specific conditions that the texts posit are no longer present; what will have been. The reason for this is set out in specific scenes. The exception that proves the rule among the historical films in formal terms, *Land and Freedom* does make concrete this 'commenting on the present' through the framing device of David Carr's (Ian Hart) death in the Liverpool of 1995, with his granddaughter (Suzanne Maddock) looking through his papers, which takes us to the first flashback, until we end with his funeral and the mourners giving the raised fist salute. Still, the raised fist functions as little more than an exercise in nostalgia; a symbol of mourning from the present.[4] What is much more common is the representation of a political crossroads and the failure of the revolutionary path taken by some, and the victory of the compromising and reformist path taken by others, leading to the present situation. Let us look at the scenes in our chosen films that present this historical moment, and consider what this tells us about Loach's political alignment. The scenes will be summarised initially, prior to being subject to a comparative analysis.

The scene in *Land and Freedom* that presents this crossroads, and which in twelve minutes acts as a miniature of schisms within the left regarding strategy and tactics that are still present to this day, is the debate on land collectivisation that takes place in the recently commandeered house of a capitalist. It commences just prior to halfway through the film, functions as its apex and is its longest scene. Non-professional actors are used by Loach in this scene, and they espouse their actual positions regarding the conflict (Porton 1996: 30), which is still very much part of general discourse in Spain. This is another reason why it is qualitatively different from the rest of the film.

A peasant woman makes the case for collectivisation, which is mostly met with approval; the lone dissenting voice among the Spanish people present belongs to Pepe, a tenant farmer. After other villagers speak, the POUM militia members, who include anarchists as well as socialists and communists, are invited to speak, and the divide regarding what is to be done is presented via Lawrence (Tom Gilroy), an American volunteer, who speaks against, essentially presenting the Communist Party perspective. Scottish, German and French comrades are in favour, and present Trotskyist and anarcho-syndicalist positions: the revolution must happen now; do not try and appease capitalist countries in the hope of support. This is a retort to Lawrence, who has just reminded the room that only Russia and Mexico support the Republic; in terms of the rest of the world, he tells them, 'they are capitalist countries and if you want their help, you have to moderate your slogans, as you're scaring them away'.

David takes a pragmatic view that winning the war must be the priority and does not particularly come down on either side, though he is closer to Lawrence's position because of his own affiliation with the CPGB. We see this later as he joins Lawrence in the International Brigade, and finds himself fighting against anarchists and revolutionaries who hold the same positions as his former comrades. However, following on from an interchange with a young soldier telling lies about the militia, he rejoins it and rips up his Party card. The villagers vote and the motion to collectivise the land is carried. However, it is the road laid out by Lawrence that is eventually taken by the Republican movement, as the Communist Party represses the POUM and forces them to surrender, with Lawrence being part of the brigade that does so, leading to the death of anarchist Blanca (Rosana Pastor), with whom David is in love. He returns to England.

To turn to *The Wind that Shakes the Barley*, Donal Ó Drisceoil, in an article responding to right-wing critiques of the film, suggests that it discusses 'the "what-might-have-beens" of the Irish revolution, not in a romantic, counterfactual manner, but by highlighting or foregrounding spurned radical political and historical possibilities' (2009: 10). While the film does present lost possibilities,

I am arguing that this 'might have been' is actually, from the 2006 perspective of the text, a case of 'what will have been'. It is most clearly seen in a section that functions as a companion to the one in *Land and Freedom* discussed above. It is seven minutes long and follows on from the showing of a newsreel that announces the Anglo-Irish Treaty, which proposes to partition the country, create an Irish Free State as a British dominion, and which requires every member of the putative new parliament to swear an oath of allegiance to the British crown. In it the two sides of the IRA that will fight in the oncoming Irish Civil War, with the government led by Michael Collins on one side and the anti-treaty rebels led by Éamon de Valera on the other, are shown making their case. Teddy O'Donovan (Pádraic Delaney), the brother of the film's main protagonist, Damien O'Donovan (Cillian Murphy), argues that the treaty is the best they can hope for, and that the alternative, in the words of British prime minister David Lloyd George, is 'immediate and terrible war'. Damien, Dan (Liam Cunningham), Finbar (Damien Kearney) and others all explicitly state that they are very near to what they have fought for and that they can't stop now. More to the point, they make the case that they are remaining loyal to the constitution of the first Dáil Éireann in 1919, which was formed by the elected Sinn Féin members from the 1918 General Election in the UK, who had refused to take their seats and had instead formed a parliament and declared an Irish Republic in Dublin. Dan reads from the constitution of the Dáil, which he carries in his pocket. It states that the nation's sovereignty extended over all of its resources. From this he makes the socialist case that 'this means all of us here and all of us in this country own every bit of this country'. He then argues that ratification of the treaty would lead to an Ireland in which only the flag and the accents of the powerful would change. He is applauded and the meeting ends. The brothers fight on different sides in the ensuing civil war and the film ends with Damien's death by a firing squad under the command of Teddy.

Prior to this, this split between what from a social democratic perspective would be called realpolitik and revolutionary struggle had been foregrounded in the text in a scene half an hour earlier, in which an Irish court acting on the authority of the Dáil had ruled that a local businessman charging exorbitant interest on a loan to a peasant must pay her a reparation. Teddy and what will become the pro-treaty faction run after the man to assuage him, as he has been paying for a lot of the weapons that they have been smuggling into the country. Teddy is hauled back into the court by the all-woman judiciary. They, Damien, Dan and others argue that the court must be respected and the ruling upheld and that the poor not being exploited is more important than keeping the local elite happy.

The similarities between the scenes in the two films are clear, and function from the present as historical lessons for the contemporary left. Kosmidou suggests that both texts are predicated upon how 'a split within a potentially revolutionary movement prevents a radical social transformation' (2012: 86). While this is true, both scenes also contain traces, especially in *Land and Freedom*, of the revolutionary event of the twentieth century where such a split did lead to the most radical social transformation: the October Revolution of 1917 in Russia. For reasons of space, I will be brief here. Following the February Revolution a variety of groups took different positions regarding what to do next in terms of social organisation; at times, even the revolutionary Bolsheviks made the case that the time was not right for the workers to seize power via the workers' councils, or soviets. There were both theoretical and practical reasons behind this. Marx and Engels had made clear that societies needed to follow a feudalist and monarchist period with a bourgeois democratic one, which had not happened in Russia; in practical terms, Russia's working class was not considered large enough or advanced enough in terms of class consciousness to take power. Still, when the time came, Lenin, Trotsky and the other Bolshevik leaders made the decision to argue that the revolutionaries must seize power. This knowledge underpins the interventions made by many militia members in *Land and Freedom*, and would have been, of course, very recent in the minds of the anti-treaty socialists in *The Wind that Shakes the Barley*. Both films look in both temporal directions.

Loach very clearly sides with the anti-treaty side and with the anti-Stalinist position of the POUM. He has stated that his and Allen's identification with the POUM was based on the latter being 'anti-Stalinist Marxists' (cited in Porton 1996: 30). Later in the same interview, having been asked about parallels with *Days of Hope*, particularly in terms of the betrayal of the left, he suggests that 'it's the story of the century, really, that there is this great force which is capable of change but it doesn't always lead to something effective' (Porton 1996: 30). The positions taken by Loach in these texts allied to this comment raise a question regarding his contemporary films: why is he not prepared to take the aleatory gamble necessary to espouse radical change? Badiou's work on the subject of the Event may provide some answers.

For Badiou, the militant subject is created through fidelity to the aleatory, revolutionary Event, which is a fundamental break in the situation, and allows that which has not been counted, what has been disavowed – in this case, the working class – to take their place as subjects of history, provided they take a gamble. His examples include the Paris Commune, the Russian Revolution, the Cultural Revolution in China and sometimes May '68. As suggested above, Badiou situates the temporality of the subject of the Event in the future anterior. Due to its conditionality, history is always yet to come in the anterior register. However, for Loach, what we instead have in the historical films is what will have been, seen from the fixed present perfect of the failure of the present. We can consider the reasons for this via Badiou's thinking regarding the different types of subject position that can be created by the Event: his thought goes through some stages, but by the time of *Logics of Worlds* (2009b: 62–5), there are three – faithful, reactive and obscure – to which he adds a fourth – the resurrected subject – which is essentially a reactivated version of the first, and which allows for the subject of the Event to be created across time.

In Badiou's terms, the subject of Loach's historical films is not reactive, as such a subject declares the opposition between capitalism and communism to be wrong, and instead works to save democracy from dictatorship of both left and right. He is certainly not an obscure subject, one that disavows the aforementioned opposition, via the blocking from view of the eventual trace with something presented as universal that is not – God or race being two examples – leading to fascism. Rather, in his historical films, Loach presents a view aligned to some degree with the faithful subject, but one infused with melancholia, in the sense that the melancholic subject clings to that which was lost – the revolution – and cannot therefore mourn. What we are arguing to be clearly missing in his contemporary-set films is the resurrected subject; instead, the spectator is presented with a despairing, mournful subject, one either permeated with capitalist realism or destroyed by it. Let us turn to those films now, in order to consider why this might be so.

I will concentrate on *I, Daniel Blake* and *It's a Free World*, in order to provide a temporal framework that is as close as possible to the current manifestation of the crisis. Both films were written by Paul Laverty, Loach's frequent collaborator since *Carla's Song*, as was *The Wind that Shakes the Barley*. While a concentration on screenwriters can be said to be overly reductionist, it is worth commenting that Laverty does not share Allen's background in revolutionary politics. Having begun training as a priest, he then worked in Nicaragua in the 1980s documenting human rights abuses. Perhaps something of a tendency to identify problems without recognising any need for systemic change, allied to faith in redemption and atonement, can be seen in his films with Loach. *It's a Free World* concerns Angie (Kierston Wareing), a single mother working for a company that organises the transfer of foreign labour into Britain. After unfairly losing her job, she decides to use her contacts to set up her own business with her friend Rose (Juliet Ellis). She is let down by her financial backers, falls out with Rose and her family, starts giving work to illegal workers, and is threatened with violence if she does not pay the wages owed to the men, who are predominantly Polish, culminating in the temporary kidnapping of Jamie (Joe Siffleet), her son, and an ultimatum from three masked men. The film ends with her in Eastern Europe attempting to import more workers, her lesson clearly not learned.

I, Daniel Blake presents the world of benefit sanctions and fit-to-work assessments. The eponymous character (Dave Johns) is a Newcastle joiner recovering from a heart attack. He is denied disability benefit and considered fit to return to work, despite his doctor telling him that he is in no fit state to do so. While at the benefits office querying this and finding out about claiming Jobseekers' Allowance, he comes to the aid of newly arrived Londoner Katie (Hayley Squires), a single mother who is being removed from the Jobcentre by security, having lost her temper after being told that she is being sanctioned for lateness. The two become friends. Katie is caught shoplifting and is forced to turn to prostitution to survive. Daniel turns down work at a garden centre on the advice of his doctor, and is reprimanded by the Jobcentre for not trying hard enough to find work. While waiting for his appeal date, he sprays 'I, Daniel Blake demand my appeal date before I starve' on the wall of the building, is arrested, and becomes depressed. On the day of his appeal, having seen the people who will decide his case, he becomes anxious, suffers another heart attack and dies. Katie reads out what he had written for his appeal at the funeral.

Yet again, pivotal scenes in the films present a different world to the one in which they are set. However, they do not directly present a road not travelled; rather, they describe and present a past that is mourned; what might have been. I will describe them initially, prior to making another comparative analysis from within the prism of Badiou's varying subject positions, those which I am adding to it, and Fisher's capitalist realism. In *It's a Free World*, it is the character of Geoff (Colin Coughlin), Angie's father, who is the memorial voice, though it is social democracy, rather than revolutionary struggle, that is being mourned.

Following a scene in which Angie and Geoff have accompanied Jamie into school to discuss his having attacked another pupil, the three of them go to the park, and the adults talk, while Jamie plays with some other boys. The scene is two-thirds into the film, and slightly less than three minutes long, though it encapsulates the changes that thirty years of neoliberalism have brought. It begins with Angie complaining about constantly being judged, accompanied with her suggesting that her father ought to be proud of her for setting up her own business. He replies, 'What shall I congratulate you on?' Geoff then discusses the world that will await Jamie when he leaves school, where he will be competing with 'Kosovans, Romanians, on starvation wages'. Angie thinks he is being racist and suggests that he should join the National Front. Geoff reacts with anger, calling them 'lying bastards'. Angie, speaking from a position of how immigration benefits capital, rather than anti-racism, mistakes her father's position here. His is the voice of labourism, as is made clear in the remainder of the conversation. He talks about the effects on the immigrants' home countries, when 'school teachers, nurses and doctors' are working as waiters in the UK for starvation wages, finishing off by stating: 'No one's getting anything out of this but the bosses and the governors. No one else is smiling.' Angie retorts 'consumers are smiling', in so doing parroting the positions of successive Tory and New Labour administrations, who privilege this nebulous economic category and reify it as a discrete entity separate from the rest of society. After getting frustrated by her father repeatedly asking her if she is paying them the minimum wage, Angie responds by talking about how he's had the same job for thirty years, while she has already had thirty jobs and been treated badly in all of them. What is of interest here is that she puts this down to individual choice, a matter of how she and her father are different, rather than an effect of political decisions. Geoff responds by suggesting that all she cares about is her and Jamie, while 'the rest of the world can go to hell'. The scene ends with her telling him that 'It's a big world out there. Do you think anyone gives a shit?'

I, Daniel Blake functions a little differently in structural terms. There is no one scene that sets out the contemporary situation in contrast to the past; rather, a number of scenes present a binary between the dignity of labour and community on one hand, and the suffocating, incomprehensible bureaucracy of neoliberalism on the other. I will discuss two of them. Following his discovery that Katie is working as a prostitute, and her plea to him to leave her alone and not show her any more love, Daniel goes to the Jobcentre to sign on, whereupon it is made clear that he has not been looking for work. He sets out his reasons via a discussion of what a waste of everyone's time it is to look for non-existent jobs that he cannot take because of his condition. Ann (Kate Rutter), the case-worker, is sympathetic to his predicament and begs him not to sign off, as he may end up on the street. He gets up, goes outside and begins the protest described above. He is cheered on by the public, in particular by a Scotsman, who offers him his coat and berates the police who take him away: he shouts, 'You should be arresting the wankers who came up with sanctions', and singles out Iain Duncan Smith, the Tory Secretary of State for Work and Pensions who was behind the new system.

Daniel's funeral contains the scene that most clearly presents the film's political position: Katie's reading of Daniel's appeal. It is a clear statement against neoliberalisation and atomisation, and in favour of social democracy; a paean to a world that Daniel had not quite realised had gone, prior to his enforced demise. The speech talks about not being a customer or service user, nor a scrounger or shirker; it states that he paid his way in life and doesn't expect charity; that he is a man and demands his rights. It is tempting to suggest that this voice from the grave represents the death of the world in which Daniel had grown up: the post-war consensus, with its safety net, 'from the cradle to the grave', as the Beveridge Report stated in 1942, leading to Clement Attlee's government founding of the welfare state, which Loach himself eulogises and mourns in *Spirit of '45*. What both Daniel's speech and Geoff's comments display is class consciousness, pride, dignity and what Gramsci termed 'good sense' (1999: 634). This is the part of common sense that does not get co-opted hegemonically in the service of capital; for Gramsci, the discourses of, for example, privatisation, outsourcing, subject-as-client as presented as common sense by neoliberal governments would therefore not be 'good sense'. The latter is 'a conception of the world with an ethic that conforms to its structure' (Gramsci 1999: 660): community, connection, duty and fairness.

However, this does not detract from the fact that the films are suffused with capitalist realism, haunted by the ghosts of the system that the revolutionaries of Loach's generation had wanted to destroy. While the struggles in Spain and Ireland were against fascism and imperialism, Badiou and Loach's generation of the left that reached its political zenith in 1968 railed against the iniquities of social democracy, which effectively in its Keynesian incarnation was the social and economic response of the majority of the ruling class to the specific conditions of the post-war period. This is not to denigrate the many gains of the post-war Labour government; instead, it explains why the Conservative governments that followed it for the next thirteen years did not seek to reverse the majority of them. Angie is a proponent of the common sense of neoliberalism, and does not realise that her situation has very specific causes, instead choosing to see it as a natural consequence of her class. The Marxian credo that social being determines consciousness does not just refer to how an individual responds to a concrete situation, but how class consciousness has a material cause. Marx was writing at a time when the onward march of history, while of course contested, seemed to be going in the right direction: by 1989, though, the metanarratives of the Enlightenment and modern periods that had aimed at revolutionising social relations were seen by neoliberalism's proponents as irrelevant to an increasingly saturated and open world: that of capitalist realism.

That being said, I am arguing that since the crisis of 2008, there has been the beginning of a return to division rather than consensus; what Badiou has named 'the mass sign of a reopening of History' (2012: 42) that neoliberalism had thought closed. Where is this in Loach's contemporary-set texts? Loach presents one subject in Angie who has no access to class consciousness, as its base has been removed by thirty years of neoliberalism; in Geoff, one who is mourning it; and in Daniel, one who is both ignorant of its demise and who has no access to its contemporary manifestations. Throughout the film he has been bemused and uncomprehending regarding the world into which sickness has thrown him; he does not understand why the word of an unqualified, contracted-out benefits advisor can trump his doctor's, nor why there is no time limit for receiving an appeal date; he cannot use a computer; he expects the bureaucracy of the state to take him at his word when he tells them he has been looking for work. Of course, Loach's intention here is to tell a story regarding the horrendous effects of current Conservative policy, not to issue a polemic regarding the ways in which such a policy and its proponents can be overcome. Furthermore, the film does fall into the trap of at least tacitly setting up a binary regarding the deserving and undeserving poor: it is at pains to show us that Daniel is a good man who helps others, that he does not drink or smoke, is creative, and can be relied upon. This is to provide audiences with a figure of identification, no doubt; however, in the context of decades of headlines regarding 'scroungers', Loach's decision to present the state-enforced decline of such a transparently good man does mean that this binary is reinforced, rather than the system being scrutinised *tout court*.

Angie, on the other hand, is clearly a product of capitalist realism; an unknowing reactive subject in Badiouian terms. Throughout the film, she associates Geoff's politics with poverty, not realising that it is the politics of the 'free world', which she accepts and, in some ways valorises, that have led to his situation. Geoff is the untimely, mournful, despairing subject; as Cathy (Maggie Hussey), Angie's mother, functions as a constant voice of criticism for her, then it is her father to whom she looks for support. When he will not provide her with this, she feels slighted, and responds by attacking his beliefs. The position which she espouses is an example of the way that ideology is made to appear natural, as fact: as stated above, she says to Geoff, 'It's a big world out there. Do you think anyone gives a shit?' He has no response.

Both films are deeply pessimistic: *It's a Free World* concludes with Angie unable to escape the structure of exploitation. All she has achieved is a purportedly higher rung on its ladder. *I, Daniel Blake*, meanwhile, presents dignity, but in death. To consider why, we will return to Badiou's Idea of Communism. If, after the reduction of actually existing socialism to a handful of states, and the consequent period of reaction that begins in the neoliberal period, the task is to '*reestablish the* [communist] *hypothesis in the ideological and militant field*' (Badiou 2009a: 87, his emphasis), then it is clear that the four films examined here do not contribute to that in the present. Specifically, the current manifestation of the crisis has not led to a presentation of the resurrected subject in Loach's work. In the historical films, the failure of the faithful subject is explored, with this failure represented didactically. The time of the subject in these texts is one of a failed anteriority, with the path taken fixed in aspic and not salvageable as praxis for the present; instead, the films are suffused with melancholia predicated on what will have been. The contemporary-set films are mournful, suffused with what might have been. The revolution is no longer achievable, which means the subject can mourn, though what is being mourned is a different object to the one clung to by the faithful subject of the historical films: the world of social democracy, which is what the left turn in the Labour Party is attempting to resurrect.

Fisher suggests that '[c]apitalist realism can only be threatened if it is shown to be in some way inconsistent or untenable; if, that is to say, capitalism's "realism" turns out to be nothing of the sort' (2009: 16). Loach's films set in the time of the most profound crisis of neoliberalism markedly fail in this task, instead choosing to set up a dialectic between the individual and the system.

The system itself (and indeed the sense of capitalist realism posited by Fisher) is left unexamined politically: what Loach does is present a moral critique, suggesting that Martin O'Shaughnessy's comment that the neoliberal period has been one in which a 'totalising leftist language has been shattered into fragments' (2008: 64) extends into the present for the veteran film-maker, with no new language rooted in the social reality of contemporary Britain employed. The concentration on the individual rather than the collective of the historical films, which is indicative of the path taken by much of the left in the fragmentary period of capitalist realism, leads to the conclusion that not only do his films present revolution as fixed in time past, but they also disavow the most modest forms of systemic change in the here and now.

Notes

1. *Bread and Roses* (2000) is the exception that proves the rule. It is set in the US and concerns janitors fighting for better conditions and the right to unionise. It is notable that the only contemporary-set film of this era that presents the collective struggle by the working class takes place outside the UK.
2. It is worth alerting the reader to the series of debates that took place in the journal *Screen* regarding the efficacy of progressive realism as a form, many of which were predicated upon differing views of this series in terms of just how radical it was. See Caughie 2000 or Fiske 1987 for useful overviews.
3. Badiou does vary what he considers to be the end date of this short century of radicalism. Sometimes he ends it around 1980, when what he refers to as the Red Years waned; sometimes at the end of the Cultural Revolution in China in 1976. From the point of view of the beginning of the neoliberal period, the earlier dates are more useful, whereas from the perspective of the long decline of the left and the beginning of the widespread belief that capitalism is the only way to organise society, the end of the Cold War makes more sense. For an exhaustive analysis of Badiou's politics, see Bosteels 2011.
4. From the point of view of authorial intention, if not the subjects presented in the scene, this scene can be read as typical of the form of left-wing melancholy that Walter Benjamin saw in the 'radical left intelligentsia', one that fused 'constipation and melancholy' (1974: 29/31). Wendy Brown refers to it as 'a mournful, conservative, backward-looking attachment to a feeling, analysis, or relationship that has been rendered thing-like and frozen in the heart of the putative Leftist' (1999: 22).

9. IT COULD HAPPEN TO YOU: EMPATHY AND EMPOWERMENT IN IBERIAN AUSTERITY CINEMA

Iván Villarmea Álvarez

'We have lived beyond our means.' This expression – *viver acima das nossas possibilidades* in Portuguese, *vivir por encima de nuestras posibilidades* in Spanish – was endlessly repeated between 2011 and 2012 in the Iberian Peninsula. Aníbal Cavaco Silva, former president of the Portuguese Republic, used it in May 2011, after the signing of a €78 billion bailout programme between the Portuguese government and the Troika formed by the European Commission, the European Central Bank and the International Monetary Fund. Later on, Fátima Báñez, former Spanish Minister of Employment and Social Security, did the same in the parliamentary debate on state budget held in May 2012, five months after the overwhelming victory of the People's Party in the 2011 Spanish general election. The sentence soon became a mantra for conservative governments, since it allowed them to justify the adoption of austerity measures without having to assume any political responsibility after years of systematic indebtedness, institutional corruption and public overspending, as Rafael Rodríguez Tranche criticised at the time (2013). The idea, however, was not new: a few years before, the same narrative had already been used in the United States to moralise a problem – the aftermath of the financial crisis – that actually had institutional roots.

The unexpected outbreak of the Great Recession, and especially its long duration, challenged the self-image of Iberian societies: the set of wishes, fictions and self-representations associated with an inclusive middle class fell apart overnight (Observatorio Metropolitano 2011: 73). At first, film-makers did not react to this conjuncture: the financial crisis and its consequences were barely represented in Portuguese or Spanish films until 2011, with the exception of a few titles that drew attention to the malfunctions of these countries prior to the recession.[1] Nevertheless, while the sentence 'we have lived beyond our means' was being turned into an ideologically loaded cliché, some filmmakers decided to depict the plight of a wide range of social collectives, such as precarious workers, unemployed people, sick people, evicted owners and tenants, Iberian emigrants in northern Europe, Latin American and African immigrants in the Iberian Peninsula and a disoriented youth with few aspirations and fewer opportunities. The choice of these characters allowed film-makers to address a series of social problems – from unemployment to evictions – that have worsened as a consequence of both recession and austerity. Thus, faced with the voices that stated the need to make cutbacks in public services, these film-makers took sides with the victims of the crisis in a new film cycle that reflected and responded to the effects of the Great Recession at a thematic, formal or allegorical level.[2]

This Iberian austerity cinema, as I suggest calling it, is characterised by a 'politics of pain and suffering' in which 'political and physical vulnerability' go hand in hand, as Dean Allbritton has stated (2014: 102).[3] Contrary to the self-blaming discourse implicit in the expression 'we have lived beyond our means', which advocated atonement for a supposed shared guilt through personal sacrifice and passive resignation, this new film cycle sought to overcome the victims' loneliness and isolation by turning 'the individual experience of precarity and vulnerability into a communal one' (Allbritton 2014: 103). In fact, at that time, the circulation of life stories through media and social networks was being interpreted as a technology of political imagination that allowed thinking and seeing things that were neither thinkable nor visible before, as explained by Germán Labrador Méndez (2012: 562–3). According to this author, certain life stories had begun to be regarded as part of major structural problems, raising to the category of a collective political issue what was previously perceived as individual risk and private life. Consequently, many events that apparently only affected specific individuals were being inscribed within a collective paradigm, introducing a human scale in processes that used to be accounted for in quantifiable magnitudes (Labrador Méndez 2012: 563–4).

This dynamic is based on the creation of 'an empathic bridge' between those who tell their stories and their audience (Labrador Méndez 2012: 563), as well as between the characters and the viewers in the specific case of cinema. These stories foster identification between the former and the latter, although their ultimate meaning varies from case to case. Allbritton has already warned that these films usually cast 'optimism, hope and sympathy as stand-ins for any action that might effect a real change upon the world' (2014: 112); and Labrador Méndez (2018) has gone even further by discussing recent Spanish disaster films as examples of disciplinary narratives that promote individual survival as the only viable option, disregarding other possibilities based on group interdependence or collective solidarity.[4] Depending on the way in which stories and characters are presented to the audience, this empathic bridge can help reinforce or dismantle the social bonds destabilised by recession. The aim of this chapter is therefore to identify and discuss the formal and narrative strategies through which life stories pervade Iberian austerity cinema, paying particular attention to those films, whether fictions or documentaries, in which the characters work as sites of enunciation, that is, as the starting point and social position from which film-makers take part, directly or indirectly, in contemporary debates on austerity policies.

Afflicted Voices

The traumatic impact of the Economic Adjustment Program in Portugal left the country knocked out for a few years. The ubiquitous gloomy *zeitgeist* was recorded in a series of non-fiction films characterised by the enveloping presence of afflicted voices, such as *Ó Marquês Anda Cá Abaixo Outra Vez* (*The M of Portuguese Cinema*, João Viana, 2013) – a reflexive work on the growing difficulties of making films in Portugal – or *Notas de Campo* (*Field Notes*, Catarina Botelho, 2017) – an abstract travelogue in which two female voices recount their experiences during the worst years of the crisis over images of increasingly dry and wild landscapes. There was even a film that echoed President Cavaco Silva's ominous words in its title: *Acima das Nossas Possibilidades* (*Beyond Our Means*, Pedro Neves, 2014), a collective portrait of several citizens living below the poverty threshold in Porto.

Two documentaries stand out within this cycle by addressing the recession as part of long-term processes of late capitalism: *Vidros Partidos* (*Broken Glasses*, Víctor Erice, 2012) and *Vida Activa* (*Active Life*, Susana Nobre, 2014). The first is a set of screen tests with former workers of a now-closed textile factory in the River Ave Valley Region, north of Portugal.[5] These workers – six men and five women between fifty and eighty years old – summarise their working life before the camera with an old picture behind: an image taken during a lunch break in the factory canteen at the beginning of the twentieth century. They recall their harsh living and working conditions while maintaining a strong emotional bond with the factory, since it is closely related to key moments in their lives. These memories, which date back to a previous stage of capitalism, bring the past to the present, in the same way as the old picture; all the interviewees look at that image and can hardly identify themselves with the people appearing in it, mainly because current working conditions have improved compared to those a century ago, but also because people in the picture represent a type of industrial worker that no longer exists in southern

Europe: a worker with a stable job and confidence in the future. Through this contrast between workers of different times, film-maker Víctor Erice echoes the current disorientation of the working class, which has lost its agency as a consequence of its inability to cope with the closure and relocation of factories. What is most remarkable in *Broken Glasses* is the apparent ease with which Erice gives a universal scope to this particular case: the story of this factory – and the story of its workers – symbolises and summarises the recent evolution of industrial capitalism from the workers' perspective.

Active Life, in turn, reflects on the way work shapes identity while unemployment undermines self-esteem. This film mostly consists of talking heads interviews with unemployed middle-aged workers: fifteen men and ten women who are 'too old to work' but 'too young for retirement', as one of them says. All the interviews were recorded at a vocational training centre in Alverca do Ribatejo, east of Lisbon, in which film-maker Susana Nobre worked while making the film; there, she helped unemployed people to improve their academic and professional profile by certifying the expertise they had acquired throughout their working life. Most interviewees were people with little school education and without computer skills, who had become unemployed after having worked for two or three decades in sectors that were then in decline. Among them, some men in their fifties and sixties look quite uneasy in front of the camera, inasmuch as they are aware that their profile is no longer required in the labour market. This is the reason why they felt nostalgia for their previous jobs, even the hardest ones, especially those who had worked for large companies in the metal industry; once again, those jobs were linked to happy memories of friendship and youth, an idea emphasised by showing work memorabilia in the transitions between interviews.

Active Life, like *Broken Glasses*, uses the methodology of oral history to let ordinary people express their own standpoints regarding macroeconomic processes of which they are a part. Nostalgia emerges in both films as a reaction to the social involution accelerated by recession in an attempt to recover 'the self-confidence of the present' that, according to Zygmunt Bauman, is at the basis of the concept of historical progress (2000: 132). This attitude, however, has not been the only response to the crisis among Portuguese workers and film-makers. Some documentary fictions, such as *As Mil e uma Noites* (*Arabian Nights*, Miguel Gomes, 2015) and *A Fábrica de Nada* (*The Nothing Factory*, Pedro Pinho, 2017), also include interviews with unemployed and aged workers with a slightly different purpose: offering people – both the characters and the audience – the possibility of developing alternative accounts of the recession, beyond resignation and victimhood, that help them to empower themselves as individual and collective subjects. In order to do so, both films combine different systems of representation with a playful and self-conscious spirit that ultimately praises the pleasure of storytelling: from objective records of strikes and demonstrations to fictional re-enactments of real events, as well as metafictional reflections on the different ways of filming the crisis and even sequences planned according to the conventions of film genres such as the fairy tale fantasy, the western or the musical.

The Nothing Factory, for example, criticises a key aspect of late capitalism – the transnational mobility of capital, here represented by factory relocation – while simultaneously making a self-criticism of the commonplaces of social cinema. The film explores the different stages of a labour dispute in a lift factory: the company's attempt to take the equipment away, the workers' resistance, the failed negotiations between both sides and the beginning of an indefinite sit-down strike that will lead the workers to occupy the factory and assume its self-management. This story, which is set in the midst of recession, actually comes from two prior sources: the real story of a factory abandoned by its owners after the Carnation Revolution that was later bought and self-managed by its workers (see Halpern 2017: 16), and Judith Herzberg's drama play *De Nietsfabriek*, originally staged in 1997 and later adapted to Portuguese in 2005. From these materials, film-maker Pedro Pinho shapes a film that revisits, refutes and reworks many clichés of social cinema; what begins as a documentary fiction played by real workers soon becomes a self-reflexive militant film pervaded by a dry and bitter humour that even dares to include a choreographed musical number on the verge of self-parody. The development of the plot, in which every new situation causes doubts among the characters, entails a gradual transformation in the film's style that echoes the film-maker's own doubts about how to represent this conflict and its effects on the characters. Thus, by embracing Brechtian aesthetics, *The Nothing Factory* establishes a link between the past and present challenges of the workers' struggle while testing different strategies to update the tradition of social cinema.

Two years before, *Arabian Nights* had already managed to extend the scope of austerity cinema with its ambitious blend of documentary footage and whimsical re-enactments. This six-hour epic project consists of three feature films composed of eleven independent episodes inspired by real events gathered by a team of journalists. This structure was intended to depict the impact of recession in the everyday life of Portuguese people in the early 2010s.[6] The claims and complaints of real unemployed workers can be heard from the opening sequence, a 25-minute prologue in which a series of disembodied voices talk about their working and personal relationships with a large shipyard that was about to close in Viana do Castelo, north of Portugal. At a given moment, film-maker Miguel Gomes joins these voices to make a reflexive and self-parodic speech – probably the most quoted passage in Iberian austerity cinema – that must be interpreted as a statement of intent regarding the aim, meaning and politics of the film:

I feel I am in the eye of the storm and at a dead end at the same time. Our current situation stems from what I consider today the dumbest idea of my life. I thought I could make a fine film, filled with wonderful and seductive stories. At the same time, I thought the film could follow, for one year, Portugal's current miserable situation. Any mutton-head understands that, more or less skilfully, one of these two films can be made. But it is impossible to make both at once. It is a matter of common sense. You cannot make a militant film which soon forgets its militancy and starts escaping reality. That is betrayal, disengagement, dandyism. Likewise, it is stupid beyond words to want to tell marvellous stories, timeless fables, fettered by the transient, the foam of days, the present's closed horizon.

In this sequence, Gomes portrays himself as a film-maker who does not know how to make 'a fine film' about recession. His creative crisis mirrors the country's situation, but simultaneously uses the aesthetic of failure to parody the inability of some film-makers to find original and meaningful ways to depict crises – in this regard, he would probably agree with Alberto Toscano and Jeff Kinkle that 'representations of crisis need not be crises of representation' (2011b: 39). Gomes introduces himself as a film-maker who is first and foremost a worker who claims his rights.[7] He thus identifies himself with the demonstrators in Viana do Castelo, but also with Scheherazade, the main character in *One Thousand and One Nights*, because both work as storytellers: a job understood by Gomes as an act of empowerment and resistance.

Susana Nobre also portrays herself as a worker in *Active Life*; a worker who loses her job, given that the film ends with the closure of the vocational training centre where she worked: the final shot shows the destruction of large amounts of paper, meaning the destruction of office work and jobs. Her onscreen presence, like Gomes's appearance at the beginning of *Arabian Nights*, has to do with another tendency in austerity cinema: the rise of diary films, both in Portugal and Spain, in which the film-makers' life stories – Elías León Siminiani's trip to India in *Mapa* (*Map*, 2012), Joaquim Pinto's treatment for hepatitis C and HIV in *E Agora? Lembra-me* (*What Now? Remind Me*, 2013) or Eloy Domínguez Seren's experience as a migrant worker in Sweden in *Ingen ko på isen* (*No Cow on the Ice*, 2015) – must be understood as allegories of recession. In all these films, the film-makers become characters who expose the position from which they speak, thereby establishing the aforementioned empathic bridge with the audience.

Suffering Bodies

Just as happens in Portuguese cinema, first-person accounts are also central to Spanish non-fiction film, especially to those works supporting anti-austerity movements and organisations – from the 15M movement to the Platform for

People Affected by Mortgages – in which film-makers directly recorded public assemblies where ordinary people took the floor to share personal issues with their fellow citizens. The strength of the voices heard in titles such as *En tierra extraña* (*In a Strange Land*, Icíar Bollaín, 2014) or *La Granja del Pas* (Silvia Munt, 2015)[8] contrasts with the weariness of the bodies depicted in family portraits, a genre with few examples in the documentary field – *Los desheredados* (*The Disinherited*, Laura Ferrés, 2017), *Niñato* (Adrian Orr, 2017) – but a much greater presence in fiction – *Hermosa juventud* (*Beautiful Youth*, Jaime Rosales, 2014), *Magical Girl* (Carlos Vermut, 2014), *Techo y comida* (*Food and Shelter*, Juan Miguel del Castillo, 2015) and *El Olivo* (*The Olive Tree*, Icíar Bollaín, 2016) in Spain; *São Jorge* (*Saint George*, Marco Martins, 2016) and *Colo* (Teresa Villaverde, 2017) in Portugal, among other titles.

The characters in these films do not look at ease in their family homes, which are usually represented as spaces of isolation and confinement. Their bodies seem trapped there, as happens to Natalia and Carlos, the protagonist couple in *Beautiful Youth*; Natalia, who is pregnant, still lives with her divorced mother and two younger siblings in a small flat south of Madrid, while Carlos takes care of his sick mother in another narrow apartment in the same city. They embody a particular social type: NEETs, young people who are not in education, employment or training, and consequently have no choice but to stay in their family homes. Lacking privacy, Natalia and Carlos meet in public spaces such as parks, walkways, vacant lots, parking lots or bus stations, non-places filmed by cinematographer Pau Esteve Birba with a dull white light that significantly contributed to set the tone of the film: an everyday naturalism completely devoid of emotion.

The narrative in *Beautiful Youth* is composed of banal conversations and domestic scenes in which nothing apparently happens, not even in the two stunning ellipses that summarise the events of several months – including the birth of Natalia and Carlos's daughter – through WhatsApp conversations and pictures taken with smartphones. The coldness of most sequences emphasises the characters' deadlock despite their efforts to improve their situation. Natalia, for instance, looks for a job as a shop assistant after giving birth, but the impossibility of finding one convinces her to migrate to Hamburg, where she works as a cleaner, babysitter and sex worker. Carlos, meanwhile, works as a bricklayer for €10 per day and plans to buy a van with a friend, even though they do not have money to do this. An unexpected possibility of getting one arises after Carlos is attacked by a petty criminal, since he expects to receive legal compensation for his injuries. When he finally does not get this, he decides to hire two thugs to beat up his aggressor in a pathetic attempt to extort money and get revenge. The characters' bodies thus become battlefields for their daily struggle: damaged and battered bodies subjected to physical and sexual abuse in their search for income. *Beautiful Youth* must therefore be interpreted as a nihilistic film, inasmuch as it hints that this type of life story – those of NEETs without prospects – may lead people to prostitution and crime.

Magical Girl goes even further with its reversal of film noir conventions. One of its characters, Luis, is an unemployed high school teacher who has a teenage daughter who is ill with leukaemia. One of her last wishes is to wear the dress of her favourite manga character, which is available from a Japanese website at a cost of 900,000 yen (about €6,400) – plus 2,500,000 yen (about €18,000) for the accompanying magic wand. Luis tries everything to get the money: he sells his books, asks a friend for a loan, requests credit by phone and is about to rob a jeweller's shop when he accidentally meets Barbara, a beautiful woman who is going through a personal crisis that threatens her marriage to a wealthy psychiatrist. They spend the night together, and then Luis blackmails Barbara to get the money for the dress. She could recount everything to her husband or even ask him for the money, but instead she decides to get involved in a sordid plot of prostitution and sadomasochism. In this unlikely noir, the femme fatale becomes the victim of blackmail, but the blackmailer has already been introduced as a victim too: with whom should the audience then empathise?

Luis's obsession with the dress – and with the money it costs – is actually an allegory of the confusion of priorities in times of crisis, considering that what his daughter really wants is simply to spend more time with him. Likewise, Barbara's decision to put her physical integrity at risk to pay her debt is an allegory of austerity that stands for the excessive and unnecessary sacrifices that Iberian societies have had to make in order to cope with recession. In this regard, *Magical Girl* takes to the extreme the ruthless logic summarised in the expression 'more pain, more gain'. The first time Barbara prostitutes herself, a man warns her that there is a safe word: 'everything will stop only when you pronounce that word', he says, 'the longer you take to say it, the more money you will make'. The second time, however, there is no safe word, as she has asked for more money: the blank paper she receives before entering the room where she will be brutally mistreated represents the helplessness and hopelessness of every society subjected to the 'shock doctrine', the term used by Naomi Klein (2008) to describe the neoliberal strategy of implementing free market policies after armed conflicts or economic shocks, taking advantage of the fact that people are then too overwhelmed to dissent or resist.

The situation seems no less desperate in Portuguese family portraits, beginning with *Saint George*. Its main character, Jorge, is a boxer who has been hired as a debt collector for a company that buys private debts and coerces people to pay them back. This job places him in an insider position halfway between creditors and debtors – as well as between employers and employees – which allows film-maker Marco Martins to address a wide variety of life stories: on the one hand, those of small businessmen on the verge of bankruptcy; on the other, those of workers distressed by the threat of unemployment. Recession is thus depicted as a problem common to all social classes in a country in which nobody seems to be solvent. Wherever Jorge goes, his colleagues always use the same sentence to convince people to pay their debts: 'help us to help you', a catchy phrase that actually conceals a fallacy, inasmuch as debt collectors help creditors, not debtors. Its systematic repetition throughout the film echoes the rhetoric of the Troika years, in which people had 'the illusion of being helped', as Mariana Liz has pointed out, while their lives were made worse (2018: 246).

Marco Martins uses Jorge as a witness narrator to peek into different social strata. Through internal focalisation, the camera follows the character's gaze and shows what he sees: a depressed, decapitalised country where people strive to continue working despite the fact that their income is never enough to pay their debts. His job is supposed to be to intimidate debtors and, if necessary, to give them a beating, but Jorge's passive and hesitant nature prevents him from taking action for most of the film. In fact, as a boxer, his main ability is to withstand the blows, a feature that may be regarded as another allegory of the country in recession. After all, Jorge is also a victim; a former industrial worker with a complicated family situation: he still lives with his father – an insensitive man who thinks his son is good for nothing – and is temporarily separated from his partner – Susana, an Afro-Brazilian immigrant who is thinking of returning to her country with their child, Nelson. Under such circumstances, Jorge takes the job as a debt collector in order to get the money needed to rent an apartment in which to live with Susana and Nelson, away from his father's scorn. His plan is simple, but the crisis is not the right time to carry it out, an idea expressed through the camerawork itself: 'the constant tight framing', Liz explains, 'highlights the sense of entrapment that defines Jorge's character – in the boxing ring, in his professional, and in his personal life. From the start, Jorge is reduced to insignificance by framing choices that see people and buildings constrain him' (2018: 244).

Jorge's family house, for example, is depicted as a hostile environment in which it is impossible to feel at home. The place is a claustrophobic apartment located in a working-class neighbourhood – Bela Vista, south of Lisbon – that appears to be permanently crowded with relatives, neighbours and former workmates. There, Jorge acts like a caged animal: he barely leaves his room, and when he does so, he has to cross several barred metal gates to reach the street. In these sequences, the *mise en scène* conveys the feeling that he is always alone, isolated, fleeing from something or hiding from someone. This impression remains when he goes to Jamaica, the neighbourhood to which Susana has moved after leaving his house: a vertical slum inhabited by African immigrants that is located in Seixal, again south of Lisbon, on the periphery of the periphery. This area is a doubly marginalised space, a racially segregated ghetto disconnected from the city's main economic flows, beginning with the closest street – an attentive observer will notice that its multi-storey blocks have been built within a large plot surrounded by other buildings. The choice of these communities as settings for the film shows the places where the victims of the crisis are confined, but also mirrors the semi-peripheral condition of the Iberian Peninsula within Europe in a historical period that has been described as a moment of rejection disguised as a moment of acceptance by Boaventura de Sousa Santos (2014: 51).

Recession has also hit middle-class neighbourhoods such as Olivais, east of Lisbon, where *Colo* is set. This film chronicles the gradual disintegration of a family: the father, who is unemployed, stays at home all day, entering a downward spiral of depression and neglect; the mother, in turn, has two different jobs, one by day and one by night, so she is absent and exhausted most of the time; and their daughter, finally, faces her own teenage anxieties without any parental support. Their sense of entrapment is also expressed through framing strategies: this time, instead of a hand-held camera on the move, as in *Saint George*, film-maker Teresa Villaverde uses static shots that enclose the characters in rigid compositions with the help of architectural elements, especially windows – an opening that lets them look outside while remaining inside. These architectural metaphors allow Villaverde to delve into the psychological effects of the crisis, such as the father's loss of self-esteem and the mother's growing alienation.

The father's inability to maintain his role as breadwinner has led him to develop erratic and paranoid behaviour, until he assumes paternity of a child that is not his, just to recover a power position within the hegemonic masculinity framework. The mother, meanwhile, gradually disengages from her family situation while normalising self-exploitation as an inherent condition of making a living. There is no wonder that their daughter decides to escape from this family life towards the end of the film, though not through imagination, like the main character in *John From* (João Nicolau, 2015) – another teenage girl who lives in the more affluent district of Telheiras, north of Lisbon, where she can still dream of seducing a neighbour in a parallel universe. On the contrary, in *Colo*, the girl ends the film alone in a fisherman's shed, far from everything and from everyone, like Jorge in *Saint George*. The use of estrangement and defamiliarisation effects, as employed in Villaverde's previous films, contributes to obscure the motives of the characters and, what is more important, to denounce the arbitrariness of the crisis, from which nobody is safe. The disintegration of this family, in which every character decides to cope with recession on their own, is the outcome of the tendency to isolation that *Arabian Nights* and *The Nothing Factory* try to counteract with their collective accounts. Arguably, then, one of the purposes of the agonistic narratives of these family portraits would be to warn the audience about the limits and risks of individual responses to the crisis.

Ambiguous Identifications

Prioritising the representation of victims has also indirectly helped to keep the sectors that have caused the crisis away from the spotlight. If we all are victims, is there no one responsible for the economic and political decisions that led us to recession and austerity? The empathic bridge has also served to reflect on social and individual responsibilities, especially in multi-protagonist films, such as the Spanish comedies *Murieron por encima de sus posibilidades* (*Dying Beyond their Means*, Isaki Lacuesta, 2014) or *Tiempo después* (*Some Time Later*, José Luis Cuerda, 2018), as well as in titles portraying different professional collectives, from bricklayers in *Os Fenómenos* (Alfonso Zarauza, 2014) to politicians in *El reino* (*The Realm*, Rodrigo Sorogoyen, 2018). In these works, the characters' life stories are used to describe the social dynamics before and after the crisis, but also to judge them retrospectively from a moral point of view, giving rise to ambiguous discourses that may blame the victims and excuse those in power.

Dying Beyond their Means – another film with this awful expression in the title – is an inter-class satire that avoids entering into dichotomies between good and bad characters, since no one is a paragon of virtue. Its five main characters are victims of recession who meet in a mental hospital and devise a plan to overcome the crisis and take revenge on those who they consider responsible for their misfortunes. Each one stands for a different social stratum: Miguel, an investor, belongs to the upper class; Albert, the owner of a pet store, to the middle class; Iván, a debt collector, and Julio, a conservative homeless man who insists on taking his son to a private school, to the working class; and finally Jordi, a drug dealer, to the underclass. Their respective life stories are introduced through flashbacks in order to explain the factors that have led them to the mental hospital, but also to parody the excesses of the socio-economic system and the complacency of the population prior to the crisis.

As the narrative progresses, the film also mocks the shortcomings of anti-austerity movements, represented here by this inter-class alliance formed by the characters, whose methods and purposes turn out to be brutal and lacking in ambition. In the long set-piece that closes the film, the characters break into a secret party full of wealthy, beautiful people with the aim of kidnapping the president of the central bank and torturing several corrupt ministers responsible for cutbacks in public services.[9] Their political claims, however, make it clear that they do not intend to change or improve the situation, but just to restore their previous privileged position – in the case of the upper class, embodied by Miguel – or, at least, the illusion of prosperity in which they lived – in the case of the popular classes, headed by Julio in this final set-piece. By presenting the characters as a gang of naive fools doomed to failure, film-maker Isaki Lacuesta hints that these people might be fighting for the wrong reasons:

it should not be a matter of returning to the status quo prior to austerity but of attempting to develop a fairer and more equitable system.

Corruption finally comes to the fore in *The Realm*, a political thriller inspired by real events taken from several case summaries (see Zas Marcos and Pinheiro 2018). Its main character, Manuel López Vidal, is an ambitious party man who has benefited for years from peddling influence and misappropriation of public funds while waiting to move up within the hierarchy of his party – an unnamed party that presents many similarities to the conservative People's Party, especially with its regional branches in Madrid and Valencia. The appearance of an incriminating recording in which he talks about illegal activities with a city councillor causes his expulsion from the metaphorical realm referred in the title: his career must be sacrificed in order to save the party. Manuel, however, refuses to step aside – why him and not any other? – and decides to gather evidences to incriminate his colleagues, in an attempt to prove that he was just a pawn in a larger system.

Throughout its first half, *The Realm* meticulously describes the power relations within the party, as well as the inner workings of its corrupt networks. Up to this point, except for Luis Bárcenas in *B* (David Ilundain, 2015),[10] corrupt politicians had usually been depicted as stereotyped supporting characters in austerity cinema.[11] Manuel, in turn, is an antihero with whom the audience can empathise, inasmuch as his illegal activities are explicitly compared with ordinary people's petty thefts: in the most questionable sequence in the film, Manuel sees how a young client keeps the extra money he has wrongly received as change after having paid his bill in a bar. This wicked comparison seems to state that corruption is, to a greater or lesser extent, an inherent attribute of Spanish society, as if Manuel's life story might be compared with anyone else's, ignoring the fact that he held a privileged position that was completely out of reach for most of the population. The issue, according to film-maker Rodrigo Sorogoyen, would not then be who is corrupt, but who is not; an ambiguous and indulgent approach that is not so far from the statement 'we have lived beyond our means'.

Manuel rebels against the system, but his reasons have nothing to do with a desire for justice or an attempt at atonement. On the contrary, he is motivated by revenge. The final sequence, in which he tries to expose the party's fraudulent accounting on a TV show, conveys a misleading message: instead of showing the party's account books, the anchorwoman corners Manuel with her questions, blaming him and missing the big picture, just as the party wanted from the beginning. This ending reproduces a usual narrative convention in conspiracy thrillers, according to which the truth remains hidden because society is never prepared to face it – consequently, why should anyone bother to try to change things? The anchorwoman's question that closes the film is supposed to be an invitation to self-criticism, but it actually induces self-blame: 'Have you ever stopped to think', she asks to both Manuel and the audience while staring at the camera, 'about what you were doing?' The way the question is asked and filmed leaves no room for empowerment: there may be some viewers who have somehow benefited from corruption and others who have not, but *The Realm* seems to suggest that the latter are also guilty of not having been able to prevent the former from doing it.

Conclusion: Exemplary Lives

Allegory has become the main rhetorical figure in austerity cinema at a time when collective certainties are constructed from individual feelings and perceptions: anything, and especially anyone, may stand for a country in recession. For this reason, many characters have been used as social signifiers to embody different attitudes and situations related to the crisis, both in documentary and fiction films. Their life stories have been adapted to cinema through several systems of representation, among which first-person monologues and internal focalisation stand out. These narratives have allowed film-makers to establish an empathic bridge between the characters and the audience in order to promote an inter-class identification with the victims of austerity, who usually play the role of civil, secular martyrs in these films. Accordingly, this technology of political imagination, as Germán Labrador Méndez has called it (2012), must be regarded as a counter-hegemonic strategy against self-blaming discourses that have ultimately helped reinforce social bonds.

Some of the titles adopting this dynamic, however, may lead to victimhood or, what is worse, to confusing self-criticism with self-blame. A few films take advantage of this empathic bridge to spread the line of argument of those in power, according to which all citizens have been more or less responsible for the crisis, regardless of the scale and impact of their actions and choices. Nevertheless, the systematic effort of Iberian film-makers to show the plight of the victims has been mainly intended to turn compassion into solidarity and empowerment, despite the fact that this strategy has sometimes bordered on sensationalism or led viewers to identify with the wrong people. After all, empathy in film does not depend on taste or ideology, but on the approach and skill with which film-makers address any kind of situation.

Notes

1. Works such as *Um Pouco Mais Pequeno que o Indiana* (*Slightly Smaller Than Indiana*, Daniel Blaufuks, 2006), *Vete de mí* (*Go Away from Me*, Víctor García León, 2006), *Concursante* (*The Contestant*, Rodrigo Cortés, 2007), *Ruínas* (*Ruins*, Manuel Mozos, 2009), *A Espada e a Rosa* (*The Sword and the Rose*, João Nicolau, 2010) and *Biutiful* (Alejandro González Iñárritu, 2010) can be

interpreted retrospectively as a premonition of the economic shift, as I have argued elsewhere (Villarmea Álvarez 2018: 9–10).
2. Many writers have taken a similar position in their books on the topic, at least among Spanish novelists, as argued by Jochen Mecke (2017: 212).
3. Albritton specifically writes on Spanish cinema, but his ideas can also be applied to Portuguese film.
4. Some of these films would be *Fin* (*The End*, Jorge Torregrosa, 2012), *Los últimos días* (*The Last Days*, Àlex and David Pastor, 2013) and *El bar* (*The Bar*, Alex de la Iglesia, 2017).
5. These screen tests are not spontaneous interviews but re-enacted speeches, a *mise en scène* technique that had previously been used in the documentary fiction 二十四城记 (*24 City*, Jia Zhang-ke, 2008), another film based on the testimonies of former industrial workers.
6. *Arabian Nights* was filmed between August 2013 and August 2014, when Portuguese macroeconomic data was at its worst: at the time, the country's GDP had been decreasing for more than two consecutive years and the unemployment rate had just reached its peak – 17.5 per cent – in the first quarter of 2013.
7. In fact, Gomes played an active role in the 2012 debate on public funding for film in Portugal (see Ribas and Cunha 2015).
8. These documentaries, according to Araceli Rodríguez Mateos (2018: 198–218), have contributed to turn the circulation of life stories into an empowerment strategy in the Spanish context.
9. The desire for revenge against bankers and politicians was a widespread fantasy in the early 2010s which appears in other Spanish films such as *El mundo es nuestro* (Alfonso Sánchez, 2012), *Justi&Cia* (Ignacio Estaregui, 2014) and *El desconocido* (*Retribution*, Dani de la Torre, 2015), as explained by Marta Álvarez (2018).
10. Luis Bárcenas worked in the accounts department of the People's Party from 1990 to 2009. His involvement in several corruption scandals led to his detention and imprisonment in 2013. The film *B* is a legal drama based on an earlier play – *Ruz-Bárcenas* (Jordi Casanovas, 2014) – which transcribed Bárcenas's testimony in the Audiencia Nacional.
11. A few examples would be the villains in *Cinco metros cuadrados* (*Five Square Metres*, Max Lemcke, 2011), *Justi&Cia* and *Dying Beyond their Means*.

10. THE DOUBLE FORM OF NEOLIBERAL SUBJUGATION: CRISIS ON THE EASTERN EUROPEAN SCREEN

Anna Batori

In 1989 popular revolutions exploded across Eastern Europe, bringing an end to the socialist state system in the region. Without doubt, no other region has embraced the adoption of neoliberal policies as enthusiastically as the post-socialist states (Appel and Orenstein 2016). Yet three decades after the fall of the Berlin Wall, Eastern Europe still faces severe economic problems. The rapid sociopolitical changes and the transformation of the welfare system brought about mass unemployment, a crisis of sovereign debt and various forms of austerity packages that all exposed the economies of European post-socialist countries. The hardship of the transformation from state socialism to neoliberal capitalism was further intensified by the 2007–08 global financial crisis that put the region at the centre of economic recession (Kattel 2010). In view of this it is not surprising that, being disappointed by the post-1989 neoliberal reforms – with relatively little chance of reaching Western development levels (Kornai 2006; Kattel 2010) – the region entered the age of what Boyer (2012: 19) defines as *nostomania* – a desire to recapture the old socialist way of life.

This chapter investigates patterns of neoliberal crisis in contemporary Eastern European cinema. By positing a post-2010 Eastern European narrative structure called the 'double form of neoliberal subjugation', this essay examines the heavily gendered visual formations through selected case studies. Dissecting four films from four different Eastern European countries – the Slovenian Damjan Kozole's *Slovenka* (*A Call Girl*, 2009), the Romanian Ruxana Zenide's *Ryna* (2005), the Czech Matěj Chlupáček and Michal Samir's

Bez doteku (*Touchless*, 2013) and the Hungarian Szabolcs Hajdu's *Bibliothèque Pascal* (2010) – the study sets up a visual-narrative analysis of neoliberal (self-)colonisation. It argues that, along with the *nostomanic* resurrection of the socialist male figure, there is a tendency in the region's cinema to feature Western male figures as powerful, authoritative and often violent characters who exploit Eastern European women by sexual trafficking and/or other forms of corporeal violence that render these females obedient to them.

It must be stated that, as diversified as the Eastern European sociopolitical and economic transformation was between 1989 and 1991, equally as different are the faces that the current neoliberal structures and crises display in the region. Thus, it would be incorrect to state that political leaderships and economic policies have identical forms in the post-socialist area. However, the collectivist past, its pronatalist ideology and gender reconfiguration policy – together with the hardship of the economic transformation and current populist tendencies – unite these countries under a common sociohistorical umbrella.

The economic doctrine of neoliberalism that originally aimed to develop market economies, and proposed practices to promote human well-being 'within an institutional framework characterized by private property rights, individual liberty, unencumbered market and free trade' (Harvey 2007b: 22), has often been labelled a 'shock therapy programme' for the post-1989 Eastern European economy and society (Dale and Hardy 2011). The prompt ascendancy of neoliberal ideology centred on privatisation, macroeconomic stabilisation, the liberalisation of domestic prices and the construction of new markets resulted in a severe decline in economic output (Dale and Fabry 2018). As Kattel puts it, the recession that East European countries experienced in the 1990s was 'worse than the Great Depression in the United States and World War II in Western Europe' (2010: 52). The massive inflow of foreign direct investments (FDI), the rise of cross-border loans, exchange rate depreciation (Appel and Orenstein 2016) and the region's incapacity to address the crisis resulted in around a 20–25 per cent decline in GDP and a 50 per cent decline in agricultural production (Berend and Bugaric 2015), which led to mass unemployment (de la Cámara 1997) and a severe social crisis. The economic crash resulted in declining living standards, growing suicide rates (Minagawa 2013), gender, race and labour force status inequalities (Heyns 2005), migration to the West from the Eastern European region (Okólski 1998) and the rise of human trafficking (Surtees 2008).

While Eastern European governments believed that Western neoliberal paradigms must be adopted in order to achieve higher wages and thus financial security and better living standards (de la Cámara 1997), most countries did not count on the price they would have to pay for neoliberal reforms and European Union membership. Their absolute dependence on the IMF, World Bank and the European Union[1] enabled Western business leaders and policymakers to exploit the region for its 'low wages, high productivity and simple taxes' (Dale and Fabry 2018), which contributed to anomic decades in the region. As Dale and Fabry put it,

> the logic of transformation was not simply to liberate the countries of the region from the shackles of communism or to unleash entrepreneurial talent [...] but to open up the economies of the region to the exigencies of global capital, while restructuring and bolstering the power of domestic elites. The outcome has been growing disillusionment, and public discontent with simplistic attempts to install a market economy and Western-style democracy [...] The capitalist triumphalism of the early 1990s has everywhere given way to the dystopian realities of an authoritarian, restrictive and reactionary mode of neoliberal capitalism. (2018: 248)

By 2008 the post-socialist region had become economically liberal, yet when compared to the West's early to mid-nineteenth-century or post-Second World War level, it was still behind Europe's developed countries (Berend and Bugaric 2015). Also, by the mid-2000s the financial flows that had fostered neoliberal changes slowly started to dry up (Appel and Orenstein 2016), and the 2007 global financial crisis eventually prompted Western banks to stop extending credit in the region. The lack of financial support, which was only reinitiated in 2009 by the Vienna Initiative, together with the declining demand for exports, pushed the post-socialist countries into a deeper crisis, with draconian austerity measures imminently on the horizon. These included reducing wages and benefits, raising taxes and cutting spending on health and welfare (Dale and Hardy 2011), while accumulating more Western debt on low interest rates.[2] The privatisation of public institutions, utilities, social welfare provision and the wholesale commodification of nature, cultural forms and history – together with the accumulated foreign debt, the monetisation of exchange and taxation and austerity measures (Harvey 2007b) – gave birth to a crisis-laden twenty-first-century Eastern Europe.

This is not to say, of course, that the neoliberal free market ideology and foreign support only caused damage. Without the support of the European Union and Western capital, the region would be still at the 1989 economic level (Berend and Bugaric 2015). Foreign companies established retail networks, high-tech industrial sectors and domestic and occidental workplaces, while the post-socialist countries' landscape was slowly shifting towards a modernised, capitalist territory. On the other hand, the neoliberal transformation and crisis caused severe economic decline, massive unemployment, migration and dependence on foreign capital (Lane 2010). As Berend and Bugaric summarise, Eastern European countries 'that joined the EU in 2004 and 2007 have declined, rather than improved since accession' (2015: 777). The current crisis led to 'a rediscovery of the economic role of nation states' (Dale and Hardy 2011) and authoritarian populism, which goes hand in hand with Euroscepticism, neoconservative and chauvinistic movements and militarism (Polyakova and Shekhovtsov 2016).

Populism and Self-Colonising Structures in Eastern Europe

The penetration of multinational companies into the Eastern European economic structure and the immense outmigration from the region into wealthier European countries set up a new centre–periphery socio-geographic structure, with the West being the object of desire and the East the marginal brother that will never catch up with its sibling. The discursive practices that blame Eastern Europe for the region's economic difficulties (Dale and Hardy 2011), and identify post-socialist countries as 'backward, inefficient, underproducing, politically juvenile, oppositional to [Western] identities and generally untrustworthy' (Dauphinée 2003: 194), only emphasise the region's suppressed socio-economic position via Orientalist readings. In this way, the post-1989 transition and European neoliberal crisis resurrected the old West–East dichotomy. With the concentrated Western geopolitical power on one side, and its 'socially stigmatized brother' (Buchowski 2006: 474) on the other, the hierarchy between the centre and periphery became more and more sharp, thus giving way to a new orientalist mindset and self-colonising social imagination.

Alexander Kiossev uses self-colonisation as a concept for cultures that succumbed to Western European cultural power without military conquest. According to him, these states stand under foreign cultural supremacy and voluntarily enter the colonial structure to become the 'extracolonial periphery'. As Kiossev summarises this process, while these nations absorbed the values of the centre,

> they imported something else: the [. . .] parodical image of themselves [. . .] they were compelled to internalize these embarrassing images precisely as they were coming from their source of recognition and were charged with its authority. All this fostered a controversial nation-building process: one that borrowed models hand in hand with resistance against the models. Such borrowings were meant to Europeanize yet at the same time they stood in the way of actual cultural emancipation as they never failed to recycle the secondary, submissive, and opaque role of small peripheral nations on the world scene, thus failing to acknowledge their sovereignty, authenticity, and autonomy. (Kiossev 2011)

In the midst of severe economic crisis, populism became a defining political strategy in Europe. While there is no doubt that the phenomenon grew out of the crisis and failure of neoliberal reforms, in the post-socialist region the burden of the socialist past further deepened the general disappointment. I argue that people in Eastern Europe have been on a quest for a leader who would stand for national values and citizens' security and protection. As Weyland (1999) emphasises, in a populist structure, the leader reaches the mass in a direct way, while building a new or old populist party with a low level of institutionalisation. In this manner, populism in Eastern Europe acts as a form of *nostomania*, a return to the old totalitarian socialist system whose main paternalistic figure promises wealth and safety to his citizens, while abusing them. The periphery–centre dichotomy and self-colonisation imaginary thus not only signal the economic recession but a certain nostalgia for the past to reset the gender-differentiated parental sociopolitical structure.

Socialist and Post-Socialist Patriarchy and Gender on Screen

Based on egalitarian ideas, socialist ideology emphasised gender equality and liberation, with several gender policies that fostered this ideological commitment. Besides maternity leave, childcare and free medical and healthcare, the system had a quota that ensured the political visibility of women (Racioppi and O'Sullivan 2009). Despite these measures, however, the socialist state apparatuses remained heavily masculine. The regimes' pronatalist policy ensured women's social representation and role as 'married working mothers', with the aim of disguising unemployment by lengthy maternity leave (Verdery 1996: 67) and a focus on the role of females as suppliers of the nations' future generation. As Katherine Verdery notes, socialist structures functioned as an extended family – a 'zadruga-state' – that was composed of families tied to a 'patriarchal authority with the father Party as its head' (1996: 64). Thus, nuclear relations and roles were embedded into a much larger social structure that made citizens dependent on the socialist father figure, while oppressing women via policies that exploited their bodies and hindered emancipation.

In her book examining the socialist films of Romania and their post-1989 transformation, Florentina C. Andreescu (2013) identifies four commonplaces that illustrate this gender dichotomy in cinema. The Other as the nexus of power, she argues, is illustrated by the nation and the socialist state, while the two other screen characters, the worker hero and the ideal female heroine, are represented as satisfied, obedient bodies within the sociopolitical structure. This heavily gendered structure can be also traced through socialist films that represent female rape. Thanks to the strict propaganda that was peculiar to the cinema industry and prescribed what could be screened and what not, sexual violence against women rarely occurred in these narratives. In the few examples we find, females passively accept their suppressed role and succumb to their male partners. Krsto Papić's *Lisice* (*Handcuffs*, 1969), for instance, tells the story of the arrest of post-Soviet communists in 1948 in the Dalmatian hinterland. The sexual assault in the film happens just after the wedding of the young and attractive Višnja (Jagoda Kaloper) and her husband, Ante (Fabijan Šovagović). While the crowd celebrates with the newly wed couple, Andrija (Adem Čejvan), the dominant male father figure and politician in the story, accidently falls and hits his head against a stone. The young Višnja takes care of his injuries in a remote room of an isolated building in the barren landscape. After he regains consciousness, Andrija realises the young bride's vulnerable position and rapes her. The long scene of the violent sexual assault is portrayed in graphic detail, with rhythmic close-ups and metaphoric cross-cutting between the assault and the celebration. Andrija's strong physique and power are emphasised via his dominant male physique – his moustache and hairy chest – and his statement that even if the woman is afraid, he will get what he wants. After the rape, Višnja is captured lying in a Jesus-like position on the floor, while the man relaxes and eats an apple on the bed. Interestingly, it is the woman who later prays to God for forgiveness and punishment. After the insult, the celebrating males attack Višnja for dishonouring her husband and kill the young woman. In the end Andrej is jailed for his political activities against the ruling powers and not for the sexual violence he committed against Višnja.

Handcuffs precisely demonstrates the socialist period's highly gendered structures: the virgin, beautiful Višnja is portrayed as a loving, obedient bride, who respects her husband and is ready to bear children with him. As a symbol of the nation, she stands for purity and the maternal future. However, after her rape by the state – as represented by the figure of Andrej and the men celebrating the wedding – she becomes a victim of ruling powers that hold her responsible for the sexual assault. In this metaphorical framework, the nation is oppressed by the state that condemns her for dishonouring the community and eventually kills Višnja.

The representation of females in films of the socialist period thus not only pinpoints the Other–coloniser and subjected–ruler dichotomies but, through sexual assault or bodily violence against them, it communicates a metaphorical message, that is, the punishment and killing of the nation by socialist powers. In the films of the transition period, however, these roles undergo a dramatic change whose main characteristic is the lack of a father figure and thus the paternalist (though abusive) state. Instead of the righteous, strong male character who would dominate cinematic narratives, the post-1989 film corpus gives way to weakening worker heroes and anomic individuals (Andreescu 2013). Lucie Pintilie's *Balanta* (*The Oak*, 1992) for instance, starts with the death of the communist ex-politician father of the main protagonist, Nela (Maja Morgenstein). She decides to donate the dead body for research and education, but the hospital rejects her offer and the wish of the deceased. The middle-aged daughter then decides to escape Bucharest and travel through Romania, where she almost gets raped by unknown factory workers in the countryside. In Pintilie's film, the body of the dead father – the corpse of the state – becomes an unwanted object, while the daughter gets into dangerous situations in which she is incapable of protecting herself. The process of emasculation – the death of the father figure and the growing tendency to portray violent males on screen – thus starts at the very beginning of the new capitalist transformation.

In her postcolonial reading of Eastern European film and literature, Anikó Imre (2012) also addresses the process of emasculation as the region's reaction to the failure to meet European ideals. In this discourse, women and other national minorities remain in an internally colonised position against the insecure colonised masculinities that inflict sexual violation on them. Indeed, the post-2000 Eastern European film corpus, which features an increasing tendency of violence against women, signals a dramatic change in gender relations in cinema that is illustrated by the resurrection of the lost socialist father figure as the Western capitalist male (Andreescu 2013). In this way, the inflicted neoliberal policy and crisis in the region go hand in hand with the repatriarchalisation of its cinematic discourse. That is, after the death of the socialist father, a new narrative has been born that shows women with a new identity on screen. Instead of heroic mothers, films often portray females in highly sexualised and subordinated contexts, with sexual trafficking and prostitution as central concerns. Whether rape – as in Titus Muntean's *Kino Caravan* (2009) and Peter Calin Netzler's *Maria* (2003) from Romania; Jan Cvitkovič's *Odgrobadogroba* (*Gravehopping*, 2005) and Matěj Chlupáček's *Bez doteku* (*Touchless*, 2005) from the Czech Republic; or Kornél Mundruczó's *Delta* (2008) from Hungary – or trafficking and prostitution – as in the Romanian Cătălin Mitulescu's *Loverboy* (2011), Myroslav Slaboshpytskyi's *Plemya* (*The Tribe*, 2014) from Ukraine or the Serbian Vinko Bresan's *Nije Kraj* (*Will Not End Here*, 2008) – or other forms of mental and physical abuse – as in Srdjan Spasojević's *Srpski Film* (*A Serbian Film*, 2012) and Maja Miloš's *Klip* (*Clip*, 2012) – women are placed in oppressed, subjected positions in Eastern European narratives.[3]

Besides the revival of the patriarchal system by violent Western male characters, the post-2000 film corpus illustrates the (self)-colonised structure and crisis-laden position of the region through the transformation of the socialist father figure into an impotent male character who is obliged to cooperate with the Western, colonising power by betraying his family. I call this narrative the 'double form of neoliberal subjugation' whereby the internally colonised, emasculated male figure uses his power to oppress his wife, daughter and other female characters on screen. These women then undergo a series of physical and sexual assaults that – portrayed in explicitly violent and pornographic sequences on screen – eventually transform their bodies and very identity into a self-colonised imaginary.

Extreme Corporeal Violence in Eastern European Cinema

Since the 2000s there has been a growing tendency in global cinema to aestheticise bodily violence on the audiovisual, narrative as well as thematic level. Called 'extreme cinema' (Horeck and Kendall 2011; Frey 2016) or 'feel-bad film' (Lübecker 2015), this trend is often associated with New French Extremity, the first wave in contemporary European cinema that used extreme graphic representation and provocative topics on screen. Western scholarship has examined this wave as a visual way of conveying a political message that goes via the body of the spectator to his or her intellect (Lübecker 2015). Thus, the symbiosis of corporeality and violence on screen, and its heightened presence in cinema, references changing socio-economic conditions, that is, the easier access to and commodification of human bodies in the capitalist age. As Ipek A. Celik Rappas argues, 'Stylistic violence may provide a commentary on the violent disposability of bodies as well as their adaptability under the post-Fordist economy obsessed with efficiency, competition and risk-taking' (Rappas 2016: 677). As the following case studies demonstrate, in the post-2000 Eastern European discourse, corporeal violence against women and its extreme visual representation on screen symbolises a double form of neoliberal subjugation – a growing tendency towards *nostomania*, populism and neoliberal dissatisfaction.

Symbolic Corporeal Transformations: *Touchless* and *Ryna*

Ruxana Zenide's *Ryna* (2005) focuses on the eponymous teenage heroine who runs her father's garage in a small village in the Romanian Danube delta. Because of her father's desire to have a son, Ryna has been brought up as a boy: she must dress as a man, not wear make-up and have short hair. While she assists her alcoholic father's illegal businesses in town, which involve initiating mechanical failures in cars at night so that they will have more clients the next day, Ryna's desire to dress as a woman and go to the local festival continually grows. At the same time, she becomes the focus of male attention in the village. Besides the mayor of the town and the young postman who have a crush on her, she takes the interest of a newly arrived French anthropologist who is looking for the roots of Latinity in Romania. The man asks Ryna to participate in his research by letting him measure her body and she eventually agrees. They slowly develop a close relationship, but after a failed attempt at a kiss, the young girl chooses to go home and returns to her father. The old man, however, decides to sacrifice Ryna's virginity on the altar of prolonging his garage business with the village, and allows her to be raped by the mayor.

The film illustrates a closed world where women's identity is prescribed as inferior (Pop 2014). Ryna stands under the control of her emasculated father whose violent behaviour chases away the girl's mother. The teenager thus gets stuck in a very patriarchal society, with male figures dominating her life. First, her repressive father, then the French anthropologist and finally the mayor take advantage of her body. While Ryna finds rescue in photography, her passion also signifies a highly gendered structure.

In the opening sequence of the film, the girl is portrayed capturing a bull that eventually attacks her so that she has to run away. This highly symbolic scene puts Ryna in opposition to the testosterone-filled social context that rules the narrative of the film. Wherever she goes, she is objectified by male power. First, her father oppresses the teenager by demanding male behaviour from her. Ryna obediently agrees to work as a car mechanic and hide any trace of her femininity. She keeps her jewellery in a box far from home and wears an oily mechanic's overall and dark clothes throughout the film. Her male iconography only changes when she goes to the festival: her pink dress and bright kerchief emphasise her female features, which leads to tragedy. While the French anthropologist uses a genuine means of getting close to Ryna, the mayor brutally rapes her in the presence of her father. Being haemophiliac, the teenager goes into hospital to be treated for blood loss, where the men of the town accuse the French doctor of rape. Dressed as a man, Ryna suddenly appears to state that the sexual violence was committed by an unknown person, and then leaves the hospital. After the rape, she thus repositions herself in the male role, which gives her a safe position in the town.

The peripheral Romanian village in *Ryna* demonstrates its entrapment in the socialist era: it is not only the naturalistic setting of the film – the dilapidated grey buildings, dusty roads and old cars – but the very realistic film form that emphasises the girl's enclosed position. The dull colours of the scenes, together with the hand-held, often claustrophobic close-ups and barely lit images that accompany Ryna's movements and her inner journey in the film, give the narrative space a suffocating atmosphere. After the rape, the rhythm of the sequences slows down, and instead of flowing camera work, *Ryna* uses fixed camera positions that capture the girl in frontal large and medium shots. These tableau-like images give the close of the film a slow pace and, together with Ryna's constant silence, create a still portrait of female subjugation in contemporary Romania.

Besides the textuality of the film, the very grid of gender hierarchy reawakens the epoch. The town is led by a corrupt totalitarian figure who, in exchange for Ryna's virginity, promises to keep the garage and save the father's business from the penetration of a multinational chain. As the main capitalist power in the film, the mayor threatens the mechanic with the establishment of a foreign company. Eventually, Ryna, the untainted young girl and the only woman in the film, pays the price of the capitalist transformation. Her body – like the nation's – is scarified by the emasculated father figure whose response to the globalist change is to sell out his daughter. Ryna thus stands in a doubly

CRISIS ON THE EASTERN EUROPEAN SCREEN

Figure 10.1   Ryna's tableau-like positioning in *Ryna* (Ruxana Zenide, 2005).

subjected position. Not knowing how to react to the neoliberal transformation, the socialist father figure betrays his own child, while he himself also stands under the supervision of the mayor.

The appearance of the French doctor – and hence the foreign power – starts the series of tragedies in Ryna's life. Dressed in his white uniform, the anthropologist's iconography stands in strong contrast to the portrayal of the other men. This colonising character – the intelligent, civilised Western doctor – takes palm-prints and photos of the locals – the uncivilised tribe – which sharpens the periphery–centre dichotomy. In this self-colonising process, the inhabitants succumb to his cultural power, as does Ryna by starting to learn French to get closer to his authority. While the girl first rejects his wish to measure her, she eventually lets the doctor touch her body, which only exacerbates her subject position in the film. From this moment, she sinks deeper into her colonised, oppressed role. Still, while the Western power's penetration into her intimate sphere is soft violence, her rape by the mayor is a brutal deed. Her self-colonising process thus ends with the violent extermination of her female body, which outlines the oppressive power-structure of the current Romanian sociopolitical establishment.

Like *Ryna*, the Czech *Touchless* represents a double neoliberal subjugation via the tropes of the emasculated father figure, the absence of the mother and a dominating capitalist power. The teenager Jolana (Teresa Vítu) lives with her mother and stepfather in Prague. During the day, she lives the life of an average schoolgirl, but at night she is persistently raped by her stepfather. At first her mother looks away and tries not to notice the change in her daughter's behaviour, but when she realises the situation, she succumbs to the wishes of the man and sacrifices Jolana on the altar of her marriage. Later, the stepfather decides to sell the girl to the manager of a brothel, where she is constantly beaten up and raped. It seems, however, that Jolana becomes identified with her subjected role to such a degree that she cannot think of herself as a free individual. When she is offered freedom, she hesitates whether to accept it and start a new life, or stay in the brothel. While the film has an open ending, *Touchless* suggests the latter: in the grid of male domination, she has taken on the role of the objectified prostitute which she cannot leave behind.

Like *Ryna*, *Touchless* represents a deeply patriarchal society with an absence of maternal roles. Jolana stands under the absolute control of her policeman stepfather, who does suspicious business with the Czech underworld. After becoming pregnant, the teenager loses the very right to her body: she is obliged to have an abortion and then work in a brothel. The last maternal bond to her mother and her own unborn child thus gets finally broken; deprived of her reproductive rights and access to her own womb, she succumbs to the will of her stepfather to become a prostitute. In the brothel, however, she acquires another father figure. Kleiner (Ondrej Malý), the German-Czech manager of the place, has an ambivalent relationship with Jolana: as the head of the business, the older man pretends to take care of the girl, but he also brutally rapes her over and over again. Stuck in this male-dominated world, Jolana is humiliated by all the protagonists in the film. Sold by her stepfather, she has to work in a deeply profit-oriented world made up of Western clients, where she faces daily psychological and mental abuse. The colleague of her stepfather who tries to save her only aggravates this crisis. First, he pretends to be a client in order to get Jolana out of the brothel. However, he then decides to claim his right to sleep with the girl. Disappointed in her 'prince', Jolana leaves the bedroom and watches while the man is thrown out of the brothel.

Touchless illustrates the mental and corporeal transformation of Jolana from an innocent schoolgirl into a prostitute. In the first half of the film, she is dressed as an average teenager with natural look and loose clothes. In the brothel, her body becomes heavily fetishised. It is not only her heavy make-up and provocative outfit that signal the change but her very behaviour in enduring the daily abuse without resistance. Her dependence on older, male, father-like figures throughout the film signals her absolute subjected role: sold by her emasculated stepfather, she steps into the world of capital acquired through female rape. Jolana's transformation thus signals the neoliberal changes in the region: from the crisis-laden socialist home, she moves into a profit-oriented space based on bodily exploitation. The highly stylised visual context that conveys her captive position – the blue-lit scenes, harsh shadows, the double-framing spatial choreography and fast zoom-ins – create an unrealistic, dream-like context, which stands in strong contrast to Jolana's natural-coloured, socialist childhood home.

Figure 10.2   Jolana's stylised double-framing position in *Touchless* (Matěj Chlupáček and Michal Samir, 2013).

Interestingly, while the *mise en scène* of the film changes – with fluorescent lights and vivid colours dominating the screen in the brothel – the gender roles depicted in *Touchless* do not alter. Whether in the socialist home or the brothel, Jolana gets stuck in her doubly subjected role by succumbing to her stepfather and then to Kleiner, the neoliberal power in the film. Because she has been socialised to subjugate herself to the male figures in this modern social context, Jolana's actions become understandable to the viewer and trigger sympathy as well as pity in the audience.

'This EU, it costs us a lot of money': *A Call Girl* and *Bibliothèque Pascal*

While *Ryna* and *Touchless* follow the paths of two teenagers, the Slovenian *A Call Girl* features a university student who decides to follow the road of prostitution in order to acquire a flat and have a stable financial background. The 23-year-old Aleksandra (Nina Ivanišin) advertises herself as the 'Slovenian Girl' (*Slovenksa*) in the newspapers and has a prosperous business with foreign clients. She soon buys a luxury flat in the heart of Ljubljana, but is threatened by the local underworld, which blackmails her to join their circle. Aleksandra escapes the city and decides to reside temporarily in her father's home in the countryside to get time to find a solution to her problems. She eventually changes her nickname to 'Naïve' and restarts her business in the city, but her income does not cover the bank loan she took out to pay for her flat. Losing her friends, clients and home, she finally moves in with her father.

As well as her struggles with the Slovenian underworld and her mortgage, Aleksandra is wanted by the police for questioning about the death of a

German politician. This narrative line runs through the whole film, as it causes a national scandal. Whether on the television or through other media platforms, Aleksandra is constantly followed by the news media, which wants to discover the identity of the 'Slovenian Girl'. The German member of the European Parliament dies of cardiac arrest after he takes Viagra before meeting Aleksandra. In the film's opening shot, the girl enters the hotel room of the gasping man and, noticing his critical state, calls reception for help. Before escaping, she takes all the man's money, and only learns of his death from the news later. In the next scene, Aleksandra is shown sitting in a cab whose driver complains about the European Union, which, according to him, only causes headache and financial trouble to Slovenians. The film's establishing shot thus makes a clear statement about abusive Western power, which is further illustrated by the visual depiction of the German politician. While Aleksandra's natural look – her black hair, white skin and slim figure – radiate elegance, the representation of the overweight, grasping old man mediates greed and wealth. The German politician is incapable of answering the girl's questions and, although she tries to help by bringing a glass of water, Aleksandra's facial expression remains numb. She lacks any emotional feedback when it comes to business, and in this regard she does not differ much from her clients.

As representative of the nation, the Slovenian Girl takes on a contradictory position in the narrative. On the one hand, she is sexually exploited by visiting Westerners, while on the other, she deliberately chooses to serve them. Aleksandra's only goal is to have enough money for her flat and her expensive lifestyle and, as an English literature university student, she steps on to the road of self-colonisation. Realising that the only way to achieve capital is through the commodification of her body, she starts playing according to neoliberal rules. She uses her English to conduct business with Western consumers, and her body to gain what she wants from society. Knowledge and corporeality thus merge in the capitalist space of the city that brings her prosperity and satisfaction.

However, as the Slovenian Girl, Aleksandra is eventually punished for her colonised, semi-subjected identity – the local prostitute who serves Western clients – and the local gangsters soon blackmail her for money. Unlike Aleksandra's clients, who are older, less attractive males from Italy, Germany and other EU countries, the pimps are young, well-built young Slovenians who demand the Slovenian Girl's income. Aleksandra's already threatened and vulnerable state, caused by the police warrant and the media pursuit, thus becomes even more complicated: while the Slovenian forces chase her, she still has to serve Western clients to pay her debt.

In this multi-layered colonising structure, Aleksandra, the female figure of the nation, succumbs to Western powers but, when threatened by her countrymen, she becomes a helpless, panicky woman. In this way, *A Call Girl* suggests, the nation is exploited by foreign influence and, while slowly going bankrupt, the Slovenian state makes no profit from the monetary exchange. Aleksandra's enclosed position is further stressed by extreme close-ups of her that align the viewer with her inner struggles and hopeless situation.

Besides the core–periphery and colonised–coloniser dichotomies, *A Call Girl* sets up a further opposition by contrasting Ljubljana with rural Slovenia. In her father's remote village, people are altruistic, genuine citizens who look out for each other. In this space, Aleksandra becomes a naïve young girl who is supported by her divorced father; the man does the housework, cleans, cooks and washes and irons his daughter's clothes. While he takes on a maternal identity, the man is deprived of his role as the head of the family; in the capitalist framework, he is incapable of supporting his daughter's studies and lifestyle, and escapes into music and drinking. As the resurrected socialist father figure, he enters an emasculated role and, even though he learns about Aleksandra's prostitution, he remains silent. For the young girl, however, the rural setting brings peace and security, which changes when, after going back to Ljubljana, she faces her father's best friend in a hotel room. After the first shock, the obese man demands that Aleksandra have sex with him, but he does not pay for the service. Thus, whenever the call girl meets Slovenian men, she is deprived of money and enters a dangerous system of bribery and greed. Like her ex-boyfriend who threatens Aleksandra by telling her father about the girl's business, her father's best friend blackmails the woman by threatening to reveal the truth to her family if she does not sleep with him. This is the end of her self-colonising process: Aleksandra decides to give up prostitution and move back to her father's village. By leaving behind the capital and its centralised Western powers, she relocates to the periphery and choses the traditional Slovenian socio-realistic context as her future setting.

In contrast to *Ryna*, *Touchless* and *A Call Girl*, Szabolcs Hajdu's *Bibliothèque Pascal* uses a cross-border narrative and physical travel to demonstrate neoliberal subjugation. The film narrates the story of Mona (Orsolya Török-Illyés), a Transylvanian single mother who is trafficked to England to work in a luxury brothel. Dressed as Joan of Arc and later as Desdemona, she must fulfil the fantasies of Western customers. Slowly, her body goes through a drastic transformation: from an Eastern European mother she turns into the fantasy of foreign consumers, with heavy make-up, extravagant costumes and witty sexual games. During her oppression, Mona also learns English by studying her erotic roles and talking to Pascal (Shamgar Amram), the head of the brothel. Thus, while she is forced to work as a prostitute, she slowly succumbs to the Western powers by colonising herself. Her daily rape and forced heroin consumption, together with the physical-psychological assault by Englishmen, transforms Mona into an object. She loses the right to her own body, which is exploited at every level.

The colonising power structures are further illustrated by the portrayal of Mona's home country, Romania, and her cell in England. The Eastern European country is depicted as a godforsaken space, with muddy roads and criminals, which creates an Orientalist image of the region. It is in this socialist Balkan space that the woman's colonising journey begins. Mona is sold by her father, who she has not seen for a long time, who asks her to accompany him to Germany where he is going to have an operation. Instead of having surgery, he exchanges his daughter for money and is eventually murdered by traffickers. Germany thus functions as a changing point in the story that seals Mona's fate in the West. Interestingly, in the dream of Mona's daughter, it is the father who saves her from the brothel at the end of the film. In this phantasmagorical scene, he arrives in England with an orchestra and opens the doors for all the prisoners in the sex club. In this way, the socialist father figure is literally resurrected in a fantasy where he overcomes the colonising Western powers to save his daughter – and hence the nation from further Western exploitation.

Conclusion

The increasing incidence of female rape, domestic violence and physical abuse in Eastern European cinema suggest a newly re-patriarchised social structure that resurrects the socialist father figure as an emasculated, impotent male who, while being colonised by Western powers himself, oppresses his female relatives through their sexual exploitation. In this patriarchal context, women stand under the double burden of internal colonisation against the older male parent while they also take on a self-colonised imaginary and succumb to Western powers. In this double form of neoliberal subjugation, *nostomania*, the basis of the Eastern European populist structure, plays a crucial role. Ryna, Jolana, Aleksandra and Mona all have a love–hate relationship with their fathers, who eventually deceive them. Hoping for the wealth and security provided by these older figures, the female protagonists have absolute trust in their male parents. Instead of supporting their daughters, however, these figures all step into business relations with Western and/or local capitalist forces that demand female sacrifice or, as in the case of *A Call Girl*, the silent supervision of their children's degradation. As a symbol of populism and *nostomania*, the socialist father figure only stands as mediator between the exploiting West and his home country. While recalling the socialist period's gender bias, these films also criticise socialism via the older male character who is incapable of protecting his female relatives, and so the nation itself.

The explicit pornographic content of the sexual and physical abuse in these films only underlines the colonised–coloniser dichotomy by causing discomfort in the viewer so as to achieve political spectatorship. Thus, like the socialist rape-films, the extreme tendency in Eastern European cinema communicates a metaphorical message that points towards the exploitative nature of the current neoliberal framework. Whether deploying a socio-realistic setting and hand-held camera work – as in the case of *Ryna* and *A Call Girl* – or a highly stylised visual setting – as in *Touchless* and *Bibliothèque Pascal* – all these art films portray women's subjugated roles via a range of film aesthetics to make audiences aware of the present, neoliberal crisis on the Eastern European screen.

Notes

1. In Eastern Europe, over 70 per cent of assets are foreign-owned (Lane 2010: 232).
2. Germany for instance, has loaned to southern Europe at historically low interest rates, and accumulated trade surpluses by using undervalued currency (Moravcsik 2012). In order to overcome the 25 per cent competiveness gap, post-socialist countries have had to cut down on wages and economic activities, which puts them into a never-ending cycle of foreign dependence.
3. Of course, this list is not exhaustive – the number of films representing violence against women would exceed the limits of the present chapter. Rather, it aims at pointing to some examples from the present and past decade that use extreme graphic violence and shock aesthetics to raise awareness of the current sociopolitical and economic crisis in the region.

11. HOUSING PROBLEMS: BRITAIN'S HOUSING CRISIS AND DOCUMENTARY

Anna Viola Sborgi

This chapter explores recent documentary production on the housing crisis in the UK and sets it within the wider context of social and economic crisis at the European level and beyond. I argue that this output not only provides an in-depth representation of growing social and economic inequality in housing, but also (through different channels of distribution and in its interconnection with the world beyond the screen, housing activism in particular) increasingly shapes the debate on the home, opening a potential platform for discussion that goes well beyond the national level.

I chose the UK as the main case study because of its paradigmatic trajectory from the egalitarian project of mass housing provision in the postwar period to the increasing erosion of this same social housing stock from the end of the 1970s to the present, within a wider process of privatisation and the dismantling of the welfare state. The potentially tragic consequences of this process, which not only includes the demolition of council estates but also their systemic neglect, a process 'captured by the phrase "managed decline"' (Watt 2009: 236), became evident in the Grenfell Tower fire. On 14 June 2017 a malfunctioning fridge-freezer ignited a fire that engulfed the tower, a 24-storey block administered by Kensington and Chelsea Tenant Management Organisation in West London, killing 72 people and injuring another 70. The fire at Grenfell not only 'stood as an awful culmination to deeply damaging policies pursued towards council housing, and the public sector more widely, since 1979' (Boughton 2018: 1) but, importantly, was also rooted in a 'colonial politics of space' in which 'ideas of race and racial inferiority served to justify the practice of profit-induced exploitation' (El-Enany 2017; 2019: 51).

While it clearly has its specificities, the housing crisis in the UK, and in London in particular, condenses a series of social and economic challenges that are part of wider transformations at the European and global level. It exists within a wider scenario of planetary gentrification (Lees et al. 2016), and is impacted by both austerity politics and a precarious labour market. Finally, it reflects wider class, gender and race inequalities under neoliberalism.

The UK's long-standing housing problem has generated a vast film and television output in which social housing has been a key space across a wide range of formats, from feature films such as *Meantime* (Mike Leigh, 1983), to television series such as *Top Boy* (Channel 4, 2011–13) and *Chewing Gum* (2015–17), essay films such as *Estate. A Reverie* (Andrea Luka Zimmerman, 2015) and documentary. As I demonstrate in this chapter, the latter has emerged as the privileged mode of enquiry into housing conditions in Britain, while at the same time participating in a long tradition that goes back to the early twentieth century but has gained new momentum in recent years as a result of different factors, from the exacerbation of the housing crisis itself to the wider accessibility of filming technology, online distribution forms and digitisation. For documentary, the latter, as Erika Balsom and Hila Peleg have noted, 'figures simultaneously as threat and promise: it is a form of derealisation against which the documentary must assert itself, and yet it offers new tools for the creation and distribution of nonfiction images, revitalising this field of practice' (Balsom and Peleg 2016: 16).

In this chapter I will look at how selected documentaries portray the housing sector as a testing ground for growing social and economic inequality along class, ethnic and gender divides. From the housing application process in *How to Get a Council House* (Channel 4, 2013–16) to the wider erosion of the housing stock in *Dispossession. The Great Social Housing Swindle* (Paul Sng, 2017), television and film portray, in different ways and with different purposes, widening inequality and social exclusion. At the same time, these transformations are not passively received, but encounter resistance from the communities affected. I explore a series of productions connected at various levels to housing activism, such as the recent inquiry into London's housing movement, *Concrete Soldiers UK* (Nikita Wolfe, 2017), and I trace the wide range of screen responses to Grenfell and its reverberations in documentaries about housing. Within a vast corpus of documentaries, I argue that the selected examples are key to engaging with different aspects of the current economic and social crisis.

A Permanent Crisis?

The term 'crisis' suggests an exceptional situation, but it is certainly not a new word in relation to housing. David Madden and Peter Marcuse point to its long-term history and suggest that perceptions of the present moment as a crisis might be due to housing problems affecting larger sectors of the population. They argue:

> The idea of crisis implies that inadequate or unaffordable housing is abnormal, a temporary departure from a well-functioning standard. But for working class and poor communities, housing crisis is the norm [. . .] For the oppressed, housing is always in crisis. The reappearance of the term 'housing crisis' in headlines represents the experience of middle-class homeowners and investors, who faced unexpected residential instability following the 2008 financial implosion. (Madden and Marcuse 2016: Kindle edition)

Although this is certainly true, housing unaffordability has reached unprecedented levels and, unless radically different planning, political and economic strategies are envisaged, this will lead to the transformation of our cities into playgrounds for the ultra-rich only. Scholars such as Anna Minton argue for the importance of keeping an integrated perspective in housing studies, since

> [h]ousing, and the different layers of society it affects, is seen as a set of separate issues when in fact it is one issue: what happens at the top affects the middle and the bottom, and vice versa, with the influx of wealth from the top displacing communities across the city, while the introduction of a market in housing benefit adds inflationary pressures on rents for everybody. (Minton 2017: xv)

Even considering the long-term nature of the UK's housing problems, specific moments in the past forty years can be connected to the acceleration of this crisis. Although they acknowledge that the privatisation of public housing has been an issue since the nineteenth century, scholars point to Margaret Thatcher's introduction of the 'right to buy' in 1980 – the right for council tenants to buy the property they lived in – as 'the decisive turning point in public policy towards housing' (Hodkinson, Watt and Mooney 2013: 2). Writing on the impact of right to buy on the reduction in London's housing stock in the early 1980s, Paul Watt argues that this policy

> has helped to 'residualise' council renting since it has shifted from 'general needs' housing catering for a broad mass of the working class to a residual tenure for the poorer working class with the direst housing needs. (Imrie, Lees and Raco 2009: 216–17)

The iconic nature of this moment is captured in several of the films I examine through the repeated use of archival footage showing Thatcher visiting and congratulating homeowners in their newly bought flats.

The current housing crisis is the result of a substantial continuity in housing policy between Conservative and Labour governments since 1979.[1] The tendency towards a progressive dismantling of social housing culminated in the Housing and Planning Act 2016, which further encouraged home ownership and deregulation in the market and in construction. The erosion of social housing and, more generally, the lack of affordable homes in the UK runs in parallel with rampant gentrification, which has been an escalating problem in Europe and at the planetary level (Madden and Marcuse 2016; Lees et al. 2016). Furthermore, the economic crisis and wider austerity experienced by the UK and other European states post-2007/2008 do not provide a favourable environment in which to solve the housing crisis, but rather exacerbate it. Finally, the UK's peculiarly unstable position within Europe after the 2016 Brexit referendum outcome might have further effects on the real estate market and, consequently, on housing policies.

The housing crisis is also, in a wider sense, the result of a long shift begun in the 1970s, from an industrial society to a growing financialisation of the economy, and increasing investment in the property market, characterised by deregulation precipitating recurrent property bubbles. As scholars have demonstrated, film and television are extremely receptive to recurrent waves of economic growth and recession at the international level, both in terms of representation and industry transformations (Negra and Tasker 2014; Webb 2014).[2] I will show how recent documentaries have responded to the current exacerbation of the housing crisis and engaged with the long-standing and systemic nature of housing injustice.

As much as the housing crisis has long-standing implications, the most recent productions must be seen within a longer tradition with an extremely wide range of manifestations. Since the 1930s, the British documentary tradition has been preoccupied with housing conditions in Britain, and especially in London. The classic contributions to this genre are Arthur Elton and E. H. Anstey's *Housing Problems* (1935) about early twentieth-century slum clearances, and Paul Rotha's progressive propaganda film about post-war reconstruction, *Land of Promise* (1946). In the 1970s Paul Watson depicted the appalling living conditions in temporary accommodation in Southwark in *The Block* (BBC1, 1972), and the radical film collective Cinema Action recorded housing struggles in the campaign documentary *Squatters* (1969/70). In the 1980s Adam Curtis investigated the technical failure of 1960s and 1970s housing projects in *Inquiry. The Great British Housing Disaster* (BBC, 1984), and in the 1990s Patrick Keiller explored the British housing situation in *The Dilapidated Dwelling* (2000).

As this brief overview shows, there has never been only one genre and format of housing documentary, and recent productions exhibit an even wider variety, an indication that the landscape is a lively and evolving one. I will be taking into account the films' aesthetics, which includes the blending of genres, as well as their production circuits, distribution formats, and finally their circulation in different venues. I will go on to analyse selected case studies within the British context to show how housing films made in Britain travel beyond national boundaries, as well as how connections can be established with similar productions at the European level. In the first part of the analysis I focus on the Channel 4 docu-series *How to Get a Council House* (2013–16), which explores the dehumanising aspects of the housing allocation process in austerity Britain. In the second part, I look at productions in line with community-based initiatives and housing activism, which not only attempt to expose housing injustice but also share the common intent of deconstructing the stigmatisation of those affected by it.

How to Get a Council House

How to Get a Council House is the only British television documentary programme to date that is entirely devoted to the current housing crisis. It is also the longest-running programme within a wider production trend for factual reality shows on housing, such as *Swap My Council House* (BBC1, 2014) or *Council House Crackdown* (BBC1, 2015–16). These can be connected to a wider line of what has been termed 'factual welfare television', exemplified by shows such as *Benefits Street* (Channel 4, 2014–15) (De Benedictis, Allen and Jensen 2017).

Made by the production company Studio Lambert, the series consists of thirteen episodes filmed over a period of three years.[3] Altogether, they cover a comprehensive range of specific topics: the application process, the waiting list, the bidding system, benefits, homelessness, evictions, housing shortages, overcrowding and dilapidated housing. The programme was filmed across the UK, with recurrent case studies such as London and Portsmouth. Five episodes out of the total thirteen are devoted to Tower Hamlets in East London. This choice reflects the specific housing emergency taking place in the area. As the borough experienced a process of rebranding following the 2012 Olympics, large numbers of people in need of council accommodation were pushed out, with new groups with better economic resources flowing into the area. Therefore, Tower Hamlets stands more widely for the progressive spreading of inequality and gentrification connected to urban regeneration.

Responses to the series in the press have varied. Reviewing Series 3, Episode 1 in the *Guardian*, Rebecca Nicholson described it as 'an unpleasant framing of a complex subject' and the overall series as 'unsubtle and crude' (Nicholson

2015). Ben Travis in the *Evening Standard* described it as a 'a tough watch with no solution', while the *Daily Mail* entitled its review: 'If you end up with this lot as neighbours, heaven help you' (Travis 2015; Connell 2015). Differences in responses to the show not only reflect the political orientation of the newspapers, but, I argue, are also to be found in a series of ambiguities in the framing of these issues.

The title promises an informative and handbook-like take on the subject, but also instils an expectation in viewers that they are about to watch a salacious programme about so-called 'benefit scroungers'. The company website's production statement further reinforces this stance of objectivity:

> This returning documentary series provides an insight into the workings of Britain's social housing system. It launched on Channel 4 in 2013 and documents, with honesty and integrity, the reality of life for the front-line workers who have to cope with a reduced stock of social housing and a growing number of desperate people seeking their help to avoid homelessness.[4]

In some respects, *How to Get a Council House* can be placed in the tradition of 'fly-on-the-wall' and observational documentary. The crew is invisible and, most of the time, those interviewed speak for themselves. As in other films in this tradition, such as *The Block*, the interviewer's voice is rarely heard. The external voice-over is always impersonal and almost robotic. At the same time, however, this is a docu-drama and the combination of an observational mode with dramatic and spectacularising aesthetics leads to ambivalences in characterisation.

The naturalistic take on the subject matter is also complicated by the soundtrack. Music, normally absent from classic 'fly-on-the-wall' documentaries, is used dramatically in the whole series to increase suspense and pathos. The editing is extremely fast-paced and emphasises a sense of emergency. As one of the tenants about to be evicted in Season 2, Episode 1 suggests, 'the clock is ticking fast', which appears in stark contrast to the quasi-immobility of the waiting process. Overall, the absence of a clearly stated point of view, instead of reinforcing the premise of objectivity, paradoxically creates ambivalence.

The System

How to Get a Council House shows how the housing allocation process is ruled by a depersonalised and computerised system. This situation is similarly played out in Ken Loach's feature film portraying Britain in the age of austerity *I, Daniel Blake* (2016).[5] But even if Daniel's world does not offer many options to survive the system, as the tragic ending of the film confirms, a tiny space for hope can still be found in the man's own attempts to make himself visible against the blindness and facelessness of the state. Hope can also be found in meaningful human connections which counteract state brutality, as shown by his friendship with single mother Katie and her two children.

By contrast, the applicants in How to Get a Council House are, with very few exceptions, alone in their struggle to secure a home. Viewers are presented with the brutality of their drama by invasive use of the camera and driven to it through a 'poverty porn' aesthetics. The representation of the housing allocation process is crudely accurate; however, while individual case studies are moving, a series of other representational strategies in the programme undermines a discourse of empathy towards the subjects represented.

Several elements in the visual aesthetics of the documentary give the impression that we are actually witnessing a game. For instance, the prices of council rents are often presented in the manner of a slot machine. The language used also conjures up the impression that the whole bidding and application process is a contest in which only the fittest survive.[6] In Series 1, Episode 1, we are introduced to a young man who has spent the previous months in an overpriced, privately rented room with no lock and who sleeps on a bedbug-infested mattress with his pregnant girlfriend. He has already placed 41 bids on a flat to no avail, and responds to the interviewer's questions with resignation, interiorising the perception of failure that has been projected on to him by society. Referring to the 'shortage of homes', he observes that 'there's going to be losers and there's going to be winners. Unfortunately, with the system that we're facing at the moment, we are the losers.'

The gaming aesthetic is further emphasised by the opening sequence, where the letters of the title stand upright on the ground as the pieces of a gigantic Monopoly board. This introduction always concludes with similar questions or statements posed by an external voice-over: 'Who deserves a house the most?', or 'The system decides who's most deserving and who is left on the street.' If the idea of the housing struggle as a Darwinian competition among vulnerable individuals were not disturbing enough, this kind of linguistic framing places the spectator in the position of judging whether the 'candidates' are 'deserving' or 'undeserving'.[7] The sense of ruthless competition increases when applicants start comparing themselves to those who seem to be luckier than them. Predictably, this becomes particularly evident when nationality comes to the fore. Series 4, Episode 3, entitled 'People Coming from Abroad', is set in Hounslow in West London, and was broadcast on 24 May 2016, just a month before the referendum on the UK's membership of the European Union. It follows three stories: 52-year-old Lisa, from Bermuda; 35-year-old Florin and his wife Liliana and their five children, from Romania; and a couple, 31-year-old Monica, from Poland, and Frederick, from Uganda, with their two children. The opening recap sequence conjures the impression of hordes of foreigners arriving through repeated images of aeroplanes landing at Heathrow. Throughout the show we are reminded that the council is facing an emergency regarding migration, with statistics explaining that half of the people sleeping rough are foreigners.[8] Lisa, a white woman who left Bermuda to access better medical care, keeps insisting that she has a priority to be housed because of her British national status; frustrated by the lack of help, she hurls racial abuse at one black council duty manager.

The Romanian family appear to be used as a case study of European migrants' 'naïve' expectations of finding council housing. The man was previously in the UK and has returned with his family. He is constantly being judged as irresponsible for bringing his five children to the UK without a secure plan, and thus labelled as 'undeserving poor'. As an EU citizen, he can only stay in the country if he demonstrates that he is actively looking for work, and a series of misunderstandings regarding his jobseeker status ensue. A council worker tries to help the family but lacks empathy and constantly scolds them. At the wife's remark that they would be able to find work if they had a home, the council officer loses her temper, rebuffing her as if she were a capricious little child: 'It doesn't work like that!'

Only the local priest Roger, who temporarily hosts the family in the homeless shelter he runs in Brentford, shows empathy. After one of several visits to the council, Roger looks into the camera and remarks that 'with little help he would give back to the community', suggesting that the man's move to the UK was caused by desperation, which 'sometimes necessitates what might appear illogical'. Florin himself repeatedly explains that in Romania he was not able to feed his children, as he was paid the equivalent of one pound per hour. But when the family is finally housed in Birmingham, about which they are thrilled, the priest too expresses doubts about the fact that they were a priority to receive housing, having put themselves in danger.

Moreover, there are several grey areas that are not fully explored, for example the fact that both Florin and Frederick are caught within the web of a precarious job market. The former does everything he can, but he is never regularly hired, while the latter is in the paradoxical situation in which, if he works, he earns less than if he stays at home, because he is employed on zero hours contracts and ends up in arrears. In addition to facing job market precarity, the Romanian family also face linguistic barriers related to the housing allocation system; it is only when an interpreter comes to the council office with them that it becomes clear that the man is actually receiving jobseeker's allowance and therefore has a right to be housed. Although one of the housing officers makes clear that 'it's a myth that immigrants get housing more easily', the episode aired at a moment of particular intensity in debates regarding migration in the lead-up to the 2016 referendum, leading to a series of racist tweets blaming the migrants in the show for obtaining social housing more easily than British nationals.

Overall, does the series further our understanding of the housing crisis? After watching the show, the viewer is certainly more literate in the mechanisms of the housing allocation process, but what is missing is an analysis of the wider context. For instance, the voices of other subjects in the housing sector, from policymakers to activists, are absent, with interviews limited to council applicants and workers. Moreover, does the series offer an accurate portrait of both? The council workers interviewed are not necessarily impassive – many of them express distress about the position they are put in – and although the show effectively highlights how council services themselves are overstretched, the fact that this situation is also a consequence of austerity cuts and wider policy decisions at the national level is never fully explored.

Although the programme claims to be on the front line of the housing crisis, it is limited both in terms of the variety of subjects interviewed, and the way applicants are characterised along a deserving–undeserving binary. With some exceptions, such as the figure of Roger, *How to Get a Council House* portrays tenants and council employees as if they are the only subjects involved in the housing crisis. Moreover, the interactions between council workers and applicants are often, though not always, impersonal. One of the recurring answers from council employees in the programme is: 'I can't change our policies, I just implement them.' In this way, tenants are largely represented as idle and undeserving. On the other hand, housing officers are seen as the 'foot soldiers' of the housing crisis, in a way that is unfair to both categories of people, who are similarly left alone to face the emergency. Although seriality allows for the comprehensive exploration of the mechanisms of the housing system, the show offers little context for the current crisis, and does not attempt to explain its wider economic, social and political causes.

Representations of social housing in factual reality television mainly mediate the organisation of society whereby vulnerable subjects are crushed between a state-owned space that they cannot access and a privately owned space that they cannot afford. The space for sharing and constructing solidarity, for community building in the broadest sense, also disappears. At a wider level, the spatial nature of the housing crisis is a crucial aspect of the neoliberal system. As David Harvey has theorised, the spatial and economic expansion of the property market represents a way to solve over-accumulation crises in contemporary capitalism, what he calls 'the spatial fix' (Harvey 2001). The loss of access to state-provided housing on the part of the most vulnerable in society that we observe in these films is, at the wider level, typical of the neoliberal system. As Anna Minton writes: 'the government has given up its democratic responsibilities, handling over responsibility for the public realm and for housing of the poor to the private sector' (Minton 2012: xxxv).

Docu-dramas about housing provide an image of the state as an impermeable and automated, Kafkaesque 'system' whose strings are pulled by invisible 'decision-makers', to borrow a phrase that recurs in *I, Daniel Blake*. Failing to problematise this depersonalisation conceals a fundamental failure of the state, at several levels, to provide a safety net for life's 'ups and downs', and to recognise housing as a fundamental human right.

Film and Housing Activism Community-based Initiatives

While *How to Get a Council House* shows that the consequence of the retreat of the state is a fight of the poor against the poor, other films show the fight for access to space and the 'right to the city' as an area for potential solidarity (Lefebvre 1968; Harvey 2012). A radically different response comes from a series of documentaries that are either directly connected to the world of housing activism or are sympathetic to the communities affected by the housing crisis. This is an evolving landscape at the time of writing, constituted by an extremely wide range of manifestations that share three aspects: they provide a space of resistance to housing displacement and injustice; they aim to rewrite the narrative from the point of view of the affected communities, rejecting the stigma often associated with council housing tenants; and, finally, they aim to express a wider engagement with the systematic nature of crisis and the concept of housing as home, as opposed to housing as real estate (Madden and Marcuse 2016: Kindle edition).

While certain films, such as Paul Sng's 2017 *Dispossession*, provide an exposé of housing at the national level, documentary production has sometimes concentrated around specific areas and case studies. Ayo Akingbade's *Street 66* (2018) narrates the life of Ghanaian housing activist Dora Boatemah (1957–2001) and her role in the community-based regeneration of Angell Town Estate in Brixton, South London. However, the area that has originated the largest amount of short and feature-length films is Elephant and Castle in South London. Undergoing the largest regeneration programme in Europe, the area was once home to the (now demolished) Heygate Estate, and still hosts the Aylesbury Estate, which is facing demolition at the time of writing. Some of these productions are collected on the *Heygate was Home* online archive, and range from campaign videos to Enrica Colusso's feature-length documentary *Home Sweet Home* (2012), an exploration of the meaning of home and regeneration mediated through the form of the personal essay film.[9]

The relationship between activism, community action and film is also articulated through the work of the London-based Rainbow Collective, a production collective that facilitates the use of film in social justice campaigns, producing a range of films in collaboration with specific communities. For instance, *Cracks in the System* (Hannan Majid and Richard York), a film made with the residents of the Ledbury Estate in South London, shows how, as of June 2018, the tenants of these system-built towers lived with arm-wide cracks in the corners of their flats, a situation that, post-Grenfell, caused the tenants distress and anxiety. The Collective also involves children aged 5–15 in animation workshops for the purpose of making films reflecting on their experiences in social housing, such as *Vauxhall Dragon* (VGERTA, 2017). In June 2018 both films were screened at a session organised by the East End Film Festival in London, entitled *Building a Movement*, which consisted of housing campaign talks and film screenings that recognised the potential of film as a campaign tool.[10]

A 'GRENFELL EFFECT'?

The deadly fire at Grenfell Tower produced an impressively wide range of media responses: news reports, witnesses' mobile phone footage, grassroots videos and documentaries, and feature-length documentaries produced for network television. This overall production is too vast to be done justice here, and to make sense of this large corpus, as I have argued elsewhere (Sborgi 2017a; 2017b; 2019), requires a long-term response and further distance from the event itself. Some preliminary considerations, however, can be made.

As films such as *Cracks in the System* show, Grenfell resonates in the most recent productions on housing, which acknowledge the importance of tracing connections between the event itself and the systemic aspects that produced it, which, if not addressed, could lead to similar disasters. Some of the documentaries made about Grenfell itself offer this reading. The three-part documentary *Failed by the State* (2017), directed by Daniel Renwick and produced in collaboration with Redfish (a Berlin-based independent journalists' organisation), is based on interviews with the local community. Starting from the premise of avoiding images of the fire itself, the film is vocal in establishing connections between the state's failings towards the community (both at the local and national level) and wider phenomena such as globalisation and gentrification. Though an in-depth treatment of these aspects is still missing, partly because the film represents an immediate reaction to the facts, it nevertheless testifies to an awareness on the part of the local community of the wider implications of the fire, and its preventability. A further reflection on this was provided in October 2018 by the BBC2 documentary *The Fires that Foretold Grenfell* (Jamie Roberts), which explored the wider history of previous fires in post-war Britain, with particular attention to tower blocks. It traced the failings in fire safety regulations and policies, showing how, 'had lessons been learned', Grenfell could have been avoided.

As I have argued elsewhere, the urgency of portraying the community response was widely felt by grassroots films produced in the early days after the fire, as is evidenced by films such as *On the Ground at Grenfell* (Nendie Pinto-Duschinsky and Stowe Films, 2017), a collective effort of 'a group of 9 young people: survivors, local residents, and volunteers'.[11] In a second phase, this necessity seems to have been intercepted by network television as well. Both the BBC and Channel 4 commissioned documentaries that dealt more specifically with the stories behind the 'faces on the memorial wall' in *Searching for Grenfell's Lost Lives* (Reggie Yates, BBC2, 2018); the role of the local community in the emergency in *Grenfell* (Ben Anthony, BBC1, 2018); the survivors' memories of life in the tower and their homes in the 15-minute virtual reality documentary *Grenfell Our Home* (Channel 4, 2018); and the longer history of the area in *Before Grenfell* (2018). Broadcast on the occasion of the first anniversary of the fire, the latter uses archive materials and interviews to show the historical origins of the extremely polarised social make-up of North Kensington with regard to wealth distribution and race, showing how this is an area where the ultra-rich live next door to some of the least wealthy communities in the country. Within the vast corpus of documentaries on social housing I have outlined above, I choose to concentrate here on two films: *Dispossession*, perhaps the most popular and most widely distributed of the recent films on the housing crisis, and *Concrete Soldiers UK*, the first film to portray activism and also the first film of this kind produced post-Grenfell.

Dispossession: The Great Social Housing Swindle

Dispossession engages with social tenants, housing activists, charity workers, photographers, journalists, academics and one politician, Scotland's First Minister Nicola Sturgeon, to provide an informative and timely survey of the housing crisis in the UK. It covers an extensive number of case studies across the country: London (the Aylesbury Estate, Balfron Tower and Cressingham Gardens), Nottingham (St Ann's) and Glasgow (the Gorbals, Govanhill and Red Road). Working-class actress Maxine Peake's voice-over represents an interesting attempt to change the point of view of narration, especially if we compare it both to classic housing documentaries such as *Housing Problems* or *Land of Promise* (where the only female voice is The Housewife) but also to more recent programmes such as *How to Get a Council House*, in which the 'authoritative' voice-over is always male. The film has a strong online media presence, and has played an important role in circulating updated information on the housing crisis via Facebook and Twitter.

The title inserts the film into previous media history as it recalls both *The Great Rock 'n' Roll Swindle,* Julian's Temple 1980 mockumentary on the Sex Pistols, and *The Great British Housing Disaster*, Adam Curtis's 1984 investigative documentary into the failures of system-built post-war housing. At the same time, the word 'dispossession' itself recalls David Harvey's theorisation of 'capital accumulation by dispossession' (Harvey 2005: 162–3) and the film deals with demolitions, endemic neglect of the housing stock, prejudices associated with social tenants, community actions to regain control of the estates,

Figure 11.1   Poster for Paul Sng's *Dispossession* (2017).

top-down regeneration projects and the most important development in housing policy in recent years, the 2016 Housing Bill and its predictable negative impact on the housing situation.

Dispossession represents an interesting case of circulation and distribution. The film was first shown in April 2017, but it was the third, sold-out screening at Picture House Central in London, followed by a post-screening debate, which became particularly memorable, as it took place the day after the Grenfell Tower fire, making the film even more timely and urgent. It was screened at the House of Commons on 23 November 2017, and a sold-out screening at Curzon Chelsea in December 2017 with the participation of Jeremy Corbyn culminated in a stage invasion by a housing activist from the Aylesbury Estate asking the Labour leader to condemn Labour-run councils' housing policies more forcefully. Later, *Dispossession* was released through a series of different channels, on iTunes, on DVD, and in an edited version on Channel 5 on 28 March 2018.

The documentary also acted as a fundraiser by devoting proceeds from promotional materials and specific screenings to a series of campaigns. For instance, on 15 April 2018 proceeds from a screening were donated to Streets Kitchen, a grassroots campaign that offers information, advice and food runs for homeless people. At the same time, Velvet Joy Productions, Sng's production company, used a Kickstarter campaign to fund the ethnographic photography book *Invisible Britain: Portraits of Hope and Resilience* (2018), which features stories and portraits of individuals across the UK who have been impacted by austerity, de-industrialisation and cuts to public services. The stories are from a diverse range of people, many of whom 'feel misrepresented in the media and out of sync with the government and politicians'.[12]

Sng's previous work *Sleaford Mods: Invisible Britain* (2015) was also devoted to a re-evaluation of British working-class culture. *Dispossession* itself attempts a systematic look at the housing crisis and is committed to countering the prejudice against social tenants that has characterised much factual reality television. Particular attention is given to interviews with tenants describing their own lived experience on estates such as Cressingham Gardens and St Ann's in Nottingham, which is far from the sink estate cliché that has been attributed to these housing developments.

CONCRETE SOLDIERS UK

Concrete Soldiers UK (Nikita Wolfe, 2017) is the first film to look at the crisis by portraying the world of housing activism in London. Based on interviews with campaigners and community members, it was the result of three years of research and came out a few months after the Grenfell Tower fire, and is dedicated to the memory of the victims. The documentary opens and closes with images of Grenfell and contains parts of a longer film of an open meeting held by Architects for Social Housing, held on 22 June 2017 in the Residents Centre of Cotton Gardens Estate in Lambeth in response to the tenants' fears about fire safety in their building.[13]

The pace of the narration, articulated through the voice-over of journalist and campaigner Andy Worthington, is much slower than in *Dispossession*, where the quantity and the pace of information that the viewer is expected to process are at times overwhelming, and image credits are not always clear. Instead, *Concrete Soldiers UK* allows for an in-depth treatment of each case and of the history of each estate, which is introduced with the name of the architect who designed it and the dates of completion. Interviewees include estate residents, activists from the campaigns 35% and SHOUT, and Architects for Social Housing (ASH), which is given prominence in the film. The film not only captures campaigns to save the estates from demolition, but also discusses alternative plans for refurbishment, some designed by ASH, and discussion over wider policy ideas, such as an increase in upfront governmental investment in social housing which would come back to the state through social rent, and which would re-envisage public housing as an asset rather than something to get rid of.

Compared to *Dispossession*, the film is more overtly political. Although it starts by clarifying that local councils have been facing cuts from the national government, it also makes clear that many of those involved in aggressive regeneration schemes are Labour councils. It is also pointed out that as estate regeneration balloting is supported by the national leadership of the Labour Party, councils not applying this provision are in breach of national party policy. The documentary not only criticises the state of housing but also shows that alternatives to demolition exist, as demonstrated by the happy ending for the newly renamed Macintosh Court, a care home designed by architect Kate Macintosh and earmarked for demolition, which was saved through a campaign carried out by the residents with the help of Macintosh herself.

Film, Home and Housing in the European Context

As I have underlined in the course of this chapter, the UK represents a particular case study in terms of housing history. However, Watt and Smets remark that, despite differences in national housing systems, in recent years 'we have also witnessed greater private sector involvement in social housing provision in the European Union' (Watt and Smets 2017: 27). Before I turn to my conclusion, I will show how the response to this emerging trend shapes film production and housing activism not only in the UK but also at the European level.

European cinema has historically explored different forms of public housing and the shortage and dilapidation of homes. For instance, these themes feature widely in post-war Italian cinema, from Vittorio De Sica's *Bicycle Thieves* (1948) to Pasolini's *Mamma Roma* (1968). More recently, Matteo Garrone's feature *Gomorrah* (2008) captures the housing development Le Vele in Secondigliano, Naples, and its criminal infiltrations, while Ruggero Gabbai's observational documentary *CityZen* (2015) portrays the deprived Zen neighbourhood in Palermo.[14]

The comparative, global approach shaping housing and urban studies (Watt and Smets 2017; Lees et al. 2016) has also been adopted in film and urbanism studies (Andersson and Webb 2016) and is evidenced by documentary production, such as the recent film *PUSH*, by Fredrik Gertten (2019), which is being distributed at European festivals at the time of writing. Comparing different case studies across the world through interviews with local people and writers and scholars such as Saskia Sassen, Joseph Stiglitz and Roberto Saviano, the film explores the different meanings of housing as both a commodity and a human right, along with the increasing unaffordability of our cities. It also relates this phenomenon to the wider financialisation of the economy, and the corrupt relationship between the political sphere and real estate. The film follows Leilani Farha, the UN Special Rapporteur on Adequate Housing, who travels around the world to report on housing conditions, and who initiated The Shift: 'a new worldwide movement to reclaim and realise the fundamental human right to housing – to move away from housing as a place to park excess capital, to housing as a place to live in dignity, to raise families and participate in community'.[15]

The growing interest in these themes and their representation on screen at the European level is also demonstrated by film events and sessions at social housing festivals, such as the International Social Housing Festival in Lyon in summer 2019. *Concrete Soldiers UK* screened at the first edition of the Movie Activism Festival in Berlin in 2018, while *Dispossession* was presented in Belgium on 29 March 2018 at a public screening organised by the Rassemblement Bruxellois pour le Droit à l'Habitat. At the same time, the European architectural world is debating alternative solutions to the current profit-driven housing system, as demonstrated by the short film *Social Housing – 'European Housing Perspectives'* (2018), produced by Karakusevic Carson Architects and directed by Jim Stephenson.[16] The film features interviews with architects comparing housing systems in different European countries and discussing projects for more inclusive housing provision.[17]

Conclusion

The films I have analysed in this chapter inform, in different ways and across different formats and platforms, responses to an exacerbating housing crisis that goes beyond the UK and represents a global emergency. At a time of great debate on the 'impact' of documentary and its possible shortfalls within a neoliberal environment (Nichols 2016), the films I have analysed testify to a grassroots vitality across a range of forms, connected to community-based action and housing activism. All these films make wide use of non-theatrical venues for screenings, in line with what has been termed 'useful cinema' (Acland and Wasson 2011). At the same time, documentary fully participates in the potentiality of digitisation, both widening the modes of production and reaching a larger audience – for instance, through streaming on the main online networks' portals following theatrical release, or via Vimeo or YouTube. Distributed across a series of channels, these films build a shared platform for housing activism at the European level and beyond.

Although there are significant differences in aesthetics and content, such films share with their twentieth-century antecedents the objective of representing 'ordinary people', and aim to 'set the story straight' against the stereotyping and sensationalism associated with representations of social housing tenants, and working-class people in general. Moreover, in many of the documentaries I explore, attention to the individual is deployed to oppose the dehumanisation of housing conditions and the often-aggressive process of urban regeneration. In doing so, they respond to a failure in representation that has been perceived as coming not just from the most populist mainstream media, but also from sources that traditionally have had a remit to represent cultural diversity and minorities and to approach social problems with a spirit of inquiry. This issue is expressed, for instance, by the transition of Channel 4 television documentary production from more experimental forms to an increasingly market-oriented approach that is reflected in the factual welfare television format exemplified by *How to Get a Council House*.[18]

The liveliness of response to these issues is fully in evidence in representations of the Grenfell Tower fire, an event that represented the tipping point of a long-standing crisis, but, at the same time, saw documentary emerge, across different formats and circuits of production, as a crucial space to give voice to those affected by the inequalities of the housing system and, at the same time, to address the wider structural implications that produce them.

Notes

1. Equally iconic, in the films I explore, is the footage of Tony Blair's first speech as prime minister at the Aylesbury Estate, which has come to symbolise the disillusion towards Labour housing policies. See analyses of this moment in Campkin 2013 and Cairns 2018.
2. On the relationship between media culture, recession and gender, see Negra and Tasker 2014. On the relationship between real estate, the economic crisis of the 1970s and the British film industry, with particular reference to London, see Webb 2014.
3. Studio Lambert is described as 'a fast-growing independent television production company based in London, Manchester and Los Angeles. It is part of All-3Media, the global production group.' The company also produces *Gogglebox*, *Undercover Boss* and *Tattoo Fixers*. Available at <https://www.studiolambert.com> (last accessed 14 June 2019). It is led by media executive Stephen Lambert, who authored the well-known BFI publication *Channel 4: Television with a Difference?* in 1982.
4. Company website available at <https://www.studiolambert.com/shows.html> (last accessed 9 June 2019).
5. The story of single mother of two Katie being moved from London to Newcastle as her only option to receive a council flat is extremely common, and could have well been a case study for *How to Get a Council House*. Fiction and reality blur.
6. The 'fittest' in this case is the most vulnerable according to the council criteria, an aspect that merges confusingly the different concepts of vulnerability with that of performance in a neoliberal sense. The idea that people who are vulnerable must compete with one another as if in a reality show is twisted and brutal.
7. Interestingly, this aspect came up also in relation to *I, Daniel Blake* (2016). A *Guardian* review by Phil McDuff labelled Daniel as the 'avatar of the deserving poor', arguing that 'to evoke the sympathy of his audience towards kindly but unfortunate souls, Loach allows the viewer to conclude that the dehumanising welfare system is only a problem if it hurts the wrong people' (McDuff 2016).
8. Hounslow is indeed a rapidly growing borough: 'there are relatively high rates of migration into Hounslow. In 2011, 43.3 per cent of the population was born outside the UK. Migration tended to be concentrated in certain areas of the borough, but this is changing with higher rates of migration. A comparison of the 2001 and 2011 Census shows that there are significantly more areas with new migration. Hounslow also has one of the most diverse populations in London.' Available at <https://www.londoncouncils.gov.uk/our-key-themes/leadership-devolution-and-democracy/social-integration/hounslow> (last accessed 11 June 2019).

9. Available at <http://heygatewashome.org/film-archive.html?fbclid=IwAR2o5Hdmqd3jnE1-bjo4ROCZn0zh7DI-Z3gACe2PhghBU0SWzEfmtYi_IN8> (last accessed 14 June 2019).
10. Available at <https://www.rainbowcollective.co.uk/housing-activism> and <http://www.eastendfilmfestival.com/programme-archive/action-housing-talks-screenings> (last accessed 14 June 2019).
11. See <https://www.onthegroundatgrenfell.com/> (last accessed 18 January 2020)
12. See *Invisible Britain* project website, available at <https://www.invisiblebritain.com/> (last accessed 14 June 2019).
13. Available at <https://architectsforsocialhousing.co.uk/2017/07/21/the-truth-about-grenfell-tower-a-report-by-architects-for-social-housing/> (last accessed 14 June 2019).
14. The housing development Le Vele is undergoing demolition at the time of writing.
15. See the film production and campaign websites: <http://www.pushthefilm.com/>, <http://www.unhousingrapp.org/the-shift> (last accessed 14 June 2019).
16. The film was produced in the occasion of the 'Social Housing – New European Projects' exhibition at the Centre for Architecture in New York, 15 February–19 May 2018.
17. The video is available at <https://vimeo.com/265195273> (last accessed 13 June 2019).
18. On the E4 platform, *How to Get a Council House* is accompanied by a whole apparatus of contact details for people affected by similar issues.

12. MISERABLE JOURNEYS, SYMBOLIC RESCUES: REFUGEES AND MIGRANTS IN THE CINEMA OF FORTRESS EUROPE

Thomas Austin

A salient social and political issue in Europe in recent years has been the increasing number of people fleeing war and poverty and attempting to gain entry to the continent. During the so-called 'refugee crisis' of 2015–16, over a million people sought asylum in European Union countries, more than double the number for the previous year.[1] As Prem Kumar Rajaram notes (2016: 2), a prevalent Eurocentric perspective on these events holds that 'it is Europe that has had the "difficult year", not migrants'.[2] Politicians such as Viktor Orbán and David Cameron responded with dehumanising language, conflating refugees with economic migrants and 'illegal immigrants' to talk of 'unknown masses' and a 'swarm' threatening to engulf the continent.[3] While newspapers and television often amplified this hysteria, the topic has since become 'only intermittently visible in mainstream Northern European news media', such that, in Bruce Bennett's phrase, 'the "refugee crisis" is in part "a representational crisis"' (2018: 15). Furthermore, a discourse of 'crisis' has been used strategically to reinforce the border regime that produced it. Nicholas De Genova writes of the Mediterranean 'deathscape':

> the invocation of tragedy was cynically conscripted to supply the pretext for reinforcing and exacerbating precisely the material and practical conditions of possibility for the escalation in migrant deaths – namely the fortification of various forms of border policing that inevitably serve to channel illegalized human mobility into ever more perilous pathways and modes of passage. (De Genova 2017: 2, 7)

As both the number of 'illegalised' people seeking to enter Fortress Europe and the death toll in the Mediterranean have mounted, some commentators have argued for a mass resettlement programme, comparable to that undertaken for 1.3 million refugees from Indochina in the aftermath of the Vietnam War.[4] Another response, from engaged film-makers working across Europe, has been to stage fictional, symbolic rescues of refugees and 'clandestines'. Here I analyse films by directors Aki Kaurismäki and Emanuele Crialese in which white characters welcome new arrivals. I also consider two works which attend more closely to the experience of people trying to reach Europe, their dangerous journeys and the problems that await them: Senegalese director Moussa Touré's *La Pirogue* (2012) and American Italian Jonas Carpignano's feature debut *Mediterranea* (2015). In all four cases, the migrant character originates from sub-Saharan Africa.

While several commentators and politicians have conflated refugees and migrants as undesirables, others have distinguished them via a racialised hierarchy wherein refugees from Syria in particular are elevated above black migrants from Africa. To cite De Genova again:

> in the European context, the very figure of migration is always already racialized, even as dominant discourses of migration in Europe systematically deny and dissimulate race as such [. . .] The struggles of migration and borders reanimate race and postcoloniality as central to adequately addressing the most fundamental problems of what 'Europe' is supposed to be, and who may be counted as 'European'. (2017: 21)

European (and also African) cinema constitutes a key cultural and public sphere in which this debate can be seen to be played out. In the analysis that follows I make no claim to have assembled a representative sample, but seek to interrogate the dynamics of migration, benefaction, privation and self-definition across the selected films.[5]

The figure of the immigrant or refugee in European cinema often functions as a 'narrative prosthesis', to borrow a term coined by David Mitchell and Sharon Snyder. In their analysis of the representation of disabled characters in literature and film, Mitchell and Snyder argue that disability offers 'a crutch upon which [. . .] narratives lean for their representational power [. . .] and analytical insight' (2000: 49). The same can be said of the refugee. His or her presence may precipitate plot events and serve to differentiate characters via their diverse reactions to the newcomer's plight, without necessarily challenging the Eurocentrism of the narratives in which they are situated. A common benefaction trope typically legitimates the well-meaning response of a white European protagonist, while those who provide the catalyst for such a display of hospitality often remain more or less marginalised.

For example, in Aki Kaurismäki's *Le Havre* (2011), Idrissa (Blondin Miguel) is a West African boy on the run having fled from a container being unloaded at the docks. His primary impact is as a narrative prosthesis, allowing shoe-shiner Marcel Marx (André Wilms) and his neighbours to display their communitarian and anti-establishment values in hiding him and helping him escape to England. Marcel is narratively rewarded at the end of the film with the miraculous recovery of his wife Arletty (Kati Outinen) from a terminal illness. Kaurismäki's self-consciously utopian film thus provides its viewers with a doubled happy ending, the implausibility of which is acknowledged in the final shot of a cherry tree blossoming out of season.[6] But *Le Havre* does little to develop Idrissa's subjectivity, and he is exclusively defined as the grateful recipient of Marcel's benefaction. (In a rare conversation, he tells Marcel that his father was a teacher. Later Marcel learns from the boy's grandfather that his father is dead and his mother is working illegally in London.)

Le Havre is more interesting for its aesthetics, which appear aberrant insofar as they confound the verisimilitude espoused by other socially engaged European film-makers such as the Dardenne brothers, Ken Loach or Laurent Cantet, but which serve Kaurismäki's political agenda. The film deploys both performative and mimetic modes,[7] in a combination of artifice and referentiality that has become a key element of Kaurismäki's signature style.[8] For instance, when Inspector Monet pays a visit to Marcel's house in his search for Idrissa, a medium long shot shows the boy hiding behind an open door while Marcel looks on from behind. The pattern of looks here registers a hierarchy of knowledge and figures it as a sight gag, in both senses of the term. The shot is both a visual joke that needs no words and a diagrammatic rendering of how vision and control are structured according to asymmetrical power relations. Monet represents the state's power to scrutinise, and if necessary interrogate and imprison Idrissa as an 'illegal immigrant'. As a *sans papiers* in flight from this threat, Idrissa is reliant on the hospitality of strangers such as Marcel. He evades surveillance by hiding behind the open door, but cannot see what Monet is doing beyond it. However, the film asserts its optimism by effectively blocking Monet's gaze. He cannot see past the door and doesn't try to enter the room, a decision that prefigures his later deliberate refusal to 'see' Idrissa at the port, allowing the boy to evade the police and sail to England. *Le Havre* aligns the audience with both Idrissa and Marcel who, standing in the background, is the only character who knows the position of both Monet and the boy. Marcel's vantage point and optical perspective inverts that of the audience, which is given a frontal perspective on the arrangement of actors and is invited to share his anxiety and hope for the best, that is, for Monet to remain blind to Idrissa's location.

Earlier in the film, Kaurismäki stages another wordless inquiry into the situation of African arrivals in Europe, visualised as a tableau. Armed police, a press photographer and a Red Cross team await as the container from Gabon with its human cargo is opened. However, when its inhabitants are revealed they are composed in both senses of the word: neatly dressed, silent and almost motionless as they sit in the shadows. The image then cuts to a series of spot-lit medium close-ups: an elderly man, a woman and a young girl, another woman with a baby, a young man, a middle-aged couple, another young man, then a boy of about 12 (later revealed as Idrissa). All are framed more or less frontally and looking directly at, or just past, the camera, almost as if posing for photographic portraits. Composition and performance afford the immigrants a quiet dignity and self-possession as they return and refute the 'othering' gazes of the (white) police officers, the photographer and, by implication, the film's viewers. At this moment the filmic rendition of the inside of the container confounds verisimilitude not only through *mise en scène* but also by enlarging this confined space into an impossible, rhetorical one.[9]

Kaurismäki has commented:

> I had written that the container with the refugees is filthy, and that some of the immigrants had died. I could not go through with that, and I thought I'd do the complete opposite. Instead, I'd show them wearing their respectable Sunday best – to hell with realism. I'd make them arrive as proud people, instead of having them lie in the container in their own filth, as some of them realistically would have done after two weeks' incarceration. (von Bagh 2011)

The political efficacy of the container sequence derives from the dialectical combination within this tableau of social veracity (the plight of undocumented immigrants) and the blatant impossibility of their figuration here. The gap between the two calls attention to the relative social positioning of (African) migrants and refugees, and the film's (Western) audiences; between the former's experience of deracination and trauma and that of a (presumably) concerned but relatively comfortable viewer whose knowledge and expectations are derived from prior mediations. It also poses the question: what would have to change in the geopolitical order to render these images realistic, and hence unremarkable? For Kaurismäki, social engagement and self-conscious fabrication (in both form and content) pivot on the interrogation of such 'impossibilities'.

Despite staging these two concise and wordless interrogations of white perspectives on the immigrant other, *Le Havre* remains a largely Eurocentric film, unable or unwilling to shift from Marcel's perspective for very long. In the process it comes close to offering a vicarious instance of what Lilie Chouliaraki (2012: 24) calls 'solidarity as self-fulfillment', which 'construes our action on refugees as the realisation of our own humanity whilst keeping the humanity of the refugee out of view'. Ultimately, however, the film's political aesthetics problematise this logic of benefaction and emotional catharsis. The doubled happy endings of Idrissa's escape and Arletty's recovery function to reward audiences who share Kaurismäki's political concerns, but they also present a variant of the Brechtian boomerang image, emphasising the currently 'unrealistic' nature of their hopes. Paul Willemen has applied Brecht's concept to Douglas Sirk's cinema of excess, which magnified audience expectations of onscreen luxury and family dysfunction. Drawing on Bernard Dort's work on *The Threepenny Opera* and Brecht's pre-epic theatre, Willemen writes:

> Brecht presented the theatre public with the image of life it wanted to see on the stage, but in order to denounce the unreality of such an image, to denounce its ideological character [. . .] 'Brecht puts on the stage what seems to be the image of the kind of exotic society that the spectator wants to see. In fact what the spectator discovers in the very unreality of such an image is himself [*sic*]. The mirror of the stage does not reflect the world of the audience any more, but the ideological disguises of the audience itself [. . .] It bounces the images of the spectacle back to us – like a boomerang.' (Willemen 1972: 129, citing Dort 1960: 190–1)

In *Le Havre*, it is the hopes of progressive audiences that are bounced back, but Kaurismäki does not do this in order to challenge them as 'ideological disguises'. Instead he takes a step beyond the boomerang image to ask: why do such images of collectivity, diversity and dignity appear so utopian in neoliberal Europe?[10]

Like both *Le Havre* and Kaurismäki's subsequent film, *The Other Side of Hope*, *Terraferma* (2011) shows a marginal white family or community working to help and restore a refugee family whose members are scattered across different countries and are trying to evade the legal authorities.[11] Director Emanule Crialese shot *Terraferma* on and around the tiny Italian island of Linosa, situated 103 miles from the Tunisian coast. Linosa's nearest neighbour, the larger island of Lampedusa,[12] is the setting for Gianfranco Rosi's celebrated documentary *Fuocoammare/Fire at Sea* (2016), which also concerns refugees and migrants attempting to reach Europe by boat.[13] For the role of Sara, a heavily pregnant refugee from Eritrea, Crialese cast Timnit T., herself a refugee and survivor of a hazardous ordeal crossing the Mediterranean. Crialese recalls:

> I was particularly struck by the story of a boat that remained adrift for three weeks, with 79 people on board: 76 died, three survived, and when I saw in the newspaper the face of Timnit, the woman who was among the survivors, I felt deeply upset [. . .] I immediately wanted to

meet her, I was still in a very early stage of the screenwriting, undecided about whether to use actors or people who had really lived through that experience.

She didn't want to tell her personal story, it was as if she wanted to create a separation between her life before the boat landing and her future life, she didn't want to give me any details about her experience. At that point, I asked her if we could reinvent a new story together, offering her the one I had written and asking her to correct it where she thought I'd got it wrong. I was able to do it because at that point the screenplay still allowed us a large degree of freedom. (de Marco 2011: n.p.)

In parallel with the Kaurismäki films discussed above, *Terraferma* addresses the guilt of (some) white Europeans, but again does so via spectacular moments of subjective violence rather than the systematic but less easily visualised workings of objective violence. For Slavoj Žižek, objective violence entails 'the often catastrophic consequences of the smooth functioning of our economic and political systems'. It is 'precisely the violence inherent to this "normal" style of things. Objective violence is invisible since it sustains the very zero-level standard against which we perceive something as subjectively violent [that is] violence performed by a clearly identifiable agent' (Žižek 2009: 1, 2, 1, 10). *Le Havre* points the finger at the chief of police and an anonymous informer who fails in an attempt to apprehend Idrissa,[14] while *The Other Side of Hope* condemns the violent and incoherent racists of Liberation Army Finland. Although its verisimilitude contrasts with Kaurismäki's more performative aesthetic, *Terraferma* similarly presents images of 'violence performed by a clearly identifiable agent'. Further, it conforms to a historically amnesiac perspective that approaches Europe's border crisis as primarily a humanitarian problem rather than a political one. The film thus reproduces a discursive schema identified by De Genova:

[The] root causes [of the crisis are] always attributed to troubles elsewhere, usually in desperate and chaotic places ostensibly 'outside' of Europe. These putative elsewheres, beyond the borders of Europe, are systematically represented as historically sanitized, which is to say shorn of their deeply European (post)colonial histories as well as disarticulated from the European political and economic interests implicated in producing and sustaining their fractured presents. (2017: 18)

Terraferma starts with 20-year-old islander Filippo (Filippo Pucillo) and his grandfather Ernesto on their fishing boat. They come across floating wreckage from a wooden boat, which has presumably sunk while carrying refugees.

Later, on a second fishing trip, the pair find an inflatable boat crowded with refugees and call the coastguard, before rescuing four African men, a woman later revealed to be Sara, and her son. The use of a hand-held camera, rapid cutting and semi-obscured shots marks this sequence out as more visually urgent than previous scenes of Filippo and his relatives. The family hide Sara and her son, and Filippo's widowed mother Giulietta helps Sara give birth to a daughter. Nevertheless, the benefaction function is not shared evenly across the family. While Ernesto is adamant that Sara should be helped, and Filippo goes along with this, Giulietta is very reluctant to offer hospitality for fear of the police, an anxiety that increases after an officious policeman impounds the family boat for aiding illegal immigration. Distraught at the loss of the boat, Filippo asks his mother: 'Is it true that saving people at sea is forbidden?' In interview Crialese answers his question: 'the law of the State goes against the moral duties of the civilian world. Leaving people to die in the middle of the sea is a sign of immense savagery, an absurd barbarity' (de Marco 2011: n.p.).

Filippo corporealises this brutality himself in a later scene when he takes a female Italian tourist on a night-time boat trip, which is interrupted by desperate African men swimming towards the boat. In a nightmarish spectacle, Filippo repeatedly beats the shipwrecked Africans with a paddle to prevent them boarding. This staging of subjective violence is followed the next day by Filippo witnessing the bodies of drowned victims washed up on the beach. In a slow-motion sequence lasting two and a half minutes, Crialese spectacularises the consequences of both Filippo's rage and fear, and the policies of the Italian state. Tourists try to aid those still alive, but uniformed carabinieri wearing white masks and gloves move the holidaymakers away to take charge of the scene.[15] Filippo flees by diving into the sea, and an underwater shot shows traces of debris from the wreck on the seafloor (a shoe, a toothbrush, a book), before settling on an ancient figure of the Virgin Mary covered in seaweed. Signalled by this icon of salvation and redemption, Filippo's guilt and urge for expiation drives the film's climactic sequence.[16]

Ernesto decides to smuggle Sara and her children to the mainland in the back of his van. Giulietta, Filippo and Ernesto share a meal with the refugees, then drive them to the ferry, but turn back because the police are searching all vehicles. Filippo takes off with the van, leaving his mother and grandfather, and boards their impounded boat with Sara's family. As they sail away from Linosa, an extended aerial shot shows the small boat moving slowly across a vast, dark sea. The disjunction in scale in this final shot opens a new space of ambiguity in a film that has largely dealt in emphatic oppositions: is this a symbol of plucky heroism or futility and insignificance? Either way, the wishful nature of Filippo's (and the film's) solution becomes clear in the image of the tiny boat on the dark sea. To recall Willemen: 'Brecht presented the theatre public with the image of life it wanted to see on the stage, but in order to denounce the unreality of such an image, to denounce its ideological character' (Willemen 1972: 129, citing Dort 1960: 190–1). But the boomerang image that *Terraferma* offers here is inadvertent rather than deliberate. The film comforts its audiences with a gesture of rescue that attempts to expiate white guilt, while avoiding a more systematic critique of the objective violence inherent in Europe's economic and political functioning.

The Eurocentric logic of a narrative prosthesis is not always deployed to celebrate the hospitality offered to refugees and migrants by white liberal characters standing as surrogates for the audience, as in the three films discussed so far. For instance, in *Happy End* (2017), Michael Haneke rejects the benefaction trope in order to concentrate on guilt, alienation and miscommunication among a dysfunctional haute bourgeoisie family living in Calais. In this schematic critique of a recurring Haneke target, nameless Africans appear onscreen at two moments, each of which serves to develop the characterisation of the white characters. The African men remain mute, massified and almost entirely lacking in agency. (One supposes that they are migrants because of the location, Calais, and their slightly anxious clustering as a small group in public space.)

In the first scene, the wheelchair-bound and suicidal grandfather Georges Laurent (Jean-Louis Trintignant) meets a group of five or six black migrants on the street. The Africans are presented as a group, un-individuated, interchangeable. Georges talks and gestures to them, at one point offering them his watch. Whatever he is asking the migrants, their response is to refuse. However, all dialogue is drowned out by the noise of traffic passing between the camera and the characters, which are placed on opposite sides of a busy road. Thus the encounter between the old man and the migrants is reduced to a dumb show. The significance of the scene is retrospectively clarified when Georges offers to pay his hairdresser to kill him; this is presumably also what he asked the Africans. They thus operate to develop a key plot line, and to fill out Georges's predicament. Their own predicaments may provide an implicit rebuke to the self-centred machinations of the Laurent family, but nothing more than that. They are not ascribed sufficient screen time to be enlarged beyond a gesture.

In the second scene, which is also the final scene of the film, the engagement celebration of Georges's daughter Anne (Isabelle Huppert) is interrupted by her son Pierre (Franz Rogowski) bringing with him another small group of silent migrants. Pierre's appearance with the uninvited Africans effectively punctures the air of smug entitlement and wealth at the feast. As a narrative prosthesis the Africans work to discomfit the presumed audiences of *Happy End*, as well as Anne and her guests, through their embodiment of a hitherto ignored humanitarian and political crisis. But in calling characters' and viewers' attention to this imbalance, Haneke prioritises a symbolic act of rupture over the subjectivity of the Africans themselves.

In contrast to *Happy End*, *Terraferma* and the two Kaurismäki films, the final two works under discussion here place the experiences of (African) migrants centre stage, relegating white European characters to marginal roles. But this does not imply that European systems of exploitation (of immigrant labour, and of Africa's natural resources) are overlooked. Rather, they are subjected to scrutiny and critique.

Moussa Touré's *La Pirogue* takes its title from the French word for a large wooden fishing boat, used in clandestine migration from Senegal and other parts of West Africa to the Spanish Canary Islands. Based on Abasse Ndione's novella *Mbëke mi*, the film has a simple, familiar format, that of a diverse group of travellers thrown together for a perilous journey, a template that Touré had previously employed in the comedy drama *TGV* (1998), in which a ramshackle bus drives from Dakar to the Guinean capital Conakry.[17] Touré has said that he made *La Pirogue* after meeting a young housepainter in Dakar who had made the six-day boat voyage to the Canaries, but was then repatriated: 'These desperate people generally think even if there's [an economic] crisis in Europe, it's still better to go there than stay in a never-ending crisis [at home].'[18] This context is also briefly summarised in a final crawl before the end credits: 'Between 2005 and 2010, lured by the mirrors of the west, more than 30,000 West Africans have attempted to brave the Atlantic Ocean aboard simple pirogues. Over 5,000 of them perished.' The anthropologist Ruben Andersson expands on the same point: 'clandestine routes from West Africa need to be seen as but one extreme response to the closed borders, economic turmoil and globalized imaginations of a new era'. The urge to migrate is an attempt to forge a connection 'between unfulfilled desires and an unresponsive external world' (Andersson 2014: 20). However, Andersson notes, the demand for cheap, illegal labour has collapsed since the Eurozone crisis: 'clandestine migrants have provided a small but supremely expendable labour force for the construction and farming sectors of new immigration [destinations] such as Italy and Spain. [But] southern Europe's economic bubble [has] burst' (2014: 20).

La Pirogue begins with an open-air wrestling match in front of a vocal crowd. This loud and colourful spectacle of Senegalese culture, (male) prowess and beauty concludes with the first of many bad omens when the wrestler backed by Baye Laye (Souleymane Seye Ndiaye), an experienced fisherman who is soon to become the reluctant captain of the migrants' boat, loses the fight. Later Baye Laye's junior partner Kaba (Babacar Oualy), who has already signed up for the trip, sits with him looking out to the Atlantic and asserts: 'There's no one left here, no more fish. They all left. What can we do here? Nothing lies ahead of us.' In the 2000s, overfishing by supertrawlers from Europe and Russia destroyed fish stocks and fishermen's livelihoods in West Africa. Andersson writes:

Fishing had long been the main métier of Yongor's Lebou inhabitants who [...] were the Senegalese capital's original population. Now a fishing crisis racked their neighbourhoods [...] Stocks had depleted in part because of an explosion in small-scale fishing, caused by Senegal's worsening economy and the motorization of pirogues. The biggest culprit in the emptying of the seas, however, was the sale of fishing rights to other states, not least Spain [...] This [...] was why so many had tried to leave in 2006, embarking in the very boats they had previously used for fishing: here there were no jobs to be had. (2014: 47)

Andersson suggests that Senegalese migrants' motives have often been misunderstood by Western journalists and politicians: 'Rather than being ignorant of the risks, migrants *embraced* [them] in a quest to affirm their masculine prowess [...] Lebou fishermen out of work had suddenly found themselves as the protagonists in a national drama: the heroic seeking of European shores in defiance of the Senegalese and Spanish governments' (2014: 59, italics in original). Male migrants' self-presentation as agentic and heroic is evident in the early stages of the film, as they assemble on the coast, and again when Lansana (Laity Fall) declares to fellow passengers on the boat: 'Je suis un homme africain qui a décidé de rentrer dans l'histoire' [I am an African man who has decided to enter history]. This is not only an assertion of autonomy, but also a riposte to French president Nicholas Sarkozy's notorious speech in Dakar in 2007, when he stated that 'The tragedy of Africa is that the African has not fully entered into history [...] They have never really launched themselves into the future.'[19] However, by the time Lansana has died of thirst, his and others' boasts have been recoded by Touré as understandable aspirations confounded by inescapable structural constraints; the passengers are unable to evade their subaltern position through an act of will.

Ultimately the boat's engine fails and it drifts aimlessly until it is spotted by a helicopter crew. Six survivors (out of the 31 who began) are escorted to the Canaries by Spanish Red Cross workers, the only white characters in the film, and then flown back to Senegal. *La Pirogue* concludes with Baye Laye and his brother Abou (Malaminé 'Yalenguen' Dramé) returning in darkness to their family compound in Dakar. A man asks Abou, 'Weren't you supposed to leave?' to which he replies 'Soon'. Abou's lie is freighted with the shame of repatriation, in the shift from a semi-public departure to a private, almost secret return. The film leaves this continuing shame to resonate beyond the final scene. As Andersson makes clear, the thousands who were repatriated from the Canaries to Senegal in the 2000s became 'walking billboards testifying to the futility of boat migration'. 'The shame of return was shattering [...] Rather than simply being disciplined, the Senegalese repatriates were put to work as human deterrents' (Andersson 2014: 39, 41). The Canaries repatriations were an instance of an emerging 'deportation regime' whereby '[rich] states increasingly defend and enact their sovereignty against those who violate the boundaries of the nation – poor migrants and refugees [who are subjected to] discrimination, abuse, and disciplinary power' (Andersson 2014: 39, 41).[20] *La Pirogue* dramatises the hopes, dangers and disappointments of the people subjected to this regime.

The economic dimensions of migration are also foregerounded in *Mediterranea*, which addresses both attempts to enter Fortress Europe and the struggle for subsistence on arrival. Shot mainly with a hand-held camera and performed by non-professionals, the film is a collaboration between director Jonas Carpignano and his leading man Koudous Seihon, an immigrant from Burkina Faso whose life experience provides the vast majority of the plot. Seihon plays Ayiva, an unmarried father who, with his friend Abas (Alassane Sy), undertakes a gruelling journey via Algeria and Libya to Calabria in southern Italy, in search of work. On the trek across the Sahara the travellers are robbed at gunpoint, and Ayiva has to call his uncle, who is already in Italy, to wire him money to pay for the sea crossing. *Mediterranea* thus begins as a migrant road movie, in the mould of *In This World* (Michael Winterbottom, 2002), *14 Kilometrós* (Gerardo Olivares, 2007) or *La Jaula de Oro* (Diego Quemada-Diez, 2013), but after the first half hour it settles on detailing the poverty, precarity and racism that confront immigrant labourers in southern Italy.

Following the night-time rescue of the migrants after their boat has sunk, an emblematic shot bearing the title 'Italy' is far from a celebration of arrival. Instead it shows exhausted and traumatised Africans gathered quietly in the yard of a detention centre. Once released, the men are situated between two cultures, that of the homeland they have left behind, and the less than welcoming environment of Calabria, where they live in a makeshift camp near the railway line and find insecure, undocumented employment on an orange farm. They are thus 'bodies out of place', racialised and conceived as already suspicious or dangerous 'in advance of their arrival' in certain social spaces in Italy.[21]

Carpignano states that 'the film is pretty much 90 per cent based on experiences that happened to [Seihon]' (Carpignano in Rapold 2015; see also E. Brown 2015). The director met and first cast Seihon when he was making the short film *A Chjana/The Plain* (2012), based on the Rosarno riots of 2010, which also feature in *Mediterranea*. As Vittorio Longhi notes (2014: 79), the shooting of three African farm labourers and the ensuing riots showed how 'attacks are not only motivated by racism, but are also linked to a deeply rooted, generalised system of exploitation of labour'. Longhi writes: 'Africans are the ideal victims of the criminal world that runs orange picking in that area of Calabria, often intimidating them to avoid paying them' (2014: 79). Following immigrants' protests against the initial attack, locals responded by attacking several Africans and setting fire to their homes. 'In a sort of collective hysteria, a "black hunt" started, which required intervention by the police [who] had to remove the Africans and take them to a reception centre to save them from the fury of the citizens' (Longhi 2014: 80). Despite this (limited) response by the authorities, it is vital to understand 'the widespread illegality in labor recruitment and retribution and the lack of institutional intervention' in southern Italy's agricultural sector as 'an added layer of control and coercion' situated within a wider European regime that both depends upon and illegalises migrant labour (Gambino 2017: 256).[22] It is this systematic exploitation and oppression of undocumented African workers that confronts Ayiva and Abas in *Mediterranea*.

Ayiva's liminality is figured by repeated shots of him looking on to a space of colour and music from the outside, unable or uncertain whether or not to cross the threshold and enter. The first iteration comes after he has met Marta, the teenage daughter of Rocco, the (white) orange farmer for whom he works. Ayiva is walking around the outside of the house when he hears music and peers through an open door to see the girl dancing along to a music video. He remains silent and watches her, unseen, for a moment before moving on. The scene is lighthearted rather than voyeuristic, but it adumbrates significant limits on Ayiva's freedom of movement, as a temporary employee rather than a relative or friend. In contrast to Marcel Marx, Waldemar Wikström and Filippo, Rocco can never be thought of as a benefactor. He is only ever Ayiva's employer. The narrow and asymmetrical nature of their relationship is made evident when Ayiva asks Rocco for help in securing a work permit. The farmer

Figure 12.1   Ayiva (left) looking for employment in *Mediterranea* (Jonas Carpignano, 2015).

expresses sympathy, recalling his own grandfather's hard life as an immigrant in New York, but has no interest in aiding Ayiva and only offers him a few banknotes.

The second figuration of Ayiva's liminality comes following the riot in which Abas has been injured, and once Ayiva has decided that they should return home. He makes a Skype call to his sister in Burkina Faso.[23] 'You don't look fine', she comments, to which he replies, 'This is what I always look like here.' Ayiva has sent his seven-year-old daughter Zena an mp3 player that he stole. Now she appears on the screen and dances to her favourite song. Separated by thousands of miles, the interface gives Ayiva virtual access to his family but also serves to heighten their physical and emotional separation. He temporarily cuts the link to hide his feelings as he cries silently.

In the subsequent and final scene, Ayiva is working at Marta's birthday party when Rocco asks him to come inside for a drink. An extended shot shows Ayiva in medium close-up, hesitating on the threshold, his face illuminated by purple and blue lights from the party as a 1980s pop song plays (Richi and Poveri's hit 'Sarà perché ti amo'). The lights, the music, the champagne and the guests' expensive cars collectively function as a metonym for the dream of Europe as a land of plenty. As Andersson writes of postcolonial Africa: 'Europe [is] rendered as a mythical repository of wealth and transformative power' (2014: 19). However, the reality for the vast majority of undocumented immigrants is a life of poverty and precarity. To paraphrase neoliberal economist Milton Friedman: 'Immigration is good for business as long as it remains illegal – because immigrants without rights are cheaper to hire' (Friedman, summarised in Gamlen 2015: 310).[24] Eventually, Ayiva walks slowly towards the party room in an out-of-focus shot, his silhouette gradually merging with the moving coloured lights as the music fades out. This last, ambiguous scene refuses any easy consolations or resolutions.

In *A History of the World in Seven Cheap Things* Raj Patel and Jason W. Moore offer an urgent reminder about the inseparability of capitalism and colonialism, both old and new. They write: 'Frontiers are [. . .] encounter zones between capital and all kinds of nature – humans included. They are always, then, about reducing the costs of doing business' (2018: 18–19). The central strategy of capitalism in its search for new frontiers to exploit has been the drive for cheapness. 'Cheap is a strategy, a practice, a violence that mobilises all kinds of work – human and animal, botanical and geological – with as little compensation as possible' (Patel and Moore 2018: 22). This persistent, systemic appetite for cheapness has both put to work and immiserated diverse peoples (and natures) in Africa, Asia and South America, and is now often the only way in which a few of their number might be granted a precarious existence inside Fortress Europe.[25]

Like *La Pirogue*, *Mediterranea* traces the manifold and contingent obstacles that confront its engaging but never simply heroic African protagonists. But the two films also map the more systemic constraints and Žižekian objective violence that both precipitate their flight and limit their options on arrival in Europe. In the process, white benefactors, so attractive to the continent's liberal film-makers, are nowhere to be found. Yet alongside a continuing paucity of substantial filmic engagements with the experiences of those making perilous journeys to the gated continent, symbolic rescues and acts of hospitality look likely to persist on European screens. As such, these well-intentioned but Eurocentric gestures of welcome might be seen to constitute a necessary, if ultimately limited, initial intervention in a prevailing climate of hostility and selective amnesia.

Acknowledgements

Thanks to Charlotte Adcock, Tereza Hadravova, Nick Hodgin and Angelos Koutsourakis.

Notes

1. 'In 2015, 1,255,600 first time asylum seekers applied for international protection in the Member States of the European Union (EU), a number more than double that of the previous year. The number of Syrians [. . .] has doubled [. . .] to reach 362,800, while the number of Afghans has almost quadrupled to 178,200 and that of Iraqis has multiplied by 7 to 121,500. They represent the three main citizenships of first time asylum applicants [. . .] accounting for more than half of all first time applicants' (Anonymous 2016).
2. In addition, as Nicholas De Genova (2002, cited in Andersson 2014: 12) has argued, grouping heterogeneous individuals under the collective rubric of 'migrants' as objects of study constitutes 'epistemic violence' to the complexity of their lived experiences.
3. David Cameron, television interview ITV, 30 July 2015, available at <http://www.itv.com/news/update/2015-07-30/pm-a-swarm-of-migrants-want-to-come-to-britain/> (last accessed 11 December 2019); Viktór Orbán, 'Orbán Viktor sajtótájékoztatója az Európai Tanács ülését követően' (Viktor Orbán's press conference following the European Council's meeting), Government of Hungary, 21 February 2016, cited in Rajaram (2016: 4). Ruben Andersson comments: '*illegal immigrant* [is] pejorative, stigmatizing, and even incorrect, implying as it does that migrants are criminals when they have usually only committed an administrative infraction. While the creeping criminalization of migration is changing this, *illegal* remains insidious when used to label *people* rather than actions' (2014: 17, italics in original). Patrick Kingsley (2016: 52) argues: 'While someone [. . .] may be best described as an economic migrant when he sets out from Nigeria, after a few weeks in Libya [typically involving imprisonment violence, and hunger] he will be someone more akin to a

refugee.' Alex Rotas (2004: 52) warns that 'the term refugee smooths over difference within the group it designates at the same time as reifying the boundary that defines its otherness'.

4. 'If Lebanon with its tiny population of 4.5 million can manage, then the world's richest continent (population 500 million) can too' (Kingsley 2016: 294). See also the 2015 speech by Francois Crépeau, UN special rapporteur, cited in Kingsley (2016: 294–5).
5. In these largely androcentric films, women are often relegated to minor roles (wife, mother, sister, daughter, prostitute). For a discussion of documentary responses to the so-called refugee crisis, see Austin 2019.
6. The cinephilic Kaurismäki calls this final image 'a perfect Ozu shot' (von Bagh 2011: n.p.). *Le Havre* recalls not just Ozu but also the fantastical fate of the homeless at the end of de Sica's *Miracolo a Milano/Miracle in Milan* (1951). It was released in the Italian market as *Miracolo a Le Havre*.
7. Kaurismäki's films thus offer a particular version of the tension that Lesley Stern locates in the cinema of Robert Bresson, which 'demonstrates its own cinematic performativity at the same time as it draws from the quotidian world of things' (2001: 324).
8. For more on the politics and aesthetics of Kaurismäki, see Austin 2018.
9. This device recalls Eisenstein's oscillation between the classical delineation of space and spatial expansions and overlaps in *Strike* (1925).
10. A rather less nuanced endorsement of progressive thinking is evident in Kaurismäki's *Toivon Tuolla Puolen/The Other Side of Hope* (2017), which also concerns a white male benefactor offering hospitality to an uninvited guest from overseas. Sherwan Haji plays Khaled, a Syrian mechanic who has lost most of his family in the bombing of Aleppo and arrives in Helsinki having stowed away on a coal freighter. Waldemar Wikström (Sakari Kuosmanen) is a middle-aged shirt salesman who leaves his business and his wife to take over a struggling restaurant. The pair meet when Khaled, fleeing deportation, is discovered sleeping behind the restaurant bins by Wikström, who then gives him a job. Khaled enjoys a more developed subjectivity than that of Idrissa. He is accorded a significant role in the narrative, and manifests ingenuity, determination and dry charm. Kaurismäki's characters are usually taciturn, but he grants Khaled an atypically lengthy account of his travails crossing Europe, including losing touch with his sister on the trek. But *The Other Side of Hope* refrains from the Brechtian devices that productively complicate the utopianism of *Le Havre*. For more on the power relations inherent in the dynamic of hospitality, see Austin 2019.
11. In *The Other Side of Hope* the community is comprised of Wikström and his staff at the struggling restaurant.
12. Matthew Carr notes, 'In 1997 Lampedusa became a destination for undocumented migrants from North Africa for the first time' (2015: 78–9). Following the collapse of the Ben Ali regime in Tunisia and Gaddafi's overthrow in Libya, both in 2011, many more Tunisians, Libyans and migrants from other parts of Africa began arriving on the island. With a booming oil economy Libya had become a migration destination in its own right, but it was also the beneficiary of a 5 billion dollar

'friendship pact' with Italy in 2008, and had been promised a further 50 billion euros by the European Commission in 2010 for its part in a 'cooperation agenda' to curtail African migration to Europe. See also Andersson 2014: 14.

13. *Fire at Sea* opens with an intertitle stating that 400,000 migrants have landed on the island in the past twenty years, and another 15,000 have died in the attempt. For further discussion of *Fire at Sea*, see Austin 2019.
14. The neighbour who informs on Marcel is played by Jean-Pierre Léaud, a totemic actor for Kaurismäki, whose acting style he imitated in *Valehtelija/The Liar* (1981), and who he also cast in *I Hired a Contract Killer* (1990) and *La Vie de Bohème* (1992).
15. Triangular dynamics between tourists, police and migrants are also traced in *Die Farbe des Ozeans/The Colour of the Ocean* (Maggie Peren, 2011).
16. A similar pattern of expiation and emotional catharsis is anticipated but crucially complicated in Luc and Jean-Pierre Dardenne's *La Promesse* (1996). Teenager Igor's attempt to make amends for his complicity in his father's exploitation of vulnerable immigrant labour is ultimately refused by Assita, the widow of Amidou, an 'illegal' worker from Burkina Faso who has died in an accident. In the last scene of the film Assita leaves Igor and walks away from him and the camera, leaving him running after her.
17. A review in the *San Diego Reader* compared *La Pirogue* to Hitchcock's *Lifeboat* (1944) 'with more tragic results' (Marks 2013).
18. Interview, 4 December, 2012, available at <http://www.dailymotion.com/video/xvlybj_myfff-2013-interview-moussa-toure-la-pirogue-the-pirogue_shortfilms> (last accessed 11 December 2019). Touré adds: 'It's hard to make a film in a country where people don't have enough to eat. Movies are not a priority in Africa.' In another interview, he states: 'In Dakar no-one has seen the film, because there are no cinemas' (Forster 2013).
19. Sarkozy continued: 'The African peasant only knew the eternal renewal of time, marked by the endless repetition of the same gestures and the same words. In this realm of fancy [. . .] there is neither room for human endeavour nor the idea of progress' (Ba 2007; see also Tchouaffe n.d.).
20. 'To implement repatriation-as-deterrence, Spain had entered into a grand bargain with Senegal [. . .] Madrid padded the steeliness of policing and deportation with financial rewards and warm diplomatic words [. . .] Between 2006 and 2010, arrivals in the Canaries dropped from thirty-two thousand to two hundred a year' (Andersson 2014: 40–1).
21. I am citing here Sarah Ahmed's discussion of 'stranger danger' (2014a: 211–12). Ahmed argues that 'The immediacy of bodily reactions is mediated by histories that come before subjects, and which are at stake in how the very arrival of some bodies [in certain spaces] is noticeable in the first place' (2014a: 212).
22. On migrant workers' and local activists' responses to the riots, and the establishment of the Campagna in Lotta (Fields of Struggle) network, see Gambino 2017: 275–81. On the Italian distribution and logistics sector, Anna Curcio and Gigi Roggero write: 'Differently from countries that invested heavily in automation and large-scale information systems, capital gains in the Italian logistics sector have

long been predicated on the exploitation of an underqualified or underpaid workforce, mostly made of migrant workers' (Curcio and Roggero 2018: n.p.).
23. In an earlier phone call, Ayiva had told his sister that the sea crossing was too dangerous for them to join him.
24. See also Gambino 2017: 260–1. Longhi writes that, despite the economic downturn, the Italian economy still needs 100,000 overseas workers per year, a figure that is expected to more than double by 2020. 'It begs the question why, if the demand for foreign workers is so great, more realistic criteria are not adopted for setting quotas and more legal permits are not granted' (Longhi 2014: 82).
25. Clearly this excludes the easy and taken for granted mobility of elites from all parts of the world.

13. FRONTLINES: MIGRANTS IN HUNGARIAN DOCUMENTARIES IN THE 2010S

Lóránt Stőhr

The refugee 'crisis' swept over Europe in 2015, resulting in a series of documentaries on the topic of migration in the continent and all over the world. The populist Hungarian government that has ruled the country since 2010 utilised the migration 'crisis' to boost its temporarily waning popularity by creating a demonic image of the refugee as the enemy of the country. As a result of the deliberate mishandling of mass migration, Hungary was one of the European countries where the flow of refugees congested and caused highly dramatic scenes in 2015. Despite the cinematic potential of these spectacular events and their impressive media coverage, no Hungarian documentaries thematised the turbulent events directly. In this chapter, I aim to provide an explanation of this telling absence and to analyse documentaries on migration and refugees before and after 2015. The overarching question is how have Hungarian documentary film-makers represented these issues in the recent xenophobic and openly anti-migration political climate, in which financial resources for socially critical documentaries are largely absent?

Freedom of expression in Hungary has gradually decreased since 2010, but some relatively independent financial support has remained available for a handful of documentary projects annually. Openly critical documentaries have not been banned yet as they were under state socialism, and their directors can operate in this underfinanced field of film-making, but government grants and television channels are cautious in their support. With regard to the complex and changing context of film production, I examine, first, the institutional background, secondly the representational strategies of Hungarian documentaries on refugees, and thirdly their reception in Hungarian society. I have two main theses concerning the film corpus under discussion. First, the emphasis of Hungarian documentaries shifted from the issue of integration into Hungarian society (2009–13) to the exploration of the physical methods and social psychological motifs of the exclusion of potential immigrants from Hungarian society (2013–17). Secondly, Hungarian documentaries have increasingly aligned the physical and ethnic boundaries between refugees and the majority of society with the increasing political and cultural gap within Hungarian society.

The Refugee Crisis and its Consequences in Hungary

From 2012 to 2015 the numbers of immigrants increased at the southern border of Hungary and there was an increase in applications for refugee status in Hungary (Bernáth and Messing 2015: 9). The refugee crisis peaked in 2015. 'More than 487,000 people arrived at Europe's Mediterranean shores in the first nine months of 2015, double all of 2014 and the highest number since record keeping began', and '[m]ore than 155,000 people crossed from Serbia into Hungary between January and August' (Banulescu-Bogdan and Fratzke 2015). Politicians did not react to the growing numbers of refugees in the country until 2015 when the Hungarian populist government, led by Prime Minister Viktor Orbán, recognised the potential to boost his party's waning popularity with anti-migrant propaganda. After the Islamist terrorist attack against the offices of *Charlie Hebdo* in Paris January 2015, the government parties (Fidesz, KDNP) and also the far-right opposition party, Jobbik, followed Orbán's new political direction in naming migrants as the main threat to the country (Bernáth and Messing 2015: 9–10). The government immediately launched a massive campaign against migration and deliberately mishandled the dramatic events of mass migration in the summer and early autumn of 2015. The government caused turmoil with its totally inadequate and inhumane management of the difficult situation of migration emerging mainly at the southern border and in Budapest. By creating chaos, Orbán's main goal was to establish himself and his government as the main guardians of order (Kallius, Monterescu and Rajaram 2016: 34) and the defenders of Hungary and the whole of Europe against the massive wave of migration. The so-called 'defence' consisted of the construction of a temporary fence at the southern borders of Hungary during the summer and autumn of 2015. The fence 'has also appeared as a defence and civilisation metaphor in Hungarian and European public discourse' (Glied and Pap 2016: 142).

Public television was brought under total and direct state control and became a media machine for state propaganda immediately after Fidesz won the election in 2010 (Magyar 2016: 209–10). Businessmen directly linked to the party have gradually acquired the majority of the commercial media companies since

2010 (Urbán 2016; Kovács 2018). The government launched an aggressive political campaign consisting of a so-called 'national consultation on immigration and terrorism', and a billboard campaign advertising the 'results' of the consultation (Barlai and Sík 2017: 153–4), followed by a referendum on the relocation quota in October 2016. Xenophobia has grown to a relatively high level since 1989, but migration was not regarded as a significant problem until the political campaign with its inflammatory language hit the country in 2015 and totally transformed public attitudes towards refugees in Hungary (Hunyadi and Molnár 2016).

The Institutional Conditions of Contemporary Hungarian Documentary Film Making

The dramatic events of mass migration and the absurd government measures in response offered several perfect topics for socially active and morally conscious Hungarian documentary film-makers. However, against all expectations based on the trend of contemporary (Western) European documentary cinema, only a handful of documentaries have been made about refugees and migration in Hungary since 2010, and only two compilations of television news on the refugee crisis in 2015. The explanation for this conspicuous absence might lie in the institutional and economic framework of contemporary Hungarian documentary film making. Until 2011 the Motion Picture Public Foundation of Hungary (MMKA), a democratically elected and governed film fund, was the main sponsor of social documentary projects, many of which were highly critical of Hungarian social affairs. The Fidesz government closed the fund in 2011 (Foktői 2016: 51–3). The Media Council, heavily influenced by government politics, took over the job of financing documentaries. It supports mainly conservative documentary projects about cultural excellence and the historical merits of the nation, while socially critical documentary works are almost absent from the list of supported films (Stőhr 2019). Film-makers rely on politically less prejudiced, but financially even less predictable sponsors, such as the Hungarian National Film Fund (MNF), HBO Europe and the University of Theatre and Film Arts (SZFE), if they want to make socially critical pieces. Until 2014 the main sponsor of Hungarian documentaries on migration was not the Hungarian government but the European Union through the European Refugee Fund and European Integration Fund.

Representation of Refugees and Migrants in Hungarian Documentary Cinema

In 1989 the borders of Eastern Europe opened, which meant, on the one hand, that Hungarians had the chance to travel abroad and emigrate, and, on the other, that Hungary became a destination for immigration. Despite the growing number of Chinese migrants and their visibility because of their businesses (fast food restaurants, shops, markets) in Hungary from 1990 onwards (Nyíri 2003: 249), the representation of non-Hungarian migrants in the media played a marginal role, and they appeared as almost fairy-tale characters in Hungarian feature films (Erőss 2019: 130). Until 2009 documentaries followed this trend, with a very few exceptions such as *Az út* (*The Way*, 1997) and *Szia nagyi, jól vagyunk!* (*Hi Granny, We Are All Fine!*, 1999). The Balkan civil war and ethnic cleansing prompted a wave of refugees towards Hungary, which was scarcely represented in Hungarian documentaries. Rare exceptions are *Végállomások* (*Destinations*, 2005) and *Bosznia, Bosznia!* (*Bosnia, Bosnia!*, 2012). Migrants did not make any documentaries about their own experiences, and thus accented cinema (Hamid Naficy) is also absent from Hungarian film culture.

To explain this conspicuous absence, we can mention Dina Iordanova's point that Europe in the post-Cold War era can be appropriately described in postcolonial terms (Iordanova 2010: 52–6). 'Eastern Europe's frontier position in Europe has made it into a type of colony for the West' (Imre 1999: 406) and it 'remains ambiguous: it is both inside and outside, not "European" enough, nor "White" enough, and in a permanent state of needing to catch up' (Grzechnik 2019: 5). Consequently, before and after 1989, Eastern Europeans looked to the West to 'catch up' with, that is, to learn its political, social and economic models. Hungarians therefore perceived themselves as inferiors in comparison to Western standards, and not as proud citizens of an 'empire'.

Before the huge wave of migration, the 'Westernised' members of Hungarian society regarded the losers from the political and economic transition, and not the scarcely visible Asian and African immigrants, as their Other (Buchowski 2006: 466). When Hungary joined the EU in 2004 and the Schengen area in 2007, Hungarian people also found themselves in 'Fortress Europe'. Despite having crossed the long-existing physical, imaginary and mental borders, Hungarians do not regard themselves as part of Europe's colonising past and do not feel any responsibility towards migrants coming from Eastern and Southern postcolonial societies. Accordingly, documentary film-makers chiefly examined the postcolonial condition in Hungary (rapidly increasing unemployment and impoverishment, privatisation of public companies to Western investors), and were less interested in the Asian and African migrants in their own country.

The funding sources and institutional background of Hungarian documentaries explain the changes in the representation of migrants and refugees. Hungary's joining the EU launched a small wave of migration documentaries between 2009 and 2013 as a result of EU funds, in which Hungarian film-makers made empathetic documentaries on immigrants integrating into society and refugees struggling in camps. After this EU-sponsored programme stopped, HBO, MNF and SZFE at least partly took over the task of supporting documentaries on migration. In the years of tightening economic, cultural and political censorship, state socialist patterns of Hungarian culture resurrected in the field of documentary film making, especially in the case of those made about such a contentious issue as migration. First, small areas of relative freedom of expression were maintained and sponsored by the state in the same way as under state socialism. Paradoxically, the biggest budget documentary on migration with the highest production standards was made during these years (*Könnyű leckék/Easy Lessons*, 2018), as a result of the relative political freedom of the MNF, guaranteed by the good relationship of its leader, Andy Vajna, with the prime minister. The SZFE also functioned as a small, underfinanced but 'independent' studio, similarly to the Béla Balázs Studio (BBS) in the 1960s and 1970s, a relatively independent though state-financed studio which was the main source of critical documentaries. Secondly, artistic strategies revived, such as ironic and allegorical representations, which avoid open violation of political taboos without surrendering social and political criticism. The films made at SZFE, in the absence of special obligations to the EU programmes, pointed to the growing hostility of Hungarian society against migrants, exposing the lies and contradiction of state propaganda through their characters' words and behaviour, as in the films of the late 1960s and 1970s.

Hungarian documentaries can be divided into three groups according to their focus on different possible aspects of migration. The first group, which I call 'integration documentaries' (partly after the name of the financing EU fund), reveal the possibilities and difficulties of integration by stressing cultural differences between the immigrants and the majority of Hungarian society. The second, 'journey documentaries' (Jørholt 2019: 282), represent the transitional situation of refugees on their risky routes to the destination country and their plight in refugee camps until they receive refugee status. The third group, 'host society documentaries', concentrate on the attitudes of the public to migrants in host societies. In the next section, I will analyse Hungarian documentaries through this typology, putting emphasis on the third group of films because this category has the closest link to the refugee crisis.

Integration

'Integration documentaries' are characterised by the film-maker's intention to understand the migrants' complex cultural and religious identity in relation to the host society. The migrant characters share their own experiences, thoughts and emotions with the viewers, to enable them to understand their unique positions and attitudes towards Hungarians. The main concern of integration documentaries is to make familiar the face of the migrants and reduce their 'Otherness' to the members of the host society. The EU-sponsored versions of integration documentaries have several main characters and storylines providing an overview of the examined problem of migration. Thus, film-makers applied the methods of Hungarian 'sociological documentary' (Hammer 2009) by showing more examples and short stories on the same phenomenon, underpinning their rhetorical aim. The three stories of *3 esküvő* (*3 Weddings*, 2009) show couples in mixed marriages – a Hungarian wife and a migrant husband – to shed light on the nature of their coexistence with regard to cultural, ethnic and linguistic differences. *Allah minden napján szaladnak a lovak* (*Every Day of Allah Horses Run*, 2011) represents the cultural and linguistic difficulties of the Muslim migrants in Budapest and their ethical dilemma of separation from their culture and their forebears. Contradicting their own 'methodology', the film-makers often represent refugees or migrants without emphasising the differences between their personal, ethnic and cultural backgrounds.

As opposed to the EU-financed 'sociological' documentaries, the feature-length *Könnyű leckék* (*Easy Lessons*, 2018), financed by the MNF and directed by a young film-maker, Dorottya Zurbó, focuses on a single protagonist's story, in the tradition of contemporary, character-driven documentaries (Cagle 2012: 54–5). The narrative arc is built on the protagonist's integration process into Hungarian society. The plot follows the last year of secondary school of Kafiya (Kafiya Said Mahdi), a Somalian girl in Budapest. The clearly defined narrative goal is her graduation, which will function as her entrance into Western culture and Hungarian society. With the irony suggested by the title, the director creates one of the main plot points in the film by revealing that Kafiya has a Christian boyfriend and has converted to Christianity. On the one hand, this is the ultimate renunciation of her family and faith; on the other, it can be interpreted as the ultimate accomplishment of her aim: integration.

The emotional drama unfolds as an inner conflict with her mother left behind in Somalia. Kafiya does not dare to talk about her life in Hungary to her mother for fear of her disapproval. The dramatic climax of the narrative is constructed by Zurbó in an intimate confession scene at a professional sound studio, where Kafiya can whisper her imaginary confession and secret feelings to her mother. The Somalian girl has a closed personality as a result of her difficult past and struggles in the present, so she could not tell her thoughts and feelings to the film-maker or other characters who are present in the filmed situations. As Zurbó mainly used the method of observational documentaries and relied on information that Kafiya revealed to others, she could have not shown her protagonist's inner thoughts and feelings without this confession scene. Kafiya's emotional struggle during her integration is expressed by the close-ups on her face and the observational footage accompanied by her confession as a voice-over narration. As a result of Zurbó's film-making strategy, the viewer can strongly empathise with Kafiya and experience her struggles.

With the stress put on the emotional drama of integration and denunciation, that is, 'the good story', the director impoverishes the analysis of the political context in the film. The protagonist hardly talks about the social situation of women in Somalia and she completely refuses to recount her long escape from Somalia to Hungary. The film-maker avoids reflecting on the official discourse on migration, which depicts it as a potential threat to the host society. There is only one short excerpt from a news programme screened in the background which refers to the current political situation in Hungary. Kafiya lives through the refugee crisis and its political aftermath, but she does not care about politics and she does not talk about the ongoing xenophobic campaign in the film. The representation of society seems to refute the statements of sociological surveys on the growing hostility against migrants. All the Hungarians presented in the film help Kafiya: the tutor and her fellows at the children's home, her boyfriend, the swimming coach and the teachers at the secondary school.

Zurbó's political strategy as a film-maker is to make it easier for Hungarian and other viewers to identify with the migrant protagonist, and thus facilitate an understanding and acceptance of refugees coming from different cultures in general. Kafiya is a conspicuously beautiful girl, whose face and eyes are very expressive, whose voice is soft and kind. Her face was on posters and printed advertisements for the film, and her photo was on the cover of the Hungarian edition of the international women's magazine *Marie Claire* when the film was released. Because of her beauty, the choice of the protagonist seems to be rather manipulative; however, the director claims to have had different intentions originally. Zurbó started creating a web documentary about refugee children living in a Hungarian foster home, but all her characters moved to Western Europe during the 2015 refugee crisis except for Kafiya, who felt too exhausted to travel further and find another country to live in. Although the story of the shoot explains why this extraordinary girl became the only representative of thousands of migrants trying to settle in Hungary, nevertheless this directorial choice eases the viewer's identification with Kafiya and the unfolding story creates an unambiguous empathy for her.

By muting the contradictions of migration and assimilation, Kafiya is presented as the 'ideal migrant' in the film, not only beautiful, extremely ambitious and diligent, but willing to adapt to European norms completely. Thus, Western viewers can easily appreciate her hard work and endurance without facing the price of her success, that is, that she has entirely sacrificed her past identity. Despite its problematic choice of protagonist, *Easy Lessons* is the first Hungarian documentary to show a migrant as a well-rounded character, emphasising her individuality and not reducing her to her social position as a migrant. Consequently, *Easy Lessons* has an ambiguous political message; on the one hand, it makes a brave stand for refugees and helps to change attitudes towards them in a hostile sociopolitical context; on the other, for less sensitive viewers, it may promote the idea of total integration to Western civilisation as the key to one's admission to society.

Journey

Interestingly, 'journey documentaries' are hardly represented in Hungarian cinema. One might assume that the Hungarian authorities would have made it difficult, and from 2015 practically impossible, for film-makers to shoot in refugee camps and on the border.[1] The one and only professional documentary, *Két világ közt* (*Caught between Two Worlds*, 2011), produced by HBO Europe, represents the confinements, difficulties and relative peace of a Hungarian refugee camp. Two less significant documentaries on the migrants' journey were part of a compilation made by local television channels. *Álljon meg a menet!* (*Stop the March!*, 2017) is a typical propaganda work that promotes the government's anti-migrant policy. The director/cinematographer of a television studio in Győr did not conduct any interviews with the refugees but used an extensive voice-over commentary that emphasises the detriments and dangers of 'illegal migrants' in Hungary. *Félúton a jobb világ felé* (*Half-Way Towards a Better World*, 2017) was made by an ethnic Hungarian television channel in Serbia, which explains how it could be shot on the border during the refugee crisis. The television programme is a compilation of empathetic interviews with refugees and coverage of the events on the Serbian side of the border, accompanied by a neutral or sometimes slightly anti-migrant voice-over narration cautiously serving the propaganda aims of the Hungarian government.

The only significant documentary on the topic, *Caught between Two Worlds* does not show migrants *en masse* (as in the compilation works), but creates vivid individual portraits of some asylum seekers in Hungary. The director, Viktor Oszkár Nagy, gives the protagonists the right to tell their own stories of flight and give their opinions on the Hungarian immigration system. Their past sufferings play an important part, but they are not overemphasised in the portrayal of the four main characters. All of them fled violence and death in their homeland. Usama (Khaled Saleh Usama) escaped from a life-threatening political situation in Lebanon with his family; Lia (Lia Kokoeva), a Georgian woman, fled with her son from the Georgian-Ossetian war; Bebe (Diary Bebe) left the Ivory Coast, where her whole family was murdered and she was brutally attacked and raped; and Ahmed (Ahmed Omar Salah) fled Somalia, leaving his wife and children behind, after many years of brutal discrimination, hiding and a severe beating. While Bebe and Ahmed recount their horrible sufferings in detail in intimate situations, the two families touch upon their miseries in their own country only briefly, supposedly with the aim of protecting their children from the past trauma.

Although the horrible past of the refugees lingers in the background, Nagy places emphasis on their present experience of the camp. He shows their monotonous everyday life: bored children watch television and play computer games, or kick a ball on a dusty football field; young men work out in the fitness room; and families walk on the dreary paths between the houses. These sequences are juxtaposed with intimate scenes showing family life and personal exchanges with fellow refugees. These scenes capture the very personal and intimate moments in refugees' lives and portray them not as a faceless flock of migrants but as individuals with their own experiences and emotions, similar to those of Hungarian viewers. The images are dominated by the faces of the refugees to enhance the intimate atmosphere and bring them closer to the viewers emotionally. The past, nevertheless, keeps emerging in the present. When two men court Bebe with a not so hidden sexual agenda and she refuses them perplexedly, the memory of her sufferings haunts the scene. Similarly, Ahmed's journey in a truck on country roads also awakens his horrible memories of Somalia.

The dramatic tension in the narrative derives from the temporariness of life in the refugee camp, as we can see in other European documentaries set in detention centres such as *Die Unsichtbaren* (*Invisibles*, 2014) *La forteresse* (*The Fortress*, 2008) and *Vol special* (*Special Flight*, 2011). The protagonists are introduced through captions with their names and the number of days remaining of the one year they are allowed to stay in the camp. After they receive refugee status in Hungary, they are given only one year to prepare to settle down in the country. Emotionally, refugees feel at home in the houses of the camp after their long flight, but rationally they are aware of the fleeting nature of this stability. They live in the transitional time and space of the refugee camp and the limbo state of refugee life. As scholars have shown, 'the perceived limbo situation of being neither "here" nor "there" became a paralysing force that prevented refugees from actively seeking employment' (Koser 2007: 245). Bebe is the only one who works, as a cleaner in the camp, while the other refugees keep trying to find jobs in vain.

The most dramatic storyline of the four main characters represents the hardships of their integration into Hungarian society. Lia and her son must leave the camp in a few weeks' time, but she is unable to find a job and rent a flat. The film stresses Lia's vulnerability and helplessness due to the lack of proper help from the Hungarian state. She complains about the burnt-out social workers who do not empathise with the refugees. While Lia is trying to make ends meet on the tight official support of the state, Ahmed's story exposes the absurdity of the Hungarian immigration system. The state does not recognise Somalian passports, therefore Ahmed's wife and children who fled to Yemen are not allowed to join him, despite his acknowledged refugee status. Though both Lia's and Ahmed's stories start before the Hungarian government's xenophobic propaganda campaign, they keep coming up against the constraints of the Hungarian immigration system.

Host Society

The 'sense of border' that had been generated by putting into practice 'a way of understanding the world that made distinctions between one entity and another, one people and another, one place and another' (Green 2012: 577) was intensified in Hungarian society by the mass movement of migrants who appeared at the southern border. The Fidesz-controlled media – including the public service radio and television channels – instilled fear of migrants among citizens to gain public support for building a fence on the border. The fortified border became a solid wall of 'the fortress of Europe' in the public imagination. The rapidly increasing number of migrants and the growing hostility towards them motivated Hungarian documentary film-makers to analyse the sense of border by portraying some representatives of Hungarian society with an ironic tone and creative filmic techniques.

The first 'host society' documentary, *Felsőbb parancs* (*Superior Orders*, 2013), is the only one that was shot in the borderland, supported by the European Refugee Fund of the EU. Viktor Oszkár Nagy reacted to the phenomenon of the increasing number of illegal border crossings at the southern border two years before the peak of the refugee crisis. This was followed by two student films, set in remote villages far away from Budapest, which examine Hungarians' attitudes towards migrants in small and closed societies. The absurd prejudices and contradictions offered by the villagers in the interviews are juxtaposed with an ironic approach in both films. *Azok* (*Those*, 2016), which was shot in 2014–15 in a wealthy north-western Hungarian village, Vámosszabadi, examines the social, psychological and political effects of a newly established refugee camp on the edge of the village. The other film, *Iborfia* (2017), portrayed the day of the infamous migrant quota referendum in 2016 in the smallest village of Hungary, which provides the title of the film. *Iborfia* revealed the contradictory views on migration of a resident of the village who had never met a migrant.

The three documentaries share the critical interpretation of the perplexed national self. All the films point out the social and political divisions of the 'host society' by stressing the polarised viewpoints and attitudes of social actors towards migrants. The political and social stance of the characters is often related to their strong emotional attachment to the state and its ethnic borders. Mabel Berezin explains this phenomenon by the various experiential dimensions that territory plays in human communities. She asserts that 'its capacity to subjectify social, political and cultural boundaries make it the core of public and private identity projects . . . Emotion is a constitutive dimension of territory' (Berezin 2004: 7). For many people, the borders of their nation represent the territory in which they can define their identity against globalisation. From a psychological perspective, territory and borders can help a community define its own collective identity and its cultural heritage set against the 'Other'. The collective fantasy about the cultural 'Other' and its imaginative expulsion as an abject help to 'reinforce the borders of the collective and personal identity' (Erős 2001: 21).

Anthropologists of state borders also support the psychological explanation for claiming borders. Pablo Vila pointed out an apparently contradictory human need for both movement and solid basis, change and permanence.

> Money, people, and culture constantly move, allowing people to anchor their identities in the new entities this process creates [. . .] However, many people feel threatened by the idea of abandoning the kinds of national, racial, and ethnic names (and the culture those names involve) that have identified them for generations. (Vila 2000: 7)

Vila therefore thinks that the 'crossing of borders' metaphor should be complemented with another one referring to 'reinforcing borders'. This other metaphor describes the attitudes of those people who fear cultural globalisation and insist on their ethnic, national or cultural characteristics, and do not support any kind of amalgamation with other ethnic or cultural groups. Hungarian documentary film-makers have pointed to the growing need for 'reinforcing borders' in Hungarian society as a result of weak individual identity strategies and strong attachment to the national self, which was boosted by the harsh anti-migrant propaganda and the building of fences on the state border.

Superior Orders takes place at the Hungarian-Serbian border, where only short sections of barbed wire had been put up at the time of shooting. Borders have been spaces of violence since their inception. Borders are the 'scars in the territorial landscape that act as reminders of "the sufferings, the crimes, the tortures" that rarely fail to accompany the founding of states as distinct entities' (Vaughan-Williams 2009: 70). Nevertheless, Wendy Brown points to the contradiction posed by building physical walls on borders in the present era of globalisation:

> Ideologically, the dangers that walls are figured as intercepting are not merely the would-be suicide bomber, but immigrant hordes; not merely violence to the nation, but imagined dilution of national identity through transformed ethnicised or racial demographics; not merely illegal entrance, but unsustainable pressure on national economies that have ceased to be national or on welfare states that have largely abandoned substantive welfare functions. (Brown 2010: 82)

Brown describes very precisely the ideology of the present Hungarian government, which is reflected in the characters' words and behaviour in the analysed documentaries.

Fences and walls are still considered to be embodiments of the state's right to apply violence against the violators of borders. The walls built on borders have become a popular topic in contemporary fiction and documentary cinema, as they make the traces of the 'violent scars in the landscapes' visible again. Contemporary documentary films, such as *The Great Wall* (2015) and *Walls* (2015), usually represent walls as the materialised signs of the opposition between impersonal power and powerless people. *Superior Orders* also presents the state border as a space of violence. Its recurring visual motif is the night-vision camera shot scanning the borderland. This helps the representatives of the state to reinforce the border on a visual level and alienates the refugees. In the last scene, the close-ups of the monochromatic, low-resolution night-vision shots show migrants as menacing aliens or targets in a video game. The highly emotional Latin American musical score, which is played by refugees (Silveira Claudicea and Ayala Manuel), gives a counterpoint to the uncanny and inhuman nature of the images.

The patched tents of the refugees scattered in the borderland on the Serbian side are controlled by the state and unpredictably governed by arbitrariness and personal interest. Migrants tell the film-maker about their regular harassment by Serbian policemen, who take their money by force. Waiting on the borders of the EU at, for instance, Melilla or Ceuta, as represented in other European documentaries such as *Bab Sebta* (2008), *Ceuta, Prison by the Sea* (2013) and *The Land Between* (2014), suggests a similar experience everywhere. Until a refugee gains a new identity within the boundaries of the EU, they will be stuck in the eternal present-time limbo defined by vulnerability and violence. The specific chronotope of the border area can expand indefinitely in time and space. Migrants wait days, weeks or months for the favourable conditions necessary for crossing. The crossing is made as quickly as possible. After they are caught by border guards or present themselves at a police station on the other side of the border, migrants must wait again in a camp for the decision of the authorities.

Superior Orders emphasises personal responsibility in host societies by juxtaposing different attitudes towards refugees. One of the two protagonists, a volunteer border guard (István Turó) who lives in Hungary near the southern border, hunts the migrants, while the other, a Hungarian pastor (Tibor Varga) who lives in Serbia close to the same section of the border, helps the refugees with food, clothing and sympathy. The title confronts the two types of ethos, the 'superior orders', that is, the ideology of nationalism and the idea of Christian love. The oppositional logic of borders determines the dominant attitudes towards refugees; thus the Hungarians inside the border are dedicated to reinforcing the ethnic-cultural borders, while Hungarians outside the border are dedicated to building bridges across these gaps.

The film attributes the different attitudes towards refugees to social role, group identity and personal character traits. The pastor was an immigrant in

South America as a child, where he experienced being an outcast in society. He turns his professional practice of Christian ethics to bridge ethnic, religious and cultural boundaries by giving food, clothing and love to the people in need. The prayers of a small group of men that he leads at the snow-covered border are a simple way of creating a temporary community. As the majority of refugees are Muslim, he first asks permission to pray for them.

In contrast, the border guard cannot express his emotions in front of the camera. His refusal to open up to the camera is a reflection of his emotional refusal of refugees. The volunteer border guards play the social role written for them by Westphalian logic, in acting 'as the bastions of the nation, protecting it from the threat of infiltration' (Green 2012: 577). The border defence helps men in the village to create their group identity based on nationalistic pride and the masculine cult of power. As a result of this strong social identity, they approach refugees with prejudices and a huge sense of superiority and regard them as abject beings.

Those, made during and after the refugee crisis, further explicates this social-psychological phenomenon resulting from the intensification of racist, discriminatory and exclusionary stances in Hungarian society. The director, Krisztina Meggyes, explores the relationship between the people of a Hungarian village and a newly established refugee camp in the neighbourhood. Meggyes creates an allegorical reading of the local story by inserting it into a fairy-tale framework illustrated by animated sequences. She understands the social construction of 'Otherness' along the already existing division within the village. The first pole of the community consists of old, poor villagers who have long been living in a relatively traditional way in Vámosszabadi. The second pole is of prosperous, middle-class families, who moved to Vámosszabadi in the 1990s and 2000s, and transformed the village into a suburb of Győr, a nearby wealthy city. The director explores the process by which the 'Westernised' part of Hungarian society creates its own 'Other' by socially stigmatising the less successful members of society (Buchowski 2006: 475–6), before the migrants started coming from Eastern and Southern countries and more or less took over the role of the 'Other'. The establishment of a refugee camp near the village could have united the community in identifying a new common enemy. However, in fact it deepened the opposition in Meggyes's interpretation. The wealthy families, feeling their children and property threatened by the migrants, became the leaders of the anti-migrant campaign, while the older and poorer members of the village differentiate themselves from the 'class enemy' by accepting the presence of the refugees in the village. The social division in the village has consequences for the interpretation of the reality of the refugee camp. The older inhabitants conquer their own fear of the unknown by encountering migrants in their own reality, while anxiety is not alleviated in the younger group, whose experiences are framed by their imaginative construction.

Meggyes shows the migrants exclusively from the villagers' mental and visual point of view as a conscious representational strategy. The representatives of the middle-class villagers try to stigmatise the migrants on physical, moral and ethnic grounds (Goffman 1963: 14–15). In their descriptions, migrants are intruders who pose both a direct physical threat and also a menace to the village. The interviewees give voice to the most typical racist fears and prejudices when they characterise African and Asian migrants as hypersexual deviants, who have come to rape 'white women', 'blond, blue-eyed children', and have high fertility rates. The second typical racist imagination presents migrants as an epidemic or as parasites carrying the plague. Finally, the villagers feel superiority to the migrants by regarding them as lazy, uncivilised savages who must be educated and taught to work. In *Those*, Hungarian society as represented by the villagers reproduces the former colonisers' worst racist prejudices to construct migrants as aliens, like the shots of the night-vision cameras in *Superior Orders*. While in Western Europe an indirect and subtle new racism is taking hold, which 'utilizes themes related to culture and nation as a replacement for the now discredited biological referents of the old racism' (Ansell 1997: 20), in Hungary people from the extreme right can still share ideas of biological inferiority and superiority (Van Dijk 2000: 33–4). As Slavoj Žižek suggests, 'impoverished European countries expect the developed West European ones to bear the full burden of multicultural openness, while they can afford patriotism' (Žižek 2016).

Meggyes also reproduces the villagers' visual point-of-view towards the migrants. The camera shows 'strangers' and 'intruders' from behind, or from a great distance, as some fearful villagers see them. Meggyes inserts comical, dream-like sequences, which ironically exaggerate the imagined fearsome character of African, Asian and South American migrants (played by film students in reality), who approach the village menacingly. This sequence can be interpreted via Sara Ahmed's understanding of strangers:

> Through strange encounters, the figure of the 'stranger' is produced, not as that which we fail to recognise, but as that which we have already recognised as 'a stranger'. In the gesture of recognising the one that we do not know, the one that is different from 'us', we flesh out the beyond, and give it a face and form. (Ahmed 2000: 3)

The narrative frame adds a political dimension to the social-psychological understanding of the villagers. The narrative climax is constructed around the 2014 local elections in the village. The issue of the refugee camp helps the middle-class villagers to articulate their own agenda and create their social identity as responsible and active citizens who are fighting against the migrants. Their group produces an atmosphere of fear, which enables their candidate to win. The story set in Vámosszabadi in fact foreshadows political events in Hungary between 2015 and 2018. The film helps the viewer understand the socio-psychological reasons why the majority of people, especially in villages, voted for Fidesz in the national parliamentary election in 2018. In this narrative, the village becomes a model of Hungary, in which a xenophobic, discriminatory and wealthy political and social group comes to power because of its hate propaganda.

Both *Superior Orders* and *Those* point to the racial stigmatisation of migrants, the psychological and technological construction of the ethnic 'Other'. In focusing chiefly on the Hungarians' mental images about and attitudes towards African and Asian people, these films hardly represent the migrants at all. The political background of the Hungarians' anti-migrant stance is more emphasised in the latter films (*Those*, *Iborfia*), while the reinforcement of physical and mental borders is increasingly linked to the reconstruction of the 'national self' in a contemporary, post-communist society under authoritarian rule.

Conclusion

Since 1989 Hungary's path has certainly not been a straight transition from Soviet-style state socialism to Western-style democratic capitalism. What is more, in 2010 the country veered back to an authoritarian regime. In accordance with this contradictory social-political transformation, Hungarian society underwent an ambivalent process of learning to come to terms with immigrants to the country. On the one hand, Hungarian society became more open to migrants, especially in the cities. On the other hand, the present populist government has been able successfully to boost xenophobia in the country, since ethnic and racist prejudices survived as a consequence of Hungary's long isolation.

In accordance with this slow and ambiguous process, film-makers also needed time to recognise the presence of migrants in Hungary and learn how to make documentaries about them. Hungary's entry into the EU advanced the recognition of the civil and artistic responsibility towards migrants, and launched a small wave of documentaries about their integration and life in limbo. Despite the film-makers' sympathetic stance, the EU-sponsored documentaries were not particularly interested in the individuality of the migrants, but rather in their difficulties in settling down and integrating. Some years later, film-makers had to face the tightening financial and bureaucratic censorship on the representation of migrants; consequently they began to analyse the host society and its xenophobic tendencies.

The absence of migrants as individual human beings has haunted the screen of Hungarian documentaries like the worst nightmare of isolated Hungarian society. Paradoxically, the 2015 crisis helped film-makers gain financial support to follow a refugee's life over a period of years, and focus on her as an individual rather than as a member of a collective (as presented in *Easy Lessons*). However, it is possible that growing authoritarian tendencies and xenophobic anger at Asian and African migrants will hinder film-makers in making further complex documentaries on asylum seekers. Hungarian documentary has taken a long time to present the individuality of a migrant on screen, but now that the film-makers have found her face, the right to show it might be taken away.

NOTE

1. Documentary film making about migrants might be punishable in Hungary since June 2018 under the so-called 'Stop Soros' law (Timmer and Docka-Filipek 2018).

14. MONGREL ATTUNEMENT IN *WHITE GOD*

Rosalind Galt

This chapter begins from the question of where we might locate political aesthetics in contemporary European cinema, and in particular the challenge of escaping the various modes of liberal realism that dominate representations of economic crisis and migration. In an attempt to avoid what Karl Schoonover has argued to be neorealism's collaboration with the hegemonic forces of the post-war transnational order (2012: xiv–xviii), my argument avoids the kind of neo-neorealist films that invoke this distancing spectacle of imperilled bodies. It considers instead the cinematic potential of an aesthetic of attunement, drawing on contemporary theories of mood. Despite the obvious importance of mood in the experience of cinema, there is relatively little attention paid to it in film theory. *Stimmung*, or attunement, forms a key part of Lotte Eisner's account of German Expressionism, and this theoretical interest in the expressive capacities of the medium proposes atmosphere as a central modality of film form (1969: 199–206). In his more recent exploration of the concept, Robert Sinnerbrink comments that 'the aesthetics of mood are curiously overlooked today' (2012: 148), arguing that the insights of classical film theorists such as Eisner and Béla Balázs have not been sufficiently taken up in relation to contemporary film.

Where we do find the two together, however, is in recent cultural studies work on mood, which often turns to cinema as a social space. Ben Highmore, for instance, writes about how light, sound and the organisation of space work to create atmospheres, using the movie theatre as an example (2013: 428–30).

If mood in this Heideggerian sense of *Stimmung* is directionless, then a film-theoretical focus on attunement could speak more directly of subject and object. In cinematic terms, it conjures questions of spectatorship, identification and the politics of the image, as well as a close attention to the formal registration of light, sound and space. As Sinnerbrink puts it, cinematic mood 'is not simply a subjective experience or private state of mind; it describes, rather, how a (fictional) world is expressed or disclosed via a shared affective attunement orienting the spectator within that world' (2012: 148).

Attunement is thus an apt concept for analysing cinematic effects. Equally relevant for my purpose, however, is the frequency with which scholars of attunement invoke the public politics of migration. Highmore discusses the moods prevalent in the UK Border Agency's immigration removal centres. Sara Ahmed considers immigration policy as a key example of public mood, in which 'governments often defend these policies as being responsive or receptive to public feeling' (2014b: 23). It seems that theories of attunement are intrinsically linked, for these European theorists, to the growth of racist immigration discourse in Europe. Subtending these examples is a political and philosophical question: does an account of these public feelings necessarily lapse into a liberal politics of winning 'hearts and minds' or does altering attunement nurture a radical potential? Ahmed certainly believes that it does, and she has argued compellingly for the feminist and anti-racist value of thinking about the social calibration and dissident uses of mood (2004: 1–8). Here, I argue that the Hungarian film *Fehér isten (White God, 2014)* provides an opportunity to bring the political frameworks of mood and those of cinema into communication, and that through this process we might analyse European cinema's attunement to the figure of the migrant.

Directed by Kornél Mundruczó in 2014, *White God* constructs an allegorical tale in which Hungary orders the registration, taxation and rounding up of mongrel dogs, that is, those whose blood is not purely Hungarian. Led by beloved but forcibly abandoned pet Hagen (Body and Luke), the dogs violently rise up against the humans who have oppressed them. *White God* imagines a national mood in which mongrels are excluded from the body politic, leaving teenage dog-lover Lili (Zsófia Psotta) violently out of tune with the world. Her project is to reattune the world. The film's project is to reattune its audience, who might have been carried away by the national mood to hate migrants and other racialised groups, and to reattune them towards a world that welcomes others. *White God* invites us to create new attunements to those bodies that are out of tune with the national mood; those whom dominant audiences have already made into strangers in Ahmed's terms (2014a: 14). This project could be read within a broad history of post-neorealist liberalism, rendering marginalised communities visible and seeking to produce empathy for the stranger. Viewed through this lens, we might see *White God* as laudable in its attempt to counter an increasingly reactionary and even fascistic European politics, but not as an especially radical text. However, I want to argue that the film's elaboration of non-human attunement offers an opportunity to see its politics in more ambiguous terms. What does it mean to be attuned to (and reattuned via) the non-human animal?

The film's first move is to disaffiliate its spectator from the mood of hatred towards mongrels. When Lili's mother goes on an extended research trip, she and her dog Hagen go to stay with her father, Dániel (Sándor Zsótér). Immediately, we encounter an upstairs neighbour who says that Hagen cannot stay, insisting that 'They've posted the ruling. They're making a list now.' Since she stands upstairs from Lili, we see her in low-angle shot, as a figure of threat, vocalising the authoritarian strategy of the list. 'Read the order,' she continues. 'Mutts have to be reported.' Soon after, a government official arrives at the door, saying, 'We've received a report . . . this is a mixed-breed street dog. It's not a Hungarian breed so you have to pay a tax.' The allegorisation of fascistic social controls is evident, from the neighbour who reports Hagen to the bureaucratic white nationalism of the pure blood tax. This mode of separation and control moves into the domestic space when her father tells Lili that Hagen must eat separate food and cannot sleep in the bedroom with them. 'He's a dog,' Dániel insists, 'and I won't sleep with dogs.' Segregation is immediate and angry, leaving Hagen to whine in the bathroom. Meanwhile father and daughter sleep uncomfortably in the same room – Dániel has to turn his back as Lili undresses. This scene's awkward mood reminds us that separation does not succeed in creating spaces of propriety. Relatively powerless humans can be made to take up socially taboo and unpleasant places, even as mutts are removed.

For Ahmed, 'To be attuned to some might simultaneously mean not to be attuned to others, those who do not share one's leanings. We can close off our bodies as well as ears to what is not in tune' (2014b: 18). *White God* works to make the oppressive politics of this effect palpable. When we are in tune with the national mood – as Dániel is – we are thus not attuned to the lifeworld of others. To be attuned in a certain direction is to be unaware of the emotions, the needs, or even the existence of those outside our sphere of attention. We might be in the world with them, but we have not noticed how they feel. When Dániel locks Hagen in the bathroom, he doesn't perceive himself as cruel; he simply doesn't think about how Hagen feels. The dog's whines annoy him, whereas Lila is stricken by her attunement to Hagen's pain. As Ahmed points out, when the attempt to screen out the non-attuned person fails, we view that person as the problem, not our own failure to include them, or even our own failure in being blind to their situation. Thus, for Dániel, as for the state, it is dogs that are the problem and that must be removed from the public sphere.

When Dániel insists on getting rid of Hagen, he refuses Lili's suggestion of finding him a good home by retorting, 'Nobody will want a stinking mutt.' This articulation of disgust is narratively unmotivated, since the dog could be a problem without being an object of revulsion, thus attuning the spectator to notice the social circulation of hostility. Louis-Georges Schwartz (2013) uses the term *cinema hostis* to name an untethered atmosphere of oppressive hostility common in recent cinema, which he sees as responding formally to experiences of contemporary capitalism. *White God* exemplifies this category's powerful effects. Racist anti-migrant feeling is here staged as a directed hostility whose object is clear but whose affective energies seem to come from nowhere. Why does nobody want a mutt? Why are foreign breeds excluded from full participation in society? In place of causality, the film constructs a mood all the more threatening for its disordered excess. Anger emanates from all the adults except Lili's vanished mother, and our spectatorial attunement to Hagen derives from our recoil against this socially mandated hostility.

The film makes it very easy to read this hostility towards mongrels in racialising terms. Susan McHugh has analysed how the historical development and social usage of terms such as 'mongrel' in the nineteenth and twentieth centuries parallels racialising discourse about humans, implying 'degeneracy, degradation, and ultimately social chaos' (2004: 129). Critics such as Lesley Pleasant have likewise drawn a connection between these epithets and *White God*'s critique of Hungary's authoritarian right-wing government (2014: 3). The rise of Viktor Orbán's Fidesz party, which has ruled Hungary since 2010, and which is characterised by populism, a weakening of democratic institutions, anti-labour reforms and strong anti-immigrant and racist rhetoric, provides an immediate context for the film's allegory. In analysing the rise of right-wing populism in Hungary, for example, Jens Becker points to 'a culture of resentment, especially against Jews, "gypsies" and "communists"' (2010: 31). Becker notes the similarities between Hungary's politics of anti-immigrant hostility and those in Austria and Italy, characterising all three as trendsetters of 'a right-wing populism which has fascistic-like references' (2010: 37–8). Indeed, as many scholars have noted, this kind of right-wing nationalism is a growing problem for Europe as a whole. András Toth and István Grajcjár identify a new wave of radical populism across Europe's periphery, arguing that 'in response to the deep, long, and structural crisis of the Europeanised economic system, there is a new type of revolutionary radical right-wing party emerging in the crisis-stricken European countries' (2015: 133). Abby Innes sees Hungary as a canary in the coalmine of European politics, suggesting that its political and economic stresses are 'a magnified version of those afflicting Western Europe' (2015: 97). Moving beyond Europe, examples abound of the rise in racist and anti-immigrant hatred encouraged by populist right-wing political parties in the United States, India, Brazil etc. Peter Wilkin considers that Hungary's illiberal governments have been empowered and encouraged by the success of similar regimes in, for example, Russia and China (2016: xiii). Thus, *White God*'s allegory of racialised hostility describes a European or even global structure as much as a narrowly Hungarian one.

This allegorical mode is certainly open to critique. We might sense something queasy and diminishing in imaginatively turning racialised categories of people into animals. In a cynical reading, I might suggest that the film uses dogs to court empathy in an allegorical switch that saves us from having to love actual people. This critique perhaps runs aground on the long history of animal-based political allegory, but it does speak to the extent to which the contemporary right-wing dehumanisation of migrants to Europe – for instance in 2015, when then British prime minister David Cameron referred to people entering the country from the Mediterranean as a 'swarm' – must be taken into account by contemporary modes of progressive thought. Animal allegories feel overdetermined and potentially uncomfortable. European moods have changed in ways that suggest high stakes for the politics of representation. *White God* also offers us cause for suspicion in its more direct representations of marginalised groups. We might be concerned, for instance, by the fact that two of the men who exploit Hagen are represented as racialised minorities in Hungary. The shopkeeper who originally sells Hagen (and on whom Hagen later takes revenge) is Turkish and Muslim, and the man who trains him to kill is referred to by a group of white men by a slur associated with Roma. Perhaps these characters speak to the circulation of the language of hatred, and they could certainly complicate any too-neat correspondence between dogs and marginalised people, but their prominence among Hagen's exploiters at least creates another uneasy ambiguity.

Meanwhile, for some animal theorists, the problem is not diminishing the status of humans but failing to respect the integrity of animals. According to this mode of thought, we should not think of animals as allegories for human politics or problems, as this process erases the animal in its own selfhood and experience, rendering it only instrumental to human-imposed meanings. Michael Lawrence and Laura McMahon theorise the way in which filming animals is often a process of 'capture and appropriation' that replicates the dominant hierarchy of power between humans and animals. Anthopomorphism is, for them, one of the main discourses of domination, in which animal performers are made to tell human stories (Lawrence and McMahon 2015: 2). This criticism is certainly apt for *White God*, insofar as it uses cinematic means to manipulate animal performances into a sentimental narrative that makes sense within an anthropocentric frame of reference (racism, xenophobia, Hungarian politics, etc.). Some critics of the film have taken exactly this stance. Robin Murray and Joseph Heumann argue that reviewers of *White God* are wrong to see in the dogs an allegory for migrants or other oppressed humans. 'For us,' they insist, 'Hagen moves beyond symbol. As a companion species whose pleasure and pain align with our own, Hagen stands in only for himself' (Murray and Heumann 2018: 301). Drawing on Donna Haraway's work, they suggest that Hagen becomes 'a full partner in worlding' (2018: 301). We might note, though, that Murray and Heumann do not simply reject the film out of hand for using dogs to speak anthropomorphically about human issues; rather, they see the film's mode of representation as more layered, suggesting that Hagen is both symbol and dog, and indeed that he might say more about the world as a dog than as a symbol.

For many domestic critics, the riskiness of *White God*'s allegory is to be found in its national context. Lóránt Stőhr argues that Mundruczó's turn to mythical forms of storytelling departs from the ability of his earlier films to critique gender roles in Hungary. For him, such universalising uses of the body as metaphor risk 'sacrificing the particular experiences of specific human lives and their contradictions' (Stőhr 2016: 150). Hajnal Király also sees in Mundruczó's films what she calls a 'mannerist formalism' (2016: 67) that turns post-communist melancholia into an aestheticised and allegorical form that turns away from the social and political altogether. By contrast, Holly Case points to a possible ethno-nationalist reading in which the downtrodden dogs embody Hungary itself, somehow abused and blamed falsely, and finally lashing out in fury (2015: 118). Allegory for these scholars might be too abstract and lose a necessary sense of Hungarian social specificity, or it might be susceptible to dangerously specific misreadings. These pitfalls tend in opposite directions but they all point to the problems of aesthetic obliqueness.

It should be clear that allegory is a risky mode for *White God*, with both the material figuration of animals and the metaphorical meanings around otherness and political marginality threatening to derail the film's good intentions. Still, it is possible to see the very plasticity of the film's allegory as its strength. Amy Taubin argues that 'The movie is remarkable for existing coherently on so many cinematic planes at once and for generating multiple metaphoric readings, all of them about power and a state-determined caste system in which the "fit" reassure themselves of their superiority by brutalising and murdering the "unfit"' (2015: n.p.). Finding a text to be rich with multiple potential interpretations is a classic way to assign value, but I would argue that there is something else at stake in the film's insistence that humans might be felt more intimately as animals and vice versa. *White God* attunes its spectator at once to dogs and to humans, in a process that is increasingly uncertain and dislocating. The film resists the more instrumentalising impulses of allegory in the unruliness of its attunements. In Mundruczó's recent film, *Jupiter's Moon* (2017), the allegory is extremely direct: the protagonist is a Syrian refugee who can fly over borders. But *White God*, where the dogs are legible as racial, national, ethnic, ecological and animal figures, asks us to attune our senses and our empathy towards a collective whose being and desires cannot be so easily exhausted by interpretation.

Are we attuned to Hagen as the figural representative of Hungary and Europe's marginalised people, or as a dog? In the introduction to their collection on the body in Eastern European cinema, Ewa Mazierska, Matilda Mroz and Elżbieta Ostrowska propose the cinematic body as the textual site of a historical relationship between the abstractly allegorical and the sensorially corporeal (2016: 13). They cite Anikó Imre's discussion of cinema's 'grim allegories' of the region's traumatic histories (2009: 215) and yet they also note how, despite the apparently conceptual mode of allegory, many discussions of Eastern European films pay attention to 'embodied viewing, that is, to the potential bodily impacts of the films on audiences' (2016: 13–14). One example, relevant to contemporary Hungarian cinema, is Steven Shaviro's analysis of *Taxidermia* (Györgi Pálfi, 2006), which he reads as 'both viscerally charged and icily allegorical' (2012: 36). This dialogic relationship is also at work in *White God*, where the bodies that animate the narrative are at once allegorical figures and corporeal dogs. Of course, *White God* is not a horror film and its bodily effects are focused more on the (supposedly) positive feelings of empathy and the thrill of bodily movement. Dogs' bodies primarily prompt affection, though the film's revolutionary climax points to some other affective regimes. In reading attunement both through *White God*'s political allegory and its use of real dogs, I want to think about how an attunement to dogs might proceed as both allegorical and corporeal, and what kind of politics might emerge from the uneasy cohabitation of these discourses.

Let us consider how *White God* attunes the spectator *to* dogs, and to the diegetic world *through* dogs. The film begins by staging Lili's attunement to Hagen and his to her. When Dániel locks Hagen in the bathroom, Lili plays her trumpet to calm him, creating attunement as a mode of harmony and connectivity. That their connection is musical is central to the film's elaboration of attunement as a cultural practice of empathy. The resonance between Lili and Hagen is contrasted to the hierarchical orchestra in which Lili plays the trumpet. These different social practices of music are contrasted in a rehearsal scene. Since she is not allowed to bring her dog into the rehearsal space, Lili hides Hagen in a closet. The conductor is autocratic and patriarchal, and the music, Lizst's *Hungarian Rhapsody No. 2*, is in this context nastily nationalistic. We are directed to critique the scene by viewing it through Hagen's optical point of view. He can see out of the closet through its slatted door, and our perspective is thus clearly marked as his by the horizontal bars briefly visible within the frame. Here, we see how attunement is a function of cinematic expressivity: in its management of point of view and shot distance, the film builds an atmosphere of frustration in the closet. Hagen barks his displeasure, revealing his presence, and both dog and girl are thrown out. When Hagen – and his voice – emerge into the larger *mise en scène* of the orchestra space, our attunement is shifted to feel the weight of social hostility. His sounds cannot be harmonised with a nationalistic soundscape, and thus we hear the sociality of attunement. Hagen's barking is out of tune with the orchestrated melody of Hungarian nationalism and Lili is rendered out of tune with the demand that she abandon her dog and submit to the coercive harmony of the nation.

As much as Lili's relationship to Hagen forms a contrast to the hostility of the wider nation to dogs, it also attunes us to its potential for an uncomfortable similarity. After Lili is thrown out of the rehearsal, Dániel makes her return and apologise to the orchestra. The conductor says, 'I'm sure Lili can explain why she had that animal', and Lili is compelled to lie and say that Hagen had bitten her father. Here we might read an allegorical staging of how cognition can be shaped in a violent manner. Everyone present knows that Lili is telling a lie – that Hagen has not bitten anyone – and this is indeed the point of the ideological enforcement. Hatred is normalised through repetition, and the visibility of power is here one of its guarantees. Lili is told that she can return to the group *if she behaves*, a coercive modification of her behaviour to adapt to desired social norms. This is surely an allegorisation of authoritarianism, but it also displays a type of behavioural training. Early in the film, Lili tells Hagen that she will never train him, even to do something so basic as sit and stay. She sees behavioural training as form of social violence, a belief that the narrative confirms when Hagen is trained by dog fighters to become a killer. But even though Lili seeks to form a relationship with Hagen that might avoid the coercive nature of training, he still belongs to her in a way that the film cannot avoid viewing as exploitative. Although it clearly doesn't want to condemn the sentimental bond of girl and dog, *White God* needs to move beyond that relationship for its political narrative to emerge.

If we are first attuned to dogs through Lili's human perspective, the film eventually departs from human focalisation to construct a canine point of view. (This mechanism is what Eva Mazierska is referring to when she locates the film as an arthouse theriophilic film; one which understands animals as superior to people and tries to present reality from their perspective [Mazierska 2017].) For example, when Lili first meets her father outside the slaughterhouse where he works, a standoff deploys a dog-centric camera height to equate Lili, Dániel and Hagen as comparable characters in this drama. All three are seen in medium shot, with Hagen's shot cutting Lili off in her midsection. Instead of a human-centred scale in which dogs might be included in shots framed to the measure of the human body (as shot scales are, after all, defined), here Hagen is featured in a shot that centres his head and upper body but that cuts off Lili's face. Later, when Hagen is abandoned by the humans, a new resonance is created that is dog–dog, rather than human–dog. Hagen is looking longingly at meat on a butcher's counter, when he hears a little woof. In a shot/reverse sequence reminiscent of a classical rom-com 'meet cute', he encounters Peggy, whines, and tilts his head interrogatively. The two dogs become effectively linked, as friends, lovers or comrades. Hagen walks into his own point-of-view shot to follow Peggy and we cut to a wide shot that reveals a larger canine community. By this later point in the film, we no longer need humans to triangulate our relationship to dogs: cinematic conventions of relationality such as identification, point of view, and a socially constructed decomposition of space are elaborated wholly in relation to canine subjectivity.

Rizvana Bradley (2018) describes attunement in terms of 'systems that structure, extend and enable sentience', and *White God* precisely extends and enables animal sentience in a way that transcends realism. Central to this fiction, in a vaguely speculative mode, is a world in which dogs can organise and think. And these impossibly revolutionary dogs are enabled by cinematic structures of knowledge and attention. From the objective canine-height camera angle of the standoff, we progress towards a full-on doggie optical point of view, as when Hagen is drugged and gradually loses consciousness. We are attuned to animal sentience through looking relations. Dog point of view is established as having agency when Hagen bursts out of the closet and disrupts the orchestra rehearsal, and this agency grows when he joins the undocumented canine community. Here, dog point of view is primary, and cinematic form is revised to centre dogs rather than humans. When Hagen is captured, he realises that the dogs are being euthanised in an initially humorous scene of animal spectatorship. A group of dogs watch a *Tom and Jerry* cartoon – with apparent cognition of the media narrative but no sense of their own peril. Through a gap in the wall, Hagen sees a kennel worker injecting another animal and, the editing implies, is able to process and comprehend the situation. By extending canine sentience, the film orients the viewer's attention and emotional understanding towards the experience of the other.

In this cinematic construction of sentience, we are attuned to fictional dogs rather than to real dogs: editing anthropomorphises Hagen and Peggy to create creatures whose understanding of their own oppression and whose resistance to it are legible to human spectators. Indeed, canine subjectivity and embodied experience are explicitly compared to that of humans. For example, one way in which we understand Lili and Hagen's attachment is by a paralleling of their experiences. Both characters are imperilled by exploitative men in a sequence in which Lili has her drink spiked by boys in a nightclub at the same moment that Hagen is drugged by a dog-fighting ring. Parallel editing connects these experiences of male violence, and we see each of them lose consciousness as the drugs take effect. In the film's use of point of view and editing, canine sentience runs on parallel tracks to human cognition. Our relationship to animal experience, however, becomes more twisty in the film's use of visual effects. *White God* deploys effects to visualise tortures that it would be unethical to film with actual dogs, and to create action sequences that real dogs could not undertake. When Hagen is sold to a dog-fighting ring, he is trained to kill. His teeth are filed to points, he is starved, and he is psychologically bent towards violence. Finally, in a brutal fight scene, he is forced to kill another dog. The use of visual effects in these scenes is designed, as many contemporary effects are, to pass unnoticed: although the gory death is clearly not real, it's hard to tell where the profilmic ends and post-production effects begin. Such uncertainty prompts a mixture of emotional responses.

Insofar as they are successfully naturalised, the effects work, like the editing, to heighten the spectator's attachment to the imperilled and hostile lifeworld of the dogs. But this attachment depends on a constant tension between the profilmic weight of the dogs and the post-production intensification of their bodies and actions. As Amy Taubin puts it, 'The dogs had to be real for us to have as visceral, kinetic, and emotional a connection to them as to the humans on-screen' (2015: n.d.). Notice how she formulates the decision to use real dogs rather than completely CGI ones in terms of attunement. The corporeality of the dog collective enables a sensory attentiveness to the political stakes of their situation, which we experience through our connection to the physicality of their bodies in motion. Like the film's combination of gritty post-communist realism with fantastic allegory, the representation of dog bodies combines the indexical affect of real dogs with a spectacularly enhanced vision of canine revolt. In both cases, the film's *mise en scène* attunes us to the weight and physicality of the diegetic world, only to complicate those realist limitations with phantasmatic possibilities. Pete Porter also argues that the sparsity of CGI makes the scenes of revolution more effective, but he goes on to propose that the attack 'gains conviction because the filmmakers accommodated the behavior of the dogs' (2017: 101). Spectators feel a bodily connection to real dogs because the film-makers were attuned to the natural behaviour of the animals with which they worked. Cross-species attunement becomes not only a textual effect but also a mode of production.

This awareness of actual dog performers is a double-edged sword for the film, however, as it can militate against its narrative effects as easily as it can enhance them. When the dogs begin their uprising, the effect of a revolution is largely created out of the mass of animals running in the streets. Observed closely, however, none of the dogs are doing anything especially threatening: they do typically rambunctious dog things such as grabbing at handbags, hoses and rubbish bags. When the humans respond with terror, then, their responses can appear to be misplaced, exaggerated or even humorous. Pleasant reads this mismatch as a formal strategy, designed to place the spectator on the side of the dogs (2014: 5). If the humans are scared for no reason, this scenario accords with the idea that authoritarian violence and hostility have demonised a marginalised social group. A less sympathetic viewer might see this effect as an unintended consequence of the fact that the dogs cannot really act aggressive when they are not, which has led to a failure of the film to be genuinely scary. There is also a more serious variant of the way in which audiences pay attention to animals. Many viewers worried about the treatment of the dogs on set, and questioned where the film used visual effects and where it displayed potentially unethical treatment of the canine actors. For these viewers, an attunement to dogs led them out of the diegesis entirely, replacing a politics of representation with one of animal rights. The dogs cannot be entirely erased from the biopolitics of their representation, and these audience concerns illustrate the permeability of animal allegory.

What happens to the spectator's layered sense of attunement to dogs-as-dogs and to dogs-as-migrants in the film's climactic scenes of revolt? These uncertain attunements have consequences for the film's political aesthetics. If this is a fantasy about the revolution of those violently excluded by an ethnonationalist state, then clearly the film has worked to attune the viewer to the rightness of this act of resistance. There is enormous pleasure in the dogs' refusal to consent to their own destruction; as they fight back, they change the public mood to one of fear, flipping the hostility that has oppressed them and turning it on the humans. The revolt begins with Hagen breaking free of the kennel worker who is taking him to be euthanised and tearing the flesh from his neck. He then moves in slow motion towards the female worker whom he witnessed killing dogs, his muzzle bloody. He makes the familiar thoughtful head tilt gesture, before knocking her to the ground but not, in this instance, killing her. We watch the dogs escape from her prone point of view, but with no particular sympathy for her plight.

At this point we are closely aligned with the dogs, even with their vengeful violence. When the state fights back and we see dozens of dogs shot by police, including Hagen's friend Peggy, our sympathies are redoubled. Here, the responses of humans seem both ridiculous and hateful – the boy who warns Lili that the dogs are rabid illustrates a pathologising language that seeks to render the dogs' revolt as a form of madness and the humans as innocent victims. But when the point of view flips back to Lili, the film's affiliations become ambiguous. She goes to the market where Hagen used to steal food and finds the butcher who chased him away dead, with his throat torn out. She vomits, still attuned to violence against humans. Where does the film imagine its spectator's affiliations to be? Does this killing horrify us, as it does Lili? Or do we remain on the side of the dogs, advocating political violence and personal revenge? At this point the film's management of our affective responses risks becoming unruly, and its political affiliations exceed the apparently secure liberalism of its premise.

The film's final scene sees Lili, Dániel and Hagen face off again, this time with Lili and Hagen on opposite sides. Lili is scared of Hagen, and when she throws a stick in an attempt to re-establish their bond as owner and pet, he won't fetch it. He is no longer a pet, and rejects even this loving version of human–dog hierarchy. What does temporarily re-establish cross-species relationality is their mutual attunement via music. Lili begins to play her trumpet – repeating the Lizst piece from the rehearsal – and the dogs stop barking. Hagen lies down first, then the other dogs, then Lili. This scene is affective, even emotionally powerful, in part because it is so ambivalent. Does it lapse into an anodyne fantasy of reconciliation, where music is a depoliticised universal language? Mazierska (2017) sees the use of music in these terms as idealistic. The dog pack surely becomes a concert audience, but I would argue that the connotations of this new collective are uncertain. Does it evoke the social hierarchy of the human orchestra? Or might it envision a utopian Hungarian space that reconstitutes the nation through the canine bodies of its outsiders? The mood cannot be resolved easily. To return to Ahmed's account of the social quality of moods, this scene attunes us to an overwhelming empathy and resonance, the sustained ability of creatures to hear one another, even and perhaps especially when action has been exhausted. In classic melodramatic fashion, it is too late for Lili and Hagen's reconnection to matter. Hagen has become something other than a pet, and the state will not forgive these revolutionaries. One of the slaughterhouse workers asks if he should call the police and Dániel says, 'Give them a little more time.' This is borrowed time, a moment of grace before the inevitable state violence in which the dogs, we imagine, will be slaughtered.

This is a strange ending for a liberal film with a pedagogy of empathy for the other. It is neither a feelgood conclusion nor quite the plea for peace and reconciliation that it might at first appear to be. Rather than bearing witness to the problems of the migrant, in the terms of a post-neorealist art cinema, or mounting the kind of self-reflexive ideological critique promised by political modernism, *White God* proposes a series of disconcerting shifts in the spectator's attunement. Its recalibrations of mood can offer a dispiriting movement from the effect of poiesis in the opening scenes of exhilarating canine motion, directing the audience towards the pleasures of revolutionary action, to the closing scene of stillness and solidarity before certain death. What remains consistent throughout the film is our attunement to the other, and both the opening and closing scenes insist on the collective subjectivity of these excluded others and on a refusal of oppressive modes of nationalism. Nonetheless, the film ends up confused about what to do with its revolutionary energies, unable to imagine anything but the reassertion of power. These political ambiguities may be what makes *White God* such a difficult film, tangled up with the both/and logic in which it speaks about the figure of the European migrant and about, with and through dogs. The film challenges public feelings, asking its spectator to attune herself to other subjectivities and then providing no easy resolution to the status of its excluded subjects. Whereas realist strategies of witnessing injustice tend to reinstall hierarchies of distance, *White God*'s mode of allegorical attunement unseats such emotional and ideological sureties. It may not succeed in elaborating a political aesthetic for Europe's dangerous present, but *White God* undermines the production of its own liberalism. In attuning the spectator to the soon-to-be-violently-excluded subjectivity of the dogs, it suggests both the challenge and the necessity of rethinking our potential for collective life.

15. LABOUR AND EXPLOITATION BY DISPLACEMENT IN RECENT EUROPEAN FILM

Constantin Parvulescu

The modus operandi of capitalism is one of constant disruptions and reconfigurations. Whether one envisions these as creative destruction (Schumpeter 1994: 82–3) or as cycles of accumulation by dispossession (Harvey 2007b: 153), dis- and re-embedding (Polanyi 1957: 71) or spectacularisation and profanation (Agamben 2007: 77), they refer to processes that generate ruptures in economic and cultural practices, which in turn create opportunity for some and updated forms of disenfranchisement for many others. Collaterally, these processes produce insides and outsides to the law, civilisation and quality of life, within or upon which capitalism can operate more ruthlessly. Various economic categories can become outsides: from land and individual savings to bodies and social relations. Capitalist disruptions operate upon them in terms of expropriations, uprooting, as well as by generating displaced, non-placed and over-placed labour groups, which may be, respectively, external to, in the blind spots of, or above the law.

This chapter analyses the presentation of these labour groups and their work at the geographical and social margins of European civilisation in four recent European films. It offers a commentary on the way these films invite viewers to reflect on practices of labour displacement, the opportunities for exploitation this displacement generates and, more generally, on the violence generated by what Marx calls the 'silent compulsion of economic relations' (1990: 899). The chapter draws on research by the contributors to the collection *Work in Cinema: Labor and the Human Condition* (Mazierska 2013), as well as Ewa Mazierska's genealogy of the representation of work in the film of the twentieth century (Mazierska 2015). It advances this research by focusing on twenty-first-century texts and on the representation of practices of accumulation by dispossession and displacement. In this sense, it considers films presenting labour migration from the so-called Third World (*Mediterranea* [Jonas Carpignano, 2015]), exploitation on post-terrestrial frontiers of capitalist production practices (*Moon* [Duncan Jones, 2009]), as well as the psychological and moral hazard created by the geographical and social uprooting of the white-collar workforce (*Toni Erdmann* [Maren Ade, 2016] and *Le Capital* [*Capital*] [Costa-Gavras, 2012]).

This selection of films covers various European national cinemas and distinct generations in European film directing: an accomplished auteur, Costa-Gavras; a mid-career female director, Ade; and two debutants, Carpignano and Jones. Moreover, these directors diverge in political orientation. Costa-Gavras and Carpignano are leftist artists,[1] Ade seems less attracted to politicised art,[2] while Jones shows interest in philosophical issues and commercial film making.[3] Under scrutiny are cinematic texts made in the post-2008 era. As such, they even more acutely record the increasingly competitive and thus oppressive post-crisis work environment, as well as a growing scepticism among Europeans regarding the capitalist free market. While *Mediterranea*'s observational (realist) drama is the predictable format for such recording, I have also chosen films that surpass this framework of representation. *Capital* is labelled a financial thriller with a touch of black humour (Lemire 2013), *Toni Erdmann* a comedy-drama (Kermode 2017) and *Moon* is a science fiction film. In the first part of this chapter, I discuss *Mediterranea* and *Moon* and their inquiry into the condition of capitalism's underdogs. The second part analyses *Toni Erdmann* and *Capital*, and reflects on the condition of the apparent winners in capitalist displacement processes.

Mediterranea

Mediterranea is perhaps the most fitting film to start this study with because, at the time of its release, its plot, as one critic put it, seemed ripped from the headlines of newspapers (Hoffman 2015). It addresses one individual story among the hundreds of thousands that contributed to the phenomenon coined as 'Europe's migrant crisis'. The film is inspired by actual events. Its director researched migration in North Africa and work conditions in Italy, and the cast of non-professional actors played real situations from their own lives (Dodman 2015). Moreover, the film is still topical at the time of writing. The concerns that it addresses have worsened with the rise of anti-immigrant rhetoric in Europe.

Mediterranea continues a long tradition of realist cinematic presentations of displacement, border crossings and manual work, as well as the efforts of agents of power to control the movement of labouring bodies. More recent contributions to this tradition include a cycle of migration-to-Europe films inaugurated by the Oscar-winning *Journey of Hope* (Xavier Koller, Switzerland, 1990) as well as the neo-Marxist social documentarism of the Dardenne brothers. *Mediterranea* also increases its reality and topicality effect by structuring its plot in dialogue with iconic news and social media representations of the condition of migrants. The main episodes of the first part of *Mediterranea* show trucks overflowing with people on African roads; men and women walking hundreds of miles through hostile desert land; calls for help from sinking boats in the Mediterranean; drowned bodies picked up by rescue forces; columns of police-escorted asylum seekers entering temporary detention centres; and charity spokespeople calling for human solidarity. The second part of the film is built around highly circulated images representing the foreign workers' precarious living and work conditions in host countries: shanty dwellings and soup kitchens; physical labour and the struggle to avoid deportation; call-centre emotional moments and Western Union money transfers; and wearisome and sometimes violent exchanges between migrants, the local population and law enforcement.

The protagonist of these episodes is Ayiva (Koudous Seihon) who has come to southern Italy from Burkina Faso. The first part of *Mediterranea* shows him struggling to cross the external borders of Europe in order to become a temporary worker on an orange farm. The second records his unsuccessful effort to cross the continent's growing and intricate internal borders, integrate and gain long-term residence in Europe. My analysis focuses on the second part because it presents work, and because the relevance of internal borders in the creation of global injustice and control of the supply of cheap labour that guarantees European economic supremacy is greater than that of external ones (Balibar 2010: 321; OECD 2014).

Mediterranea's plot emphasises the existence and effect of internal borders by having its characters constantly talk about work stability (and not salary and welfare, as anti-immigrant discourse has it). Ayiva and those in his situation are given a three-month deadline to obtain permanent employment – a 'contract'. Otherwise they will be deported or will have to reside illegally. The contract is a second passport that allows the migrant worker to cross the main internal barrier to European residence, integration, rights and social security. At the same time, it is an apparatus of control that is instrumental in setting up a more accurate labour selection service than an external border (Loshitzky 2010: 3). More problematically, however, it creates internal no-man's lands, as well as deceptive narratives of transcendence. These no-man's lands are spaces of exception within a jurisdiction where rights do not apply equally to each individual. Despite being in Europe, Ayiva does not have the rights of European citizens. He has no social or economic buffers, and must accept whatever job is available on the market. Moreover, he is exposed to harsh competition, as new and available workers await at every corner, willing to accept increasingly radical and inhumane forms of exploitation.

As the global supply of Ayivas seems endless, the European dream generates an oppressive form of hope (Loshitzky 2010: 22), or cruel optimism as Lauren Berlant has it. In Berlant's terms, Ayiva is the victim of an attachment to compromised conditions of possibility (2011: 10). *Mediterranea* shows that the European dream is for him an investment of desire in an object or a narrative that, at a certain moment in time, becomes a means of oppression. Moreover, the dramatic format of the film suggests that there is no clear way out of this predicament, as its ending shows an Ayiva with no clear vision as to what to do after his three-month deadline expires.

In *Mediterranea*, there are two scenes that insightfully reflect the oppressive effects of hope. The first is a conversation Ayiva has with his employer about obtaining a work contract. The second is an interaction between Ayiva and his employer's teenage daughter. Both scenes have the function of making Ayiva (and the viewer) more aware of his condition. The first shows Ayiva asking his employer whether he can offer him the much-desired work contract. They drive in a truck to his employer's house after a long day in the orange orchard. Ayiva can have this conversation with his boss because he has won his sympathy, and because Ayiva honestly believes that European labour culture rewards those who work hard like him. But, predictably for a migration drama, the employer's answer is negative. He acknowledges Ayiva's merits, offers him a fifty-euro tip, another small job, and even mentions that Italian immigrants to America have gone through similar experiences. But the ultimate reason why his answer is negative will be fully understood by Ayiva and the viewer only during the last sequence of the film.

Before revealing it, let us take a look at the second key scene. It is also a night scene, unfolding at a time when characters reflect on the work done during the day. While Ayiva is loading crates of oranges on to a truck, the daughter of his employer approaches him and spills their contents on to the ground. Surprised, Ayiva wonders why she does this. Her reply is to lift another crate and empty it. She asks Ayiva whether he likes Italy and suggests that if he does he should continue putting oranges back into the crates, something that the puzzled but docile Ayiva does.

The episode, which precedes the conversation on the truck, prepares the ground for understanding the employer's refusal to offer Ayiva a work contract. Ayiva's interaction with his daughter is a denunciation of the way the African workforce is regarded behind closed doors and screens of political correctness. In a broader sense, it gestures towards the condition of displaced workers as *things*. My use of *things* draws on Roberto Esposito's approach to the concept. Esposito aims to show how, by linking citizenship and rights to private property, Roman law becomes a useful tool for explaining contemporary capitalist relations. He defines a *thing* as that which does not have ownership over other things, including oneself, and which, as such, belongs to a person, the latter being defined by way of ownership of things (Esposito 2015: 26, 17).

Ayiva might regard himself as a person, as one who is his own property, and who strives towards improving his condition. However, in the eyes of the girl – and by extension of other Europeans – he is not. He is a human tool, whose efficiency is fuelled by the illusion that, ethically and legally, he is human. The girl's actions suggest that, within the European social and economic imaginary, informed by capitalist relations of production, Ayiva is just a labouring body, rented or owned by his employer for a period of time. As an owned thing without rights in an economic no-man's land, he not only stands at the mercy and even mockery of his employers, but also cannot function without offering his body, unconditionally, as thing, to them.

This is how the entire picture of displaced labour comes to the fore in the film. Work is put in the service of a narrative of hope, but its actual function is to reinforce the status of the displaced worker as a human thing. Social exclusion completes the picture. Ayiva's outside-ness is visually marked by skin colour, language, second-hand clothing fit for physical labour, as well as by the dire living conditions he endures in Italy. He sleeps on the cold floor of what looks like a former pigsty. The dwelling lacks elementary sanitation and, tellingly, doors, because, as things, the displaced do not have any valuable private property to protect. Exclusion is also documented by the violence directed against labourers like Ayiva by a segment of the local population, headed by what seems to be the organised crime in town. The internal border becomes here a frontline. The local hooligans' xenophobic violence leads to vehement protests from the African community. They occupy streets demanding, 'Stop killing us!' but their protests fail to bring any positive change to their condition. They only generate street battles with the police and the hooligans. Ayiva's best friend is almost beaten to death, and many others are injured.

The protests take place immediately after Ayiva's conversation with his employer. Frustrated, Ayiva takes an active part. But his physical manifestation, the film intelligently suggests, is not to be seen as an expression of hope for change, but as a reflection of powerlessness. Ayiva vandalises property – perhaps belonging to workers like him – and only puts his safety in peril. The only concise message his revolt conveys is his incapacity to define his oppressor and the object of his revolt (see Žižek 2009: 9–10, 63–6) which cannot be traced back to a person, a company or a government, but only to opaque agencies defining his situation, which bear names such as transnational and decentred networks of power.

The last sequence of the film shows a resigned Ayiva helping at the lavish birthday party of his employer's daughter. It is here that he fully understands why his employer denied him a contract. He notices that among the important guests are the same gangsters who led the hooligans who terrorised the displaced labour force. The visual reference to organised crime is Carpignano's gesture towards putting a face to the invisible power network that supports the functioning of internal borders and that administers their undemocratic no-man's lands. The gangsters' presence at the party suggests that it is not sheer exploitation on the part of his employer that makes him reject Ayiva's demand for a work contract. It is the fact that the employer is himself included in a broader economic system of exploitation whose most visible arm is local organised crime.

MOON

Moon takes the reflection on the exploitation of uprooted labour beyond the boundaries of Earth, the present, values still respected in *Mediterranea*'s no-man's lands, and especially the understanding of what it means to be human. The title of the film indicates that, in the future, there will be demand for labour on Earth's satellite, and that, in the logic of capitalist exploitation, the company that sends labour to the moon will do everything possible to minimise costs, including biological ones. The venture is located on the dark side of Earth's satellite, invisible to humanity's scrutiny, hinting at ethical and legal transgressions related to the administration of the displaced workforce.

Moon's workforce is Sam (Sam Rockwell), the only person inhabiting the lunar base. Unlike *Mediterranea*'s Ayiva, he doesn't seem to be disadvantaged in terms of conditions of work and race. Sam is white and educated, and has a contract: three years in solitude on the moon followed by a substantial financial reward once he is back to Earth. He has a skilled maintenance and managerial job with the heroic touch to it of overseeing a mining operation that extracts a potent source of clean energy that is vital for Earth's survival. While *Mediterranea* shows work and life reduced to basic bodily operations and needs, *Moon* depicts a cutting-edge work-life environment, which includes the services of a sophisticated AI called Gerty (Kevin Spacey). Gerty not only manages the infrastructure and functioning of the base, but also substitutes for family, friends, co-workers, health services, society and household help. For example, one of the initial sequences of *Moon* shows the robotic arm of Gerty cutting Sam's hair. Other sequences present Gerty coaching, treating and entertaining Sam.

In spite of the fact that *Moon* is shot in a studio, employs Hollywood visual style and relies on special effects, it shares several representational strategies with *Mediterranea*. The most important is plot structure. *Moon* also tells the story of a character who comes to understand his condition and develop class consciousness. This includes becoming aware of the economic, legal and ethical circumstances that enable his exploitation and that are essentially linked to his displacement. Another important similarity is that both films have protagonists who regard work as a tool to improve their condition in the first act of the plot, lose faith in this belief in the second, try to rebel against their situation in the third, and cope with failure and uncertainty at the denouement. Protagonists do not transgress socially or economically. At best, they sharpen their skills to deal with oppression.

Sam's emerging class consciousness is that he comes to understand that he is a clone, that his alleged family on Earth with whom he regularly shares video calls is a simulation staged by Gerty, that his memories are implants, and most importantly that he has never lived on Earth and never will, because his three-year work contract on the lunar base represents his life. From the day of his inception he has been poisoned by Gerty in such a way that, when he approaches the end of his tenure on the moon, he will become lethally ill, be terminated, all traces of his existence erased, and be replaced by a new Sam with a similar identity and lifespan, animated by the same cruel optimism of returning to a good life on the planet.

Though a white-collar worker, Sam is more a thing than Ayiva, who has a second life in Burkina Faso, an actual home to return to and in which to regain personhood. Trapped on the moon, Sam is a humanoid machine who runs on hope for a better life beyond his temporary displacement. That a work cycle on the lunar base cannot last for more than three years reveals the central role played by hope in the deceptive narrative of the ethics of work that structures capitalist economic relations. The life cycle of Sam ends in three years because, in the view of those who made and use him, the costs of maintaining his hope alive and beyond questioning his predicament are higher than those of creating a new Sam.

The technological sophistication of the lunar base indicates a disturbing dimension of progress. Improved (bio)engineering and information technology seems not to reduce human exploitation, but only to render it more imperceptible. Technology creates distance between labourer and the object of their labour. This displacement increases with the sophistication of the employed technology, and, as *Moon* shows, is accompanied by an act of dispossession. The more powerful the machine, the fewer rights the human labourer has, which, in Sam's case, refers to the loss of the right to life. Long takes of Sam's machine-mediated labour suggest this dispossession. Similarly, the moon's no-man's land conditions are referenced by long takes of its barren and lifeless landscapes, by the close observation of the artificial laboratory environment in which Sam lives, as well as by the fact that all his social interactions are mediated by electronic devices such as screens, microphones and speakers, and more generally by a ruthless instrumental rationality, which goes so far as to make decisions in terms of profitability over the life and death of an employee.

* * *

In the second part of this study, I focus on *Toni Erdmann* and *Capital*. My purpose is to explore the effect of displacement on workers who are apparently situated on the winning side of the global capitalist order and are instrumental in perpetuating its relations of production. This will help me suggest that dispossession affects various levels of society. The protagonists of *Toni Erdmann* and *Capital* are highly educated Western Europeans active in the knowledge economy. More concretely, they work in high finance and consultancy, occupy leadership positions, and speak sophisticated shop talk. They wear designer apparel, have assistants, are driven in limousines, visit select nightclubs and, perhaps most importantly, are in possession of passports that allow them to cross whatever state border tries to control their movement, usually by flying business class.

Whereas *Moon* and *Mediterranea* show that, in the era of globalisation, the idea of free movement applies much more to capital and goods than to people, *Toni Erdmann* and *Capital* present a global bourgeoisie that moves as freely around the globe as foreign direct investment, oil tankers, containers, long-range nuclear missiles and carbon dioxide. This global bourgeoisie has an acute sense of class and has willingly exchanged national or ethnic belonging for loyalty to their company and pride in their profession. This sense of pride is nurtured not only by their privileged lifestyle and by the fact that they do not have to face racist prejudice, exclusion or undemocratic treatment at borders, but also because, in today's economic context, their work is treated with fear and respect all over the world, as it has become synonymous with job-creation and economic development. My analysis of these two films brings to the fore both their aforementioned similarities, as well as their differences. The three most notable differences are the type of displacement each film addresses; the costs protagonists have to pay for being able to truly enjoy their status; and the role gender plays in cinema's approach to capitalist realities.

Toni Erdmann

The protagonist of *Toni Erdmann* is Ines (Sandra Hüller), a young woman of German origin deployed by her company to Bucharest, Romania, at the margins of the European Union. She works in international consultancy, a signature white-collar nomadic profession requiring long stays abroad and constant resettlement. Moreover, she specialises in outsourcing and relocations, her job contributing to the migration of capital around the globe, as well as labour exploitation. Although when compared to Ayiva and Sam, Ines's class privileges and quality of life are exponentially higher, *Toni Erdmann* does not present her as happy, but as an insecure workaholic. The film also suggests that the main cause of Ines's misery is displacement, understood both as geographical uprooting and as an outcome of relations of production specific to the era of immaterial labour.

The main markers of Ines's uprooting are her dark-grey, corporate, two-piece business suit, her mobile phone and her rigid body language. These markers are noticeable during her first appearance on screen in a quick long shot through the window of her mother's house in Germany (her parents have been separated for years). Her mother's family has prepared a celebration for her, but Ines hardly finds time to connect with them. She withdraws into the garden, talks on the phone and solves problems related to her projects in places as far away as Bucharest and Shanghai. Even if she might be physically in one place, she is, by means of technology, in the anywhere or everywhere of her job.

While her ubiquitous global presence confers professional glamour on her, Ines has only apparently developed the skills to deal with it. She copes well with many aspects of the lifestyle of the global bourgeoisie, except one that she is not able to control, and that brings her condition closer to that of Sam and Ayiva. It is her becoming a 24/7 worker. Aided by global communications and the growing immateriality of labour, the heterotopia of displacement with its lack of allegiances to natural communities, commons, family or friends delivers the white-collar labourer into the hands of their employer and links the meaning of their life to their career. As such, working in a series of non-places (Augé 1992: 122) makes it harder for the labouring subject to defend the boundaries between their existence as the employed labour force of a corporation and forms of human activity that emerge from other important human needs and require other forms of emotional, corporeal and intellectual engagement.

Unlike Sam and Ayiva, who come to be aware that they deliver their bodies and skills to an employer, the more educated and worldly Ines seems less aware of the dispossession caused by the increased socialisation of white-collar labour. While *Mediterranea* and *Moon* include episodes in which their protagonists enjoy leisure time and the company of friends and family, this is less the case with Ines, who embodies the radical individualism of the neoliberal order. She lives by and for herself, having a utilitarian relationship to everyone she comes into contact with. All family encounters become chores; on the phone she talks only about work, and her evening outings are also business-related.

Bucharest is her dark side of the moon. Her everyday activity unfolds in an environment that is not rooted in the actual place she lives in. Ade has chosen to show Bucharest as a non-place, as a background replicating a global scenery of corporate headquarters, rented apartments, shopping malls and nightclubs, all populated by G20-country expats or their local clones. Ines has developed various mechanisms to deny her emotional and intellectual dispossession by displacement. The most important operation of this mechanism is to link her condition and the abstract (and gated) environment she is part of to a global meritocracy. She feels worthier not only because she is skilled, well paid and has a personal assistant, but also because she believes she works hard and delivers quality intellectual output, even though this output could be questioned as unethical, since it implies firing people and corrupting local business and government representatives.

Enter Ines's father (Peter Simonischek). According to him, Ines could and should be happier. His efforts to lighten up his daughter's life initiate and develop the plot of *Toni Erdmann*, which, unlike the more pessimistic stories of *Mediterranea* and *Moon*, presents a project of re-embedding a consciousness which, due to displacement, has lost touch with what the father thinks is a wholesome and emancipated way of life. His aim is to reconnect Ines with aspects of human character that her high-achieving, individualist persona has repressed. Not surprisingly, he is a music teacher. In the universe of 24/7 work and intellect-driven activity, art is expected to heal the career-obsessed subjects of present-day knowledge economies. Art is expected to offer them stress relief and a new context of self-understanding; to galvanise their senses and corporate creativity (Brewer 2016).

Toni Erdmann is the name that Ines's father invents for himself in his effort to relieve his daughter from corporate objectification. Under this name, he travels to Bucharest and, unasked, interferes with her business operations and surrogate private life. Since he is not able to directly dialogue with his daughter on topics related to happiness and a wholesome life, his effort to help adopts a strategy of disruption. It consists of generating absurd and inappropriate situations related to Ines's work. They are aimed at questioning the corporate logic that governs her life, reframing it, and pushing Ines towards reconsidering her relationship to herself, her employer, other people, and her environment.

The film offers a partial happy ending. In a twisted way, the father's plan succeeds and his daughter unwinds. His insistent mockery of the corporate world breaks through her mechanisms of denial and persuades her to confront her condition. The turning point is presented in a scene in which Ines sings Whitney Houston's hit 'The Greatest Love of All'. She does this at the insistence of her father during her only non-work-related encounter with Bucharest locals. Because the chorus of the song concludes that this greatest love is love for oneself, Ines realises that, in her context, this individualist imperative has become unsustainable or needs redefinition.

In the next scene she decides to act against it. Nakedness is the visual metaphor that the film uses to emphasise her dispossession. Ines organises a party at her house and decides to come out. This means receiving her guests with no clothes on. She tells them that it is a nudist party and consequently demands that they undress too, which some even do. Nakedness indicates her realisation that she has no life outside of work and that her identification with her job has turned her into a crippled and selfish individual whose self-esteem depends only on her performance as an employee. The party thus suggests that she is ready to make changes. They include not only changing employers but a promise to take one step back.

CAPITAL

In spite of Ines's perhaps ethically questionable profession and its centrality to reproducing global inequality, *Toni Erdmann* is not an anti-capitalist film. Although, in a comic register, it includes a scene of chasing evil spirits, its story is not built around a Faustian pact-with-the-devil as is *Capital*. Considering anthropological studies that equate excesses in finance and financial consultancy with hypermasculinity, one can speculate that the gender of *Toni Erdmann*'s protagonist influenced the film's more indulgent presentation of the corporate world (Figlio 2011: 2). Cinematic female executives are expected to develop less insensitive business personas than Marc Tourneuil, the protagonist of *Capital*. On screen, they tend to be less possessed by corporate ambition and instead more equipped to take one step back and play by more ethical and humane rules.[4]

Unlike *Toni Erdmann*, *Capital* does not provide redemption for its protagonist, but a model of adaptation to and enjoyment of displacement. It also helps one notice that displacement can be approached in a more abstract way. While the protagonist of *Capital* moves intensely around the world (on the Paris–London–Tokyo–New York axis of glamour), this is not the displacement that is relevant to Marc's condition. This means, on the one hand, that *Capital* helps one see displacement also as a movement on the social ladder. In Marc's case this is a rise to the highest economic and power position on the continent, to the Elysium of the 0.1 per cent. On the other hand, the film allows one to understand dispossession generated by displacement not necessarily as objectification, as *Toni Erdmann* proposes, but also as *perversion* (a concept I will explain below).

The vertical displacement that *Capital* presents comes in the form of a rise-to-power story. The costs of this displacement are the protagonist's conversion into a corporate player. This is Marc's adaptation as well as his perversion. Originally Marc is a left-leaning economist, who once wanted to become a university professor, a critic of capitalism, a fighter for society's improvement and a winner of the Nobel Prize. However, he has given up these dreams for the thrill of playing the corporate power game, with its big bonuses and aristocratic lifestyle. The thriller elements of the film are not related to Marc's activist war against the financial system, but to his efforts to gain and maintain the chairmanship of the bank. He fights off hostile takeovers, internal disloyalty, femmes fatales and, most importantly, his own values.

Gender is also a means to encode his adaptability. Marc reacts differently to the stress and frustration associated with displacement than Ines. *Capital* never shows Marc close to a nervous breakdown. He deals with challenges by fully internalising the identity of his corporate persona. While, at the start of the film, there are at least three Marcs – the romantic intellectual, the family man and the ethical banker – when he delivers his final monologue at the end of the film, only one Marc remains, the ironic and manipulative corporate player. His character arc shows that he has discarded the surplus that builds the human subject and not recovered it as Ines did. Marc turns into what Slavoj Žižek (2018) calls a well-rounded ideological pervert – a person who has rationally cleansed himself of any distraction from his ideological or life project and draws pleasure from this identification. Marc's loyalty to the ideology of power and profit is no longer challenged by irrational excesses or ethical dilemmas. His drives and interests have been instrumentalised to serve his struggle to maintain himself at the top of the high finance game.

From this point of view, *Capital* resembles *Mediterranea*. Both Ayiva and Marc's efforts are to break through certain boundaries, learn the tough survival game of a new environment, and give their best to improve their condition. The similarities stop here, however, the most important difference being that Marc enjoys his displacement and that his enjoyment is only partially linked to the fact that he makes more money in a month than Ayiva does in a lifetime. His bliss and exuberance are the result of his perverse identification with the ideological construct of the capitalist corporate subject and his full adaptation to the rules of its power game – a transgression that the more melancholic Ayiva and Ines cannot undergo. To Marc they are losers. While he embraces the game with a joyful Yes, they look over their shoulder and wonder whether the game is fair or whether happiness and human fulfilment have other sources than economic activity.

Marc's story shows that displacement becomes a happy story if one views the dispossession it requires as a gain. And this is a political issue, as it means identification with the type of subjectivity that serves and drives the functioning of unleashed capitalism. In one of the final scenes of the film, before his crowning as uncontested CEO of the bank, Marc abandons the two people who still regarded him as more than a corporate player. Considering the gender codes of corporate dramas mentioned above, it is not a surprise that these two characters are women. One is his wife, concerned with the demise of Marc the moral person and family man. The other is an executive of his bank, concerned with the disappearance of Marc the ethical economist and the intellectual.

The way Marc rationalises the selling of his soul to the corporate mindset comes best to the fore in a final dialogue with his executive colleague. She wants to remind him of a previous commitment to write a book denouncing what she calls the predatory practices of banks, the dictatorship of the market, and the negative effects of speculation on economic, social and political environments. The transformed Marc reacts to her reminder with an indulgent smile and suggests that such a project would be either useless or nothing more than a scheme within a scheme, and just another strategy within an all-encompassing economic game, to which Marc refers to as the big prostitution. Everything is merely a game, an unjust but planetary one, as Marc puts it; and because we are all in it as players and prostitutes, we need to be honest with ourselves and admit that our main desire is to enjoy it and win. His conclusion: the game is the sole generator of value, dividing the world into winners and losers. All ethical and political concepts that refer to exploitation, unemployment or unsustainability are, in Marc's vision, nothing but strategies for obstructing one's opponents' tactics and for situating oneself in a more advantageous position.

Marc's argument indicates that, in order to function properly, perversion requires taking distance from the non-playing world – ethically, emotionally, as well as empirically. This assumed dis-placement is shown in many finance films with the help of high-rise architecture (King 2017: 18; Meissner 2012). *Capital* uses the same procedure in its final sequence, but adds an ironic touch. It not only locates the board meeting in a building towering over the 'everyday' life of Paris and the working world, but also gestures towards bankers' superstructural condition by means of dialogue. In the high remoteness of the boardroom, Marc is so far away from common sense and ethics that he can make the main shareholders of the bank cheer for joy when he tells them that he is an updated (perverted) version of Robin Hood, who steals from the poor and gives to them, the rich. Additionally Marc cynically reflects for himself and for the audience that he has to say these words and act accordingly because the game of greed is all about disconnection and playing it for the fun of winning, at least for as long as there is a game.

Conclusion

This chapter has shed light on cinema's take on various forms of displacement produced by capitalism's quest for the extraction of value. The selected films criticise a hegemonic trend of opinion in Europe and around the globe – criticised by David Harvey in his landmark essay 'Neoliberalism as Creative

Destruction' – that endorses updated understandings of the Schumpeterian 'gale' of creative destruction as responsible for the dynamism of industries and long-term economic growth, and which, as Harvey revealingly notices, have been first carried out in the peripheries before being turned into a model to be implemented at the centre (2007a: 26).

The films analysed in this chapter reveal the downsides of these processes and draw attention to the price paid by such choices of economic roadmaps. These downsides include disruptions within 'divisions of labour, social relations, welfare provisions, technological mixes, ways of life, attachments to the land, habits of the heart, ways of thought' (Harvey 2007a: 23) and, I would add, human solidarity. While Harvey's thesis is that these updated forms of disruption have been aimed at undoing what human solidarity has achieved at the level of political organisation (the welfare state and its politics of inclusion), the broad social spectrum of the victims of disruption presented in the selected films is indicative of the social and economic dynamics one can expect in the future (Snyder 2016: 8). The films show that the insides of the law and social and economic justice are shrinking in the era of accelerated capitalism. Processes of disruption and displacement that led to the practices of abuse of yesteryear – as presented in *Mediterranea* – can morph into future forms of exploitation imposed upon those who think of themselves as belonging to the inside of the global order, such as Ines from *Toni Erdmann* and Sam from *Moon*.

My analysis has made use of the concepts of uprooted labour, borders (internal and external), cruel optimism, hope and corporate perversion. They served me to comment on the issues addressed by these films and to outline the effects of the process of dispossession by displacement. All four selected films indicate that freer movement of capital, goods and information around the globe has not been matched politically in terms of movement of persons and even less of intercultural understanding and dialogue. In fact, the selected films gesture towards a closure of the European political imagination caused by global capitalism. They testify that this aforementioned liberalisation of economic practices depends on the oppression of the less privileged. They also show that the so-called demolishing of barriers and disruption of antiquated structures with the aim of making room for free enterprise, coupled with efforts to enhance the circulation of capital, have been accompanied by the establishment of new borders, internal and external, as well as economic and political no-man's lands permissive of unfettered exploitation.

Critics of capitalism such as Hardt and Negri believe, however, that these no-man's lands can constitute, as zones of exception, breeding grounds for progressive forms of disruption in the service of the oppressed (2000: 216–17). These oppressed are expected to make use of their experiences within the indeterminacy of these zones of exception and undermine the legal, intellectual and perverted moral infrastructure that allows capitalism to increasingly generate inequality around the globe. Each film I have analysed hints at moments in which the exploited revolt and challenge the legitimacy of such apparatuses of oppression. *Mediterranea* presents the insistent challenges posed by human bodies against the borders that undemocratically control their movement. It also presents the street riots of displaced workers targeting a system of internal borders that relies on the complicity of local economic enterprise, government, population and organised crime.

Moon's Sam rebels against corporate practices that literally kill him. By means of a shuttle, he crosses the border between Moon and Earth, between the inhuman and the human, and tries to reclaim his right to life. The film does not offer an optimistic ending. It suggests that Sam will probably be detained as an illegal immigrant and his whistle-blowing about the practices of his company will remain unheard. In *Toni Erdmann* the rebel is Ines's father. In one of the dramatic moments of the film, he dresses up in a traditional furry Bulgarian costume used in exorcism rituals. His purpose is to challenge and ridicule neoliberal corporate decorum and perhaps exorcise his career-possessed daughter.

Capital also includes scenes that show Marc revolting by means of physical and verbal violence. But since *Capital* is a film presenting adaptation to displacement, these are framed as imagined. They show what the ethical Marc would do in the spirit of social and economic justice, but refrains from doing because he is teaching himself to play the corporate power game. In these imagined sequences he wants to punish finance's elitism and greed, and help a friend who has lost his job. Moreover, if one reads *Capital* against the grain, and assumes that it follows the Marxist thesis that capitalism is doomed to self-destruction, one can argue that it is Marc's very adaptation that proves to be subversive, and not the denunciatory book he once planned to write. Such a reading would conclude that Marc's determination to become a modern Robin Hood follows the logic of accelerating the demise of capitalism by increasing its degree of corporate perversion and by 'liberating' it from the ethical and sustainability constraints that make it both socially acceptable and economically viable.[5] This reading is confirmed by Marc's admission in the last sequence of the film that the game can go on only as long as there is a game and the system does not fall apart. When he makes this statement, Marc winks to the audience, suggesting that, both for him and them, the memory of the 2008–09 meltdown is still fresh, and that, indeed, the game itself can make the system implode.

Notes

1. Prior to *Capital*, Costa-Gavras authored the migration dramedy *Eden is West* (France, 2009) and *The Axe* (France, 2005) about the effects of long-term unemployment. Carpignano's second feature, *The Ciambra* (2017), shows that he follows a similar path.

2. In *Little White Lies*, available at <https://lwlies.com/interviews/maren-ade-toni-erdmann/> (last accessed 20 December 2018).
3. See an interview with Minnesota Public Radio, available at <https://www.mprnews.org/story/2009/04/27/duncanjones> (last accessed 20 December 2018).
4. For example, in *Working Girl* (Nichols, USA, 1988) or *Equity* (Mennon, USA, 2016), as well as female executives in *Margin Call* (Chandor, USA, 2012).
5. An insight that hints at the doctrine of accelerationism summarised in Land 2017.

16. A HUSHED CRISIS: THE VISUAL NARRATIVES OF (EASTERN) EUROPE'S ANTIZIGANISM

Dina Iordanova

There is a serious crisis across Europe today, a crisis of racism. It is particularly palpable in Eastern Europe, where openly racist talk and actions emanate from a range of people who practise hate speech on a daily basis – from football fans to yoga teachers to real estate agents – at their workplace, in their social interactions and on social media. Yet it is a crisis that remains unacknowledged – mainly because the objects of racism and hate speech are the Roma, aka Gypsies. This is a crisis of antiziganism, a hushed one.

Take Jan Gebert's acclaimed documentary, *Az prijde válka* (*When the War Comes*, 2018). Set in Slovakia, the film follows the leader of a paramilitary group, Petr Švrček, a clean-cut youngster who is articulate and polite. We see him taking exams and helping older people around town, and on weekends training the other youngsters of his 'army' in the nearby woods. Is this training just for recreation purposes or has it real-life application? What is the war that these young people are preparing for? Who is the enemy that they will counter with their advanced fighting skills? This is never clearly identified. Viewers in Eastern Europe, however, know the answer – it will be a war against the Roma, against the refugees, against the 'foreign', against all those who are not 'us'. In fact, it is not a war that is still to come – rather, it is a war that has already quietly started and that such groups are involved with. My attention in this investigation is focused on the reality of antiziganism and the war against the Roma – one that is not officially recognised but that rages across the countries of Eastern Europe – and on the way it has been represented in cinema of the past decade.

Roma are mistreated in Western and Eastern Europe alike, albeit in different ways. In Western Europe, actions against Roma that verge on human rights abuse (demolition of settlements, deportations without the chance to be heard, restrictions on welfare) are carried out by official enforcement bodies such as the police or welfare officers. They are reported on – mainly in human rights monitoring and Roma media, with little in the mainstream sources – but rarely cause much public outcry. For example, from 2003 until at least 2005, illegal selective deportations of Roma from Kosovo, Serbia and Montenegro were carried out in a particularly inhumane manner across Germany (Howden and Kuehnen 2005). The only case that seems to have sparked widespread protests was that of Kosovo teenager Leonarda Dibrani in 2010, who was dragged out by police from a school bus in France to be deported. This triggered mass student demonstrations, to no avail, as Dibrani was still deported. Later, the French police were known to be continually involved in actions demolishing Roma settlements across the country, such as La Petite Ceinture in Paris (Rubin 2013).

In general, the Roma are regarded as an East European problem, as a population that is 'foreign' to the West and that needs to be relocated back where it belongs; and indeed most deportations affect the Roma who come from countries that are not members of the EU, such as Kosovo. In Britain it took years of deportations and selective human rights abuses on an ethnic basis before the scandal of the Windrush Caribbeans became public and led to attempts to correct these injustices. Nothing like this is on the horizon for the Roma, many of whom are in a similar legal limbo and treated equally appallingly in the West.

In Eastern Europe, publicly and legislatively Roma are supposed to be treated equally, in terms of housing, education or health, even though there are investigative films that show this is not the case, such as *Scoala noastra* (*Our School*, 2011) or *Cambridge* (2015). Yet there is widespread racism that proclaims the Roma to be a major social problem. States do not normally engage in direct Roma-bashing, but at the same time they tolerate it and normally leave citizens from the main ethnic group to practise it at will. Vocal local anti-Roma activists openly reproach the state for not daring to act against alleged Roma criminality for fear of the European Community, as the EU membership position of these countries is fragile. Thus, West European countries act openly against the Roma without being punished, while East European countries cannot do this and instead leave the dirty work to paramilitaries. Racism is present in both regions, and indeed the extent of antiziganism is similar to that of antisemitism. This is one of the most serious crises in Europe but it remains little acknowledged and spoken about.[1]

I structure my investigation in three parts. First I discuss some films that aim to combat the prevalent antiziganism and that remain hushed in the ghetto of arthouse cinema. Secondly, I analyse an antiziganist film trilogy from the Czech

Republic and the inventive ways that have been deployed for its silencing. And third, I discuss the presence of racist and antiziganist videos on YouTube.

Hushed in the Arthouse Ghetto

In this section I discuss three films that aim to present the Roma ordeal in contemporary Eastern Europe.[2] The films are characterised by a realist approach – shot in authentic settings, using non-professional actors and real stories, and rather dominated by pessimistic yet authentic gloom, fear and desperation. There is also a belief on the part of the directors that if they show the difficulties of the day-to-day existence of concrete Roma protagonists, this may lead to better understanding. These films point at Europe in crisis, and yet they remain insufficiently acknowledged – hushed in the ghetto of arthouse cinema – and have not succeeded in influencing public discourse, either at home or internationally.

Just the Wind

Hungarian Benedek Fliegauf's *Csak a szél* (*Just the Wind*, 2012) is the earliest in this recent lineage, though it follows in the footsteps of many other similar East European films.[3] The film is based on a true story of deadly pogroms against Hungarian Roma; the opening screen reads:

> In Hungary in the years 2008–2009 a group of offenders committed acts of violence against Romanies. 16 homes were attacked with Molotov cocktails and 63 shots were fired with shotguns and rifles. 55 people were victims of these crimes, 5 were severely injured, 6 killed. Suspects are currently the subject of criminal proceedings. Though it draws on facts, this film is not a documentary.

Just the Wind follows the daily routines of members of a Roma family who live in an isolated makeshift house in a remote forest at the edge of town. There has been a racist pogrom against their neighbours and people have been killed in their beds. The protagonists (a mother and two teenage children) know they may be next in line, but hope to survive for another few months until the time they can depart and join the father, who has already obtained asylum in Canada. But by the end of the film they have also become victims; the last shots are set in the local morgue instead of the transatlantic flight of their dreams.

Just the Wind's extraordinary cinematic achievement is in the depiction of unsettling fear – its protagonists' condition from beginning to end, an uncontrollable stress coming from perennial alertness, from a permanently activated flight or fight mode – which is conveyed through a masterful combination of close-up shots, hand-held camerawork, sound and editing. Even if the reactions of the family members to the threat are different – the grandfather has given up, the teenage daughter tries to blend in as much as possible, the mother toils away at her two low-paying jobs and tries to keep the loan sharks at bay, whereas the young boy is rebellious – they will all end up victims.

An Episode in the Life of an Iron Picker

While *Just the Wind* shows a police force that does not protect vulnerable Roma, the Bosnian *Epizoda u zivotu beraca zeljeza* (*An Episode in the Life of an Iron Picker*, Danis Tanovic, 2013) shows a medical establishment that withdraws healthcare. The Roma family in the film play themselves; the day-to-day chores that take them through the winter are chronicled with documentary realism. They lead a hand-to-mouth existence in a remote mountain hamlet; four people – two adults and two children – survive on the paltry income that the father, Nazif, makes from dealing in scrap metal. Senada, the mother, is pregnant with her third child. Something goes wrong, however, and she is in terrible pain. It is an ordeal to get her to the hospital and once there, they learn that the foetus has died in the womb; her life is at risk. Rather than being rushed to the operating theatre, however, doors are closed for the Roma woman, as she has got no medical insurance and is not able to pay the bill for the operation. The ethical principles of the medical profession do not seem to apply in her case: Roma patients are not regarded as fully fledged people. Even though not overtly spelled out, the medics in the film act out of an unspoken but widespread conviction that the Roma are breeding too much anyhow. It is all the more painful knowing that the docudrama is based on a real story.

Goat

The Slovak film *Koza* (*Goat*, 2015) delivers one of the best portrayals of Roma's limited opportunities. Its slow continuous shots, exquisite framing and wintry aesthetics make it reminiscent of the tableaux in Ulrich Seidl's *Import/Export* (2007). Former lightweight Olympic boxing champion Peter Baláž, nicknamed 'Koza' ('Goat'), plays himself in a story that chronicles his own life. The Olympic glory long forgotten, he and his partner Misa live in dilapidated conditions. He is a loser now, with no chance of winning a fight, trapped in a downward spiral on the provincial boxing circuit. A fallen man in every respect, he is unable to convince his girlfriend to keep the child that they have conceived. No endurance is left in this small muscular man's body; he can no longer fight, and there is no respite for him, and no cushioned exit into retirement. The incessant disoriented travelling between bouts, on snowy provincial roads, instils a feeling of freezing and discomfort from beginning to end. His is a modern-day slavery: his manager calls him a 'dumb cripple' and looks to sell him down the chain.

Goat is an existential tale of a beaten protagonist, one who takes blow after blow after blow. There is no direct condemnation of police nor of medics nor of exploitative managers, and not even an explicit mention that the protagonist is a Rom – it is obvious to those who come from this region. A man who cannot expect respite from anywhere; he must be a Rom.

Reception

What about the reception of these realist chronicles? Each of these films made a splash in its respective country at the time of its release, and the works have been recognised for their sensitivity and civility. However, even where these films are held in great esteem by cinephiles, they only had limited circulation and were seen by limited audiences, both within the countries of their making and internationally.

These films, however, have played at numerous festivals; all were in competition at Berlinale, the grand festival that claims to be politically engaged. *The Iron Picker* won Silver Bear, Ecumenical Jury and Best Actor awards (for Nazif Mujic),[4] *Just the Wind* got the Amnesty International Award and *Goat* was nominated for best director. Each of the films also received awards from or played at various other festivals around the world – Toronto, Mar Del Plata, Istanbul, Jerusalem, Hong Kong – and they have had some theatrical distribution internationally. None of this seems to have been enough. The accolades were not sufficient to make a difference to the actual subjects or to the prevailing public discourse. The pressing social matters that these films address remain hushed in the arthouse ghetto.

Nazif Mujic, the actor who plays himself in *The Iron Picker*, used the trip to Berlin in February 2013 to apply for asylum in Germany. After all, the discrimination his family had suffered was documented in the acclaimed film. However, he was turned down and deported back to Bosnia, where he is known to have sold the award from the festival to avoid destitution. He died in extreme poverty in February 2018 at the age of 47, precisely five years after winning at Berlinale.[5]

Hushed out of Shame: *Bastards*

I first learned about *Bastardi/Bastards* – a privately produced, widely popular Czech anti-Roma film trilogy – during a visit to Moravia in 2013. My host, a film academic who was, at the time, also a member of the Czech film funding body, told me about it one day when we walked down the street – while the town looked calm, he said, in fact tensions between Czech and Roma were running high and the relations were marked by extreme hatred. This same hatred was the hallmark of *Bastards*. Comparing *Bastards* to the hugely popular output of neo-Nazi rock group Orlik and musician Daniel Landa, my friend summarised: 'Czechs are ashamed of this unbelievably racist series [. . .] *Bastardi* is not a "B" movie, but rather a "C" or "D" one, and no one wants to take it seriously, because this would legitimize it [. . .] We are trying to act as if it doesn't exist.'[6] It is this last statement – 'trying to act as if it doesn't exist' – that gives the key to understanding another of the discursive configurations that mark the hushed character of the crisis I am outlining. While hugely popular at home, this work of antiziganism is barely known beyond the borders of former Czechoslovakia, not least due to the efforts of people like my friend, who intentionally work to hush the fact of its embarrassing existence. But does hushing help to dissipate the crisis?

Bastards is an authorial project of Tomás Magnusek, a prolific young Czech writer, actor and film director. The whole enterprise seems to be driven by personal conviction: the protagonist in *Bastards*, Tomas Majer, is an alter ego for Magnusek. Majer is a teacher who takes a job at a segregated 'practical school'[7] where, some months previously, his sister, Jana Majerova, also a teacher, has been raped and murdered. The police have made no arrests and Majer suspects that the culprits are among the teenage Roma boys in the school. What follows is a story of revenge, in which Majer takes it upon himself, in a context where the authorities will not do their job, and where teachers like his sister are left vulnerable and exposed, to protect innocent citizens. The two sequels evolve into a franchise in which, once again, Majer and other vigilantes restore order, confronting and punishing the uncontrollable youths who keep creating havoc. The films are made to a television aesthetics standard; the camerawork, lighting, music and editing are not particularly different from other European TV series. It is not the artistic value of *Bastards*, however, that is my focus of interest, but rather the context of the film's production, dissemination and reception. I believe that the particularities of *Bastards*' handling in the public space once again – albeit differently – reveal the symptomatic hushing of the crisis related to the Roma in Eastern Europe at large.

The first instalment of *Bastards* – a film produced on a private basis with no state support – was extremely successful; the opening weekend generated about 70,000 euros and eventually the film ranked as the most successful Czech film of 2010. The revenues it generated, as well as sponsorships from various businesses that invested in it, generated a solid funding stream that permitted the immediate shooting and release of *Bastardi 2* just a year later. The same scenario was then repeated once again the next year, enabling the release of *Bastardi 3* in 2012. Beyond the theatrical release, all three films have been made available for free on YouTube, with no English or other subtitles. By the end of 2018, *Bastardi 1* had been viewed more than a million times on YouTube, *Bastardi 2* had about 780,000 views, and *Bastardi 3* 840,000 views.[8]

Outside the Czech Republic this film is little heard about, and one can see that special efforts have been made for things to stay that way. The film has not played at any film festivals internationally, and all the published reviews I was able to find about it were in the Czech language.[9] On IMDb, one can find short and cryptically written synopses for each of the films, provided by the Czech Film Centre; there are no viewers' reviews whatsoever – quite unusual for a film that is apparently high in popularity – and I am inclined to think that the user reviews may have been disabled or removed. On the YouTube locations of the films, the comments feature is disabled.[10] The IMDb links to an 'official site' for *Bastards* (<http://filmbastardi.cz/>) but on clicking through one finds an empty domain. It seems that the Czech Film Centre has also taken over the way the sequels are presented on IMDb: the main keywords related to *Bastards 2* are 'racist as protagonist' and 'psychopath as protagonist', and the synopsis for *Bastards 3* references justice and social responsibility.

A similar approach – one in which activists mobilised in various ways to prevent the spread of a hateful film that was posted on YouTube with full fanfare – was applied in the Netherlands around the time of the release of the infamous anti-Islamic video *Fitna* (2008), which the right-wing Dutch politician Geert Wilders posted on YouTube. These actions were put under academic scrutiny by a team of media scholars and sociologists, whose research showed that the activists' actions indeed managed to diminish *Fitna*'s international exposure (Müller, Van Zoonen and Hirzalla 2014). Similarly, only a few people abroad now know of the *Bastards* series, and this is due, in part, to the efforts of anti-racist Czech intellectuals who have managed to turn the film series into a hushed home secret. The question is, however, whether this diminishes or eradicates support for racism within the country.

The situation with *Bastards* is representative of the conflicted public discourse in many of the countries of Eastern Europe. On the one hand, domestic nationalist parties and movements, whose agendas often border on racism and who are vocal proponents of antiziganism, enjoy popular support and have their own undisturbed media presence. On the other, there are those – typically intellectuals' – voices who denounce racism; due to their higher position in society they manage to prevail in the official media and – as we saw with the example of *Bastards* – to control the spread and limit the damage of hateful material. Populist politicians who have made it on to the international scene generally fall within the latter group, but not always out of conviction – they denounce antiziganism mainly in order to be seen as complying with the expectations of the European Community. With the growing populist and nationalist tendencies across Eastern Europe, even this may change. And if it does, the hushing will be swept away by a full-blown crisis.

HUSHED IN FULL VIEW: POGROM VIDEOS ON YOUTUBE

There is another 'filmed' genre that represents antiziganism in action – video reportage of pogroms against Roma – and it is found in full view on YouTube. These videos are an extreme example of racial animosity; they provide a global platform where hate speech thrives, and reveal the true depth of the crisis. Yet this genre is also hushed – not because such videos are, sooner or later, taken down, but because the circumstances of their making, posting, popularity and particularities of removal are not publicly discussed nor denounced.[11]

Typically, these are short videos showing street confrontations and vigilante groups taking action against groups of Roma who are, allegedly, involved in illegal activities that the authorities do nothing about. The videos are mainly shot with hand-held camera, often lacking in any professionalism, and are poorly edited and put together – even though in some cases they have been set to music. In recent years, I have repeatedly come across such material, which originates from a variety of countries across Eastern Europe – Hungary, Slovakia, Bulgaria, Romania. As these videos are not fully fledged films, so to speak, and thus do not fall within the sphere of my scholarly interests, I only registered their existence and did not keep a systematic record of their content. This is something I now regret, as the content on YouTube fluctuates and different material pops up in response to searches done at different times. A number of these videos also seem to have been taken down – the record would have been of vital importance for my claim that such videos are, in fact, abundant. In the process of research, my thinking evolved, and I now believe it is essential to consider the pogrom videos (and the discourse that goes along with them) as part of this investigation. I picked out two videos that were posted in June 2018 and are available on YouTube at the moment of writing, six months later. These examples are from the Ukraine, but I do not want to single out this particular country, as I hope my discussion so far has provided sufficient evidence that hateful treatment of the Roma is characteristic of all countries in the region.

Representatives of National Warbands Clear Out a Roma Tabor in Golosyvski Park

First, there is this 12-minute video, dated 7 June 2018, which I found posted on two different YouTube channels.[12] What does one see in this video? On an ordinary Thursday, a group of about twenty men armed with battle-axes, sledgehammers and bludgeons walk into a forest, wearing balaclavas and black T-shirts marked 'National Warbands'. The cameraman follows and provides occasional commentary. On the way, he stops for a brief impromptu 'interview' with two women, apparently members of the Roma community, who try to rush out of the forest salvaging some belongings. On arrival at the camp – consisting of about twenty primitive makeshift huts between the trees – the boys jump into action and quickly break apart all the dwellings. The destruction of the slum takes just a few minutes, during which action the cameraman excitedly circles around and shouts, 'davay, davay, patsany!' ('Go on, go on, boys!'). Most residents have escaped but a few are still around and look on; resident Maria watches the destruction, dumbfounded. 'Do you have a passport?', the cameraman asks in patronising voice. 'Of course I do. In the house,' she responds.[13] A bearded pogrom master comes into a close-up to display a nauseated grimace – this is his way of suggesting that the stench one feels is supposedly unbearable. The men are in a hurry to finish the job soon so that they can go for a barbecue. A white kitten is rescued from one of the huts and cuddled by the heroes in balaclavas. The police arrive just as the destruction is complete and are shown around by the warband guys who inform them about what has been achieved. The brigade takes a proud group photo for a job well done. They have protected the environment.

Six months after the date of this filmed pogrom the video posted on the first YouTube channel (12ion) had been viewed 197,343 times and had generated 2,433 comments. The video posted on the second channel (EuroMaydan) had been seen 117,422 times and had generated more than 500 comments, bringing the total number of views to more than 300,000 and the comments to almost 3,000. The video itself is not translated, but this does not prevent international viewers from sending congratulatory comments from across the world (e.g. 'Nice job from Finland'; 'Hail from the USA!'; 'Proud of you Ukrainian dudes!'). The majority of the other comments are domestic congratulations, usually coming with references to the inaction of the authorities, as well as expressing doubts about whether corruption in the higher echelons of power could be tackled the same way. One can also see comments expressing abhorrence and pointing out the racism of the action and of the other comments, but these are significantly fewer in number.

History of the Roma Problem in Kiev and Its Solution

This video, posted a day later (8 June 2018), evolves around the same pogrom footage but represents a longer edited (19 minutes) version of it. *History of the Roma Problem in Kiev and Its Solution* is posted on the YouTube channel of the National Corps – an organisation that operates under the slogan Power, Welfare, Order – and is watermarked with their emblem.[14] Opening with a secondary title, 'The Facts', the video purports to provide contextualisation and justification for the violence by bringing in editorial interventions that give the material a certain slant and present it as environmental protection. It is edited to reportage standards, and identifies speakers by name, including the cameraman, Oleksandr Kulakov.[15] It is prefaced by a seemingly objective background summary that references the growing problem of illegal settlements by Roma migrants and the inaction of the authorities, and presents the destruction of the settlement as the only possible solution for protecting Kiev's environment and leisure areas. There is a lengthy description that sets up the pogrom as an example of civil action to protect the 'green zones' of the city, and denounces the behaviour of the police who at first appeared supportive but have since raised charges against the patriots. There is also a call for the further dissemination of the material via social media channels such as Instagram. In line with the videomakers' desire to maintain law and order, the music rights have been cleared. The commentary revolves around some of the tropes found on social media, mainly that Roma are unable to lead civilised lives and ought to be removed to the Zakarpatie region. It uses improvised interviews with Roma, where the person asking the questions maintains a patronising tone – Why is this 13-year-old boy not able to speak Ukrainian or Russian? Why is this woman not working? – while simultaneously treating the man who is working as if he has taken a more worthy person's job.

The reportage also covers the actions of the National Corps on the day after the pogrom, when the fighters return to clear away the remnants of the slum. The camera zooms in on the rubble to show found *compromats* ('compromising materials') such as syringes, dirty cooking utensils and a nunchaku, suggesting drug abuse, filth and violence. Wearing protective white clothing, the boys joke about the previous day's clearance; the vermin have been removed. The commentary towards the end of the video states: 'Our work gave results; the Roma are gathering around the south train station in Kiev.' A band of Roma, perhaps an extended family, are shown squatting in the open air in front of the city's train station and are described as 'preparing to leave'. The interviewer turns to an old woman and asks, in a patronising tone: 'What is stopping you from getting out of here and allowing us to restore order?' She tries to give an answer, stretching her arms, but her voice is cut out. The members of her group are dishevelled and do not look clean or healthy; it is not a pretty sight. The 'interviewer' continues his monologue: 'Have you heard what happened in the park? Do you want a repetition of what happened? You have only a few days to get out.'

An important narrative element that runs through this video is the footage of newborn kittens that are rescued from the debris. The kittens are shown on several occasions, first discovered in all their vulnerability, then pulled out and held gently, caressed by the gloved hands of the muscular warband members and, later on, in their new dwelling at the offices of the National Corps. Roughly the same amount of screen time is given to Roma and to the kittens, and the way the footage of these two visual tropes is edited clearly aims to build a contrast: the first are ugly and dirty intruders who must be excised, the second are sweet and cuddly little wonders that must be given loving care. This video was made public on 10 June 2018, three days after the pogrom. By comparison to the raw footage of the pogrom, it has attracted a much smaller number of views (20,000 views as opposed to 300,000).

You Are Not Human, You Should Be Exterminated

A third video, a nine-minute-long reportage from a Roma settlement in Uzhgorod in the Ukraine, produced by a 'European Media Center', was posted by Venerastudio channel in January 2012, and at the time of writing has been on YouTube for seven years.[16] This is a report by journalist Mila Nedelska and cameraman Vlad Vishnevskiy shot in a Roma settlement where a pogrom – allegedly by Berkut forces – has taken place the previous morning.[17] It shows a poor slum with muddy streets and makeshift houses. The female reporter, wearing a white fur coat, is surrounded by many Roma who speak over one another, rushing to complain, express anxiety and condemn the attackers. Piecing together the evidence, one understands that the settlement was attacked early in the morning, with the attackers rushing into the houses of people, some of who were still sleeping, shouting abuse and death threats. An old woman cries and swears: 'My children do not steal [. . .] What have we done?' The journalists are taken into several houses, which, even if cluttered, are modest and clean. Old and young, healthy and ill are consistent in the evidence: they are scared to death. The attackers promised to come back. A short epilogue to the video reports the death of one of the witnesses, a bed-ridden tuberculosis sufferer. According to the report, it has not been possible to confirm who precisely carried out the pogroms, so they ask the police. Apparently, as the alleged attackers belong to Berkut – a semi-autonomous government-affiliated force – it is an awkward issue.

The reporters appear to be independently sponsored by the European Union and certainly display bravery in making a report that aims to give voice to the victims. There is something profoundly wrong with the way this video is posted, though. The title of the report – *You Are Not Human; You Should Be Exterminated* – quotes lines used by the racist attackers. However, a title like this seems to work as a magnet for viewers who share the philosophy of the invaders. It is no wonder, therefore, that most of the 140 comments that the video has generated are probably the purest example of extreme hate speech that one can come across.

The importance of YouTube

'I love YouTube', says cultural anthropologist Grant McCracken. 'As an anthropologist, it gives me access to everything. I do not have to leave the house. Everything happening in the world gets into a video that's uploaded onto YouTube. That makes YouTube the raw feed of popular culture. It's anything and everything, completely non-curated' (McCracken 2016: 41). And indeed, the videos I have just discussed give access to aspects of life that in other circumstances would likely have stayed in the shadows. It is particularly important for the nationalists to show their actions; video is great for this purpose and YouTube is their key medium in not only making the 'raw feed of popular culture' available, but also providing a platform for forthright hate speech at the very site where the deeds are displayed.

These videos, and the many other videos that they stand in for, belong to the 'blaming the victim' category, in which groups that are socially weak, disempowered and impoverished are presented as a menace of overwhelming proportions, as extensively discussed by scholars over time (Ryan 1972; Said and Hitchens 1988). Finding such videos in full view on YouTube directly feeds into further fostering the discourse that puts the blame squarely on those who are target of the violence, while glorifying (directly or indirectly) the actions of those carrying out the pogroms. My spontaneous reaction, in the process of finding, watching and then describing these examples of racism and antiziganism, is similar to the impulse of my Czech friend: their very existence is shameful; these examples of hate speech must be banned from public space. YouTube should be alerted about the presence of this hateful stuff right away; it should take the videos down and have the comments disabled.

Before I reach for the 'flag up' button, however, I am having second thoughts. Will the removal of these videos and comments resolve anything? It will certainly hide the ugly facts from sight. But it will not eradicate the racism; it will just tuck it away. If taken down, the videos I discuss here will no longer be available, and thus we will have no public record of the reality of the pogroms, nor the size of the problem. This is what has happened to those other pogrom videos that I have seen sporadically over the years and that are no longer there. Taking this material down without any public record of what was taken down makes it impossible to be aware of the extent of the crisis, which, as I tend to believe, is significantly wider than is visible on the surface. Disabling the comments will remove hate speech from the public space but will not change the fact that there are significant numbers of individuals out there who feel that they are entitled to practise hate; nor will it alter the fact that the Roma are at the receiving end of such hate speech more than any other group.[18]

What about YouTube's Hate Speech Policy? It clearly states parameters that these videos fall under *bona fide*.[19] What about their enforcement routines (Lapowski 2017)? A news item about YouTube's resolve to combat racism was published in *Romea*, a Czech Roma-themed online news source (ČTK 2017). According to this, in 2017 YouTube was in process of hiring more than 10,000 staff to monitor hate speech and enforce standards. If such numbers were indeed hired, I find it hard to imagine what these 10,000 employees might be busy with. What other standards would they be busy enforcing as a priority as to allow the hateful material to stay up for months? I also find it hard to believe that no one has flagged up these videos to YouTube's attention; after all, there are a number of international NGOs whose job it is to protect Roma rights. No information is publicly available on which videos are flagged up nor how many times a video has been reported; YouTube does not report statistics on what has been taken down. Could it be that YouTube has been alerted about these racist videos and has simply decided to apply their 'demonetisation' approach, namely is to block advertising revenue so that those who post such material are not able to benefit financially from a possible advertising stream? One would think it would be clear to YouTube that those who post racist videos are not after advertising revenues. They do not care about generating income but about engaging publicly in hateful practice, in full view.

Conclusion

In this chapter I have discussed material from a variety of Eastern European countries – the Czech Republic, Ukraine, Hungary, Slovakia, Bosnia, and so on. But I could have easily used material from other countries – the hushed crisis I am talking about is equally prevalent across the region. It is often the case that the problems are reduced and explored as if they are typical of one country; correspondingly, the attempts to resolve them are also focused nationally. Indeed, the nation-state is still the framework for social measures. However, working within issue-based film studies, I want to foreground the importance of the transnational approach in studying representation. The Roma are a transnational group, and a migratory group at that. One can see aspects of their movements and the way they are treated only once matters are explored supranationally.[20]

It is, then, inappropriate to regard the problems of antiziganism as specific to Eastern Europe; in fact, it is an ideology that is present Europe-wide, as is the mistreatment of Roma. Film-makers have recorded a miscellany of human rights abuses against the Roma for the past two decades, from illegal detentions on the Dutch-German border as far back as 2001, through deportations of Roma from Germany in 2003 and thereafter, to the more recent destruction of Roma shantytowns in Paris and across France and the practice of separating children from their parents in France.[21] It is important to note that one can find a number of videos on YouTube that report actions of Roma removal from different West European countries by law-enforcement officers; such videos are likely to be watched with mixed feelings by antiziganists in Eastern Europe: joy over the destruction of settlements, envy that this is done by the police rather than by paramilitaries, and hatred of the Roma who will soon be deported to their neighbourhoods.[22] And indeed, Roma are usually rounded up in the West and deported to Eastern Europe, where they are believed to 'belong', but where they will be most certainly exposed to danger, a practice that undermines the key premises of the Geneva Convention.

I believe the size of this crisis to be of much bigger proportions than publicly acknowledged. I also believe that antiziganism is Europe's most systematically hushed and overlooked problem. This is why I argue that it is of the utmost importance to talk about these matters as often and as much as possible, with the aim of counteracting ignorance and raising concern. If awareness were improved, we would hopefully not see people such as the posh British comedian Jack Whitehall visiting the training fields of paramilitaries in the Ukraine and treating them as if they are just some innocuous goofy boys obsessed with militarised drills.[23] His seems an innocent encounter – but in fact it is celebrating people who today may entertain an eccentric Englishman, but on other days will engage in racist pogroms.

It would also be good to see the term antiziganism used more often, alongside instances in which antisemitism is discussed, because nowadays these two behaviours and ideologies go hand in hand. For some reason, however, talk of antisemitism is loud and uncompromising, whereas talk about antiziganism is muted and conditional. Everybody knows the meaning of antisemitism; those who know the term antiziganism are few and far between, and those who use it are an even smaller group. If the films I discussed here were about Jews, they would most likely receive more awards, would have a wider festival exposure and theatrical distribution, and what they show would be condemned much more vocally. Just as the world marks the 80th anniversary of Kristallnacht and repeats 'never again', one should ensure that this pledge applies equally to all those endangered by groups who seek to obliterate them.

Last but not least, I also appeal to social scientists and educationalists who still find it difficult to adopt film in the context of their work. For social scientists (politologists, sociologists), film does not have the same evidentiary power as a published report or a research paper, even if – as evidenced by the discussion so far – it may chronicle adverse actual events or else reveal serious social trouble. They continue to discount film – even documentary film – as a fantasy medium that is unsubstantiated by default. No wonder, then, that someone like Nazif Mujic, whose life story is the subject of a shocking film that chronicles humiliation and abuse, is rejected by an asylum court and left to die in poverty at the age of 47 in a Europe where an extensive network of social agencies is established to safeguard human rights and provide support to the needy.

I wonder how often matters of antiziganism are discussed by educationalists in the context of their work. It is likely that many teachers and college professors in various countries are trying to address these problems. But do they make good use of the medium of film to raise awareness? Three versions of the anti-racist Hungarian short *Their Skin Was Their Only Sin: Roma Serial Killings in Hungary 2008–2009*, for example, have been posted on YouTube.[24] These films address precisely the same deadly pogroms against Roma that are the subject of *Just the Wind*, which we discussed above. The two shorter versions (of 3 and 2 minutes' length) have gained slightly over 4,000 views; the 10-minute-long version has been viewed 4,539 times, giving the film a total of less than 9,000 views. The comments are disabled (one can only speculate about the content), but the 'likes' and 'dislikes' are still there, and they show a ratio of 3 to 1 in favour of the 'dislikes' (165:48). Even this minor detail gives enough information about the balance of public opinion. So in the course of five years, the anti-racist film has been viewed less than 9,000 times, whereas the viewership for pogrom videos over six months is in the hundreds of thousands. Would this be the case, I wonder, if teachers routinely suggested that their students view the anti-racist video in class? It is inexcusable for racist pogrom videos to have clocked hundreds of thousands of views while anti-racism films remain in obscurity. Can we make sure that our students are more exposed to the anti-racist efforts of film-makers? It should not be so difficult for us all – academics, educators, social scientists and film-makers – to work together to bring the hushed crisis into the daylight and confront it.

NOTES

1. In what is claimed to be the most comprehensive survey of victimisation suffered by Europe's minority and immigrant communities, the EU's Fundamental Rights Agency said that for Roma 'racially motivated crime is an everyday experience' (European Union 2000). *The Guardian*'s Ian Traynor quotes Morten Kjaerum, director of the Vienna-based agency that authored the report: 'They emerge as the group most vulnerable to discrimination' (Traynor 2009).
2. Films that chronicle the discrimination and destitution of Roma are also made across Europe, for example, *A Ciambra* (2017), by Jonas Carpignano.
3. At least two other important films were made in Hungary on the same issue, Eszter Hajdú's feature-length documentary *Judgment in Hungary* (2013) and the short *Their Skin Was Their Only Sin – Roma Serial Killings in Hungary 2008–2009* (2013). These pogroms are also discussed in Murer 2020.
4. *The Iron Picker* received somewhat better international exposure than the other two films – not least, a DVD of it is available to acquire on Amazon, with English subtitles.
5. His death was reported by Agence France Presse, but I have not been able to find a European newspaper that picked up the news. It was published, however, by the *South China Morning Post* in Hong Kong ('Award-winning actor Nazif Mujic dies penniless after selling trophy to feed his starving children', 19 February 2018).
6. My colleague also lamented the fact that the series' creator, Magnusek, enjoys quite high visibility in Czech public life and at one point was even elected head of the writers' union. 'We consider his work the worst expression of racism entrenched in Central Europe's mentality', he added.
7. According to the Wikipedia entry on education in the Czech Republic, the 'special schools' were a segregational educational arrangement for developmentally disabled children. 'Many children of Romani heritage were made to study at these schools despite lack of disability; due to institutional and social discrimination, Romani students often failed to meet academic standards and were segregated from

8. *Bastardi* is available at <https://www.youtube.com/watch?v=VNk-dlJZtGk> and can also be viewed in full via Facebook. *Bastardi 2* is available at <https://www.youtube.com/watch?v=bjO6UkbkfD0> and *Bastardi 3* at <https://www.youtube.com/watch?v=yx9XF-UHErk> (last accessed 12 October 2019).
9. Except for a single review by a Czech-Roma student, whose commentary on the hateful nature of *Bastards* is published on a Roma site: Martina Šafářová, 'Czech film series "Bastards" humiliates Romani people', Romea, 30 March 2015, translated by Gwendolyn Albert, available at <http://www.romea.cz/en/news/czech/czech-film-series-bastards-humiliates-romani-people> (last accessed 12 October 2019). The piece claims that the Roma teenagers who took part in the film were manipulated and misled by the film-makers.
10. However, when I first did research on *Bastards 1* in 2016, there were more than 700 comments.
11. As far as I can tell, most pogrom videos are removed, often after a 'successful' run over a period of some months during which they are seen and applauded by tens or hundreds of thousands of viewers.
12. Available at 12июн <https://www.youtube.com/watch?v=APw2BNuI4mk> and from EuroMaydan <https://www.youtube.com/watch?v=X73xIGsQLvw> (last accessed 25 April 2019). I spent some time deliberating and consulting over how to translate the term *Наудружини* and settled on 'National Warband', as it seems to me that this most closely relates to the intended meaning of the group's name. It is of importance that 'National' here is abbreviated to *Naz*, as in 'Nazi'. I translated *зачищають* as 'clear out', but the verb on its own can safely be translated as 'cleanse'.
13. The question about the passport is representative of a popular discourse on the Roma; they are regarded as alien people who have come from who knows where and are not really in possession of the same citizenship rights. Destroying her passport along with Maria's dwelling is an example of a rights deprivation that is, in the view of these people, bringing the status quo into line with what it should be.
14. Available at <https://www.youtube.com/watch?v=rFKBktmBy28> (last accessed 25 April 2019). The National Corps is the parent organisation for the National Warbands. Notably, the first video, which contains raw footage of the pogrom, does not seem to have been posted on the National Corps' YouTube channel. Here one finds only the video that is edited and 'contextualised' discursively.
15. Notably, in the video, ethnic Ukrainians are mainly identified by their full name and position; the Roma are identified by first name only and the label 'Gypsy'.
16. *Ви не люди, вас треба убивати/You Are Not Human, You Should Be Exterminated* (<https://www.youtube.com/watch?v=yiwrRYmQPMg>) has had nearly 82,000 views. During the month I was working on this text, December 2018, the video was still being actively watched. On 9 December 2018 it had been seen 73,000 times, while on 25 April 2019 the number of views had grown to 81,608.

17. Berkut was a notorious special branch of the Ukrainian police within the Ministry of Internal Affairs, which was founded at the beginning of the post-Soviet period in 1992 and was dissolved in 2014 after it became associated with the kidnapping and brutal treatment of Euromaidan protesters. Berkut was created to fight organised crime but later was known for operating semi-autonomously in various regions, where it was also involved in antisemitism. For more, see Kuzio 2000.
18. In any case, as I feel it is as much my duty as anybody else's to combat hate speech, and even if I know that protection for the Roma is next to non-existent, I am planning to report these videos.
19. According to this, 'if the primary purpose of the content is to incite hatred against a group of people solely based on their ethnicity, or if the content promotes violence based on any of these core attributes, like religion, it violates our policy'. Available at <https://support.google.com/youtube/answer/2801939?hl=en;> (last accessed 20 December 2018.
20. One rare instance of journalism that approaches matters transnationally is Kirsti Melville's two-part project for Australia's ABS, 'The New Untouchables: Home and Abroad' (2011).
21. As seen in films such as *Gelem, Gelem* (Germany, 2001), *Kenedi Is Coming Home* (2003), *Spartacus and Cassandra* (2014), *Trapped by Law* (2015) and *Chakaraka* (2015).
22. In France, for example, the police are charged with destroying and clearing away Roma settlements, and have done so at places such as La Petite Ceinture and La Courneuve in Paris.
23. In the second season of *Travels with My Father* (2018).
24. The posts were made by X Kommunikációs Központ in July 2013. The first version is available at <https://www.youtube.com/watch?v=HMjVjZDx7ug>; the second at <https://www.youtube.com/watch?v=bzc2N9MirPI>, and the third at <https://www.youtube.com/watch?v=DLwXpe_J3B0> (last accessed 12 October 2019).

BIBLIOGRAPHY

Abel, Marco (2005), 'Images for a post-Wall reality: new German films at the 55th Berlin Film Festival', *Senses of Cinema*, 35, <http://sensesofcinema.com/2005/festival-reports/berlin2005/> (last accessed 19 December 2019).
Abel, Marco (2008), 'The cinema of identification gets on my nerves', *Cineaste*, <https://www.cineaste.com/summer2008/the-cinema-of-identification-gets-on-my-nerves> (last accessed 9 July 2019).
Abrantes, Pedro (2013), 'Vidas desativadas reflexão sobre o documentário de Susana Nobre', *Le Monde Diplomatique Edição Portuguesa*, November, <https://pt.mondediplo.com/spip.php?article977> (last accessed 30 January 2019).
Acland, Charles R., and Haidee Wasson (eds) (2011), *Useful Cinema*, Durham, NC: Duke University Press.
Agamben, Giorgio (2007), *Profanations*, New York: Zone Books.
Agence France Presse (2018), 'Award-winning actor Nazif Mujic dies penniless after selling trophy to feed his starving children', *South China Morning Post*, 19 February, <https://www.scmp.com/news/world/europe/article/2133791/award-winning-actor-nazif-mujic-dies-penniless-after-selling> (last accessed 5 January 2019).
Aglietta, Michel (2012), 'The European vortex', *New Left Review*, 75 (May/June), 15–36.
Ahmed, Sara (2000), *Strange Encounters. Embodied Others in Postcoloniality*, London: Routledge.
Ahmed, Sara (2004), *The Cultural Politics of Emotion*, Edinburgh: Edinburgh University Press.
Ahmed, Sara (2014a), *The Cultural Politics of Emotion*, 2nd edn, Edinburgh: Edinburgh University Press.

Ahmed, Sara (2014b), 'Not in the mood', *New Formations: A Journal of Culture / Theory / Politics*, 82, 13–28.
Alestalo, Matti (2000), 'The Finnish welfare state in the 1990s', in Stein Kuhnle (eds), *The Survival of the European Welfare State*, London: Routledge, 58–69.
Alexander, Jeffrey C., Ron Eyerman, Bernhard Giesen, Neil J. Smelser and Piotr Sztompka (eds) (2004), *Cultural Trauma and Collective Identity*, Berkeley: University of California Press, 155–95.
Alexievich, Svetlana (2016), *Secondhand Time*, trans. Bela Shayevich, London: Fitzcarraldo Editions.
Allbritton, Dean (2014), 'Prime risks: the politics of pain and suffering in Spanish crisis cinema', *Journal of Spanish Cultural Studies*, 15:1–2, 101–15.
Álvarez, Marta (2018), 'De la reivindicación a la ira: espacios de crisis en el cine español contemporáneo', *Iberoamericana. América Latina – España – Portugal*, 18:69, 81–102.
Anderson, Benedict (2006), *Imagined Communities*, rev. edn, New York: Verso.
Andersson, Johan, and Lawrence Webb (eds) (2016), *Global Cinematic Cities: New Landscapes of Film and Media*, New York: Wallflower Press.
Andersson, Ruben (2014), *Illegality, Inc.: Clandestine Migration and the Business of Bordering Europe*, Berkeley: University of California Press.
Andreescu, Florentina C. (2013), *From Communism to Capitalism. Nation and State in Romanian Cultural Production*, New York: Palgrave Macmillan.
Anonymous (2016), 'Record number of over 1.2 million first time asylum seekers registered in 2015', Eurostat news release, 4 March.
Anonymous (2018), 'On a ridgeline: notes on the "yellow vests" movement', *Viewpoint Magazine*, 6 December, <https://www.viewpointmag.com/2018/12/06/on-a-ridgeline-notes-on-the-yellow-vests-movement/> (last accessed 5 October 2019).
Ansell, Amy Elisabeth (1997), *New Right, New Racism. Race and Reaction in the United States and Britain*, Basingstoke: Macmillan.
Appel, Hilary, and Mitchell A. Orenstein (2016), 'Why did neoliberalism triumph and endure in the post-communist world?', *Comparative Politics*, 48:3, 313–31.
Archer, Neil (2008), 'The road as the (non-)place of masculinity: *L'Emploi du temps*', *Studies in French Cinema* 8:2, 137–48.
Arter, David (1999), *Scandinavian Politics Today*, Manchester: Manchester University Press.
Astruc, Alexandre (1968), 'The birth of a new avant-garde: la caméra-stylo', in Peter Graham (ed.), *The New Wave: Critical Landmarks*, Garden City, NY: Doubleday, 17–23.
Augé, Marc (1992), *Non-Places: An Introduction to Anthropology of Supermodernity*, New York: Verso.
Austin, Thomas (ed.) (2018), *The Films of Aki Kaurismäki: Ludic Engagements*, New York: Bloomsbury.
Austin, Thomas (2019), 'Benefaction, processing, exclusion: documentary representations of refugees and migrants in Fortress Europe', *Studies in European Cinema*, 16:3, 250–65.
Ayers, Alison J., and Alfredo Saad-Filho (2015), 'Democracy against neoliberalism: paradoxes, limitations, transcendence', *Critical Sociology*, 41:4–5, 597–618.

Ba, Diadie (2007), 'Africans still seething over Sarkozy speech', Reuters, 5 September, <http://uk.reuters.com/article/uk-africa-sarkozy-idUKL0513034620070905> (last accessed 6 December 2019).
Bacon, Henry (2015), *The Fascination of Film Violence*, Basingstoke: Palgrave Macmillan.
Badiou, Alain (2003), *L'Ethique: essai sur la conscience du mal*, Caen: Editions Nous.
Badiou, Alain (2006), *Being and Event*, trans. O. Feltham, London: Continuum.
Badiou, Alain (2007), *The Century*, trans. A. Toscano, Cambridge: Polity.
Badiou, Alain (2009a), 'Must the communist hypothesis be abandoned?', *The Yearbook of Comparative Literature*, 55, 79–88.
Badiou, Alain (2009b), *Logics of Worlds*, trans. A. Toscano, London: Continuum.
Badiou, Alain (2012), *The Rebirth of History*, trans. G. Elliott, London: Verso.
Balibar, Étienne (2010). 'At the borders of citizenship: a democracy in translation?', *European Journal of Social Theory*, 13:3, 315–22.
Balibar, Étienne, and Immanuel Wallerstein (2011), *Race, Nation, Class: Ambiguous Identities*, London: Verso.
Balsom, Erika and Hila Peleg (eds) (2016), *Documentary Across Disciplines*, Boston: MIT Press.
Banulescu-Bogdan, Natalia, and Susan Fratzke (2015), 'Europe's migration crisis in context: why now and what next?', Migration Policy Institute, 24 September <http://www.migrationpolicy.org/article/europe-migration-crisis-context-why-now-and-what-next> (last accessed 4 February 2019).
Barlai, Melani, and Endre Sík (2017), 'A Hungarian trademark (a Hungarikum): the moral panic button', in Melani Barlai, Birte Fähnrich, Christina Griessler and Markus Rhomberg (eds), *Migrant Crisis: European Perspectives and National Discourses*, Vienna and Zürich: LIT Verlag, 147–69.
Basu, Laura (2018), *Media Amnesia: Rewriting the Economic Crisis*, London: Pluto Press.
Bataille, Georges (1967 [1949]), *La Part maudite*, Paris: Editions de Minuit.
Bauman, Zygmunt (2000), *Liquid Modernity*, Cambridge: Polity.
Bauman, Zygmunt (2004), *Wasted Lives: Modernity and Its Outcasts*, Chichester: John Wiley.
Bauman, Zygmunt (2007), *Liquid Times: Living in an Age of Uncertainty*, Cambridge: Polity.
Bauman, Zygmunt, and Carlo Bordoni (2014), *State of Crisis*, Cambridge: Polity.
Bauman, Zygmunt, and Leonidas Donskis (2016), *Liquid Evil*, Cambridge: Polity.
Bazin, André (1967), 'The evolution of the language of cinema', in André Bazin, *What Is Cinema?*, vol. 1, ed. and trans. Hugh Gray, Berkeley: University of California Press, 23–40.
Becker, Jens (2010), 'The rise of right-wing populism in Hungary', *SEER: Journal for Labour and Social Affairs in Eastern Europe*, 31:1, 29–40.
Benjamin, Walter (1974), 'Left-wing melancholy (on Erich Kästner's new book of poems)', *Screen*, 15:2, 28–32.
Bennett, Bruce (2018), 'Becoming refugees: *Exodus* and contemporary mediations of the refugee crisis', *Transnational Cinemas*, 9:1, 13–30.

Berend, Ivan T., and Bojan Bugaric (2015), 'Unfinished Europe: transition from communism to democracy in Central and Eastern Europe', *Journal of Contemporary History*, 50:4, 768–85.

Berezin, Mabel (2004), 'Territory, emotion and identity: spatial re-calibrationing a new Europe', in Mabel Berezin and Martin Schain (eds), *Europe Without Borders: Remapping Territory, Citizenship and Identity in a Transnational Age*, Baltimore, MD: Johns Hopkins University Press, 1–30.

Berlant, Lauren (2007), 'Nearly utopian, nearly normal: post-Fordist affect in *La Promesse* and *Rosetta*', *Public Culture*, 19:2, 273–301.

Berlant, Lauren (2011), *Cruel Optimism*, Durham, NC: Duke University Press.

Bernáth, Gábor, and Vera Messing (2015), 'Bedarálva. A menekültekkel kapcsolatos kormányzati kampány és a tőle független megszólalás terepei' [Eliminated. The government campaign about migrants and independent voices], *Médiakutató*, 16:4, 7–17.

Bhabha, Homi K. (1990), 'DissemiNation: time, narrative, and the margins of the modern nation', in Homi K. Bhabha (ed.), *Nation and Narration*, London: Routledge, 291–322.

Biendarra, Anke (2011), 'Ghostly business: place, space, and gender in Christian Petzold's *Yella*', *Seminar* 47:4, 465–78.

Blakely, Grace (2019), 'The next crash: why the world is unprepared for the economic crisis ahead', *New Statesman*, 6 March, <https://www.newstatesman.com/politics/economy/2019/03/next-crash-why-world-unprepared-economic-dangers-ahead> (last accessed 6 December 2019).

Bloch, Ernst (1988), *The Utopian Function of Art and Literature*, trans. J. Zipes and F. Mecklenburg, Cambridge, MA: MIT Press.

Bloodworth, James (2019), *Hired: Six Months Undercover in Low-wage Britain*, London: Atlantic Books.

Blyth, Mark (2013), *Austerity: The History of a Dangerous Idea*, Oxford: Oxford University Press.

Bohle, Dorothee, and Béla Greskovits (2012), *Capitalist Diversity on Europe's Periphery*, Ithaca, NY: Cornell University Press.

Bordwell, David (1985), *Narration in the Fiction Film*, Madison: University of Wisconsin Press.

Bordwell, David (2005), *Figures Traced in Light: On Cinematic Staging*, Berkeley: University of California Press.

Bosteels, Bruno (2011), *Badiou and Politics*, Durham, NC: Duke University Press.

Boughton, John (2018), *Municipal Dreams. The Rise and Fall of Council Housing*, London: Verso, 2018.

Bourdieu, Pierre (1997), 'Marginalia: some additional notes on the gift', in Alan Schrift (ed.), *The Logic of the Gift: Toward an Ethic of Generosity*, London: Routledge, 231–41.

Bourdieu, Pierre (1998), 'The Myth of "globalization" and the European welfare state', in Pierre Bourdieu, *Acts of Resistance: Against the New Myths of Our Time*, trans. Richard Nice, Cambridge: Polity Press.

Bourdieu, Pierre, and Loïc Wacquant (2001), 'New liberal speak: notes on the new planetary vulgate', *Radical Philosophy*, 105 (January/February), 2–5.

Boyer, Dominic (2012), 'From algos to autonomos: nostalgic Eastern Europe as post-imperial mania', in Maria Todovora and Zsuzsa Gille (eds), *Post-Communist Nostalgia*, Oxford: Berghahn, 17–29.

Bradley, Rizvana (2018), 'Kathleen Collins's *Losing Ground*: the lost object of black ecstatic experience', paper presented at Society for Cinema and Media Studies (SCMS) Conference, Montreal.

Brecht, Bertolt (2015), *Brecht on Theatre*, 3rd edn, ed. Marc Silberman, Steve Giles and Tom Kuhn, London: Bloomsbury.

Brennan, Teresa (2000), *Exhausting Modernity: Grounds for a New Economy*. London: Routledge.

Brewer, Kristie (2016), 'Art works: how art in the office boosts staff productivity', *The Guardian*, 21 January, <https://www.theguardian.com/careers/2016/jan/21/art-works-how-art-in-the-office-boosts-staff-productivity> (last accessed 20 December 2018).

Brown, Emma (2015), 'Discovery: Jonas Carpignano', *Interview*, 24 November, <https://www.interviewmagazine.com/film/discovery-jonas-carpignano#_> (last accessed 6 December 2019).

Brown, Wendy (1999), 'Resisting left melancholy', *boundary 2*, 26:3, 19–27.

Brown, Wendy (2006), 'American nightmare: neo-liberalism, neo-conservatism and de-democratisation', *Political Theory* 34:6, 690–714.

Brown, Wendy (2010), *Walled States, Waning Sovereignty*, New York: Zone Books.

Brown, Wendy (2015), *Undoing the Demos: Neoliberalism's Stealth Revolution*, New York: Zone Books.

Bruckner, René Thoreau (2009), 'Lost time: blunt head trauma and accident-driven cinema', *Discourse*, 30:3, 373–400.

Bruckner, René Thoreau, James Leo Cahill and Greg Siegel (2009), 'Introduction: cinema and accident', *Discourse*, 30:3, 279–88.

Buchowski, Michał (2006), 'The specter of orientalism in Europe: from exotic other to stigmatized brother', *Anthropological Quarterly*, 79:3, 463–82.

Burch, Noël (1981), *Theory of Film Practice*, Princeton: Princeton University Press.

Butler, Judith (2006), *Precarious Life: The Powers of Mourning and Violence*, London: Verso.

Çağlayan, Emre (2018), *Poetics of Slow Cinema: Nostalgia, Absurdism, Boredom*, Basingstoke: Palgrave.

Cagle, Chris (2012), 'Postclassical nonfiction: narration in the contemporary documentary', *Cinema Journal*, 52:1, 45–65.

Cahill, James Leo (2009), 'How it feels to be run over: early film accidents', *Discourse*, 30:3, 289–316.

Cairns, Graham (2018), *Reification and Representation Architecture in the Politico-Media-Complex*, London: Routledge.

Cammaerts, Bart (2015), 'Neoliberalism and the post-hegemonic war of position: the dialectic between invisibility and visibilities', *European Journal of Communication*, 30:5, 522–38.

Campkin, Ben (2013), *Remaking London: Decline and Regeneration in Urban Culture*, London: I. B. Tauris.
Candeias, Mario (2011), 'Organic crisis and capitalist transformation', *World Review of Political Economy*, 2:1, 48–65.
Carr, Matthew (2015), *Fortress Europe: Inside the War on Immigration*, updated edn, London: Hurst.
Case, Holly (2015), 'Hope and scandal in Hungary', *Dissent* 63:3, 118–25.
Caughie, John (2000), *Television Drama: Realism, Modernism, and British Culture*, Oxford: Oxford University Press.
Chakrabortty, Aditya (2018), 'Immigration has been good for Britain. It's time to bust the myths', *The Guardian*, 17 May, <https://www.theguardian.com/commentisfree/2018/may/17/immigration-good-for-britain-bust-myths-austerity> (last accessed 6 December 2019).
Chouliaraki, Lilie (2012), 'Between pity and irony – paradigms of refugee representation in humanitarian discourse', in Kerry Moore, Bernhard Gross and Terry Threadgold (eds), *Migrations and the Media*, New York: Peter Lang, 13–31.
Ciment, Michel (2006), 'The state of cinema', *Unspoken Cinema: Contemporary Contemplative Cinema*, 30 October, <http://unspokencinema.blogspot.com/2006/10/state-of-cinema-m-ciment.html> (last accessed 4 February 2019).
Ciobanu, Claudia (2018), 'That 400,000 Romanians live in the UK is a tragedy for their homeland', *The Guardian*, 30 May, <https://www.theguardian.com/commentisfree/2018/may/30/romanians-uk-tragedy-homeland-corruption-poverty> (last accessed 6 December 2019).
Clark, Timothy J. (1999), *Farewell to an Idea: Episodes from a History of Modernism*, New Haven: Yale University Press.
Colvin, J. Brandon (2017), 'The other side of frontality: dorsality in European art cinema', *New Review of Film and Television Studies*, 15:2, 191–210.
Connell, Claudia (2015), 'If you end up with this lot as neighbours, heaven help you', *Daily Mail*, 7 July, <https://www.dailymail.co.uk/tvshowbiz/article-3151627/If-end-lot-neighbours-heaven-help-CLAUDIA-CONNELL-reviews-night-s-TV.html> (last accessed 14 June 2019).
Connolly, William E. (1994), 'Tocqueville, territory and violence', *Theory, Culture, Society*, 11:19, 19–41.
Cooper, Sarah (2007), 'Mortal ethics: reading Levinas with the Dardenne brothers', *Film-Philosophy*, 11:2, 66–87, <http://www.film-philosophy.com/2007v11n2/cooper.pdf> (last accessed 9 April 2019).
Coville, Peter (2018), '"A Minister for Loneliness" is a sticking plaster for the ills of neoliberalism', *Open Democracy*, 22 January, <https://www.opendemocracy.net/uk/peter-coville/minister-for-loneliness-is-sticking-plaster-for-ills-of-neoliberalism> (last accessed 6 December 2019).
Crouch, Colin (2004), *Post-Democracy*, Cambridge: Polity.
Crouch, Colin (2011), *The Strange Non-Death of Neoliberalism*, Cambridge: Polity.
Csoma, Emőke (2012), 'Frozen Land', in Pietari Kääpä (eds), *Directory of World Cinema: Finland*, Bristol: Intellect, 160–62.
ČTK (2017), 'YouTube wants to combat disinformation and hatred, hiring thousands to remove harmful content', *Romea.cz*, 12 July, <http://www.romea.cz/en/news/

world/youtube-wants-to-combat-disinformation-and-hatred-hiring-thousands-to-remove-harmful-content> (last accessed 30 December 2018).

Curcio, Anna, and Gigi Roggero (2018), 'Logistics is the logic of capital', *Viewpoint Magazine*, 25 October 2018, <https://www.viewpointmag.com/2018/10/25/logistics-is-the-logic-of-capital/> (last accessed 6 December 2019).

Czaika, Mathias, and Hein de Haas (2014), 'The globalization of migration: has the world become more migratory?', *International Migration Review*, 48:23, 283–323.

Dale, Gareth, and Adam Fabry (2018), 'Neoliberalism in Eastern Europe and the former Soviet Union', in D. Cahill, M. Cooper, M. Konings and D. Primrose (eds), *The SAGE Handbook of Neoliberalism*, London: Sage, 234–48.

Dale, Gareth, and Jane Hardy (2011), 'Conclusion: the "crash" in Central and Eastern Europe', in G. Dale (ed.), *First the Transition, then the Crash: Eastern Europe in the 2000s*, London: Pluto Press, 251–64.

Dalton, Stephen (2015), '"Roukli": Film review', *Hollywood Reporter*, 3 December, <https://www.hollywoodreporter.com/review/roukli-film-review-845702> (last accessed 4 February 2019).

Dardenne, Luc (2005), *Au Dos de nos images, 1991–2005*, Paris: Seuil.

Dauphinée, Elizabeth (2003), 'Faith, hope, neoliberalism: mapping economies of violence on the margins of Europe', *Dialectical Anthropology*, 27:3–4, 189–203.

Davies, William (2016), *The Limits of Neoliberalism: Authority, Sovereignty and the Logic of Competition*, London: Sage.

Davis, Glyn (2016), 'Stills and stillness in Apichatpong Weerasethakul's cinema', in Tiago de Luca and Nuno Barradas Jorge (eds), *Slow Cinema*, Edinburgh: Edinburgh University Press, 99–111.

De Benedictis, Sara, Kim Allen and Tracey Jensen (2017), 'Portraying poverty: the economics and ethics of factual welfare television', *Cultural Sociology*, 11:3, 337–58.

De Genova, Nicholas (2002), 'Migrant illegality and deportability in everyday life', *Annual Review of Anthropology*, 31, 419–47.

De Genova, Nicholas (2017), 'Introduction: the borders of "Europe" and the European question', in Nicholas De Genova (ed.), *The Borders of 'Europe': Autonomy of Migration, Tactics of Bordering*, Durham, NC: Duke University Press, 1–35.

De la Cámara, Carmen (1997), 'The labor market in Central and Eastern Europe: transformations and perspectives', *Eastern European Economics*, 35:1, 76–93.

De Luca, Tiago, and Nuno Barradas Jorge (2016), 'Introduction: from slow cinema to slow cinemas', in Tiago de Luca and Nuno Barradas Jorge (eds), *Slow Cinema*, Edinburgh: Edinburgh University Press, 1–22.

de Marco, Camillo (2011), '*Terraferma* is a film about the freedom to go elsewhere', *Cineuropa*, 6 September, <http://cineuropa.org/ff.aspx?t=ffocusinterview&l=en&tid=2351&did=209120> (last accessed 6 December 2019).

Dean, Jodi (2016), *Crowds and Party*, London: Verso.

Deleuze, Gilles (1989), *Cinema 2: The Time-Image*, trans. Hugh Tomlinson and Robert Galeta, Minneapolis: University of Minnesota Press.

Delfi (2014), 'Veiko Õunpuu alustab uue mängufilmi võtetega', *Delfi. Publik*, 9 June, <http://publik.delfi.ee/news/kino/veiko-ounpuu-alustab-uue-mangufilmi-votetega?id=68843429> (last accessed 4 February 2019).

della Porta, Donatella (2017), 'Progressive and regressive politics in late neoliberalism', in Heinrich Geiselberger (ed.), *The Great Regression*, Malden, MA: Blackwell, 26–39.
Della Sala, Vincent (2012), 'Europe's autumn? Popular sovereignty and economic crisis in the European Union', *The Whitehead Journal of Diplomacy and International Relations*, 13:1, 35–44.
Derrida, Jacques (1992a [1991]), *Given Time: 1. Counterfeit Money*, trans. Peggy Kamuf, Chicago: University of Chicago Press.
Derrida, Jacques (1992b), *The Other Heading: Reflections on Today's Europe*, Bloomington: Indiana University Press.
Dixon, Wheeler Winston, and Gwendolyn Audrey Foster (2002), 'Introduction: toward a new history of the experimental cinema', in Wheeler Winston Dixon and Gwendolyn Audrey Foster (eds), *Experimental Cinema: The Film Reader*, London: Routledge, 1–16.
Doane, Mary Ann (2006), 'Information, crisis, catastrophe', in W. H. K. Chun and A. W. Fisher (eds), *New Media, Old Media: A History and Theory Reader*, New York: Routledge, 251–64.
Dodman, Benjamin (2015), '*Mediterranea* explores the perilous journey to Europe', *The Atlantic*, 21 May, <https://www.theatlantic.com/entertainment/archive/2015/05/cannes-review-mediterranea/393776/> (last accessed 20 December 2018).
Dort, Bernard (1960), *Lecture de Brecht*, Paris: Seuil.
Douzinas, Costas, and Slavoj Žižek (2010), 'Introduction: the idea of communism', in Costas Douzinas and Slavoj Žižek (eds), *The Idea of Communism*, London: Verso, vii–x.
Drakulić, Slavenka (1996), *Cafe Europa: Life After Communism*, London: Penguin.
Duménil, Gérard, and Dominique Lévy (2002), 'The nature and contradictions of neoliberalism', *Socialist Register*, 38, 43–71.
Eatwell, John, and Murray Milgate (2011), *The Fall and Rise of Keynesian Economics*, Oxford: Oxford University Press.
Edensor, Tim (2005), *Industrial Ruins Space, Aesthetics and Materiality*, Oxford: Berghahn.
Eelmaa, Taavi, and Veiko Õunpuu (2011), *60 Seconds of Solitude in Year Zero*, Tallinn.
Eisner, Lotte (1969), *The Haunted Screen: Expressionism in the German Cinema and the Influence of Max Reinhardt*, trans. Roger Greaves, Berkeley: University of California Press.
El-Enany, Nadine (2017), 'The colonial logic of Grenfell', *Verso Blog*, 3 July, <https://www.versobooks.com/blogs/3306-the-colonial-logic-of-grenfell> (last accessed 28 September 2019).
El-Enany, Nadine (2019), 'Before Grenfell: British immigration law and the production of colonial spaces', in Daniel Bulley, Jenny Edkins and Nadine El-Enany (eds), *After Grenfell: Violence, Resistance and Response*, London: Pluto Press, 50–61.
Elsaesser, Thomas (2005), *European Cinema: Face to Face with Hollywood*, Amsterdam: Amsterdam University Press.
Erős, Ferenc (2001), *Az identitás labirintusai. Narratív konstrukciók és identitásstratégiák* [Labyrinths of identity. Narrative constructions and identity strategies], Budapest: Janus-Osiris.

Erőss, Gábor (2019), *A történelmi film szociológiája* [Sociology of the historical film], Budapest: L'Harmattan.
Esposito, Roberto (2015), *Persons and Things: From the Body's Point of View*, Chichester: John Wiley.
European Union (2000), *Charter of Fundamental Rights of the European Union*, <https://www.europarl.europa.eu/charter/pdf/text_en.pdf> (last accessed 28 September 2019).
Farocki, Harun (2002), 'Workers leaving the factory', trans. Laurent Faasch-Ibrahim, *Senses of Cinema*, 21, <http://sensesofcinema.com/2002/harun-farocki/farocki_workers/> (last accessed 28 September 2019).
Federici, Silvia (2013), 'Permanent reproductive crisis: an interview with Silvia Federici', ed. Marina Vishmidt, *Mute*, 7 March, <http://www.metamute.org/editorial/articles/permanent-reproductive-crisis-interview-silvia-federici> (last accessed 30 January 2019).
Fekete, Liz (2018), *Europe's Fault Lines*, London: Verso.
Feldner, Heiko, Fabio Vighi and Slavoj Žižek (2014), 'Introduction', in Heiko Feldner, Fabio Vighi and Slavoj Žižek (eds), *States of Crisis and Post-Capitalist Scenarios*, Farnham: Ashgate, 1–7.
Figlio, Karl (2011), 'The financial crisis: a psychoanalytic view of illusion, greed and reparation in masculine phantasy', *New Formations*, 72, 33–46.
Finn, Daniel (2017), 'Luso-Anomalies', *New Left Review* 106, 5–32.
Fisher, Jaimey (2011), 'Globalization as uneven geographical development: the "creative" destruction of place and fantasy in Christian Petzold's ghost trilogy', *Seminar* 47:4, 447–64.
Fisher, Mark (2009), *Capitalist Realism: Is There No Alternative?*, Winchester: O Books.
Fisher, Mark (2014), *Ghosts of My Life*, Alresford: zero books.
Fiske, John (1987), *Television Culture*, London: Routledge.
Flanagan, Matthew (2008), 'Towards an aesthetic of slow in contemporary cinema', *16:9*, 6:29, <http://www.16-9.dk/2008-11/side11_inenglish.htm> (last accessed 4 February 2019).
Foktői, János (2016), 'Az állam szerepe a magyar filmművészet és filmipar 2004 és 2014 közötti alakulásában, különös tekintettel a mozgóképörökség megőrzésére és hasznosítására' [The state's role in the trends of the Hungarian film art and industry between 2004 and 2014, especially in safeguarding and exploiting the motion picture heritage], PhD dissertation, University of Theatre and Film Arts, Budapest, <http://szfe.hu/wp-content/uploads/2017/02/Fokt%C5%91i-J%C3%A1nos-DLA-dolgozat.pdf> (last accessed 4 February 2019).
Forrest, Tara (2015), *Realism as Protest Kluge, Schlingensief, Haneke*, Vienna: Transcript-Verlag.
Forster, Siegfried (2013), 'Moussa Touré: "*La Pirogue* est une claque à ceux qui nous gouvernent"', RFI, 25 February, <http://www.rfi.fr/afrique/20130225-moussa-toure-fespaco-la-pirogue-une-claque-ceux-nous-gouvernent> (last accessed 6 December 2019).
Foucault, Michel (1977), *Discipline and Punish: The Birth of the Prison*, New York: Vintage.

Frey, Mattias (2016), *The Transgressive Rhetoric of Today's Art Film Culture*, New Brunswick, NJ: Rutgers University Press.
Fukuyama, Francis (1992), *The End of History and the Last Man*, New York: Free Press.
Gagyi, Ágnes (2016), '"Coloniality of power" in East Central Europe: external penetration as internal force in post-socialist Hungarian politics', *Journal of World-Systems Research* 22:2, 349–72.
Gambino, Evelina (2017), 'The "Gran Ghetto", migrant labor and militant research in southern Italy', in Nicholas De Genova (ed.), *The Borders of 'Europe': Autonomy of Migration, Tactics of Bordering*, Durham, NC: Duke University Press, 255–82.
Gamlen, Alan (2015), '"An inborn restlessness": migration and exile in a turbulent world', *Oxford Migration Studies*, 3:3, 307–14.
Gaudreault, André, and Philippe Marion (2015), *The End of Cinema? A Medium in Crisis in the Digital Age*, trans. Timothy Barnard, New York: Columbia University Press.
Ghodsee, Kristen (2017), *Red Hangover: Legacies of Twentieth-Century Communism*, Durham, NC: Duke University Press.
Ginsborg, Paul (2003), *Italy and Its Discontents: Family, Civil Society, State: 1980–2001*, New York: Palgrave.
Glied, Viktor, and Norbert Pap (2016), 'The "Christian fortress of Hungary" – the anatomy of the migration crisis in Hungary', *Yearbook of Polish European Studies*, 19, Warsaw: Centre for Europe, University of Warsaw, 133–50.
Goffman, Erving (1963), *Stigma*, London: Penguin.
Götz, Norbert, and Carl Marklund (2014), *The Paradox of Openness: Transparency and Participation in Nordic Cultures of Consensus*, Leiden: Brill.
Graeber, David (2001), *Towards an Anthropological Theory of Value: The False Coin of Our Own Dreams*, Basingstoke: Palgrave.
Graeber, David (2018), 'The revolt of the caring classes', 9 April, <https://www.youtube.com/watch?v=o-WWw1wydwI> (last accessed 30 January 2019).
Gramsci, Antonio (1999), *Selections from the Prison Notebooks*, trans. Q. Hoare & G. Nowell-Smith, London: Electric Book Company.
Gray, Carmen (2012), '60 Seconds of Solitude in Year Zero', *AnOther*, 3 January, <http://www.anothermag.com/current/view/1661/60_Seconds_of_Solitude_in_Year_Zero> (last accessed 4 February 2019).
Gray, Richard (1987), *Constructive Destruction: Kafka's Aphorisms*, Tübingen: Max Niemeyer Verlag.
Green, Sarah (2012), 'A sense of border', in Thomas M. Wilson and Hastings Donnan (eds), *A Companion to Border Studies*, Chichester: Wiley-Blackwell, 573–92.
Grisebach, Valeska (2006), 'Sehnsucht: Helden des eigenen Lebens – Interview', *Piffl Medien*, <http://www.piffl-medien.de/sehnsucht/html/interview.html> (last accessed 3 June 2019).
Grundmann, Roy (2010), 'Between Adorno and Lyotard: Michael Haneke's aesthetic of fragmentation', in Ray Grundmann (ed.), *A Companion to Michael Haneke*, London: Blackwell, 371–19.
Grzechnik, Marta (2019), 'The missing second world: on Poland and postcolonial studies', *Interventions*, 21:7, 1–17.

Hadzidavic, Habiba, and Hilde Hoffmann (2017), 'Moving images of exclusion: persisting tropes in the filmic representation of European Roma', *Identities*, 24:6, 701–19.
Hall, Stuart (2011), 'The neo-liberal revolution', *Cultural Studies*, 25:6, 705–28.
Halpern, Manuel (2017), 'Pedro Pinho. O Operário em Construção', *Jornal das Letras, Artes e Ideias*, 1225, 16–17.
Hammer, Ferenc (2009), 'A megismerés szerkezetei, stratégiái és poétikái. Szocio-doku a BBS-ben' [Structures, strategies and poetics of cognition. Socio-docu in Béla Balázs Studio], in Gábor Gelencsér (ed), *BBS 50. A Balázs Béla Stúdió 50 éve*, Budapest: Műcsarnok-BBS.
Hanman, Natalie (2019), 'Naomi Klein: "We are seeing the beginnings of the era of climate barbarism"', *The Guardian*, 14 September, <https://www.theguardian.com/books/2019/sep/14/naomi-klein-we-are-seeing-the-beginnings-of-the-era-of-climate-barbarism?CMP=Share_iOSApp_Other> (last accessed 5 October 2019).
Hardt, Michael, and Antonio Negri (2000), *Empire*, Cambridge, MA: Harvard University Press.
Harvey, David (2001), 'Globalization and the "spatial fix"', *geographische revue*, 2, 23–30.
Harvey, David (2005), *The New Imperialism*, Oxford: Oxford University Press.
Harvey, David (2007a), 'Neoliberalism as creative destruction', *The Annals of the American Academy of Political and Social Science*, 610, 21–44.
Harvey, David (2007b), *A Brief History of Neoliberalism*, Oxford: Oxford University Press.
Harvey, David (2010), *The Enigma of Capital and the Crises of Capitalism*, Oxford: Oxford University Press.
Harvey, David (2012), *Rebel Cities*, London: Verso.
Hatherley, Owen (2015), *The Ministry of Nostalgia*, London: Verso.
Heartfield, James (2009), 'Demobilising the nation: the decline of sovereignty in Western Europe', *International Politics*, 46:6, 712–31.
Henley, Jon (2018), 'Poland provokes Israeli anger with Holocaust speech law', *The Guardian*, 1 February, <https://www.theguardian.com/world/2018/feb/01/poland-holocaust-speech-law-senate-israel-us> (last accessed 6 December 2019).
Hewitt, Gavin (2011), 'Portugal reaches deal on EU and IMF bail-out', BBC, 4 May, <http://www.bbc.co.uk/news/business-13275470> (last accessed 30 January 2019).
Heyns, Barbara (2005), 'Emerging inequalities in Central and Eastern Europe', *Annual Review of Sociology*, 31, 163–97.
Higbee, Will (2014), 'Hope and indignation in Fortress Europe: immigration and neoliberal globalization in contemporary French Cinema', *SubStance*, 43:1, 26–43.
Highmore, Ben (2013), 'Feeling our way: mood and cultural studies', *Communication and Critical/Cultural Studies*, 10:4, 427–38.
Hiltunen, Kaisa (2017), 'The aesthetics and politics of melancholy in the films of Aku Louhimies', in Maja Mikula (ed.), *Remembering Home in a Time of Mobility: Memory, Nostalgia and Melancholy*, Newcastle upon Tyne: Cambridge Scholars Publishing, 111–32.
Hjort, Mette (2005), *Small Nation, Global Cinema: The New Danish Cinema*, Minneapolis: University of Minnesota Press.

Hodkinson, Stuart, Paul Watt and Gerry Mooney (eds) (2013), 'Social housing, privatisation and neoliberalism', *Critical Social Policy* 33:1, special issue.
Hoffman, Jordan (2015), '*Mediterranea* review – horribly topical drama about African migrants in Italy', *The Guardian*, 21 May, <https://www.theguardian.com/film/2015/may/21/mediterranea-review-jonas-carpignano-cannes-critics-week-sidebar> (last accessed 20 December 2018).
Hollahan, Eugene (1992), *Crisis-Consciousness and the Novel*, Newark: University of Delaware Press.
Horeck, Tanya, and Tina Kendall (2011), 'Introduction', in Tanya Horeck and Tina Kendall (eds), *The New Extremism in Cinema. From France to Europe*, Edinburgh: Edinburgh University Press, 1–27.
Horkheimer, Max, and Theodor W. Adorno (2002 [1944]), *Dialectic of Enlightenment: Philosophical Fragments*, ed. Gunzelin Schmid Noerr, trans. Edmund Jephcott, Stanford, CA: Stanford University Press.
Howden, Daniel, and Eva Kuehnen (2005), 'Germany is accused of racism as 50,000 Roma are deported', *The Independent*, 19 May, <https://www.independent.co.uk/news/world/europe/germany-is-accused-of-racism-as-50000-roma-are-deported-5345369.html> (last accessed 18 December 2018).
Hunyadi, Bulcsú and Csaba Molnár (2016), 'Central Europe's faceless strangers: the rise of xenophobia', *Nation in Transit Brief*, Freedom House, <https://freedomhouse.org/report/special-reports/central-europe-s-faceless-strangers-rise-xenophobia-region> (last accessed 4 February 2019).
Hyde, Lewis (2012), *The Gift: How the Creative Spirit Transforms the World*, Edinburgh: Canongate.
Imre, Anikó (1999), 'White man, white mask: Mephisto meets Venus', *Screen*, 40:4, 405–22.
Imre, Anikó (2009), *Identity Games: Globalization and the Transformation of Media Cultures in the New Europe*, Cambridge, MA: MIT Press.
Imre, Anikó (2012), 'Introduction. Eastern European cinema from *No End* to the end (as we know it)', in Anikó Imre (ed.), *A Companion to Eastern European Cinemas*, Chichester: Wiley-Blackwell, 1–21.
Imre, Anikó (2016), 'The case for postcolonial postsocialist media studies', in Andrea Virginás (ed.), *Cultural Studies Approaches in the Study of Eastern European Cinema: Spaces, Bodies, Memories*, Newcastle upon Tyne: Cambridge Scholars Publishing, 2–25.
Imrie, Rob, Loretta Lees and Mike Raco (eds) (2009), *Regenerating London. Governance, Sustainability and Community in a Global City*, London: Routledge.
Inman, Philip (2018), 'UK manufacturing has lost 600,000 jobs in a decade, says union', *The Guardian*, 4 June, <https://www.theguardian.com/business/2018/jun/04/uk-manufacturing-has-lost-600000-jobs-in-a-decade-says-union> (last accessed 6 December 2019).
Innes, Abby (2015), 'Hungary's illiberal democracy', *Current History*, 114, 95–100.
Iordanova, Dina (2010), 'Migration and cinematic process in post-Cold War Europe', in Daniela Berghahn and Claudia Sternberg (eds), *European Cinema in Motion. Migrant and Diasporic Film in Contemporary Europe*, Basngstoke: Palgrave Macmillan, 50–75.

Irigaray, Luce (1997), 'Women on the market', in Alan Schrift (ed.), *The Logic of the Gift: Toward an Ethic of Generosity*, London: Routledge, 174–89.
Iversen, Martin, and Lars Thue (2008), 'Introduction: creating Nordic capitalism: the business history of a competitive periphery', in Susanna Fellman, Martin Iversen, Hans Sjögren and Lars Thue (eds), *Creating Nordic Capitalism: The Development of a Competitive Periphery*, Basingstoke: Palgrave Macmillan, 1–20.
Jameson, Fredric (1971), *Marxism and Form: Twentieth-Century Dialectical Theories of Literature*, Princeton: Princeton University Press.
Jameson, Fredric (1972), *The Prison House of Language: A Critical Account of Structuralism and Russian Formalism*, Princeton: Princeton University Press.
Jameson, Fredric (1998), *Brecht and Method*, London: Verso.
Jappe, Anselm (2006), *As Aventuras da Mercadoria para Uma Nova Crítica do Valor*, trans. J. M. Justo, Lisboa: Antígona.
Jonung, Lars, Jaakko Kiander and Pentti Vartia (2009), *The Great Financial Crisis in Finland and Sweden: The Nordic Experience of Financial Liberalization*, Cheltenham: Edward Elgar.
Jørholt, Eva (2019), 'Refugee from globalization. "Clandestine" African migration to Europe in a human (rights) perspective', in Mette Hjort and Eva Jørholt (eds), *African Cinema and Human Rights*, Bloomington: Indiana University Press, 280–302.
Judis, John B. (2016), 'Us v them: the birth of populism', *The Guardian*, 13 October, <https://www.theguardian.com/politics/2016/oct/13/birth-of-populism-donald-trump> (last accessed 6 December 2019).
Kääpä, Pietari (2010), 'Imaginaries of a global Finland: patterns of globalisation in Finnish cinema of the 21st century', *Scandinavian-Canadian Studies*, 19:2, 262–83
Kääpä, Pietari (2012), *Directory of World Cinema: Finland*, Bristol: Intellect.
Kääpä, Pietari and Gustafsson, Tommy (2015), *Nordic Genre Film*, Edinburgh: Edinburgh University Press.
Kallius, Annastiina, Daniel Monterescu and Prem Kumar Rajaram (2016), 'Immobilizing mobility: border ethnography, illiberal democracy, and the politics of the "refugee crisis" in Hungary', *American Ethnologist*, 43:1, 25–37.
Kananen, Johannes (2014), *The Nordic Welfare State in Three Eras: From Emancipation to Discipline*, Farnham: Ashgate.
Kapur, Jyostna, and Keith B. Wagner (2011), 'Introduction. Neoliberalism and global cinema: subjectivities, publics, and new forms of resistance', in Jyostna Kapur and Keith B. Wagner (eds), *Neoliberalism and Global Cinema: Capital, Culture, and Marxist Critique*, New York: Routledge, 1–16.
Karjatse, Tõnu (2017), 'Isikliku apokalüpsise võimatusest maailmakinos', *Vikerkaar*, 7/8, 144–56.
Kattel, R. (2010), 'Financial and economic crisis in Eastern Europe', *Journal of Post Keynesian Economics*, 33:1, 41–59.
Kearney, Richard (1999), 'On the gift: a discussion between Jacques Derrida and Jean-Luc Marion', in John Caputo and Michael Scanlon (eds), *God, the Gift and Postmodernism*, Bloomington, IN: Indiana University Press, 54–78.
Kermode, Mark (2017), '*Toni Erdmann* review', *The Guardian*, 5 February, <https://www.theguardian.com/film/2017/feb/05/toni-erdmann-observer-film-review> (last accessed 20 December 2018).

Kershaw, Ian (2018), *Roller-Coaster: Europe 1950–2017*, London: Allen Lane.
Kettunen, Pauli (2001), 'The Nordic welfare state in Finland', *Scandinavian Journal of History* 26:3, 225–47.
Kideckel, David A. (2002), 'The unmaking of an East Central European working class', in C. M. Hann (ed.), *Postsocialism: Ideals, Ideologies and Practices in Eurasia*, London: Routledge, 114–32.
Kideckel, David A. (2009), 'Citizenship discourse, globalization and protest: a post-socialist-postcolonial comparison', *Anthropology of East Europe Review* 27:2, 117–33.
Kildal, Nanna, and Stein Kuhnle (2005), *Normative Foundations of the Welfare State: The Nordic Experience*, London: Routledge.
Kilumets, Margit, and Valner Valme (2015), 'Veiko Õunpuu: me peaksime kadaka-sakslusest üle saama', *Kultuur.err.ee*, 16 September, <https://kultuur.err.ee/308036/veiko-ounpuu-me-peaksime-kadakasakslusest-ule-saama> (last accessed 4 February 2019).
King, Alasdair (2017), 'Film and the financial city', *Studies in European Cinema*, 14, 7–21.
Kingsley, Patrick (2016), *The New Odyssey: The Story of Europe's Refugee Crisis*, London: Guardian Books and Faber and Faber.
Kiossev, Alexander (2011), 'The self-colonizing metaphor', *Atlas of Transformation*, <http://monumenttotransformation.org/atlas-of-transformation/html/s/self-colonization/the-self-colonizing-metaphor-alexander-kiossev.html> (last accessed 21 January 2019).
Király, Hajnal (2016), 'Playing dead: pictorial figurations of melancholia in contemporary Hungarian cinema', in Ewa Mazierska, Matilda Mroz and Elżbieta Ostrowska (eds), *The Cinematic Bodies of Eastern Europe and Russia Between Pain and Pleasure*, Edinburgh: Edinburgh University Press, 67–88.
Kiwa (2016), 'Autor', *Sirp*, 9 December.
Klein, Naomi (2008), *The Shock Doctrine: The Rise of Disaster Capitalism*, London: Penguin.
Klinger, Barbara (1994), *Melodrama and Meaning: History, Culture, and the Films of Douglas Sirk*, Bloomington: Indiana University Press.
Koepnick, Lutz (2013), 'Cars', in Roger F. Cook, Lutz Koepnick, Kristin Kopp and Brad Prager (eds), *Berlin School Glossary: An ABC of the New Wave in German Cinema*, Bristol: Intellect, 75–82.
Kolker, Robert Phillip (1983), *The Altering Eye: Contemporary International Cinema*, Oxford: Oxford University Press.
Kornai, János (2006), 'The great transformation of Central Eastern Europe', *Economics of Transition*, 14:2, 207–44.
Koser, Khalid (2007), 'Refugees, transnationalism and the state', *Journal of Ethnic and Migration Studies*, 33:2, 233–54.
Kosmidou, Eleftheria Rania (2012), *European Civil War Films: Memory, Conflict and Nostalgia*, New York: Routledge.
Kosuth, Joseph (2002 [1969]), 'Art after philosophy', in Peter Osborne (ed.), *Conceptual Art*, London: Phaidon, 232–4.

Koutsourakis, Angelos (2019), 'Modernist belatedness in contemporary slow cinema', *Screen*, 60:3, 388–409.
Kouvelakis, Stathis (2011), 'The Greek cauldron', *New Left Review*, 72 (November/December), 17–32.
Kovačević, Nataša (2018), *Uncommon Alliances: Cultural Narratives of Migration in the New Europe*, Edinburgh: Edinburgh University Press.
Kovács, András Bálint (2007), *Screening Modernism: European Art Cinema, 1950–1980*, Chicago: University of Chicago Press.
Kovács, Zoltán (2018), 'Sudden cataclysm in Hungarian media: almost all pro-government outlets in one hand', *Index*, 28 November, <https://index.hu/english/2018/11/28/fidesz_media_unification_meszaros_habony_vajna_liszkay/> (last accessed 4 February 2019).
Kracauer, Siegfried (1997), *Theory of Film: The Redemption of Physical Reality*, Princeton: Princeton University Press.
Krastev, Ivan, and Stephen Holmes (2019), *The Light That Failed: A Reckoning*, London: Allen Lane.
Kuzio, Taras (2000), 'The non-military security forces of Ukraine', *Journal of Slavic Military Studies*, 13:4, 29–56.
Kynge, James (2009), *China Shakes the World: The Rise of a Hungry Nation*, London: Phoenix.
Labrador Méndez, Germán (2012), 'Las vidas subprime: la circulación de historias de vida como tecnología de imaginación política en la crisis española (2007–2012)', *Hispanic Review*, 80:4, 557–8.
Labrador Méndez, Germán (2018), 'Mundos de crisis: narrativas disciplinarias e imaginación colectiva en el contexto peninsular después de 2008', *Simposio Internacional La crisis en España, diez años después*, Universität Regensburg, 13 October 2018.
Lambert, Stephen (1982), *Channel 4: Television With a Difference?*, London: BFI.
Land, Nick (2017), 'A quick and dirty introduction to accelerationism', *Jacobin Magazine*, 25 May, <https://jacobitemag.com/2017/05/25/a-quick-and-dirty-introduction-to-accelerationism/> (last accessed 20 December 2018).
Landry, Olivia (2019), *Movement and Performance in Berlin School Cinema*, Bloomington: Indiana University Press.
Lane, David (2010), 'Post-socialist states and the world economy: the impact of global economic crisis', *Historical Social Research/Historische Sozialforschung*, 35:2, 218–41.
Lapavitsas, Costas (2010), 'Germany: A euro laggard', *Guardian*, 22 March, <https://www.theguardian.com/commentisfree/2010/mar/21/germany-a-euro-laggard> (last accessed 5 October 2019>.
Lapowski, Issie (2017), 'Tech companies have the tools to confront white supremacy', *Wired*, 14 August, <https://www.wired.com/story/charlottesville-social-media-hate-speech-online/> (last accessed 5 October 2019).
Lawrence, Michael, and Laura McMahon (2015), 'Introduction', in Michael Lawrence and Laura McMahon (eds), *Animal Life and the Moving Image*, London: BFI/Palgrave, 1–19.

Lees, Loretta, Hyun Bang Shin and Ernesto López-Morales (eds) (2016), *Planetary Gentrification*, Bristol: Polity.
Lefebvre, Henri (1995), *Introduction to Modernity*, trans. John Moore, London: Verso.
Leigh, Jacob (2002), *The Cinema of Ken Loach: Art in the Service of the People*, London: Wallflower.
Lemire, Christy (2013), 'Capital', *RogertEbert.com*, 1 November, <https://www.rogerebert.com/reviews/capital-2013> (last accessed 20 December 2018).
Lévi-Strauss, Claude (1977 [1949]), *The Elementary Structures of Kinship*, trans. James Bell and John von Sturmer, Boston: Beacon Press.
Levinas, Emmanuel (1969), *Totality and Infinity, an Essay on Exteriority*, trans. Alphonso Lingis, Pittsburgh, PA: Duquesne University Press.
Levinas, Emmanuel (1978), *Autrement qu'être ou au-delà de l'essence*, Paris: Livre de Poche.
Lewis, Simon L., and Mark A. Maslin (2015), 'Defining the anthropocene', *Nature* 519, 171–80
Lieven, Anatol (2019), 'Get real', *Prospect*, midwinter, 40–4.
Liz, Mariana (2018), 'After the crisis: Europe and nationhood in 21st century Portuguese cinema', in James Harvey (ed.), *Nationalism in Contemporary Western European Cinema*, Basingstoke: Palgrave Macmillan, 235–56.
Loftsdóttir, Kristín, and Lars Jensen (eds) (2016 [2014]), *Crisis in the Nordic Nations and Beyond: At the Intersection of Environment, Finance and Multiculturalism*, London: Routledge.
Longhi, Vittorio (2014), *The Immigrant War: A Global Movement Against Discrimination and Exploitation*, trans. Janet Eastwood, Bristol: Policy Press.
Lordon, Frédéric (2018), 'End of the world?', Verso blog, 7 December, <https://www.versobooks.com/blogs/4153-end-of-the-world> (last accessed 6 December 2019).
Lorey, Isabel (2015), *State of Insecurity*, London: Verso.
Loshitzky, Yosefa (2010), *Screening Strangers: Migration and Diaspora in Contemporary European Cinema*, Bloomington: Indiana University Press.
Lübecker, Nikolaj (2015), *The Feel-Bad Film*, Edinburgh: Edinburgh University Press.
Lykidis, Alex (2015), 'Crisis of sovereignty in recent Greek cinema', *Journal of Greek Media and Culture* 1:1, 9–27.
Madden, David, and Peter Marcuse (2016), *In Defense of Housing: The Politics of Crisis*, London: Verso.
Mademli, Geli (2019), 'From the crisis of cinema to the cinema of crisis: a "weird" label for contemporary Greek cinema', *Frames Cinema Journal*, <https://framescinemajournal.com/article/from-the-crisis-of-cinema-to-the-cinema-of-crisis-a-weird-label-for-contemporary-greek-cinema/> (last accessed 3 June 2019).
Magagnoli, Paolo (2013), 'Capitalism and creative destruction', *Third Text*, 27:6, 723–34.
Magnus, Riin (2014), 'Eesti 1920.–1930. aastate vaatefilmid kohateadvuse muutuste tähistena', in Linda Kaljundi and Helen Sooväli-Sepping (eds), *Maastik ja mälu. Pärandiloome arengujooni Eestis*, Tallinn: TLÜ Kirjastus, 246–68.
Magyar, Bálint (2016), *Post-communist Mafia State: The Case of Hungary*, trans. Bálint Bethlenfalvy, Ágnes Simon, Steven Nelson and Kata Paulin, Budapest: Central European University Press.

Mai, Joseph (2010), *Jean-Pierre and Luc Dardenne*, Urbana: University of Illinois Press.
Mair, Peter (2014), *Ruling the Void: The Hollowing of Western Democracy*, London: Verso.
Malik, Kenan (2018), 'A fear of cultural loss is fuelling anger with elites across Europe', *The Observer*, 9 December, <https://www.theguardian.com/commentisfree/2018/dec/09/fear-cultural-loss-fuelling-anger-with-elites-across-europe> (last accessed 6 December 2019).
Mallard, Grégoire (2011), 'The gift revisited: Marcel Mauss on war, debt, and the politics of reparations', *Sociological Theory*, 29:4, 225–47.
Marcus, Laura (2014), *Dreams of Modernity: Psychoanalysis, Literature, Cinema*, Oxford: Oxford University Press.
Marghitu, Stefania (2018), '"It's just art": auteur apologism in the post-Weinstein era', *Feminist Media Studies*, 18:3, 491–4.
Marks, Scott (2013), 'Review: *La Pirogue*', *San Diego Reader*, 24 April, <http://www.sandiegoreader.com/weblogs/big-screen/2013/apr/24/review-emla-pirogueem/> (last accessed 6 December 2019).
Marmeleira, José (2017), 'Quem canta seus males espanta', *Público*, 22 September, <https://www.publico.pt/2017/09/22/culturaipsilon/noticia/um-filme-que-encheu-uma-fabrica-de-gente-1785774> (last accessed 30 January 2019).
Martin-Jones, David (2009), *Scotland: Global Cinema: Genres, Modes and Identities*, Edinburgh: Edinburgh University Press.
Marx, Karl (1844), *Comments on James Mill, Éléments D'économie Politique*, <http://www.marxists.org/archive/marx/works/1844/james-mill/> (last accessed 4 February 2019).
Marx, Karl (1990 [1867]), *Capital*, vol. 1, London: Penguin.
Marx, Karl, and Friedrich Engels (1947 [1846]), *The German Ideology, Parts I and III*, New York: International Publishers.
Marx, Karl, and Friedrich Engels (2008 [1848]), *The Manifesto of the Communist Party*, trans. Samuel Moore in cooperation with Friedrich Engels, London: Pluto Press.
Masco, Joseph (2017), 'The crisis in crisis', *Cultural Anthropology*, 58:15, 65–76.
Mauss, Marcel (2012 [1925]), *Essai sur le don. Forme et raison de l'échange dans les sociétés archaïques*, Paris: Presses Universitaires de France.
Mazierska, Ewa (ed.) (2013), *Work in Cinema: Labor and the Human Condition*, Basingstoke: Palgrave.
Mazierska, Ewa (2015), *From Self-fulfilment to Survival of the Fittest: Work in European Cinema from the 1960s to the Present*, Oxford: Berghahn.
Mazierska, Ewa (2017), 'From multivoicedness to solipsism and beyond: images and voices of animals in contemporary arthouse European cinema', paper presented at 'Multivoicedness and European Cinema: Representation, Industry, Politics' conference, Cork, 10–11 November.
Mazierska, Ewa (2018), 'Capitalist realism in European films about debt', in Ewa Mazierska and Lars Kristensen (eds), *Contemporary Cinema and Neoliberal Ideology*, London: Routledge, 105–20.
Mazierska, Ewa, and Lars Kristensen (2014), 'Introduction', in Ewa Mazierska and Lars Kristensen (eds), *Marx at the Movies: Revisiting History, Theory and Practice*, Basingstoke: Palgrave Macmillan, 1–26.

Mazierska, Ewa, Matilda Mroz and Elżbieta Ostrowska (eds) (2016), *The Cinematic Bodies of Eastern Europe and Russia Between Pain and Pleasure*, Edinburgh: Edinburgh University Press.
McClanahan, Annie (2017), *Dead Pledges: Debt, Crisis, and Twenty-First-Century Culture*, Stanford: Stanford University Press.
McCracken, Grant (2016), 'Opinion', *B: Netflix*, 49, 39–41.
McDuff, Phil (2016), '*I, Daniel Blake* shows us the virtuous "deserving poor" – how conservative', *The Guardian*, 2 November, <https://www.theguardian.com/commentisfree/2016/nov/02/i-daniel-blake-poor-conservative-ken-loach-welfare-system> (last accessed 11 June 2019).
McHugh, Susan (2004), *Dog*, London: Reaktion.
Mecke, Jochen (2017), 'La crisis está siendo un todo un éxito . . . estético: discursos literarios de la crisis y éticas de la estética', in Jochen Mecke, Ralf Junkerjürgen and Hubert Pöppel (eds), *Discursos de la crisis. Respuestas de la cultura española ante nuevos desafíos*, Madrid/Frankfurt: Iberoamericana/Vervuert.
Meissner, Miriam (2012), 'Portraying the global financial crisis: myth, aesthetics, and the city', *NECSUS European Journal of Media Studies*, 1, 98–125.
Miller, Matthew D. (2012), 'Facts of migration, demands on identity: Christian Petzold's "Yella" and "Jerichow" in comparison', *The German Quarterly*, 85:1, 55–76.
Minagawa, Yuka (2013), 'The social consequences of postcommunist structural change: an analysis of suicide trends in Eastern Europe', *Social Forces*, 91:3, 1035–56.
Minton, Anna (2012), *Ground Control. Fear and Happiness in the Twenty-first Century*, London: Penguin.
Minton, Anna (2017), *Big Capital: Who Is London For?*, London: Penguin.
Mitchell, David T., and Sharon L. Snyder (2000), *Narrative Prosthesis: Disability and the Dependencies of Discourse*, Ann Arbor: University of Michigan Press.
Mitric, Petar, and Katharine Sarikakis (2019), 'European cinema: spectator- or spectactor-driven policies', in Yannis Tzioumakis and Claire Molloy (eds), *The Routledge Companion to Cinema and Politics*, London: Routledge, 421–31.
Möller, Olaf (2007), 'Vanishing point', *Sight and Sound*, 17:10, 40–2.
Moravcsik, Andrew (2012), 'Europe after the crisis: how to sustain a common currency', *Foreign Affairs*, 9:3, 54–68.
Mouëllic, Gilles (2013), *Improvising Cinema*, Amsterdam: Amsterdam University Press.
Mouffe, Chantal (2005), *On the Political*, London: Routledge.
Müller, Floris, Lisbet Van Zoonen and Fadi Hirzalla (2014), '*Fitna*, fear-based communication and the moderating role of public debate', *Middle East Journal of Culture and Communication*, 7, 82–100.
Murer, Jeffrey Stevenson (2020), *Repeating Hate: Narratives of Loss and Anxiety among the Hungarian Far-Right*, Basingstoke: Palgrave.
Murphet, Julian (2017), *Faulkner's Media Romance*, Oxford: Oxford University Press.
Murray, Robin L., and Joseph K. Heumann (2018), *Ecocinema and the City*, New York: Routledge.
Nagib, Lúcia (2016), 'Politics of slowness and the traps of modernity', in Tiago de Luca and Nuno Barradas Jorge (eds), *Slow Cinema*, Edinburgh: Edinburgh University Press.

Näripea, Eva (2012), 'National space, (trans)national cinema: Estonian film in the 1960s', in Anikó Imre (ed.), *A Companion to Eastern European Cinemas*, Chichester: Wiley-Blackwell, 244–64.
Nayman, Adam (2011), 'Interviews | suicide girl: Athina Rachel Tsangari', *Cinema Scope*, 45, <http://cinema-scope.com/cinema-scope-magazine/interviews-suicide-girl-athina-rachel-tsangari-attenberg> (last accessed 6 February 2019).
Negra, Diane, and Yvonne Tasker (eds) (2014), *Gendering the Recession: Media and Culture in an Age of Austerity*, Durham, NC: Duke University Press.
Neimanis, Astrida (2009), 'Bodies of water, human rights and the hydrocommons', *Topia: Canadian Journal of Cultural Studies*, 21, spring, 161–82.
Nestingen, Andrew (2013), *The Cinema of Aki Kaurismäki: Contrarian Stories*, New York: Columbia University Press.
Nichols, Bill (2010), *Introduction to Documentary*, 2nd edn, Bloomington: University of Indiana Press.
Nichols, Bill (2016), *Speaking Truths with Film: Evidence, Ethics, Politics in Documentary*, Berkeley: University of California Press.
Nicholson, Rebecca (2015), '*How to Get a Council House* review – "like a dystopian quiz show with the prize a squalid, flea-infested flat"', *The Guardian*, 6 July, <http://www.theguardian.com/tv-and-radio/2015/jul/06/how-to-get-a-council-house-review-squalid-flat> (last accessed 11 June 2019).
Nineham, Chris (2017), *How the Establishment Lost Control*, Alresford: zero books.
North, Michael (2011), *The Political Aesthetic of Yeats, Eliot and Pound*, Cambridge: Cambridge University Press.
Notermans, Ton (2015), 'An unassailable fortress? Neo-liberalism in Estonia', *Localities*, 5, 103–38.
Nyíri, Pál (2003), 'Chinese migration to Eastern Europe', *International Migration*, 41:3, 239–65.
Observatorio Metropolitano (2011), *La crisis que viene. Algunas notas para afrontar esta década*, Madrid: Traficantes de Sueños.
Ó Drisceoil, Donal (2009), 'Framing the Irish Revolution: Ken Loach's *The Wind That Shakes the Barley*', *Radical History Review*, 104, 5–15.
OECD (2014), 'Migration policy debates', *OECD.org*. May, <https://www.oecd.org/migration/OECD%20Migration%20Policy%20Debates%20Numero%202.pdf> (last accessed 20 December 2018).
Okólski, Marek (1998), 'Regional dimensions of international migration in Central and Eastern Europe', *Genus*, 54:1–2, 11–36.
Orr, John (1993), *Cinema and Modernity*, Cambridge: Polity.
O'Shaughnessy, Martin (2008), 'Ethics in the ruins of politics: the Dardenne brothers', in Kate Ince (ed.), *Five Directors: Auteurism from Assayas to Ozon*, Manchester: Manchester University Press, 59–83.
O'Shaughnessy, Martin (2014), 'The crisis before the crisis: reading films by Laurent Cantet and Jean-Pierre and Luc Dardenne through the lens of debt', *SubStance*, 43:1, 82–95.
O'Shaughnessy, Martin (2015), *Laurent Cantet*, Manchester: Manchester University Press.

O'Shaughnessy, Martin (2018), 'Putting the dead to work: making sense of worker suicide in contemporary French and Francophone Belgian film', *Studies in French Cinema* 19:4, 314–34.
Osseiran, Souad (2017), '"Europe" from "here": 'Syrian migrants/refugees in Istanbul and imagined migrations into and within "Europe"', in Nicholas De Genova (ed.), *The Borders of 'Europe': Autonomy of Migration, Tactics of Bordering*, Durham, NC: Duke University Press, 185–209.
Osteen, Mark (2008), 'Noir's cars: automobility and amoral space in American film noir', *Journal of Popular Film and Television*, 35:4, 183–92.
Õunpuu, Veiko (2008), 'Kõik ei ole nii, nagu näib', *Teater. Muusika. Kino*, 2, 126–7.
Outinen, Sami (2010), 'The Left, Social Security and Neoliberalism in Finland Since 1970s', PhD thesis, Department of Political and Economic Studies, University of Helsinki.
Page, Joanna (2009), *Crisis and Capitalism in Contemporary Argentine Cinema*, Durham, NC: Duke University Press.
Parvulescu, Anca (2012), 'Old Europe, New Europe, Eastern Europe: reflections on a minor character in Fassbinder's *Ali, Fear Eats the Soul*', *New Literary History*, 43:4, 727–50.
Parvulescu, Anca (2014), *The Traffic in Women's Work: East European Migration and the Making of Europe*, Chicago: University of Chicago Press.
Parvulescu, Constantin (2015), *Orphans of the East: Postwar Eastern European Cinema and the Revolutionary Subject*, Bloomington: Indiana University Press.
Patel, Raj, and Jason W. Moore (2018), *A History of the World in Seven Cheap Things: A Guide to Capitalism, Nature and the Future of the Planet*, London: Verso.
Peil, Tiina, and Helen Sooväli (2005), 'Estonian national landscapes – the sum and its parts', in Tiina Peil and Michael Jones (eds), *Landscape, Law and Justice. Proceedings of a conference organized by the Centre for Advanced Study at the Norwegian Academy of Science and Letters, Oslo, 15–19 June 2003*, Oslo: Novus, Instituttet for sammenlignende kulturforskning, 49–60.
Perry, Ted (2006), *Masterpieces of Modernist Cinema*, Bloomington: Indiana University Press.
Pleasant, Lesley (2014), 'Seeing beings: "Dog" looks back at "God": unfixing *Cania familiaris* in Kornél Mundruczó's film *Fehér isten / White God (2014)*', *Humanities*, 6:82, 1–22.
Polanyi, Karl (1957 [1944]), *The Great Transformation*, Boston: Beacon Press.
Polyakova, Alina, and Anton Shekhovtsov (2016), 'On the rise: Europe's fringe right', *World Affairs*, 179, 70–80.
Pop, Doru (2014), *Romanian New Wave Cinema: An Introduction*, Jefferson, NC: McFarland.
Porter, Pete (2017), 'Revenge of the herds', *Society and Animals*, 25, 99–103.
Porton, Richard (1996), 'The revolution betrayed: an interview with Ken Loach', *Cineaste*, 22:1, 30.
Powell, Jason L., and Jon Hendricks (2009), *The Welfare State in Post-Industrial Society: A Global Perspective*, New York: Springer.

Puar, Jasbir (2012), 'Precarity talk: a virtual roundtable with Lauren Berlant, Judith Butler, Bojana Cvejić, Isabell Lorey, Jasbir Puar, and Ana Vujanović', *TDR*, 56:4, 163–77.
Rabaté, Jean-Michel (2016), '"A cage went in search of a bird": how do Kafka's and Joyce's aphorisms move us?', in David Bradshaw, Laura Marcus and Rebecca Roach (eds), *Moving Modernisms: Motion, Technology, and Modernity*, Oxford: Oxford University Press, 143–58.
Racioppi, Linda, and Katherine O'Sullivan (2009), 'Gender politics in post-communist Eurasia', in Linda Racioppi and Katherine O'Sullivan (eds), *Gender Politics in Post-Communist Eurasia*, East Lansing: Michigan State University Press, 1–47.
Rajaram, Prem Kumar (2016), 'Europe's "Hungarian solution"', *Radical Philosophy* 197, 2–7.
Ramos Martínez, Manuel (2013), 'Cinema in Dispute: Audiovisual Adventures of the Political Names "Worker", "Factory", "People"', PhD thesis, Goldsmiths, University of London.
Rancière, Jacques (2009), *The Emancipated Spectator*, trans. G. Elliot, London: Verso.
Rancière, Jacques (2010), *Dissensus: On Politics and Aesthetics*, ed. and trans. S. Corcoran, London: Continuum.
Rancière, Jacques (2013), 'The populism that is not to be found', in Alain Badiou, Pierre Bourdieu, Judith Butler, Georges Didi-Huberman, Sadri Khiari and Jacques Rancière, *What is a People?*, trans. Jody Gladding, New York: Columbia University Press, 101–5.
Rapold, Nicolas (2015), 'Interview: Jonas Carpignano', *Film Comment*, 13 November, <https://www.filmcomment.com/blog/interview-jonas-carpignano/> (last accessed 28 September 2019).
Rapold, Nicolas (2017), 'Interview: Michael Haneke', *Film Comment*, 19 December, <https://www.filmcomment.com/blog/interview-michael-haneke/> (last accessed 28 September 2019).
Rappas, Ipek A. Celik (2016), 'Corporeal violence in art-house cinema: Cannes 2009', *Continuum: Journal of Media & Cultural Studies*, 30:6, 670–8.
Redrobe [Beckman], Karen (2009), 'Doing death over: industrial safety films, accidental motion studies, and the involuntary crash test dummy', *Discourse*, 30:3, 317–47.
Redrobe [Beckman], Karen (2010), *Crash: Cinema and the Politics of Speed and Stasis*, Durham, NC: Duke University Press.
Rees, John (2016), 'Ken Loach talks Daniel Blake, Jeremy Corbyn and Leon Trotsky', *Counterfire*, 4 October, <https://www.counterfire.org/interview/18543-ken-loach-talks-daniel-blake-jeremy-corbyn-and-leon-trotsky> (last accessed 17 July 2019).
Rhodes, John David, and Brian Price (2010), 'Introduction', in John David Rhodes and Brian Price (eds), *On Michael Haneke*, Detroit, MI: Wayne State University Press, 1–14.
Ribas, Daniel, and Paulo Cunha (2015), 'Nós por cá . . . As causas do desencanto do povo (e do cinema) português', *A Cuarta Parede*, 26 August, <http://www.acuartaparede.com/nos-por-ca-desencanto-cinema-portugues> (last accessed 21 January 2019).

Rigatelli, Sara (2018), 'Yle: Tuntematon ohjaaja – Elokuvatähdet kertovat Aku Louhimiehen poikkeuksellisesta vallankäytöstä: Hän alistaa ja nöyryyttää ihmisiä', *YLE*, <https://yle.fi/uutiset/3-10115456> (last accessed 21 April 2019).
Rodríguez Mateos, Araceli (2018), 'Precarity and vulnerability. Documentaries on the crisis in Spain', in Constantin Parvulescu (ed.), *Global Finance on Screen: From Wall Street to Side Street*, Abingdon: Routledge, 198–218.
Rodríguez Tranche, Rafael (2013), 'Vivir por encima de nuestras posibilidades', *El País*, 16 May, <https://elpais.com/elpais/2013/05/07/opinion/1367943599_530998.html> (last accessed 17 January 2019).
Rohdie, Sam (2015), *Film Modernism*, Manchester: Manchester University Press.
Römpötti, Tommi (2015), 'Fathers and sons reunited: road movies as stories of generational continuity', in Pietari Kääpä and Tommy Gustafsson (eds), *Nordic Genre Film*, Edinburgh: Edinburgh University Press, 133–46.
Ross, Andrew (2009), *Nice Work If You Can Get It: Life and Labor in Precarious Times*, New York: New York University Press.
Rotas, Alex (2004), 'Is "refugee art" possible?', *Third Text*, 18:1, 51–60.
Rubin, Alissa J. (2013), 'France says deportation of Roma girl was legal', *New York Times*, 19 October, <https://www.nytimes.com/2013/10/20/world/europe/france-says-deportation-of-roma-girl-was-legal.html> (last accessed 18 December 2018).
Rubin, Gayle (1997), 'The traffic in women: notes on the "political economy" of sex', in Linda Nicholson (ed.), *The Second Wave: A Reader in Feminist Theory*, London: Routledge, 27–62.
Rushing, Robert A. (2017), 'Planes, trains, automobiles, bicycles, spaceships and an elephant: images of movement from Neorealism to the commedia all'italiana', *California Italian Studies*, 7:1, 1–24.
Rushton, Richard (2019), '*Chevalier* and the rules of the European game', *Studies in European Cinema*, 16:3, 218–31.
Ryan, William (1972), *Blaming the Victim*, London: Penguin.
Šafářová, Martina (2015), 'Czech film series "Bastards" humiliates Romani people', *Romea*, 30 March, trans. Gwendolyn Albert, <http://www.romea.cz/en/news/czech/czech-film-series-bastards-humiliates-romani-people> (last accessed 10 January 2019).
Said, Edward, and Christopher Hitchens (eds) (1988), *Blaming the Victims: Spurious Scholarship and the Palestinian Question*, London: Verso.
Santos, Boaventura de Sousa (2014), *Portugal: Ensaio contra a Autoflagelação*, São Paulo: Cortez Editora.
Sborgi, Anna Viola (2017a), 'An update on Grenfell', *Mediapolis – A Journal of Cities and Culture*, 3:2, 30 September, <http://www.mediapolisjournal.com/2017/09/an-update-on-grenfell/> (last accessed 28 September 2019).
Sborgi, Anna Viola (2017b), 'The day social housing hit mainstream media', *Mediapolis – A Journal of Cities and Culture*, 3:2, 27 September, <http://www.mediapolisjournal.com/2017/09/the-day-social-housing-hit-mainstream-media> (last accessed 28 September 2019).

Sborgi, Anna Viola (2019), 'Grenfell on screen', in D. Bulley, J. Edkins and N. El-Enany (eds), *After Grenfell: Violence, Resistance and Response*, London: Pluto Press.
Schoonover, Karl (2012), *Brutal Vision: The Neorealist Body in Postwar Italian Cinema*, Minneapolis: University of Minnesota Press.
Schumpeter, Joseph A. (1994 [1942]), *Capitalism, Socialism and Democracy*, London: Routledge.
Schwartz, Louis-Georges (2013), 'Cinema hostis, or historicizing the time and movement images', paper presented at 'Historical Materialism' conference, London, 7–10 November.
Screpanti, Ernesto (2014), *Global Imperialism and the Great Crisis: The Uncertain Future of Capitalism*, New York: Monthly Review Press.
Self, Robert (1979), 'Systems of ambiguity in the art cinema', *Film Criticism*, 4:1, 74–80.
Sennett, Richard (1998), *The Corrosion of Character: The Personal Consequences of Work in the New Capitalism*, New York: W.W. Norton.
Sepp, Edith (2019), 'Me peame rääkima Eesti filmi tulevikust', *Eesti Päevaleht*, 5 February.
Sequeira Brás, Patricia (2017), 'Crisis and catastrophe in cinema and video art', *Paletten Art Journal*, 307/308, <https://paletten.net/journal/2017/7/20/university-of-disaster> (last accessed 6 December 2019).
Shaviro, Steven (2012), 'Body horror and post-socialist cinema: György Pálfi's *Taxidermia*', in Anikó Imre (ed.), *A Companion to Eastern European Cinemas*, Chichester: Wiley-Blackwell, 25–41.
Shaviro, Steven (2015), *No Speed Limit: Three Essays on Accelerationism*, Minneapolis: University of Minnesota Press.
Shklovsky, Victor (1965), 'Art as technique', in Lee T. Lemon and Marion J. Reis (eds), *Russian Formalist Criticism: Four Essays*, Lincoln, NE: University of Nebraska Press, 3–24.
Sinnerbrink, Robert (2012), '*Stimmung*: exploring the aesthetics of mood', *Screen*, 53:2, 148–63.
Smith, John (2016), *Imperialism in the Twenty-first Century*, New York: Monthly Review Press.
Smith, Justin E. H. (2019), *Irrationality: A History of the Dark Side of Reason*, Princeton: Princeton University Press.
Sng, Paul (ed.) (2018), *Invisible Britain: Portraits of Hope and Resilience*, Bristol: Policy Press.
Snyder, Benjamin H. (2016), *The Disrupted Workplace: Time and the Moral Order of Flexible Capitalism*, Oxford: Oxford University Press.
Solar Films Website (2005), *Paha Maa, Solar Films Inc*, <https://solarfilms.com/en/portfolio-posts/paha-maa/> (last accessed 26 March 2019).
Srnicek, Nick, and Alex Williams (2015), *Inventing the Future Postcapitalism and a World Without Work*, London: Verso.
Stam, Robert (1999), 'Palimpsestic aesthetics: a meditation on hybridity and garbage', in May Joseph and Jennifer Natalya Fink (eds), *Performing Hybridity*, Minneapolis: University of Minnesota Press, 59–78.

Stam, Robert, Richard Porton and Leo Goldsmith (2015), *Keywords in Subversive Film/Media Aesthetics*, Chichester: Wiley-Blackwell.
Stephens, Philip (2018), 'Populism is the true legacy of the global financial crisis', *Financial Times*, 30 August, <https://www.ft.com/content/687c0184-aaa6-11e8-94bd-cba20d67390c> (last accessed 6 December 2019).
Stern, Lesley (2001), 'Paths that wind through the thicket of things', *Critical Inquiry* 28:1, 317–54.
Stőhr, Lóránt (2016), 'Conflicting forces: post-communist and mythical bodies in Kornél Mundruczó's films', *Studies in Eastern European Cinema*, 7:2, 139–52.
Stőhr, Lóránt (2019), *Személyesség, jelenlét, narrativitás. Paradigmaváltás a kortárs magyar dokumentumfilmben* [Subjectivity, presence, narrativity. Change of paradigm in contemporary Hungarian documentary], Budapest: Gondolat.
Streeck, Wolfgang (2014), *Buying Time: The Delayed Crisis of Democratic Capitalism*, London: Verso.
Suchsland, Rüdiger (2007), 'Liebe in Zeiten der Heuschrecken', *Telepolis*, 15 September, <https://www.heise.de/tp/features/Liebe-in-Zeiten-der-Heuschrecken-3415306.html> (last accessed 9 July 2019).
Suomen Elokuvasäätiö (2018), *Guidelines for the Prevention of Sexual Harassment in the Film and Television Industries*, suomen elokuvasäätiö, <https://ses.fi/fileadmin/dokumentit/Guidelines_for_the_prevention_of_sexual_harassment_in_the_film_and_tv_industries.pdf> (last accessed 12 April 2019).
Surtees, Rebecca (2008), 'Traffickers and trafficking in Southern and Eastern Europe: considering the other side of human trafficking', *European Journal of Criminology*, 5:1, 39–68.
Sztompka, Piotr (2004), 'The trauma of social change: a case of postcommunist societies', in Jeffrey C. Alexander, Ron Eyerman, Bernard Giesen, Neil J. Smelser and Piotr Sztompka, *Cultural Trauma and Collective Identity*, Berkeley: University of California Press, 155–95.
Tamas, Gaspar Miklos (2000), 'On post-fascism: how citizenship is becoming an exclusive privilege', *Boston Review*, <http://bostonreview.net/archives/BR25.3/tamas.html> (last accessed 28 September 2019).
Tamm, Marek (2018), 'Rahvuste tegemine. Humanitaarteaduslik vaade', *Keel ja Kirjandus*, 1–2, 15–29.
Taubin, Amy (2015), 'God bites dog', *Artforum International*, March, <https://www.artforum.com/print/201503/Kornél-Mundruczó-s-white-god-50268> (last accessed 6 December 2019).
Tazzioli, Martina (2018), 'Crimes of solidarity: migration and containment through rescue', *Radical Philosophy*, 2.01, 4–10.
Tchouaffe, Jean Olivier (n.d.), '*La Pirogue*', <https://www.austinfilm.org/program-notes-la-pirogue> (last accessed 3 April 2020).
Teder, Tarmo (2009), 'Laupäeval hakkab "Püha Tõnu kiusamine"', *Sirp*, 9 October.
Teinemaa, Sulev (2011), 'Vastab Veiko Õunpuu', *Teater. Muusika. Kino*, 11, 4–14.
Timmer, Andria D., and Danielle Docka-Filipek (2018), 'Enemies of the nation: understanding the Hungarian state's relationship to humanitarian NGOs', *Journal of International & Global Studies*, 9:2, 40–57.

Tõnson, Margit (2010), 'Bodhisattva of compassion is doomed to fail', *KinoKultura: New Russian Cinema*, special issue 10: Estonian Cinema, <http://www.kinokultura.com/specials/10/tonytemptation.shtml> (last accessed 4 February 2019).
Tooze, Adam (2018), *Crashed: How a Decade of Financial Crises Changed the World*, London: Allen Lane.
Toscano, Alberto, and Jeff Kinkle (2011a), *Cartographies of the Absolute*, Winchester: Zero Books.
Toscano, Alberto, and Jeff Kinkle (2011b), 'Filming the crisis: a survey', *Film Quarterly*, 65:1, 39–51.
Toth, András, and István Grajczjár (2015), 'The rise of the radical right in Hungary', in Péter Krazstev and Jon Van Til (eds), *The Hungarian Patient: Social Opposition to an Illiberal Democracy*, Budapest: Central European University Press, 133–63.
Travis, Ben (2015), '*How to Get A Council House*, Channel 4: a heart-breaking look at harsh reality', *Evening Standard*, 6 July, <http://www.standard.co.uk/stayingin/tvfilm/how-to-get-a-council-house-channel-4-a-heartbreaking-look-at-harsh-reality-10369717.html> (last accessed 11 June 2019).
Traynor, Ian (2009), 'Gypsies suffer widespread racism in European Union', *The Guardian*, 23 April, <https://www.theguardian.com/world/2009/apr/23/eu-roma-racism-discrimination> (last accessed 5 October 2019).
Trilling, Daniel (2018), 'Five myths about the refugee crisis', *The Guardian*, 5 June, <https://www.theguardian.com/news/2018/jun/05/five-myths-about-the-refugee-crisis> (last accessed 6 December 2019).
Trotter, David (2007), *Cinema and Modernism*, London: Blackwell.
Tuch, Andrei (2019), 'Welcome to Estonia's new neo-Nazi government', *Estonian World*, 12 March, <https://estonianworld.com/opinion/andrei-tuch-welcome-to-estonias-new-neo-nazi-government/?fbclid=IwAR2mk7rBQdzaFsfB5yRp1LXxTNKdImhlZgthoU_Tr-PmMpOfmFOmTNPyKeg> (last accessed 18 May 2019).
Tuumalu, Tiit (2009), 'Püha Tõnu kiusamine. Intervjuu Veiko Õunpuuga', *Postimees: AK*, 3 October.
Tuumalu, Tiit (2014), 'Veiko Õunpuu teeb uut filmi teistmoodi', *Postimees*, 10 June.
Urbán, Ágnes (2016), 'Recent changes in media ownership', Mertek Media Monitor, <http://mertek.eu/wp-content/uploads/2016/11/mertek_media_owners2016.pdf> (last accessed 4 February 2019).
Van Dijk, Teun A. (2000), 'New(s) racism: a discourse analytical approach', in Simon Cottle (ed.), *Ethnic Minorities and the Media*, Buckingham: Open University Press, 33–49.
Varoufakis, Yanis (2013), *The Global Minotaur*, London: Zed Books.
Varoufakis, Yanis (2018), 'Our plan to revive Europe can succeed where Macron and Piketty failed', *The Guardian*, 13 December, <https://www.theguardian.com/commentisfree/2018/dec/13/plan-europe-macron-piketty-green-new-deal-britain> (last accessed 6 December 2019).
Vaughan-Williams, Nick (2009), *Border Politics. The Limits of Sovereign Power*, Edinburgh: Edinburgh University Press.
Veciana, Alejandro (2015), 'NYFF interview: Athina Rachel Tsangari', *Film Comment*, 7 October, <http://filmcomment.com/blog/nyff-interview-athina-rachel-tsangari> (last accessed 6 February 2019).

Verdery, Katherine (1996), *What Was Socialism and What Comes Next?*, Princeton: Princeton University Press.
Vila, Pablo (2000), *Crossing Borders, Reinforcing Borders: Social Categories, Metaphors, and Narrative Identities on the U.S.-Mexico Frontier*, Austin: University of Texas Press.
Villarmea Álvarez, Iván (2018), 'Rostros y espacios de la austeridad en los cines ibéricos (2007–2016)', *Iberoamericana. América Latina - España – Portugal*, 18:69, 13–36.
Virtanen, Leena (2018), 'Minusta tehtiin pornonäyttelijä', Matleena Kuusniemi syytti Aku Louhimiestä A-Studion keskustelussa – Louhimies pyysi monta kertaa anteeksi toimintaansa, *Helsingin Sanomat*, <https://www.hs.fi/kulttuuri/art-2000005610365.html> (last accessed 12 April 2019).
von Bagh, Peter (2011), 'Aki Kaurismäki: the uncut interview', *Film Comment*, (September/October), <http://www.filmcomment.com/article/aki-kaurismaki/> (last accessed 6 December 2019).
von Moltke, Johannes (2005), *Heimatfilm: No Place Like Home*, Berkeley: University of California Press.
Walker, Shaun (2019), '"A whole generation has gone": Ukrainians seek a better life in Poland', *The Guardian*, 18 April, <https://www.theguardian.com/world/2019/apr/18/whole-generation-has-gone-ukrainian-seek-better-life-poland-elect-president> (last accessed 6 December 2019).
Wallerstein, Immanuel (2004), *World-systems Analysis: An Introduction*, Durham, NC: Duke University Press.
Warwick Research Collective (2015), *Combined and Uneven Development Towards a New Theory of World-Literature*, Liverpool: Liverpool University Press.
Watt, Paul (2009), 'Housing stock transfers, regeneration and state-led gentrification in London', *Urban Policy and Research*, 27:3, 229–42.
Watt, Paul (2009), 'Social housing and regeneration', in Rob Imrie, Loretta Lees and Mike Raco (eds), *Regenerating London. Governance, Sustainability and Community in a Global City*, London: Routledge, 216–17.
Watt, Paul, and Peer Smets (2017), *Social Housing and Urban Renewal – A Cross-National Perspective*, Bingley: Emerald Publishing.
Webb, Lawrence (2014), *The Cinema of Urban Crisis: Seventies Film and the Reinvention of the City*, Amsterdam: Amsterdam University Press.
Weyland, Kurt (1999), 'Neoliberal populism in Latin America and Eastern Europe', *Comparative Politics*, 31:4, 379–401.
Wheatley, Catherine (2009), *Michael Haneke's Cinema: The Ethic of the Image*, Oxford: Berghahn.
Wheatley, Catherine (2011), 'Not politics but people: the "feminine aesthetic" of Valeska Grisebach and Jessica Hausner', in Robert von Dassanowsky and Oliver C. Speck (eds), *New Austrian Film*, Oxford: Berghahn, 136–50.
Wilkin, Peter (2016), *Hungary's Crisis of Democracy: The Road to Serfdom*, Lanham, MD: Lexington Books.
Willemen, Paul (1972), 'Towards an analysis of the Sirkian System', *Screen*, 13:4, 128–34.

Wilterdink, Nico (1993), 'An examination of European and national identity', *European Journal of Sociology/Archives Européennes de Sociologie*, 34:1, 119–36.
Wimmer, Andreas, and Nina Glick Schiller (2003), 'Methodological nationalism, the social sciences, and the study of migration: an essay in historical epistemology', *International Migration Review*, 37:3, 576–610.
Wodak, Ruth (2015), *The Politics of Fear: Analyzing Right-Wing Popular Discourse*, London: Sage.
Wright, Steve (2002), *Storming Heaven: Class Composition and Struggle in Italian Autonomist Marxism*, London: Pluto Press
Yamin, Farhana (2019), 'Die, survive, or thrive?', in *This is Not a Drill: An Extinction Rebellion Handbook*, London: Penguin, 21–7.
Zas Marcos, Mónica, and Marcos Pinheiro (2018), 'De los regalos de Púnica al yate de Gürtel: la corrupción real escondida en El reino', *eldiario.es*, 3 October, <https://www.eldiario.es/cultura/cine/regalos-Punica-Gurtel-corrupcion-reino_0_821018248.html> (last accessed 4 February 2019).
Žižek, Slavoj (2009), *Violence: Six Sideways Reflections*, London: Profile Books.
Žižek, Slavoj (2016), 'The sexual is political', *The Philosophical Salon* <http://thephilosophicalsalon.com/the-sexual-is-political/> (last accessed 4 February 2019).
Žižek, Slavoj (2018), *Like a Thief in Broad Daylight: Power in the Era of Post-Humanity*, London: Penguin.

INDEX

Note: Page numbers in italics are illustrations and those followed by n are notes.

'accelerationism', 108
Active Life (Nobre, 2013), 11, 76–92, 152–3
Ade, Maren, 18
Adorno, Theodor W., 36, 123, 125, 137, 137–8
  Aesthetic Theory, 72
aesthetics and politics, 18–21
aesthetics of crisis, 25–42
Ahmed, Sarah, 213n, 228, 232, 233
Akingbade, Ayo, 189
Alexievich, Svetlana, 68
alienation, 37–8, 63, 73–4
Allah minden napján szaladnak a lovak (2011), 220
Allbritton, Dean, 151–2
Allen, Jim, 138, 144
Álljon meg a menet! (2017), 222
Álvarez, Iván Villarmea, 8, 10–11
Anderson, Benedict, 132, 135n
Andersson, Ruben, 206–8, 210, 211n
Andreescu, Florentina C., 168–9

Anstey, E. H., 183
anthropomorphism, 235–6
'anti-democratic populism', 6–7
antiziganism, 18, 260–76
Arabian Nights (Gomes, 2015), 77–78, 153, 154–5, 159, 163n
Archer, Neil, 75n
Argentine cinema, 81
Argentinian factory, 88–9
Art Cinema and neoliberalism, 25–42
arthouse ghetto, 262–4
As Luck Would Have It (Iglesia, 2011), 110
As Mil e uma Noites (Gomes, 2015), 77–8, 153, 154–5, 159, 163n
Asian cinema, 67
Astruc, Alexander, 26
Attenberg (Tsangari, 2010), 39, 110
austerity, 7–13
  Britain, 185–6
  Finland, 96
  Greece, 32

oppositional politics, 139
Portugal, 76–7, 91, 91–2n
Austin, Thomas, 15, 17–18, 20
Austria, Freedom Party, 13
auteur apologism, 101–3
auteurism, 5, 99, 104n
authoritarian populism, 13–14
Autumn Ball (Õunpuu, 2007), 124, 127, 128
awards, 102, 264, 273
Az prijde válka (Gebert, 2018), 260
Azok (Meggyes, 2016), 224, 227–9

Baccalaureat Graduation (Mungiu, 2016), 4–5
Badiou, Alain
  capitalist realism, 147–8
  Event, 143–4, 145
  'the Idea of Communism', 137
  'intervallic period', 139
  Logics of Worlds, 144
  Other, 45
  'short century', 140, 149n
Balanta (Pintilie, 1992), 169–70
Balsom, Erika, 181
Báñez, Fátima, 150
Bárcenas, Luis, 163n
Bastardi (Magnusek), 264–6, 275n
Bastards (Magnusek), 264–6, 275n
Basu, Laura, 7–8, 22n
Bataille, Georges, 50, 53
Batori, Anna, 5
Bauman, Zygmunt, 3, 70–1, 121, 128, 129, 153
Bazin, André, 109
BBC television, 12, 138, 191
Beautiful Youth (Rosales, 2014), 156–7
Becker, Jens, 234
Before Grenfell (Channel 4, 2018), 191
Belgium, 44
Benefits Street (Channel 4, 2014–15), 184
Benjamin, Walter, 149n
Bennett, Bruce, 198
Berend, Ivan T., 166
Berezin, Mabel, 224

Berkut, 270, 276n
Berlant, Lauren, 60–1, 75, 108, 117, 247
Berlin School, 8–9, 105–18
Berlinale, 264
Bez doteku (Chlupáček and Samir, 2013), 173–5, *175*
Bhabha, Homi K., 14–15
  'DissemiNation: Time, Narrative, and the Margins of the Modern Nation', 132
Bibliothèque Pascal (Hajdu, 2010), 177–8
Biendarra, Anke, 114
Blair, Tony, 196n
Bloch, Ernst, 137
The Block (Watson, BBC, 1972), 183, 185
Bloodworth, James, 8, 10
bodies and gestures, 48–9, 53–5
borders, crossing, 224–9
Bordoni, Carlo, 119, 129
Bordwell, David, 40
Bosnia, 263
Bourdieu, Pierre, 11–12, 22n, 51–2, 81–2
Boyer, Dominic, 164
Bradley, Rizvana, 239
Bread and Roses (Loach, 2000), 149n
Brecht, Bertolt, 29–31, 41n, 126, 202, 204–5, 212n
Brennan, Teresa, 60–1
Bresson, Robert, *L'Argent*, 96
Bretton Woods system, 138
Brexit, 15–16, 183
Britain
  housing crisis, 12, 180–97
  Labour Party, 136–49
Broken Glasses (Erice, 2012), 152–3
Brown, Wendy, 3, 36, 37, 149n, 225–6
Bruckner, Pascal, 10, 114
  'Lost Time: Blunt Head Trauma and Accident-Driven Cinema', 107
Bugaric, Bojan, 166
Building a Movement, 190
Buñuel, Luis, 40
Burch, Nöel, 25–6

Cahill, James Leo, 109
Cain, James M., *The Postman Always Rings Twice*, 115, 116
A Call Girl (Kozole, 2009), 175–7, 178
Cambridge (2015), 261
Cameron, David, 198, 211n, 235
Cantet, Laurent, 19, 63, 69–72, 75n
Capital (Costa-Gavras, 2012), 18, 245, 251, 254–6, 258
capitalism
  capitalist realism, 137–8, 145, 148
  car crashes, 108
  and colonialism, 210
  culture industry, 126–7
  'disaster capitalism', 8
  Estonia, 120–1, 135n
  and globalisation, 257–8
  Greece, 110
  Hungary, 229
  and industry, 81
  'light capitalism', 70–1
  modernism, 42n, 61–2
  and neoliberal policies, 26–8
  Yella (Petzold, 2007), 113–14
Capitalism: Our Improved Formula (Solomon, 2010), 5
car crashes, 8–9, 105–18, *116*
Carla's Song (Loach, 1996), 140
Carnival of Souls (Harvey, 1962), 113
Carpignano, Jonas, 15, 17–18, 20, 199, 208–10, 245, 249
Carr, Matthew, 212n
Case, Holly, 236
Caught between Two Worlds (Nagy, HBO Europe, 2011), 222–3
CGI, 240
A Chajna (Carpignano, 2012), 208
Chakrabortty, Aditya, 15–16
Channel 4, 12, 184, 184–5, 191, 195
Channel 5, 192
Charlie Hebdo attack, 216
Chevalier (Tsangari, 2015), 10, 20, 32–41, 37
China, 81
Chinese migration, 218
La Chispa de la Vida (Iglesia, 2011), 110
Chouliaraki, Lilie, 201–2

Cinema Action, 183
cinema hostis, 234
cinema of excess, 202
Clark, Timothy J., 61–2
climate crisis, 20–1
Colo (Villaverde, 2017), 159
colonialism, 15, 20, 67, 74, 75n, 210
  postcoloniality, 4–5
Communist bloc, 65–6, 68, 75n
Concrete Soldiers UK (Wolfe, 2017), 12, 193–4, 195
consumption crisis, 27–8
Copenhagen Declaration on European Identity 1973, 13
Corbyn, Jeremy, 192
Costa-Gavras, 245, 258n
Coville, Peter, 9–10
Cracks in the System (Majid and York, 2018), 189–90
Crialese, Emanuele, 15, 199, 202–3
crisis
  of cinema, 108–10
  of creativity, 121–5
  definition of, 25
  on Eastern European screen, 164–79
  narrative, 28
  of neoliberalism, 26–8, 119–35
Crouch, Colin, 41n
  Post-Democracy, 5–6
  The Strange Non-Death of Neoliberalism, 7
Csak a szél (Fliegauf, 2012), 262–3, 264
Csoma, Em ke, 99
Curcio, Anna, 213–14n
Curtis, Adam, 183
Czech Film Centre, 266
Czech Republic, 18, 173–5, 264–6, 274–5n

Daily Mail, 185
Dale, Gareth, 165–6
Dardenne, Jean-Pierre, 12–13, 213n
Dardenne, Luc, 12–13, 44–5, 213n
Dardenne brothers, 43–59, 246
Davies, William, 41
Days of Hope (Loach, BBC, 1975), 138, 143

De Genova, Nicholas, 198–9, 211n, 203
De Sica, Vittorio, 212n
de-democratisation, 32–6
defamiliarisation, 29–31
de-industrialisation, 1–2, 2–3, 8–9, 21n, 84–5, 90
Deleuze, Gilles, 69
'democratic antipopulism', 6–7
derealisation, 181
Derrida, Jacques, 17, 50–2, 55, 137
Detroit, 84–5, 90
Deux jours, une nuit (Dardenne, 2014), 44, 46, 57
Dibrani, Leonarda, 261
The Dilapidated Dwelling (Keiller, 2000), 183
disability, 199
'disaster capitalism', 8
Discourse, 'Cinema and Accident', 106
displacements, 28, 29–30
  labour, 244–59
Dispossession. The Great Social Housing Swindle (Sng, 2017), 12, 189, 191–3, *192*, 195
documentaries
  Britain's housing crisis, 12, 180–97
  'host society', 224–9
  Hungary, 215–30
  'integration', 219–21
  'journey', 222–3
  'sociological', 220
documentary, Britain's housing crisis, 12, 180–97
Dogtooth (Lanthimos, 2009), 110
Dort, Bernard, 202
Drakulić, Slavenka, 65
Drisceoil, Donal Ó, 141
DVDs, 192
Dying Beyond their Means (Lacuesta, 2014), 160–1

E Agora? Lembra-me (Pinto, 2013), 155
East End Film Festival, London 2018, 190
East Germany, 8–9, 110, 113–15, 117–18 *see also* Germany
Easy Lessons (Zurbó, 2018), 220–1, 221

Eelmaa, Taavi, 122–3
Eisenstein, Sergei, 65
Eisner, Lotte, 231
Eliot, T. S., 63
Elton, Arthur, 183
empathy and empowerment, 150–63
L'Emploi du temps (Cantet, 2001), 63, 69–72
Empty (Õunpuu, 2006), 124, 127–8
The Enchanted One (Gomes, 2015), 77–8
Engels, Friedrich, 67
An Episode in the Life of an Iron Picker (Tanovic, 2013), 263, 264, 274n
Epizoda u zivotu bereca zejeza (Tanovic, 2013), 263, 264, 274n
Erice, Víctor, 152–3
Esposito, Roberto, 248
Estonia, 5, 119–35, 134–5n
Estonian Film Institute, 119
European Capital of Culture, Tallinn, 2011, 122
European Integration Fund, 217
European Media Center, 270
European project, 14–15
European Refugee Fund, 217, 224
European Union
  asylum seekers, 23n, 211n
  Charter of Fundamental Rights, 63
  Eastern Europe, 175–8
  Estonia, 120
  Fundamental Rights Agency, 274n
  Hungary, 64–5, 217–20, 229
  Kovacevic on, 17
  migrants, 187, 226
  and neoliberal policies, 32
  oppositional politics, 139
  Roma, 261
  social housing, 194
  Visions of Europe (2004), 1
Eurozone, 32
Eurozone debt crisis, 8, 11, 78, 206
Evening Standard, 185
Every Day of Allah Horses Run (2011), 220
'extreme cinema', 170

INDEX

A Fábrica do Nada (Pinho, 2017), 11, 76–92, 153, 154, 159
Fabry, Adam, 165–6
Facebook, 191
'factual welfare television', 184, 195
Failed by the State (Renwick, 2017), 190
Family Life (Loach, 1971), 138
Fanon, Frantz, 14–15
Farocki, Harun, 65
   Arbeiter verlassen die Fabrik/Workers Leaving the Factory, 84
'feel-bad film', 170
Fehér isten (Mundruczó, 2014), 19, 231–43
Felsőbb parancs (Nagy, 2013), 224, 225–9
Félúton a jobb világ felé (2017), 222
Fidesz party, 15, 216–17, 217, 224, 234
La Fille Inconnue (Dardennes, 2016), 44, 57–8
Le Fils (Dardennes, 2002), 46–9, 47, 53
financial crisis (2008), 7, 44
Financial Times, 13
Finland, 11, 93–104
   welfare state, 94–6
'Finnish melancholia', 99
FIPRESCI Critics Award, Cannes, 2017, 87
Fire at Sea (Rosi, 2016), 202–3, 213n
The Fires that Foretold Grenfell (Roberts, BBC, 2018), 190
Fisher, Jaimey, 108
Fisher, Mark, 9, 137–8, 145, 148
Fitna (YouTube, 2008), 266
Fliegauf, Benedek, 262–3
foreign direct investments (FDI), 165
Forrest, Tara, 72
Fortress Europe, 15, 20, 218, 224
   refugees and migrants in, 198–214
France
   Eurozone debt crisis, 32
   Macron, Emmanuel, 139
   and multiculturalism, 31
   neoliberalism, 11
   populism, 23n
   Roma, 261, 272, 276n
Free Range (Õunpuu, 2013), 127

Freudianism, 26
Friedman, Milton, 120, 210
Frozen Land (Louhimies, 2005), 11, 94, 96–101, 101, 103
Fukuyama, Francis, 136
Fuocoammare (Rosi, 2016), 202–3, 213n

Gagyi, Agnes, 6–7
Galt, Rosalind, 19
games, 33–37, 41
Le Gamin au vélo (Dardennes, 2011), 44, 56–7
Garnett, Tay, 115, 116
Gaudreault, Andre, *The End of Cinema? A Medium in Crisis in the Digital Age*, 109
gender, 168–70, 212n, 251–6
Gerbert, Jan, 260
German cinema, 110
German Expressionism, 231
Germany
   Bibliotheque Pascal (Hajdu, 2010), 178
   de-industrialisation, 117–18
   economy, 8–9, 110, 179n
   oppositional politics, 139
   Roma, 261, 272
   see also East Germany
Gertten, Fredrik, 194
Ghost Trilogy, 105
gifts, 43–59, 47, 54
'gig' economy, 8
Ginsborg, Paul, 115
globalisation, 2–3, 9, 224–5
   'negative', 127–34
Goat (2015), 263–4, 264
Godard, Jean-Luc, 107
Gomes, Miguel, 77–8, 153, 154–5
'good life', 75
Graeber, David, 91
Grajczjár, István, 234
Gramsci, Antonio, 146–7
   War of Manoeuvre, 136
'Grândola Vila Morena', 77–8
Gray, Richard, 73
Great Recession, 150–1

308

Greece, 10, 32–41, 110, 139
Greek cinema, 110
Grenfell (Anthony, BBC, 2018), 191
'Grenfell effect', 190–1
Grenfell Our Home (Channel 4, 2018), 191
Grenfell Tower disaster 2017, 12, 180–1, 190–3, 196
Grisebach, Valeska, 8–9, 106, 111–13, 117
Grundmann, Roy, 72
Guardian, 24n, 184, 196n, 274n

Haider, Jorg, 13
'Haiderization of Europe', 13
Hajdu, Szabolcs, 177–8
Half-Way Towards a Better World (2017), 222
Hall, Martin, 12
Handcuffs (Papić, 1969), 168–9
Haneke, Michael, 19–20, 31, 63, 72–5, 75n, 139, 205
Happy End (Haneke, 2017), 19, 63, 72–5, 205
Haraway, Donna, 236
Hardt, Michael, 257
Harvey, David, 120, 121, 188, 191
  'Neoliberalism as Creative Destruction', 256–7
Harvey, Herk, 113
hauntology, 137, 147
Le Havre (Kaurismäki, 2011), 20, 200–2, 203, 212n
HBO Europe, 217, 218–19, 222
Heimatfilm, 112
Hermosa juventud (Rosales, 2014), 156–7
Herzberg, Judith, *De Nietsfabriek*, 87, 154
Hespanha, Tiago, 78
Heumann, Joseph, 235–6
Heygate was Home online archive, 189
Highmore, Ben, 231–2
Hiltunen, Kaisa, 99, 102–3
History of the Roma Problem in Kiev and Its Solution (YouTube), 268–9
Hollahan, Eugene, 25

Horkheimer, Max, 123, 125
'host society' documentaries, 224–9
Housing and Planning Act 2016, 183
Housing Bill 2016, 192
housing crisis
  activism community-based initiatives, 189–90
  Britain, 12, 180–97
  Europe, 194–5
  'right to buy', 182–3
  'system, the', 185–9
Housing Problems (Elton and Anstey, 1935), 183
How to Get a Council House (Channel 4, 2013–16), 12, 184, 184–9, 195, 196n
Huillet, Daniele, *Trop tot/Trop tard/ Too Early/Too Late*, 84
human trafficking, 165
Hungarian documentary film making
  institutional conditions of contemporary, 217
  migrants, 215–30
Hungarian National Film Fund (MNF), 217, 218–19, 220
Hungary, 6, 15–16, 64, 65, 262–3, 273–4
  Fidesz party, 15, 216–17, 217, 224, 234
  Media Council, 217
  'refugee crisis' (2015–16), 216–17

I, Daniel Blake (Loach, 2016), 12, 144–8, 185–6, 189, 196n
Iberian Austerity Cinema, 150–63
Iborfia, 224
'the Idea of Communism', 137, 148
Iglesia, Álex de la, 110
IMDb, 266
Import/Export (Seidl, 2007), 263
Imre, Anikó, 4, 22n, 170, 237
Iñárritu, Alejandro González, 107
Industrial Revolution (Hespanha and Lobo, 2014), 11, 76–92, 92n
Ingen ko på isen (Seren, 2015), 155
Die innere Sicherheit (Petzold, 2000), 105

Inquiry. The Great British Housing Disaster (Curtis, BBC, 1984), 183
Institute for Public Policy Research, UK, 20
'integration documentaries', 219–21
International Social Housing Festival, Lyon, 194–5
Invisible Britain: Portraits of Hope and Resilience, 192
Iordanova, Dina, 18, 218
Ireland, 12
Italian cinema, 194
Italian Communist Party, 88
Italian Marxism, 88, 90
Italian Neorealism, 26
Italy, 208–10, 213–14n, 245–9
It's a Free World (Loach, 2007), 144–8
iTunes, 192
Iversen, Martin, 96

Jameson, Frederic, 29–30
Jancsó, Miklós, 65
Je pense à vous (Dardennes, 1992), 44
Jensen, Lars, 3
Jerichow (Petzold, 2008), 8–9, 106, 115–17, *116*, 117–18
Jimmy's Hall (Loach, 2014), 140
Jobbik Party, 216
John From (Nicolau, 2015), 159
Jones, Duncan, 245
'journey documentaries', 222–3
Journey of Hope (Koller, 1990), 246
Judis, John B., *The Populist Explosion*, 13–14
Jupiter's Moon (Mundruczó, 2017), 236
Just the Wind (Fliegauf, 2012), 262–3, 264

Kääpä, Pietari, 98, 102
Kafka, Franz, 19, 73, 75n
Kananen, Johannes, 95
Kapitalism: Reteta Noastra Secreta (Solomon, 2010), 5
Karakusevic Carson Architects, 195
Kattel, R., 165
Kaurismäki, Aki, 15, 20, 99, 104n, 199, 200–3, 212n

Keiller, Patrick, 183
Kershaw, Ian, 13, 21n
Két világ közt (Nagy, HBO Europe, 2011), 222–3
Kettunen, Paul, 95
Keynes, John Maynard, 137, 147
Kickstarter campaign, 192
The Kid with a Bike (Dardennes, 2011), 44, 56–7
Kingsley, Patrick, 211–12n
Kinkle, Jeff, 155
    Cartographies of the Absolute, 85
Kiossev, Alexander, 4, 167
Király, Hajnal, 236
Kiwa, 120–1, 122
Kjaerum, Morten, 274n
Klein, Naomi, 8, 20, 157
Klinger, Barbara, 102
Koepnick, Lutz, 107
Könnyű leckék (Zurbó, 2018), 220–1, 221
Kosmidou, Eleftheria Rania, 140, 142–3
Kosovo, 261
Koutsouakis, Angelos, 19, 42n
Kovačević, Nataša, 17
Kovács, András Bálint, 39
Koza (2015), 263–4, 264
Kracauer, Siegfried, 106
Krigul, Ülo, 122
Kulturindustrie, 125
Kuusniemi, Matleena, 101
Kuutamolla (Louhimies, 2002), 96

Laar, Mart, 5
labour displacement, 244–59
labour market, 21n
    refusal of work, 87–9
    work ethics, 81–3
Labrador Méndez, Germán, 151–2, 162
Lampedusa, Italy, 202–3, 212–13n
Land and Freedom (Loach, 1995), 140–3
Land of Promise (Rotha, 1946), 183
Landry, Olivia, 8–9
Lanthimos, Yorgos, 110

The Last Ones (Õunpuu, 2020), 134
Laverty, Paul, 144
Lawrence, Michael, 235
Lefebvre, Henri, 60
Lehman Brothers, 76
Leigh, Jacob, 138
Levinas, Emanuel, 45, 46–7, 58, 59
Lévi-Strauss, Claude, 52
Lewis, Simon L., 20
Lieven, Anatol, 23n
'light capitalism', 70–1
Linna, Väinö, 93
Linosa, Italy, 202
Lisice (Papić, 1969), 168–9
Loach, Ken, 12, 135–49, 185–6
Lobo, Frederico, 78, 83, 92n
Loftsdóttir, Kristín, 3
London, 12
Longhi, Vittorio, 208–9, 214n
Longing (Grisebach, 2006), 8–9, 106, 111–13, 114, 117–18
Lorna's Silence (Dardennes, 2008), 44, 45–6
Louhimmie, Aku, 10, 11, 93–104
Lovers and Leavers (Louhimies, 2002), 96
Lübecker, Nikolaj, 72
Lumière brothers, 64, 84
Lykidis, Alex, 10, 19–20, 110
Lynch, David, 107

Machtergreifung (seizure of power), 16
Macron, Emmanuel, 139
Madden, David, 182
Magical Girl (Vermut, 2014), 157
Magnusek, Tomás, 265, 274n
Malik, Kenan, 13
Map (Siminiani, 2012), 155
Mapa (Siminiani, 2012), 155
Marcuse, Peter, 182
Marghitu, Stefania, 102
Marie Claire, 221
Marion, Jean-Luc, 51
Marion, Philippe, *The End of Cinema? A Medium in Crisis in the Digital Age*, 109
Martínez, Manuel Ramos, 78
Martins, Marco, 157–8

Marxism
　'accelerationism', 108
　alienation, 124
　capitalism and self-destruction, 258
　capitalist realism, 147
　commodities, 55
　globalisation, 2–3, 9
　individuality, 71
　Italian, 88
　labour displacement, 244
　Loach, Ken, 12
　modernity, 67
　Õunpuu, Veiko, 121
　rise of the left, 139
　and social realism, 26
　stagnant population, 64
　value production, 89, 91, 92n
Masing, Uku, 133
Maslin, Mark A., 20
Mateos, Araceli Rodríguez, 163n
Mauss, Marcel, 12
　Essai sur le don (The Gift), 49–53
Mazierska, Ewa, 121, 237, 238, 242, 244–5
　Work in Cinema: Labor and the Human Condition, 244–59
McCabe, Colin, 41n
McClanahan, Annie, 11, 84–5, 90
　Dead Pledges: Debt, Crisis and Twenty-First-Century Culture, 75
McCracken, Grant, 270
McDuff, Phil, 196n
McHugh, Susan, 234
McMahon, Laura, 235
Media Council, Hungary, 217
Mediterranea (Carpignano, 2015)
　African labourers, 17–18, 208–11
　capitalism, 245
　dangerous journeys, 15, 199
　labour displacement, 209, 245–51, 254–8
　mise en scène, 20
Meggyes, Krisztina, 227–9
Merkel, Angela, 110, 139
#MeToo movement, 104n

migrants, 14–16, 23n, 198, 215
  asylum seekers, 23n
  in the cinema of Fortress Europe, 198–214
  financial crisis 2008, 165
  housing crisis, 187, 196n
  in Hungarian documentaries, 215–30
  scapegoating, 3, 13, 15–16, 27–8, 31
  as 'swarm', 198, 211n, 235
migration
  financial crisis 2008, 165
  housing crisis, 187, 196n
Milanovic, Branco, 75n
Minton, Anna, 182, 188
Miracle in Milan (de Sica, 1951), 212n
Miracolo a Milano (de Sica, 1951), 212n
mise en scène, 20, 46–7, 158, 175, 201, 238, 240
Mitchell, David, 199
modernism, 19, 60–75
  reactionary, 63
modernist anti-psychologism, 42n
modernist cinema, 25–6, 42n
Moffat, Kate, 10, 11
mongrel attunement, 231–43
Montenegro, 261
Moon (Jones, 2009), 18, 245, 249–51, 257, 258
Moore, Jason W., *A History of the World in Seven Cheap Things*, 210
Motion Picture Public Foundation of Hungary (MMKA), 217
Mouellic, Gilles, *Improvising Cinema*, 125
Movie Activism Festival, Berlin, 195
Mroz, Matilda, 237
Mujic, Nazif, 264, 273, 274n
Müller, Heiner, 73, 75n
Mundruczó, Kornél, 19, 231–43
Mungiu, Cristian, 4–5
Murieron por encima de sus posibilidades (Lacuesta, 2014), 160–1
Murphet, Julian, 61
Murray, Robin, 235–6

Nagy, Viktor Oszkár, 222–3, 224
Naked Harbour (Louhimies, 2012), 11, 94, 96–101
Näripea, Eva, 5, 19
narrative cinema, 65
narrative crisis, 28
National Corps, 268–9
Ndione, Abasse, Mbeke mi, 206
Nedelska, Mila, 270
'negative globalisation', 127–34
Negri, Antonio, 257
neoliberal subjugation, 164–79
Netherlands, 266
New French Extremity, 170
New Opportunities programme, Portugal, 79, 82
Nicaragua, 12
Nicholson, Rebecca, 184
Nixon, Richard, 138
No Cow on the Ice (Seren, 2015), 155
Nobre, Susana, 78, 79–83, 87, 152–3
Nordic countries, 11, 93–4
North, Michael, 63–4
nostomania, 164–5, 168, 178
The Nothing Factory (Pinho, 2017), 11, 76–92, 153, 154, 159

The Oak (Pintilie, 1992), 169–70
obsolescence, 86–7
On the Ground at Grenfell (Pinto-Duschinsky and Stowe Films, 2017), 190
online media, 191, 195
Orbán, Viktór, 15, 23n, 66, 198, 216, 234
O'Shaughnessy, Martin, 12–13, 149
Osseiran, Souad, 23n
Osteen, Mark, 117
Ostrowska, Elzbieta, 237
Other, 45–6, 58, 218–19, 225, 227–9
  women as, 169
The Other Side of Hope (Kaurismäki, 2011), 202–5, 212n
Õunpuu, Veiko, 5, 19, 119–35
Our School (2011), 261
Ozu, Yasujirō, 212n

Page, Joanna, 81
Paha maa (Louhimies, 2005), 11, 94, 96–101, 101, 103
Papić, Krsto, 168–9
Parvulescu, Anca, 17, 18
Parvulescu, Constantin, 4, 18
Patel, Raj, *A History of the World in Seven Cheap Things*, 210
patriarchy, 168–70
Peake, Maxine, 191
Peleg, Hila, 181
People's Party, Spain, 150, 163n
Petzold, Christian, 8–9, 105–8, 113–17
Pinho, Pedro, 78, 87–9, 153, 154
Pintilie, Lucie, 169–70
Pinto, Joaquim, 155
La Pirogue (Touré, 2012), 15, 199, 206–8
The Plain (Carpignano, 2012), 208
Pleasant, Leslie, 234, 240–1
pogrom videos on YouTube, 267–72
Poland, 6
populism, 234–5
   'anti-democratic', 6–7
   authoritarian, 13–14
   'democratic antipopulism', 6–7
   and self-colonising structures in Eastern Europe, 167–8
Porter, Pete, 240
Portugal
   austerity and unemployment, 8, 10–11
   Carmo, 92n
   debt crisis, 76–8, 78–9, 91
   Economic Adjustment Program, 152
   labour displacement, 83–5
   New Opportunities programme, 79, 82
   political parties, 91n
   Sócrates, José, 79, 91–2n
Portuguese Austerity Cinema, 150–63
postcoloniality, 4–5
post-democracy, 5–7, 41n
'post-fascism', 16
post-Fordism, 76–92
POUM, 143
Pound, Ezra, 63
'poverty porn', 186

Price, Brian, 72
Pro Finlandia Medal 2017, 102, 104n
Prologue (Tarr, 2004), 1, 21n, 63, 63–8, 64
La Promesse (Dardennes, 1996), 43, 53–5, 54, 213n
The Promise (Dardennes, 1996), 43, 53–5, 54, 213n
proto-postmodernism, 137–8
psychological realism, 38–40
Püha Tõnu kiusamine (Õunpuu, 2009), 127, 129–31, 130, 133
PUSH, 194

Rabaté, Jean-Michel, 73
racism, 228, 260–76
Rainbow Collective, 189–90
Rajaram, Prem Kumar, 14–15, 198
Rancière, Jacques, 23n
Rappas, Ipek A. Celik, 170
Rassemblement Bruxellois pour le Driot à l'Habitat, 195
reactionary modernism, 63
The Realm (Sorogoyen, 2018), 161–2
Rebellion (RTÉ, 2016), 93
Redfish, 190
Redrobe, Karen, 105, 109, 111, 117
   Crash, 107
'refugee/migrant crisis', 14–16, 198, 215
   Hungary, 216–17
refugees and migrants, 23n
   asylum seekers, 23n
   in the cinema of Fortress Europe, 198–214
   financial crisis (2008), 165
   housing crisis, 187, 196n
   in Hungarian documentaries, 215–30
   scapegoating, 3, 13, 15–16, 27–8, 31
   as 'swarm', 198, 211n, 235
El reino (Sorogoyen, 2018), 161–2
Renwick, Daniel, 190
Representatives of National Warbands Clear Out a Roma Tabor in Golosyvski Park (YouTube), 267–8
The Restless One (Gomes, 2015), 77
Revolução Industrial (Hespanha and Lobo, 2014), 11, 76–92, 92n

Rhodes, John David, 72
Riff-Raff (Loach, 1991), 12
Roggero, Gigi, 213–14n
Roma, 16, 18, 260–76
Romania, 5, 24n, 168–9, 170–3
Romanians, 187
Romea, 271–2
Römpötti, Tommi, 95, 100
Rosi, Gianfranco, 202–3
Ross, Andrew, 128–9
Rotas, Alex, 212n
Rotha, Paul, 183
Roukli (Õunpuu, 2015), 5, 122, 123–7, 129–33
Roukli Filmiuhistu/Roukli Film Association, 123–4
RTÉ, 93
Rushing, Robert, 117
Russian Formalism, 29
Ryna (Zenide, 2005), 170–3, *173*

Said, Edward, 14–15
Saint George (Martins, 2016), 157–9
Santos, Boaventura de Sousa, 159
São Jorge (Martins, 2016), 157–9
Sarkozy, Nicholas, 207, 213n
Sátántangó (Tarr, 1994), 1
Sborgi, Anna Viola, 12
scapegoating, 3, 13, 15–16, 27–8, 31
Schengen area, 218
Schoonover, Karl, 231
Schwartz, Louis-Georges, 234
Scoala noastra (2011), 261
Screen journal, 149n
Screpanti, Ernesto, 2–3, 6, 7, 9, 21n, 22n
Searching for Grenfell's Lost Lives (Yates, BBC, 2018), 191
Sehnsucht (Grisebach, 2006), 8–9, 106, 111–13, 114, 117–18
Seidl, Ulrich, 40, 263
Seihon, Koudous, 208–9
Self, Robert, 30
self-employment, 8
self-reflexivity, 84, 116, 242
Senegal, 206–8, 213n
Sequeira Bras, Patricia, 11

Serbia, 216, 222, 225–6, 261
Seren, Eloy Dominguez, 155
sexual violence, 168–70, 173–5, 178–9
shame, 264–6
Shaviro, Steven, 108, 117, 237
Shklovsky, Victor, 31
Le Silence de Lorna (Dardennes, 2008), 44, 45–6
Silva, Aníbal Cavaco, 150
Silva Melo, Jorge, 87
Siminani, Elías León, 155
Sinnerbrink, Robert, 231–2
Sirk, Douglas, 202
60 Seconds of Solitude in Year Zero (Õunpuu, 2011), 5, 122–3
Sleaford Mods: Invisible Britain (Sng, 2015), 193
Slovakia, 260, 263–4
Slovenia, 175–7
Slovenka (Kozole, 2009), 175–7, 178
'slow cinema', 126–7
Smets, Peer, 194
Smith, John, 21n
Sng, Paul, 189, 192–3, *192*
Snyder, Sharon, 199
Social Housing - 'European Housing Perspectives' (Stephenson, 2018), 195
'sociological documentary', 220
Sócrates, José, 79, 91–2n
Solomon, Alexandru, 5
Somalia, 221, 223
The Son (Dardennes, 2002), 46–9, 47, 53
La Sortie de l'Usine Lumière à Lyon (Lumière, 1895), 64, 84
Spain, 8, 10–11, 12, 110, 213n
  People's Party, 150, 163n
Spanish Austerity Cinema, 150–63
Squatters (Cinema Action, 1969/70), 183
Srnicek, Nick, 82
Stam, Robert, 127
The State I Am In (Petzold, 2000), 105
Stephens, Philip, 13
Stephenson, Jim, 195

Stimmung, 231–43
Stőhr, Lóránt, 15, 236
'Stop Soros' law, 230n
Stop the March! (2017), 222
'stranger danger', 213n, 228
Straub, Jean-Marie, *Trop tot/Trop tard/ Too Early/Too Late*, 84
Street 66 (Akingbade, 2018), 189
Studio Lambert, 184, 196n
Sturgeon, Nicola, 191
sub-Saharan Africa, 199
suffering bodies, 155–9
Sügisball (Õunpuu, 2007), 124, 127, 128
Superior Orders (Nagy, 2013), 224, 225–9
symbolic corporeal transformations, 170–5
Syria, 23n, 199, 212n
Syriza, 139
Sztompka, Piotr, 22n

Tamas, Gaspar Miklos, 16
Tamm, Marek, 132
Tarr, Béla, 1, 19, 21n, 63, 63–8, 139
Taubin, Amy, 236, 240
Taxidermia (Pálfi, 2006), 237
television, 138, 216–17
The Temptation of St Tony (Õunpuu, 2009), 127, 129–31, *130*, 133
Terraferma (Crialese, 2011), 202–5
Terratreme, 11, 78, 92n
TGV, 206
Thatcher, Margaret, 182–3
Their Skin Was Their Only Sin: Roma Serial Killings in Hungary 2008–2009 (YouTube), 273–4
This is a Crisis: Facing Up to the Age of Environmental Breakdown, 20
Those (Meggyes, 2016), 224, 227–9
3 esküvő (2009), 220
3 Weddings (2009), 220
The Threepenny Opera, 202
Thue, Lars, 96
Time Out (Cantet, 2001), 63, 69–72
Tolstoy, Leo, *The Forged Coupon*, 96, 100, 103

Toni Erdmann (Ade, 2016), 18, 245, 251, 251–4, 257
Toscano, Alberto, 155, 258
  Cartographies of the Absolute, 85
Toth, András, 234
Touchless (Chlupáček and Samir, 2013), 173–5, *175*
Touré, Moussa, 15, 199, 206–8, 213n
Tower Hamlets, London, 184
Trading Cities (Homem and Pinho, 2014), 92n
Tranche, Rafael Rodríguez, 150
Transylvania, 177–8
Travis, Ben, 185
Traynor, Ian, 274n
Trilling, Daniel, 14
Trotsky, Leon, 67, 139
Trotter, David, 66
Trump, Donald, 5
Tsangari, Athina Rachel, 10, 20, 32–41, 110
Tühirand (Õunpuu, 2006), 124, 127–8
Tuntematon sotilas (Louhimies, 2017), 93, 101
The Turin Horse (Tarr, 2011), 1
Twitter, 191
Two Days, One Night (Dardennes, 2014), 44, 46, 57

UK Border Agency, 232
Ukraine, 18, 267, 273, 276n
unemployment, 63–8, 165
Union of Estonian Film Journalists, 124
United Nations, 24n
United States
  austerity, 150
  'capitalist realism', 138
  economics, 22n
  financial crisis 2008, 7
  home foreclosures, 84–5, 90
  subprime mortgage crisis (2006), 76, 138
University of Theatre and Film Arts (SZFE), 217, 218–19
The Unknown Girl (Dardennes, 2016), 44, 57–8

The Unknown Soldier (Louhimiess, 2017), 93, 101
Unt, Mati, 124

Vajna, Andy, 219
Varoufakis, Yanis, 2, 21n
Vauxhall Dragon (VGERTA, 2017), 190
Velvet Joy Productions, 192
Verdery, Katherine, 168
Vida Activa (Nobre, 2013), 11, 76–92, 152–3
Vidros Partidos (Erice, 2012), 152–3
Vienna Initiative, 166
Viimased (Õunpuu, 2020), 134
Vila, Pablo, 225
violence
  extreme corporeal, 170
  neoliberalism, 43–4
  objective, 203
  sexual, 168–70, 173–5, 178–9
Virilio, Paul, 107
Visions of Europe (2004), 1, 63
Vuosaari (Louhimies, 2012), 11, 94, 96–101

Wallerstein, Immanuel, 3
War of Manoeuvre, 136, 140
Warwick Research Collective, 67
Watson, Paul, 183
Watt, Paul, 182, 194
Weber, Max, 11
West Africa, 206–7
Weyland, Kurt, 168
What Now? Remind Me (Pinto, 2013), 155

Wheatley, Catherine, 72, 112
When the War Comes (Gebert, 2018), 260
White God (Mundruczó, 2014), 19, 231–43
Whitehall, Jack, 273
Wilders, Geert, 266
Wilkin, Peter, 235
Willeman, Paul, 202, 204–5
Williams, Alex, 82
Wilterdink, Nico, 17, 23n
The Wind that Shakes the Barley (Loach, 2006), 140, 141–3
Windrush Caribbeans, 261
Wodak, Ruth, 13
women, 168–70, 212n, 251–6
Workers Leaving the Lumière Factory (Lumière, 1895), 64, 84
Worthington, Any, 193

xenophobia, 215–17, 229

Yamin, Farhana, 20–1
Yella (Petzold, 2007), 8–9, 106, 107, 113–15, 117–18
YLE, 101
You Are Not Human, You Should Be Exterminated (YouTube), 270
YouTube, 18, 265–74, 275n

Zenide, Ruxana, 170–3
Zentropa, 63
Žižek, Slavoj, 203, 211, 228, 255
Zurbó, Dorottya, 220–1

EU representative:
Easy Access System Europe
Mustamäe tee 50, 10621 Tallinn, Estonia
Gpsr.requests@easproject.com

www.ingramcontent.com/pod-product-compliance
Lightning Source LLC
Chambersburg PA
CBHW051804230426
43672CB00012B/2622